KV-637-752

CHILDREN'S UNDERSTANDING OF SOCIETY

Studies in Developmental Psychology
Published Titles

Series Editor
Charles Hulme, University of York, UK

The Development of Intelligence
Mike Anderson (Ed.)

The Development of Language
Martyn Barrett (Ed.)

The Social Child
Anne Campbell and Steven Muncer (Ed.)

The Development of Memory in Childhood
Nelson Cowan (Ed.)

The Development of Mathematical Skills
Chris Donlan (Ed.)

The Development of Social Cognition
Suzanne Hala (Ed.)

Perceptual Development: Visual, Auditory, and Speech Perception in Infancy
Anne Slater (Ed.)

The Cognitive Neuroscience of Development
Michelle DeHaan and Mark H. Johnson (Eds.)

Connectionist Models of Development
Philip T. Quinlan (Ed.)

Children's Understanding of Society

Edited by

Martyn Barrett and Eithne Buchanan-Barrow
Department of Psychology, University of Surrey,
Guildford, UK

FRANCIS CLOSE HALL
LEARNING CENTRE
UNIVERSITY OF GLOUCESTERSHIRE
Swindon Road, Cheltenham GL50 4AZ
Tel: 01242 714600

Psychology Press
Taylor & Francis Group
HOVE AND NEW YORK

First published 2005
by Psychology Press
27 Church Road, Hove, East Sussex BN3 2FA

Simultaneously published in the USA and Canada
by Psychology Press
270 Madison Avenue, New York NY 10016

Psychology Press is a part of the Taylor & Francis Group

Copyright © 2005 Psychology Press

Typeset in Times by Garfield Morgan, Rhayader, Powys
Printed and bound in Great Britain by TJ International Ltd, Padstow,
Cornwall
Cover design by Bob Rowinski at Code 5 Design

All rights reserved. No part of this book may be reprinted or reproduced or
utilised in any form or by any electronic, mechanical, or other means, now
known or hereafter invented, including photocopying and recording, or in
any information storage or retrieval system, without permission in writing
from the publishers.

The publisher makes no representation, express or implied, with regard to the
accuracy of the information contained in this book and cannot accept any
legal responsibility or liability for any errors or omissions that may be made.

This publication has been produced with paper manufactured to strict
environmental standards and with pulp derived from sustainable forests.

British Library Cataloguing in Publication Data
A catalogue record for this book is available from the British Library

Library of Congress Cataloging-in-Publication Data
Children's understanding of society / [edited by] Martyn Barrett and
Eithne Buchanan-Barrow.
    p. cm.
  Includes bibliographical references and index.
  ISBN 1-84169-298-0
  1. Social perception in children. I. Barrett, Martyn D. II.
Buchanan-Barrow, Eithne, 1944–

BF723.S6C47 2004
155.4'18–dc22

                                                              2004009867

ISBN 1-84169-298-0

Contents

List of contributors   xi

1.   **Emergent themes in the study of children's understanding
of society**   1
Martyn Barrett and Eithne Buchanan-Barrow
    Early studies on children's understanding of society   2
    More recent emphases in the study of children's understanding
        of society   3
    An overview of the book   5
    References   15

2.   **Children's understanding of the school**   17
Eithne Buchanan-Barrow
    The school as a micro-society   17
    School rules   19
    The role of the teacher   23
    The role of the headteacher   27
    Academic and classroom processes   28
    Perceptions of the school   30
    School councils   32
    School as social system   33
    Conclusion   36
    References   38

3. **Children's understanding of economics**   43
    Paul Webley
        Introduction: The meaning of "economics"   43
        Children's understanding of economic concepts   44
        Children as economic agents   54
        Conclusions   62
        References   64

4. **Children's understanding of politics**   69
    Anna Emilia Berti
        From political socialisation to political (or civic)
            development   71
        Understanding political institutions   75
        The understanding of political values and ideologies   88
        Conclusion   97
        References   99

5. **Children's understanding of the law and legal processes**   105
    Stephen J. Ceci, Faith A. Markle, and Yoo Jin Chae
        Basic developmental competencies   106
        How the legal system understands children   121
        Concluding remarks   126
        References   128

6. **Children's understanding of gender roles in society**   135
    Kevin Durkin
        Theories of gender role development   137
        Understanding gender roles in the media   154
        Conclusions   159
        References   160

7. **Children's understanding of social class and occupational
    groupings**   169
    Nicholas Emler and Julie Dickinson
        Introduction   169
        Social reproduction   170
        Perceptions of social class as a contrast between wealth and
            poverty   171
        The child's theory of labour: Occupations and earnings   174
        Income and prestige   175
        Occupational choice   177
        Explanations and justifications   179
        Childhood construction of a theory of distributive social
            justice   180

Limits to consensus—class-based differences   183
Constructing accounts of social inequalities: A sociogenetic
    view   185
The constructivist critique of social transmission: A critical
    appraisal   187
Some concluding observations on social class and the
    unequal distribution of social knowledge   192
References   193

8. **Children's understanding of racial groups**   199
    Lawrence A. Hirschfeld
    The problem of cognitive architecture   200
    The development of social categories   202
    Embodied social categories   205
    The emergence of racial thinking   206
    Race and reality   210
    Conclusion   216
    References   218

9. **Children's understanding of ethnic belonging and the development
    of ethnic attitudes**   223
    Alida Lo Coco, Cristiano Inguglia, and Ugo Pace
    Ethnic identity from childhood to adolescence   223
    Ethnic belonging and ethnic attitudes   232
    Relations between ethnic identification and ethnic
        attitudes   243
    References   245

10. **Children's understanding of, and feelings about, countries and
    national groups**   251
    Martyn Barrett
    Children's geographical knowledge of their own country and other
        countries   252
    Children's feelings about countries, and their emotional
        attachment to their own country   256
    Children's knowledge of national emblems, and the significance
        that they attribute to these emblems   259
    Children's knowledge of, and beliefs about, national groups, and
        the development of national stereotypes   262
    Children's feelings towards the people who belong to their own
        national in-group and to national out-groups   266
    Children's national self-categorisation and the development of
        subjective identification with the national in-group   271
    Theoretical frameworks   275
    References   280

11. The development of societal cognition: A commentary   287
Giyoo Hatano and Keiko Takahashi
    Is societal cognition unique?   289
    Is societal cognition a privileged domain?   292
    How does societal cognition develop?   295
    Why do we have to study societal cognition?   299
    Conclusion   301
    References   301

Author index   305
Subject index   319

In loving memory of our fathers

William Henry Barrett
and
George William Michael O'Shea

List of contributors

Martyn Barrett, Department of Psychology, University of Surrey, Guildford, Surrey GU2 7XH, UK

Anna Emilia Berti, Dipartimento di Psicologia dello Sviluppo e della Socializzazione, Università degli Studi di Padova, Via Venezia 8, 35131 Padova, Italy

Eithne Buchanan-Barrow, Department of Psychology, University of Surrey, Guildford, Surrey GU2 7XH, UK

Stephen J. Ceci, Department of Human Development, Cornell University—NG25 MVR Hall, Ithaca, NY 14853, USA

Yoo Jin Chae, Department of Human Development, Cornell University—NG25 MVR Hall, Ithaca, NY 14853, USA

Julie Dickinson, Department of Organisational Psychology, Birkbeck College, Malet Street, London WC1E 7HX, UK

Kevin Durkin, Department of Psychology, University of Strathclyde, 40 George Street, Glasgow G1 1QE, UK

Nicholas Emler, Department of Psychology, University of Surrey, Guildford, Surrey GU2 7XH, UK

Giyoo Hatano, Human Development and Education Program, University of the Air, Wakaba, Mihama-ku, Chiba, 261-8586 Japan

Lawrence A. Hirschfeld, Department of Anthropology, University of Michigan, Ann Arbor, MI 48109, USA

Cristiano Inguglia, Dipartimento di Psicologia, Università degli Studi di Palermo, Viale delle Scienze, 90128 Palermo, Italy

Alida Lo Coco, Dipartimento di Psicologia, Università degli Studi di Palermo, Viale delle Scienze, 90128 Palermo, Italy

Faith A. Markle, Department of Human Development, Cornell University—NG25 MVR Hall, Ithaca, NY 14853, USA

Ugo Pace, Dipartimento di Psicologia, Università degli Studi di Palermo, Viale delle Scienze, 90128 Palermo, Italy

Keiko Takahashi, Department of Psychology, University of the Sacred Heart, 4-3-1 Hiroo, Shibuya-ku, Tokyo 150-8938, Japan

Paul Webley, School of Psychology, University of Exeter, Washington Singer Laboratories, Perry Road, Exeter EX4 4QG, UK

CHAPTER ONE

Emergent themes in the study of children's understanding of society

Martyn Barrett and Eithne Buchanan-Barrow
Department of Psychology, University of Surrey, UK

All children are born into, and grow up within, particular societies. Each of these societies contains many different institutions and is regulated by some kind of common economic, political, and legal systems. These societal institutions and systems facilitate, shape, regulate, and constrain many of the activities and behaviours in which individuals engage throughout the course of their everyday lives. For the developing child, a crucial aspect of the process of growing up is to acquire an understanding of these societal institutions and systems, so that by the time adulthood is attained, he or she will be able to function appropriately within the particular society in which he or she lives, and can engage with and participate in (and possibly even change) the various societal institutions, systems, and processes that influence and govern the lives of individuals within that society.

In addition, the societies within which children grow up are internally differentiated in a number of ways, for example, in terms of gender groups, social class groups, occupational groups, racial groups, ethnic groups, national groups, etc. A further important task facing the developing child is to learn about the various groups that characterise his or her own society, to establish a sense of personal identity in relationship to some of the available groups, and to internalise those norms, values, representations, and practices that are relevant for the groups to which a sense of personal belonging is established.

This book offers the reader a state-of-the-art review of the research literature on children's societal cognition. Taken together, the chapters provide a systematic overview and evaluation of the research that has been conducted into the development of children's understanding of the various institutions and economic, political, and legal systems that characterise the society in which they live, and into the development of children's understanding of several large-scale social groupings that characterise most contemporary societies, including gender, social class, occupation, race, ethnicity, and nationality.

EARLY STUDIES ON CHILDREN'S UNDERSTANDING OF SOCIETY

Early research into children's societal understanding (e.g., Adelson, 1971; Adelson, Green, & O'Neil, 1969; Adelson & O'Neil, 1966; Berti & Bombi, 1979, 1981, 1988; Burris, 1983; Connell, 1971, 1977; Danziger, 1958; Furth, 1978, 1980; Hess & Torney, 1967; Jahoda, 1962, 1963, 1979, 1981; Piaget, 1928; Piaget & Weil, 1951; Strauss, 1952; Tapp & Levine, 1977; Torney, 1971; Weinstein, 1957) tended to rely upon either open-ended verbal interviewing or written questionnaires to gather their data from children, with the responses that were collected by these means subsequently being content-analysed. Many early researchers used these methods to try and identify distinctive age-related stages in the development of children's societal understanding. It was commonly claimed that such developmental stages were indeed present, with each individual stage being characterised as a qualitatively unique way of thinking about the phenomena under question. The developmental stages that were proposed were also typically postulated to occur in a constant order of succession through childhood. Stage-based theories were proposed to explain children's understanding in a large number of different societal areas, including politics (e.g., Connell, 1971), economics (e.g., Berti & Bombi, 1981), the law (e.g., Tapp & Levine, 1977), occupational groups (e.g., Furth, 1978, 1980), and national groups (e.g., Piaget & Weil, 1951).

Some of these early researchers went still further in their theoretical claims, arguing that the stages that they had identified in their data mapped directly on to Piagetian stages of development, with egocentric and preoperational characteristics being exhibited in children's societal thinking up to 6–7 years of age, concrete operational characteristics being exhibited between 6–7 and 10–11 years of age, and formal operational characteristics and relatively decentred abstract thinking being exhibited from 11 years of age onwards (e.g., Berti & Bombi, 1981, 1988; Burris, 1983; Connell, 1971; Piaget & Weil, 1951). It was also often tacitly assumed, and sometimes explicitly argued (e.g., Berti & Bombi, 1981, 1988; Tapp & Levine, 1977), that the stage-sequences that were being proposed were universal, and that influences from the child's sociocultural context were minimal and could only either accelerate or decelerate the rate at which the child progressed through the sequence of stages. The assumption underlying many of these stage-based accounts was that the development of societal cognition proceeds through the child reflecting upon his or her own personal experience, actively constructing explanations of the observed phenomena using his or her current cognitive capacities and skills (see, e.g., Furth, 1978, 1980). Furthermore, these cognitive capacities and skills were often assumed to be domain-general rather than domain-specific (being grounded in the universal Piagetian stages of cognitive development).

MORE RECENT EMPHASES IN THE STUDY OF CHILDREN'S UNDERSTANDING OF SOCIETY

However, this traditional Piagetian picture has now been largely superseded, as the various chapters in this book testify. In particular, there are four noticeable emphases that now appear with some regularity in the more recent research literature. Taken together, these four emphases represent a major shift away from the traditional Piagetian position, and reveal that contemporary researchers are conceptualising the development of societal cognition in children in a very different manner.

First, there is an increasing acknowledgement that, in societal fields in particular, the child does not always have first-hand personal experience of the relevant phenomena and institutions (e.g., of teachers' decision-making in schools, of profit generation in shops and banks, of procedures in courts of law, of the political decision-making process, etc.; see, for example, the chapters in this book by Buchanan-Barrow, by Webley, by Ceci, Markle, & Chae, and by Berti). Consequently, it is now commonly acknowledged that the child's own personal experience *cannot* always function as the source of their societal knowledge. Instead, it is now recognised by many researchers that children are sometimes very heavily reliant upon indirect and socially mediated sources of information for learning about many societal phenomena, with television, parent and peer discourse, and the school curriculum possibly being the most important sources of information.

Second, it has become increasingly clear in recent years that children's understanding in many different societal areas can exhibit variation as a function of the particular sociocultural context within which the child lives. Findings indicating the existence of systematic variability as a function of children's own socioeconomic status, ethnicity, nationality, etc. have now been obtained in relationship to children's understanding of the school, of economics, of social class, of ethnic groups, and of national groups (see the chapters by Buchanan-Barrow, by Webley, by Emler & Dickinson, by Lo Coco, Inguglia, & Pace, and by Barrett). Variations in children's patterns of understanding as a function of their own sociocultural context is, of course, to be expected if children's knowledge in societal domains is heavily dependent upon the provision of information to the child by salient social-isation agents such as television, parents, peers, and teachers.

Third, there are a number of researchers currently working within this field who, rather than using a Piagetian approach, are instead using a naïve theory (sometimes also called a folk or lay theory) approach to the study of children's societal cognition. According to this approach, during the course of development, children construct naïve theories to explain phenomena in particular domains. These theories are specialised for particular types of conceptual content (i.e., are domain-specific rather than domain-general); provide cause-and-effect explanations of the phenomena within that par-ticular domain; involve hypothetical constructs of unobservable factors or processes; and are subject to change during the course of development. Moreover, children's naïve theories are usually implicit rather than explicit; thus, children may not be able to consciously access and verbalise these theories. Verbal interviewing is therefore likely to underestimate children's understanding. Instead, in order to reveal the structure of the child's thinking, the child needs to be presented with scenarios, stories, or vignettes in which variables are manipulated and about which the child has to make predictive judgements. In several societal domains (e.g., economics, gender, social class, and race), researchers have now begun to use this alternative to the traditional Piagetian approach (see, for example, the chapters by Webley, by Durkin, by Emler & Dickinson, and by Hirschfeld), and it seems likely that further advances in the study of children's societal cognition will emerge from the broader application of this post-Piagetian theoretical and methodological approach to the study of children's thinking about societal institutions, systems, and groups.

Fourth, there has been a growing recognition in recent years that chil-dren's cognitions concerning societal institutions, systems, and groups are not always emotionally neutral; instead, these cognitions are often accom-panied by, or associated with, very strong emotions. These emotions sometimes appear to result from the child's own subjective identification with a particular social group (e.g., with a particular gender, ethnic, or national group). Developmentally, it has been found that such emotions are sometimes present prior to the child's acquisition of factual knowledge or understanding within a particular area. Hence, there is a possibility that these emotions serve a significant motivational role in the acquisition of societal understanding. Whether or not, and how, these emotions do impact upon the child's cognitive functioning is unclear at the present time, but the recognition that societal cognition is often emotionally "hot" is a theme that developmental researchers working within this field are currently beginning to address (see especially the chapters by Durkin, by Lo Coco et al., and by Barrett).

Hence, some important conceptual and theoretical shifts have recently taken place in this field of research. The aims of the various chapters within this book are threefold: (1) to take stock of the existing literature in this field; (2) to identify the theoretical developments that are currently taking place in the study of children's societal cognition; and (3) to mark out the territory that needs to be explored by future studies in this area.

AN OVERVIEW OF THE BOOK

Chapter 2, by Eithne Buchanan-Barrow, opens the substantive part of this book with a review of the research that has been conducted on children's understanding of the school. As Buchanan-Barrow notes, for most children, entering school as a pupil often constitutes their first experience of a major societal institution beyond that of the family. Furthermore, insofar as the school itself is a micro-society, operating with its own system of rules, conventions, and power relations, it is possible that children's understanding and beliefs about other societal institutions, which will be encountered in later life, may be influenced by their early experiences of school. Therefore, in addition to examining children's perceptions of specific areas of school life, such as school rules, the roles of teachers and headteachers, academic and classroom processes, and school councils, this chapter reviews children's overall understanding of the school as a community or a social system.

Clearly, children often have first-hand personal experience of many aspects of the school, as they are prominent and, indeed, essential role-players in any school system. However, their comprehension of less evident aspects of the school context, such as the hierarchical power structure, has also been found to develop with age, as children make sense of the school system. Some aspects of children's understanding appear more intuitive and implicit rather than substantive and explicit, suggesting that naïve theories might underpin their comprehension. However, as yet, no studies have specifically examined children's thinking about school from a naïve theory perspective. Buchanan-Barrow also argues that the particular sociocultural context of children influences their school perceptions. Variations in children's understanding of such specific areas as teachers' roles, or more generally in their overall comprehension of the school, have been linked not only to variation across cultures and socioeconomic classes, but more narrowly to differences in school ethos or organisation in schools within cultures, thus hinting at the complexities involved in children's developing societal understanding.

Chapter 3, by Paul Webley, reviews the research literature on children's understanding of economics. Economics is a further area in which children often have the opportunity of first-hand personal experience. Consequently,

Webley's review focuses on the child's understanding of his or her own economic behaviour as well as on the child's understanding of the adult economy. After an initial review of the more traditional approach, examining children's comprehension of economic concepts, such as money, prices, supply and demand, profits, and banks, there is an extensive review of research investigating children as economic agents. The studies cover such areas as children's understanding of pocket money, their own savings, and the autonomous economic world of childhood, including the so-called playground economy, in which children develop such behaviours as swapping.

It is notable that, while Webley acknowledges the important role in children's developing economic understanding played by domain-general cognitive changes, he also points out the increasing input from both direct and indirect sources of information with age. As children get older, with respect to direct experience, they have greater economic independence, with generally increasing amounts of their own money (either pocket-money or earnings) and more freedom to spend it. However, children also have greater exposure to indirect sources of information as well, such as formal education, media, commercial savings literature, parental discourse, etc. There is also evidence of cross-cultural and within-cultural differences in economic understanding, which may relate to variations in direct and indirect sources of information, as a consequence of differences in the economies or socioeconomic classes in which the children are living.

Webley also examines the naïve theory perspective with respect to children's understanding of economics. Recent studies that have been conducted using this perspective have indicated that children do indeed hold implicit beliefs about cause-and-effect economic relationships, and that these beliefs underlie their comprehension of concepts such as demand, supply, and price. However, Webley also warns against too simplistic an approach to children's economic understanding. He argues that economic concepts should not be treated as givens but should be related to the wider social context, as children's economic thinking must also reflect the more general principles shaping the society in which they are developing.

Chapter 4, by Anna Emilia Berti, focuses on children's understanding of politics, including political institutions and their operation, political values, and ideologies. The chapter begins with a general overview of the many different theoretical perspectives that have been used in this area over the years, including the political socialisation, lifespan developmental, Piagetian, contextualist, and social representations approaches, in an attempt to find an appropriate and productive research framework for this topic. Despite the difficulties of dealing with such varied perspectives, some general developmental trends in children's political understanding have emerged from the studies that have been conducted. Young children (6–7 years) first understand general societal roles, such as teachers, before developing a comprehension of the political role, such as "chief" or "boss" (7–9 years), with its added aspect of power/authority; finally, around the age of 10–12 years, children become aware of the political domain with an increasingly developed understanding in adolescence. Berti's chapter also reviews the more limited research that has been conducted into children's understanding of political values and ideologies, such as rights, tolerance, and commitment to ideologies.

This is clearly an area where children often have very limited personal experience, with politics being predominantly a field of adult activity. It is therefore likely that much of children's understanding is constructed from information derived from indirect sources. As Berti points out, the developmental trends that have been found may result from a multiplicity of processes and influences, including educational input, cognitive development, role-taking or decision-making opportunities, exposure to political issues, and participation in societal institutions, in addition to more general influences, such as parental and peer discourse or the media. Furthermore, all these possible influences may be unevenly distributed according to the child's own nationality, ethnicity, and/or socioeconomic class. Political knowledge and understanding is likely to be closely linked to the power and status of various groups, and membership of lower socioeconomic groups or subordinate ethnic minority groups may mean that children have less opportunity to acquire political knowledge. However, while there is some cross-cultural research into children's political understanding, there is very little examination of other influences that might stem from the child's particular sociocultural context. In addition, this area might well benefit from the more extensive application of the naïve theory perspective. As Berti concludes, there is considerable scope for future developmental research in this area.

Chapter 5, by Stephen Ceci, Faith Markle, and Yoo Jin Chae, deals with children's understanding of the law and legal processes. This chapter discusses the extant research literature on two very different groups of children. The first of these is the majority of children who have no particular experience of the law, and who are thus largely dependent on indirect sources of information. The second group is the minority of children who do have personal experience of the law, either because they are witnesses or victims of crimes, or because they are perpetrators of crimes. Because of the problems entailed in dealing with young children in the legal process, whether as victims, witnesses, or defendants, research has tended to concentrate on the latter group, with relatively little research examining the understanding of the majority of children as they make sense of an important aspect of society.

The chapter begins with an examination of various general developmental competencies that affect children's understanding of the law, including their conceptual, memory, and language limitations, with the latter two particularly relevant to children actually participating in legal processes. There is evidence that more specialist skills, such as the ability to reason in ways appropriate to the legal context, are also generally lacking in young children. With a focus on the minority of children actually participating in legal processes, there is an examination of the way in which the legal system understands children, reviewing the typical court processes in the US and in the UK.

Given the concentration of research on child participants in the legal system, whether as victims, witnesses, or defendants, there is inevitably an emphasis in this chapter on the issue of the child's own direct experience. However, studies examining children's indirect sources of information, particularly television, are also reviewed. With respect to the majority of children who do not have first-hand contact with the legal system, one possible major indirect source of information about the law is police and crime drama that is shown on television. This can result in an inaccurate and distorted understanding of legal process, as these programmes present fictional rather than veridical accounts of the law. The research suggests that the sociocultural context of the child may also be a factor in children's understanding of the law. For example, ethnic minority children (in the US) have been found to have greater problems with language in court processes. Overall, this is another area of children's societal understanding that offers considerable opportunities for further developmental research.

Chapters 6 to 10 shift the focus of the book away from children's understanding of societal institutions, systems, and processes and towards their understanding of the large-scale social groupings by which many societies are differentiated internally. The groupings, which are considered in turn, are gender, social class, occupation, race, ethnicity, and nationality.

Chapter 6, by Kevin Durkin, reviews the literature on children's understanding of gender. He begins by drawing attention to the emotionally "hot" nature of children's cognition concerning gender: children acquire very strongly felt views about gender norms and gender self-presentation, as well as about their own gender identification. Durkin also points out that gender role development is almost certainly multifaceted and multi-determined by biological, social learning, social-cognitive, and cognitive-developmental factors. One particular theoretical approach, gender schema theory, has recently been extended into the proposal that, during the course of development, children construct a naïve social-psychological theory about the nature of social life and social activities in which their concepts of gender roles are embedded. This naïve theory enables children to make inferences and predictions about other people's behaviour in situations where there is only limited information available.

However, this naïve theory itself operates within a context characterised by intergroup relations. Children strive to achieve a positive self-concept from their own gender identification, and in order to achieve a positive self-image they typically engage in in-group favouritism, out-group denigration, and out-group stereotyping. As Durkin shows, these kinds of gender biases have been found in children from at least as young as 5 years of age. The argument is that at least some of the strong emotions that are associated with gender stem from this basic motivational need for positive self-esteem. In addition, the gender stereotypes that children acquire normatively attribute different types and levels of emotionality to males and to females. Consequently, once the child's gender identity has been incorporated into the self-concept, this in itself is also likely to predispose the child to exhibit and experience particular gender-related emotional displays and reactions.

Throughout his chapter, Durkin draws attention to the fact that a number of socialisation agents, including parents, peers, the school, and the mass media, are all likely to play a significant role in influencing children's understanding of gender. The popular mass media are an especially important influence within many contemporary Western societies, and there is evidence that television in particular can play a major role in children's gender socialisation. However, as Durkin points out, the impact of television upon children is neither direct nor invariant. He examines the role that is played by children's own selective attention and preferences for particular programme types, and their active inferential processing of televised material. It is clear that children are active and discerning viewers who attend selectively to televised material and interpret it in accordance with their own naïve social-psychologies of gender.

Chapter 7, by Nicholas Emler and Julie Dickinson, returns to some of the themes raised by Webley in Chapter 3, exploring children's perceptions of wealth, poverty, and labour as a source of personal income. However, the principal focus of their discussion is the child's understanding of social class and employment. As Emler and Dickinson note, the economic position that an individual occupies as an adult is, in general, highly predictable from the social class into which that individual has been born, and this typically occurs because of the choices that the individual makes in childhood and adolescence. Moreover, these choices themselves are influenced by the beliefs, conceptions, and attitudes that individuals acquire about employment and social class.

Emler and Dickinson review the general developmental trends that have been found to occur in children's understanding of social class. The research indicates that young children may be aware of social class differences but do not usually recognise the link with the different kinds of jobs that people do. The connection between social class and employment usually starts to be made at about 8 or 9 years of age, while from 11 years of age, children start to explain the differences between the jobs done by rich and poor people in terms of the different skills, abilities, educational

achievements, and effort that are needed for these jobs. By middle adolescence, a minority of individuals finally begin to explain social class
differences in terms of power, prejudice, exploitation, and life chances. A
similar shift occurs at around 11 years of age in children's understanding of
occupational choice and opportunity structure: up to about 11, children
tend to consider occupational possibilities primarily in terms of personal
interests, but after 11 they also begin to understand that the individual's
social class background and academic achievement influence the jobs that
can be taken up by individuals. It is noteworthy that, in many societies,
children make the transition from primary to secondary education at the age
of about 11 or 12, when they start to prepare themselves for the educational
qualifications that they will need for entry into the labour market. The
change in socioeconomic understanding that occurs at this age might not be
unconnected with this educational transition.

Emler and Dickinson note that, throughout the developmental process,
the child is gradually constructing and elaborating naïve theories of labour
and of distributive social justice. However, the research indicates that these
naïve theories can vary according to the child's own socioeconomic background. For example, middle-class children perceive much larger income
differentials, generate many more explanations and justifications of these
income inequalities, and are much more committed to these inequalities,
than working-class children. Furthermore, these differences are not related
to age. Emler and Dickinson argue that these differences in understanding
offer strong evidence against the Piagetian account of the development of
societal cognition, and necessitate a social transmission account instead.
According to the latter account, the social worlds that are inhabited by
middle-class and working-class children make available very different
patterns of explanations, arguments, and ways of conceptualising their own
and other people's economic circumstances. A social transmission account
can, of course, readily explain why media representations influence children's conceptualisations and understanding of occupations. It also helps to
explain why the economic positions occupied by adults tend to be highly
predictable from the social class origins of those individuals, i.e., why there
is a pattern of societal reproduction across successive generations.

Chapter 8, by Lawrence Hirschfeld, examines children's understanding
of racial groups. He challenges the commonplace assumption that race is a
biological given, and simply involves sorting people into categories based
on their physical characteristics. Instead, he argues that race is a cultural
construction. He points out that 3- to 4-year-old children are typically
inconsistent in sorting people into racial categories, that racial misidentification at this early age is common, and that race itself plays little part in
predicting playmate choice amongst preschoolers. Instead, it is not until
children enter elementary school that their sorting by race becomes reliable,

and it is at this point that race also comes to shape their social interactions, predicting their patterns of social inclusion and exclusion. However, even 3-year-old preschool children display patterns of racial prejudice when they are tested using verbal methods. Hirschfeld argues that this discrepancy between their verbally expressed attitudes and their real-life behaviour is due to the different modalities of the information that is employed. He suggests that verbal (rather than visual) information is initially used to build a knowledge of race, and children do not begin to consistently identify the relevant physical differences associated with race until about 6 years of age.

Hirschfeld argues that even 3-year-olds hold a naïve theory that race is fixed at birth, inherited, immalleable, and impervious to environmental influence, but this naïve theory is derived from socially mediated information available within the child's own culture rather than from direct visual observation. This naïve theory specifies how race is related to physical appearance and behaviour, and hence serves to generate both racial stereotypes and racial prejudice. Note that this theory is *not* constructed via a process of empirical generalisation based upon a process of identifying visual similarities in appearance amongst a set of category exemplars. Instead, race is an "ambient" belief that is available in, and supported by, the cultural context within which the child lives. Hirschfeld claims that the child is particularly attuned to the types of differentiations that are made by the racial system of categorisation. However, in other cultures that recognise different social category systems from race (e.g., in South Asian cultures, where caste is privileged instead), the distinctions are acquired in place of race during early childhood. Hence, the particular naïve theory that is acquired by the child (and that drives the child's pattern of stereotypes, prejudices, and evaluations) is culturally specific.

In Chapter 9, Alida Lo Coco, Cristiano Inguglia, and Ugo Pace also examine the development of prejudice in childhood. However, their approach to this phenomenon is from the perspective of the child's own subjective identification with a particular ethnic group (rather than from the perspective of the child's naïve theory of racial groups). As such, their focus is much more directly upon the emotionally "hot" nature of children's cognitions about ethnicity. They begin by noting that ethnic identification is not merely a cognitive act, but a complex process involving feelings of belonging to a particular group, patterns of self- and other-evaluation, self-esteem, and the internalisation of the cultural norms, values, traditions, and practices that are characteristic of the ethnic group (the crucial distinction between race and ethnicity being that, while race is defined in terms of putative biological and physical characteristics, ethnicity is instead defined in terms of shared cultural traditions and a sense of common identity).

As Lo Coco et al. note, early studies suggested that different patterns of ethnic identification were exhibited by ethnic majority and minority group children, with majority group children exhibiting in-group identification and preference, but minority group children exhibiting either a more ambivalent attitude towards their own in-group or in some cases actually displaying out-group identification and preference. However, in more recent studies, patterns of identification have altered, with ethnic minority children commonly exhibiting strong in-group identification. This change occurred in the wake of the emergence of the civil rights, Black power, and "Black is beautiful" movements within Western societies during the 1960s and 1970s. In other words, a historical, political, and cultural shift in the status and evaluation of minority ethnic groups appeared to impact upon patterns of ethnic understanding and preference in ethnic minority children.

Lo Coco et al. review the theoretical accounts that have been put forward to explain the development of children's attitudes towards ethnic groups. The social reflection view, that children come to acquire the ethnic attitudes displayed by their parents and by other significant figures in their environment via observational learning and imitation, has not been substantiated by empirical research. The alternative Piagetian view, that the child's general cognitive abilities determine his or her perceptions of ethnic groups, emphasises the watershed that appears to occur at 5–7 years of age: in many studies, it has been found that in-group favouritism and out-group denigration reach a peak at this age, with prejudice against out-groups subsequently declining between 7 and 11 years of age. This reduction in prejudice is attributed to the development of the child's cognitive capabilities across this age range. However, as Lo Coco et al. point out, there are also studies reported in the literature that have failed to find a decline in ethnic prejudice across middle childhood and, indeed, some studies have even found an increase in prejudice between 7 and 11 years of age. In other words, contrary to the claims made by cognitive-developmental theorists, there is in fact considerable variability in the development of ethnic understanding and attitudes in middle childhood.

A more recent theoretical approach derives from social identity theory. According to this account, patterns of prejudice are linked to motivational factors, in particular to the need for positive self-esteem, which can often be achieved by engaging in in-group favouritism and out-group denigration. However, Lo Coco et al. argue that, in addition to this motivational factor, the child's judgements are also influenced by the prevailing attitudes, evaluations, and conditions that prevail within their own social environment, as well as by the child's own cognitive and sociocognitive capacities (note that this is a similar argument to the arguments made in relationship to the child's understanding of both gender and nationality: cf. the chapters by Durkin and by Barrett). Crucially, the relative social status of the various ethnic groups within a given society, the nature of the boundaries that exist between those groups, and the social discrimination that may be experienced by the members of minority groups, can all influence the strategies of adaptation to the societal structure that are adopted by the child. Hence, patterns of ethnic understanding and preference need to be examined in conjunction with the specific social, political, and economic conditions that prevail within the child's own society. As Lo Coco et al. note, there is now good evidence that children's development varies as a function of all these factors, and that children's ethnic attitudes are in fact educationally malleable under appropriate conditions.

Chapter 10, by Martyn Barrett, reviews the research literature on children's understanding of countries and national groups. He too emphasises the emotionally "hot" nature of children's societal cognition: from as young as 5 years of age, children often evince very strong feelings concerning national groups, particularly concerning the national in-group and traditional national "enemy" out-groups. Barrett reviews the research that has been conducted on the development of children's knowledge of, and feelings about, their own and other countries (including their emotional attachment to their own country), on children's knowledge of national emblems (including the significance that they attribute to these emblems), on the development of children's knowledge, beliefs, and feelings about the people who belong to different national groups, and on the development of children's subjective identification with their own national group.

One of the most striking findings to emerge from this review is the considerable variability that can occur in children's development as a function of the specific national and sociocultural context within which they grow up. For example, there are systematic differences in children's geographical knowledge of other countries according to their social class, gender, geographical location, and ethnicity. In addition, children's attitudes towards national in-groups and out-groups can exhibit quite different developmental patterns depending upon the child's national context (with some children displaying significant reductions in in-group favouritism and out-group prejudice between 5 and 11 years of age, others displaying no developmental changes in their national attitudes, and still others displaying an increase in out-group prejudice across this age range). Furthermore, even within a single country, there are systematic differences in the levels of national identification exhibited by children who grow up in the capital city vs other locations within the nation, between children who belong to different ethnic groups, and between children according to their sociolinguistic situation.

In addition to this wide-ranging variability in development, Barrett's review also shows that socially mediated representations of nations and national groups, including those purveyed by the mass media and by the state educational system, impact upon children's knowledge and under-standing in this area. Indeed, it is clear that there are, in fact, multiple influences upon children's understanding of countries and national groups, including societal influences, familial influences, personal experiences, and cognitive-motivational factors (cf. the arguments made by Durkin and by Lo Coco et al. in relationship to gender and ethnicity). Barrett argues that previous theoretical formulations (including cognitive-developmental theory, social identity theory, self-categorisation theory, and social identity development theory) have underestimated the role played by many of these factors, with the primary emphasis having been given to either cognitive and/or motivational factors. Barrett argues that it is essential to adopt a much more inclusive and multilayered theoretical framework if the goal is to formulate an empirically adequate theoretical account of children's understanding of, and attitudes towards, countries and national groups.

In the final chapter of this book, Chapter 11, Giyoo Hatano and Keiko Takahashi offer a discussion of, and some reflections upon, the contents of the preceding chapters. They examine whether societal cognition is unique, that is, whether it is similar to or different from cognition about, for example, the physical and biological domains. They note that societal cognition differs from many other types of cognition in that it is linked to the moral and emotional functioning of the individual. Societal cognition is also different from other forms of cognition in that the actions and properties of societal institutions and groups can be given both intrinsic and extrinsic teleological explanations (where intrinsic teleology concerns the functioning of an entity for the sake of its owners or constituent com-ponents, and extrinsic teleology concerns the functioning of that entity for the sake of others external to it). However, at the same time, societal cognition may be similar to other forms of cognition, insofar as it probably contains both core, privileged components (which facilitate the rapid and effortless acquisition of some societal knowledge), and peripheral, non-privileged components (which are much more laboriously acquired using domain-general learning mechanisms).

Hatano and Takahashi draw attention to the fact that, throughout the various chapters of this book, three major sources of societal knowledge are identified by the different authors: the child's participation in cultural practices; the educational programmes to which children are exposed in school; and the mass media, particularly television. As far as the mass media are concerned, they note that this source of information can be invaluable for learning about those societal institutions, processes, or groups with which the individual has very little direct first-hand contact. However, the mass media are a double-edged sword in that they frequently purvey inaccurate, biased, or partial representations, and hence can actually lead the developing individual to acquire distorted societal beliefs or judgements. In addition, Hatano and Takahashi draw attention to a fourth major influence upon children's societal cognition, which is the children themselves. They argue that children are agents in the development of their own societal cognition, actively constructing their own knowledge from their experiences within society.

In their commentary, Hatano and Takahashi highlight the fact that, traditionally, developmental psychologists have tended to shy away from the investigation of societal cognition, preferring to focus their attention upon children's physical, biological, and psychological cognition instead. However, they argue that there is a vital need for developmentalists to focus much more attention on the societal domain, for both theoretical and practical reasons. Theoretically, societal cognition offers a vital opportunity to examine cognitive functioning linked to moral and emotional functioning. But practically, and more importantly from a moral perspective, research into children's societal cognition also provides the necessary foundation for the facilitation of the development of children as economically and politically literate, engaged, and responsible citizens. As the editors of this volume, we concur wholeheartedly with Hatano's and Takahashi's judgement of the theoretical and practical importance of studying children's societal cognition.

REFERENCES

Adelson, J. (1971). The political imagination of the young adolescent. *Daedalus, 100*, 1013–1050.

Adelson, J., Green, B., & O'Neil, R. (1969). Growth of the idea of law in adolescence. *Developmental Psychology, 1*, 327–332.

Adelson, J., & O'Neil, R. (1966). Growth of political ideas in adolescence: The sense of community. *Journal of Personality and Social Psychology, 4*, 295–306.

Berti, A. E., & Bombi, A. S. (1979). Where does money come from? *Archivio di Psicologia, 40*, 53–77.

Berti, A. E., & Bombi, A. S. (1981). The development of the concept of money and its value: A longitudinal study. *Child Development, 52*, 1179–1182.

Berti, A. E., & Bombi, A. S. (1988). *The child's construction of economics.* Cambridge: Cambridge University Press.

Burris, V. (1983). Stages in the development of economic concepts. *Human Relations, 36*, 791–812.

Connell, R. W. (1971). *The Child's Construction of Politics.* Carlton, Australia: Melbourne University Press.

Connell, R. W. (1977). *Ruling class, ruling culture.* Melbourne, Australia: Cambridge University Press.

Danziger, K. (1958). Children's earliest conceptions of economic relationships. *Journal of Social Psychology, 47*, 231–240.

Furth, H. G. (1978). Young children's understanding of society. In H. McGurk (Ed.), *Issues in childhood social development* (pp. 228–256). London: Methuen.

Furth, H. G. (1980). *The world of grown-ups.* New York: Elsevier.

Hess, R. D., & Torney, J. V. (1967). *The development of political attitudes in children.* Chicago: Aldine.

Jahoda, G. (1962). Development of Scottish children's ideas and attitudes about other countries. *Journal of Social Psychology, 58,* 91–108.

Jahoda, G. (1963). The development of children's ideas about country and nationality, Part I: The conceptual framework. *British Journal of Educational Psychology, 33,* 47–60.

Jahoda, G. (1979). The construction of economic reality by some Glaswegian children. *European Journal of Social Psychology, 9,* 115–127.

Jahoda, G. (1981). The development of thinking about economic institutions: The bank. *Cahiers de Psychologie Cognitive, 1,* 55–73.

Piaget, J. (1928). *Judgment and reasoning in the child.* London: Routledge & Kegan Paul.

Piaget, J., & Weil, A. M. (1951). The development in children of the idea of the homeland and of relations to other countries. *International Social Science Journal, 3,* 561–578.

Strauss, A. L. (1952). The development and transformation of monetary meanings in the child. *American Sociological Review, 17,* 275–286.

Tapp, J. L., & Levine, F. J. (Eds.). (1977). *Law, justice and the individual in society.* New York: Holt, Rinehart & Winston.

Torney, J. V. (1971). Socialization of attitudes toward the legal system. *Journal of Social Issues, 27,* 137–154.

Weinstein, E. A. (1957). Development of the concept of flag and the sense of national identity. *Child Development, 28,* 167–174.

CHAPTER TWO

Children's understanding of the school

Eithne Buchanan-Barrow
Department of Psychology, University of Surrey, Guildford, UK

Undoubtedly one of the most influential of social contexts experienced by children is the school. Children's first contact with the school begins with their entry into an elementary school, typically around the age of 5–6 years. Most children will continue their schooling into adolescence, though possibly with a transfer at some stage into a secondary school, and are likely to be members of one or more schools for some 10 years or more. Children therefore experience the particular context of the school for the major part of their childhood. Furthermore, the importance of the school as an environment for children is enhanced by its statutory requirement to provide the main context for children's formalised cognitive development. Indeed, the school has been specifically designed as a system that will provide the most effective environment for promoting children's intellectual growth.

THE SCHOOL AS A MICRO-SOCIETY

However, in addition to fostering children's cognitive development, the school also offers a vital context for social development. Children experience it as their first social system after the family, thereby gaining a new and different perspective on the vital interaction between self and system, and learning to relate both to adults outside the family and also to their peers. Minuchin and Shapiro (1983) describe school children as "members of a small society, in which there are tasks to be done, people to relate to

17

and rules that define the possibilities of behaviour . . . (affecting) aspects of social behaviour and development" (p. 198). They believe that there is an important connection between the individual's long-term social functioning and his/her experience in school, as a consequence of both the significance and the length of the impact that school makes on the lives of children, despite later influences from subsequent social experiences and contexts. Therefore, this early system-knowledge may well be a developmental pointer to institutional understanding in adulthood and, as a consequence, variations in school experiences may contribute to differences in social system-understanding in adult life (Emler, Ohana, & Moscovici, 1987).

The primary school contains many of the aspects of a structured, small-scale society. First, the sense of system is evident, even for a very young child. Schools have a real physical presence with names, possibly uniforms, geographical locations, and boundaries. There are also specially designated roles for all participants, which exist only within the school, such as headteacher, teachers, pupils, etc.; even though they may not be very clearly defined for the youngest pupils, children are generally aware of them from the earliest years. The system of the school therefore makes demands on each member, but equally each participant has expectations of the system. Second, there is also a sense of belonging to a community, which is actively fostered in the children in particular, with frequent references to the school as a society with communal needs and requirements. Competition with other schools, either directly in interschool activities or implicitly through school league tables, also contributes to this feeling of community. Third, conventionally there is a hierarchical power structure, mainly involving headteacher and teachers, but also possibly including some parents and school governors. Decisions by those adults with authority are taken on behalf of the community as a whole and, while children are unlikely to be appraised directly of the organisational structure involved, they are nevertheless regularly made aware of the collective will through new rules or decisions announced in assembly. Finally, and perhaps most importantly of all, there are rules to regulate the system, both explicit and implicit, including a large number of socioconventional rules particular to the school concerned.

However, while the school is undoubtedly an important social context for children, the focus on research in schools has been mainly on the educational context, given the important requirement to foster children's formalised cognitive development. There has been a sustained body of research into all aspects of the school's educational environment, such as children's progress and attainments, teaching styles and practices, curriculum matters, class sizes, school ethos, school design, classroom environments, reading methods, number concept, etc., across the full age-range, with the aim of maximising the academic functioning of the school.

Research has also been conducted into social and behavioural aspects of school life, with particular emphasis on bullying. There have also been extensive studies of teachers' practices, beliefs, and expectations. However, most of this research has been based on teachers' perceptions or observational data or on the analysis of the wealth of educational statistics that are regularly gathered about schools. On the other hand, there has been relatively little research into the specific focus of this chapter, the perceptions of school held by children. However, it is important to know something of children's thinking about the school-as-context during a crucial period in their cognitive development. If schooling is to achieve its important academic and social goals, it is essential to ascertain from school children how they make sense of their school experiences and, even more crucially, whether they value them (Silberman, 1971). Furthermore, children's assessments of their schooling may make a pertinent and important contribution to the debate about the educational system.

This discussion and review of children's understanding of the school will deal with two broad areas of research: (1) children's perceptions of specific areas of school life, such as school rules, the roles of teachers and headteachers, school councils, etc; and (2) more generally, children's understanding of the school as a complex social environment.

SCHOOL RULES

An essential early task in children's social understanding is to grasp the distinction between the two separate domains of social thinking, the moral and the socioconventional (Turiel, 1983). All rule understanding is based ultimately on factual knowledge about the social world; however, moral rule understanding does not depend on this informational content alone, but derives its force from an important and highly valued set of principles, which are held to be rule-, authority-, and context-independent. By contrast, conventional rules are held to be constructs of certain social groupings and/or contexts, designed to regulate social interactions within particular cultures or social units. These shared understandings, such as religious strictures, dress conventions, table manners, politeness rules, etc., are held to be relativistic and dependent on context, role, and possibly on authority as well. As they are consensually constructed, their wrongness is not self-evident and must be learnt, and these rules can be changed. As a consequence of this proposed distinction between two sorts of social judgement, there has been sustained interest in investigating children's ability to differentiate between moral and conventional rules. Some researchers have included further distinctions between rules: prudential rules, which are concerned with children's safety (Schweder, Turiel, & Much, 1981; Tisak & Turiel, 1986, 1988); academic rules (Blumenfeld, Pintrich, & Hamilton,

1987); or second-order conventions, which are conventional rules with major or moral-like consequences (Turiel, 1983). However, the overwhelming interest has been in the dichotomy of moral and socioconventional rules.

Research suggests that very young children, and certainly most preschool children, display competent skills of rule differentiation, acquired within the social context of the family in interaction with their caregivers and their peers (Dunn & Munn, 1985; Smetana & Braeges, 1990; Smetana, Schlagman, & Adams, 1993). Therefore the ability to discriminate between moral and socioconventional rules appears to be fairly well established before entry into school. However, on entry into the new social context of the school, children are confronted with a complex and varied system of rules that may present a challenge to their developing comprehension, despite the early competency of their rule discrimination. With respect to socioconventional rule understanding, such rules are very evidently dependent on the society to which they apply, and in each new context, children must internalise a fresh set of rules. Therefore, on entering school, young pupils are challenged by a large range of diverse socioconventional rules, which make greater demands on their comprehension than moral rules (Smetana, 1993) because their wrongness is less evident and therefore requires more explanation and elucidation. Some school rules, such as second-order conventions (Turiel, 1983), may have a moral-like function discernible to children. Furthermore, children may become aware of the safety aspects of prudential rules (Schweder et al., 1981), such as rules to prevent running in school for fear of injury to self or others, or they may comprehend the educational necessity of some academic or classroom rules (Blumenfeld et al., 1987). The more evident purpose of these rules should facilitate their internalisation. Many school rules, however, have obscure or arbitrary function, such as rules structuring interactions between teachers and children in the classroom, and thus may strain the child's comprehension further. Additionally, children's understanding may become burdened by the sheer volume of new rules, particularly in the case of the youngest children. However, while the children's rule understanding would be facilitated by knowledge of the purpose of each rule, many school rules are simply presented as strictures and never adequately justified or explained to children.

On the other hand, even moral rule understanding, despite the belief that it is context-free once established, is not acquired in a vacuum, and children's comprehension of moral rules may also be affected by the change of context (Buchanan-Barrow & Barrett, 1998a). Some school rules do have clear moral import, such as those concerned with protecting others from harm or with stealing. Therefore, such rules echo similar moral strictures that will have been internalized, by children prior to school entry. However, given the differences in size, complexity, and organisation between the family and the school as social entities, adapting to the school context must present a severe test of young children's moral rule understanding, particularly on first entry to school.

With respect to children's understanding of school rules, some studies with school-aged children have used school scenarios to examine the ways in which children fine-tune their capacity to differentiate between the two types of rules in middle childhood (Blumenfeld et al., 1987; Weston & Turiel, 1980). However, one study specifically addressed the problem faced by children when dealing with school rules that are underexplained or simply less comprehensible (Buchanan-Barrow & Barrett, 1998a). They probed children's differentiation skills beyond the simple dichotomy between moral and socioconventional rules by examining the ability of primary school children to deal with some typically obscure and unexplained school rules; for example, a rule that children must never cross a yellow line in the playground. Asked to discriminate between three types of school rule (moral rules, socioconventional rules with discernible justification, and socioconventional rules without clear purpose), the children, aged 5–11, displayed competent and complex rule-discrimination abilities, with minimal age differences. Their responses effectively ranged the rule types along a continuum, with moral transgressions seen as the most serious, followed by socioconventional rules with evident function, and finally unexplained socioconventional rules. This suggests that children do possess a considerable capacity for dealing with the various types of school rule, but that their differentiation is assisted by an understanding of the purpose of any rule.

However, children's rule understanding in the context of the school is further complicated by the problem of authority. Power or authority is an important aspect of school life and children have to grapple with the intricacies of the organisational and power structure of the school. In particular, they have to accept that a number of adults can wield considerable authority over them. In addition, there is also a direct connection between those in power or authority, such as the headteacher and other teachers, and the school rules. The exercise of power, which helps to define those in authority, is largely achieved through the existence of the school rules, which, in turn, those in authority seek to enforce. The comprehension of rules is therefore inextricably enmeshed with the understanding of power or authority. Thus, children are confronted with the interaction of two central components of the school system, power/authority and the system of rules, which they are required to understand, not only in isolation, but more generally and importantly in conjunction.

There is some evidence that even very young children are capable of the complex task of internalising the intricacies of rules while also comprehending the authority that legitimises them. Some children's earliest experience of school is with the nursery or kindergarten, and although generally smaller in scale and less formal in structure than the elementary school, it is nevertheless a challenging new social context for the young child, with both rules and an authority structure. Corsaro (1990) observed 3- to 4-year-old children's adjustment to the system of the nursery school, particularly examining the interactions between children with regard to rules. He found clear indications that very young children comprehend that rule knowledge is not simply about content but that it involves an understanding that rules are applied and interpreted within a social context. Corsaro describes how children learn to circumvent the rules; for example, a child would share a forbidden toy with another child, while both children made strenuous efforts to ensure that the misdemeanour remained out of the sight of the teachers. Thus, in this conspiratorial manipulation of the rules and deliberate avoidance of the attention of the member of staff, the children were displaying a comprehension of the authority structure of the school.

These links between rules and authority have also been examined in older children. Studies have revealed that primary school children's thinking about authority, such as the authority of teachers, is influenced by social organisational concepts (Laupa, 1991; Laupa & Turiel, 1986), becoming increasingly differentiated with age in respect to authority status and function (Laupa, 1995). With reference to the authority of the headteacher, Laupa and Turiel (1993) found children aged 5–12 years were generally unwilling to accept any sanction on their behaviour by their headteacher in settings outside their school, although they understood fully his/her authority within school. The children demonstrated an awareness that their headteacher's power, though considerable within the school, did not extend beyond the school boundaries. With respect to teachers, Emler et al. (1987), investigating the understanding of 7- to 11-year-old Scottish and French children of the teacher's power to make and change rules in school, found that most children felt that such authority was not without limits. Furthermore, the majority of children made some reference to other rule-makers in school with higher authority, such as the headteacher. However, although Emler et al. concluded that primary school children are capable of interpreting teachers' actions in terms of the formal requirements of their specific organisational role, they found that the children's understanding appeared to be based more on intuition than on detailed knowledge, as they were not always able to give reasons for their thinking.

Although the majority of the children in Emler et al.'s study were agreed on the general rule-making powers of their teachers, there were some differences between the Scottish and French children. These might have emanated from national differences in the French and Scottish educational systems, but they might also be attributed to variations in the physical, educational, or social contexts of the two schools, regardless of cultural differences. Research examining French school children's discourse on rules and responsibilities would suggest that the particular social organisation of the school may influence children's rule understanding (Ohana, 1986). Ohana examined children's discourse as a function of the type of school attended and found that the talk of children from so-called "traditional" schools differed from that of children in "experimental" schools, suggesting that the two sets of children held different understandings of such areas as authority, rule function, and the requirements made by the system on both pupil and staff, as a consequence of variations in organisation between the two schools.

In addition to dealing with the context-based authority of teachers, children have to comprehend that generally schools have no external authority sources, even in the case of such an important and concerned group of adults as the parents. While acknowledging that the headteacher and teachers did have the power to change socioconventional rules in school, children aged 5–11 denied such authority to the parents, thus revealing a clear sense of the boundaries of power in school (Buchanan-Barrow & Barrett, 1998a).

However, with respect to moral rules, some confusion becomes apparent. While almost all the children denied all adults, whether teachers or parents, any jurisdiction over moral rules, there were indications of some misunderstandings in the youngest children's thinking about adult authority in this area. With regard to pushing a child off the climbing frame, whereas the large majority of the children said that the headteacher could not authorise this action, the younger children (aged 5–7) were significantly more likely than the older children (aged 9–11) to claim that this violation would be acceptable if sanctioned by the head. It would appear that the change of social environment from family to school, particularly with the additional and crucial element of the headteacher's exceptional position of authority, had affected the youngest children's comprehension of moral rules and led some of them to report that the rules were dependent on the headteacher's authority. This would support the view that even moral understanding is not totally independent of context (Buchanan-Barrow & Barrett, 1998a). It also underlines the complexity of the task of rule and authority understanding that confronts children as they start school.

THE ROLE OF THE TEACHER

On entry to school, children are confronted with a system in which there are specially designated roles for all participants that exist only within the school, such as headteacher, teachers, pupils, etc. One of the most visible organisational roles in school is likely to be that of the teacher. The class teacher is the child's first point of contact with the school system; through the discourse of the teacher, children will begin to construct their first understandings of the school. Furthermore, the class teacher is the agent responsible for delivering the educational aspects of the school. The importance of this aspect of the teacher's role is likely to be rapidly assimilated by the child, as the extent, type, and quality of contact between pupil and teacher will assist the child to appreciate this particular task. Additionally, parental discourse will reinforce the child's perception of the importance of the class teacher.

Emler et al. (1987), in their study of Scottish and French children's perceptions of the roles of teachers, asked children about the way the teachers perform in the classroom, in addition to their rule-making powers. The children's responses suggested that they had grasped one of the basic fundamentals of the teacher's role in the classroom, as they reported that teachers should offer more support to the less able children in the class. For example, when asked about the teacher's distribution of help to pupils, most of the children expected that the teacher would give more assistance to a child with language difficulties than to other children, and furthermore they overwhelmingly accepted this as fair. Thus the children comprehended that teachers are expected to offer help to pupils proportionately according to their individual needs.

Some studies have investigated children's perceptions of the role of the teacher indirectly while examining academic processes and attainment. A cross-cultural study examined the perceptions of Scottish and Hungarian school children, aged 12–15 years, of their schools and teachers, probing for any influences on the children's motivation and approaches to learning (Entwistle, Kozeki, & Tait, 1989). The reports of the Scottish pupils suggested that they saw their schools as being more formal than the Hungarian children's assessment of their schools. Perhaps as a consequence of this perceived greater formality, the Scottish pupils' perceptions of the pupil–teacher relationship were more likely to be based on respect for teachers, while the Hungarian children's responses showed that control was more generally achieved through informal personal relationships between pupils and staff. Differences in the children's perceptions of the learning environment of their respective schools appeared to result in differing understandings of the role of the teacher, echoing the findings of Ohana (1986).

The importance of investigating school children's perceptions of school is underlined by the apparent links revealed in the study by Entwistle et al. (1989) between the children's assessment of school ethos and learning environment and their approaches to learning and school motivation. The British children were more likely to report a heavy workload and a lack of freedom in learning, which may have emanated from the more formal teacher–pupil relationships reported by the children. On the other hand, the Hungarian children's attitudes towards school were more closely associated with perceptions of a greater freedom in learning, which may have been fostered by the more informal relationships they had with their teachers. As children's attitudes to school work must be a crucial element in their academic performance, the links between children's perceptions of the learning environment and their motivations to school work, as revealed by this study, underline the importance of systematic examination of children's perceptions of school, in order to ensure that all factors affecting academic outcomes are investigated.

Children spend most of their time in school receiving tuition from teachers. Inevitably, then, they must develop their own opinions as to the qualities exhibited by the good teacher. Two studies have used qualititative approaches to examine pupils' perceptions of the performance of their teachers. Children aged 7–17 years old in Trinidad were asked to write essays describing a "good" teacher (Kutnick & Jules, 1993). Content analysis of the essays revealed that children of all ages did judge teachers according to a key aspect of teaching, that is, by their ability to describe, deliver, and explain the content of their lessons. However, the children also tended, less directly, to assess good teachers by their physical presence, such as their general appearance and clothing. The children also reported other important qualities, which were more pastoral than academic; they valued the trustworthiness of their teacher and also mentioned as essential the teacher's care of their pupils. While these traits were general across the age-range, there were some differences in emphasis associated with age. Younger pupils were more focused than older children on the more obvious and immediate aspects, such as the appearance of the teacher, the particular subjects taught, and the administration of physical punishment. Children in the middle age ranges were also largely preoccupied with classroom matters; they mentioned the types of classroom control used by teachers, including disciplinary measures, and other various aspects of the teaching process. However, they also revealed a growing understanding that good teachers needed to be aware of the individual and to deal with the particular needs of each pupil, echoing the responses of the Scottish and French school children in the study by Emler et al. (1987). Finally, the oldest pupils were much less focused on the actualities of the classroom and offered a more mature understanding of the role of the good teacher. They believed that good teachers should be well trained and highly motivated, that they should be alert to the needs of their pupils, and that they should be skilled in engaging the pupils in the learning process. They also mentioned that good teachers should be adept in training their pupils for further education and employment. In pointing out that teachers need to be skilled in preparing their pupils for the wider world, these older children revealed an understanding that one of the essential purposes of schooling is to produce employable adults.

In a very similar study, again using the content analysis of essays, Dutch school children (aged 7, 10, 13, and 16 years), were also asked to describe the characteristics of good teachers (Beishuizen, Hof, Van Putten, Bouwmeester, & Asscher, 2001). In addition to the children's thinking, the views of primary and secondary school teachers were sought, in order to examine any discrepancies between the perceptions of school children and teachers. Correspondence analysis was used to explore any patterns linking the conceptual items that had been revealed by the content analysis, and this analysis produced two dimensions. The items ranged on the first dimension juxtaposed the personality of the teacher versus the ability of the teacher. On the first dimension, the primary school children (7- and 10-year-olds) were more focused on the ability of the teacher, responding that good teachers were first and foremost skilled instructors. On the other hand, the secondary school children (13- and 16-year-olds) emphasised the personality of the teacher. Their responses suggested that good teachers established personal relationships with their pupils, echoing the views of similarly aged Hungarian school children (Entwistle et al., 1989). These perceptions of the older children were similar to those held by the teachers, both primary and secondary; the teachers also felt that the key task for the good teacher was to build relationships with their pupils. With respect to the second dimension, the items juxtaposed the dependence of the children on the teacher versus the independence of the children. While the younger children's responses revealed their dependence on their teacher, the older children indicated a greater sense of independence in their perceptions of the respective roles of pupil and teacher.

Despite the different national samples in these studies of the role of the good teacher, they suggest a roughly similar developmental trend in the children's perceptions. The youngest children are more concerned with the absolute basics of teaching, valuing such aspects as competent and effective instruction in a well-ordered classroom. The older children, as they become more settled in school life, are able to take a broader view of good teachers. Their responses suggest a developing awareness that the teacher has a crucial task in preparing pupils for the world beyond school, either for employment or for further education. Thus, the older children are not only indicating a more mature view of the role of the teacher but also their growing understanding of the wider purpose of schooling. However, in all studies, children recognised the importance of good relationships between pupils and teachers. These findings have also emerged in further qualitative, sociological studies; pupils emphasise how essential it is that they have teachers who are understanding and who are prepared to listen (Garner, 1993; Wallace, 1996). Furthermore, children also describe the worst sort of teaching as a simple recital of information by a teacher who does not seek any involvement from the pupils in his/her class, thus suggesting a mature comprehension of the art of good teaching (Wallace, 1996). However, this is an area of research that requires further systematic examination by more quantitative methods: in particular, the suggested developmental patterns need further exploration.

THE ROLE OF THE HEADTEACHER

There is evidence that children develop an early understanding that social groups and societies may be under the authority of a single individual or "boss" with considerable authority over the workings of the group. Children appear to acquire the concept of the boss at an early age and it has been found in studies of children's political cognition (Berti, 1988; Greenstein, 1960). Berti and Bombi (1985) investigated children's ideas about the boss in specific areas of society, asking working-class Italian children, aged 4–11 years, about the headteacher and the factory boss. They found that around the age of 7–8, most children understand that the school requires a boss, but that they do not always equate this role with the headteacher. By 8–9, most children comprehend that the headteacher has the important role of authority in the school, but also report some misconceptions such as attributing ownership of the school to the headteacher. However, by the end of the primary school years, around the age of 11, most children come to understand that the state "owns" the school and the headteacher conducts his/her role on behalf of the state. This "civil servant" role is a fairly accurate reflection of the Italian headteacher, whose role is administrative, with no teaching duties.

In Britain, however, headteachers do undertake teaching duties, not only in classrooms, but they also frequently address all the pupils in school assemblies. As a consequence, the role of the headteacher may be a more prominent one for British school children. There is evidence that young British school children display an early grasp of the centrality and importance of the headteacher (Buchanan-Barrow & Barrett, 1996, 1998b). Children aged 5–11, when asked about such aspects of school life as who make the rules, or who can get the rules changed, responded that the headteacher did. Even the very youngest children were confident of the headteacher's supremacy, though this may have been more intuitive than substantive, as they were often confused over the specifics of the head's role. The preeminence of the headteacher is to be expected; the headteacher generally has very high visibility in school life and is also prominent in school discourse. However, around the age of 7–8, children reveal a developing understanding of the hierarchy of power in schools, and report that teachers are also involved in the organisation of the school, thus reflecting very similar findings by Emler et al. (1987; see above).

ACADEMIC AND CLASSROOM PROCESSES

How do children view the academic work procedures and behavioural structures in school? Most school children have to function within systems of reward and punishment designed to elicit good academic work and conduct. Research suggests that children generally understand the purpose of such systems and acknowledge their effectiveness in school life. Studies of British school children have found that they generally approve of teachers' use of praise and reward for good work and behaviour and that they value teachers' assessments over those of their peers (primary school children, aged 8–11, Merrett & Tang, 1994; secondary school children, Houghton, Merrett, & Wheldall, 1988). The children also reported that they viewed a letter to their parents, whether detailing a child's good effort or reporting on bad behaviour, as an important and effective method of obtaining good conduct, thus indicating that the children also valued or feared the assessments of their parents. In general, for the older children, private praise (i.e., by the teacher) was valued above public praise (i.e., awards and prizes), as perhaps further indication of the importance children place on the quality of pupil–teacher relationships (Beishuizen et al., 2001; Entwistle et al., 1989)

Emler et al. (1987), in their investigation of the thinking of Scottish and French children about their schools, examined children's perceptions of the criteria used by teachers to assess academic work. The children were asked whether the teacher should reward effort (i.e., hard work but incorrect answers) or success (correct answers despite minimal effort). Most of the French children (78%), regardless of socioeconomic status (SES), reported that the teacher would reward success. However, although a majority (54%) of the Scottish children also predicted that success would be the more likely, there was an important difference between the working-class and middle-class children. The middle-class Scottish children were more likely than the working-class Scottish children to predict that the teacher would reward effort over success, and this tendency increased with age. Furthermore, when the children were then asked to assess the fairness of their predicted decision, whether success or effort, they were significantly more likely to regard as unfair a decision to reward success than a decision to reward effort, with no differences associated with nationality or class. Therefore, while a majority of the children tended to accept that the norm was for the teacher to evaluate their work according to its content, they were not totally happy with a strictly academic approach. Even at this young age, the children were evidently concerned with the fairness of academic procedures.

The study by Emler et al. (1987) would suggest that children do develop an understanding that there are differences in ability between children and that teachers should therefore be more careful in their attribution of success and failure when assessing pupils' work. Similar findings emerged in a study of the evaluations of American children aged 7–8 years and 10–11 years of various motivating strategies commonly used by teachers (Nolen & Nicholls, 1993). With respect to strategies designed to increase motivation in children who were not performing well, the younger group of children were more likely than the older group to endorse the strategies of attributing low effort (i.e., not working hard enough) and giving punishment (i.e., finish work before having free time) to pupils who are failing. With respect to strategies designed to maintain motivation in children who were doing well, the younger group were more likely to support the use of rewards (i.e., prizes and/or privileges) and the attribution of superiority (i.e., display their work to the rest of the class) to high achievers. The older group of children, on the other hand, perhaps more cognizant of the role played in performance by ability, were less keen to endorse strategies that may have been unfair to less able pupils or unlikely to add to the motivation of the very able. Overall, the older children tended to reject a simple reward/punishment structure and revealed an understanding of the complexities involved in developing motivation strategies to deal with all types of pupils.

This more differentiated understanding of motivation was also revealed in a study of the thinking of Japanese and American children, aged 11–12 years (Hamilton, Blumenfeld, Akoh, & Miura, 1989). In an interview schedule using both closed and open-ended questions, the children were asked about their actions and their feelings in various areas of classroom life, including academic achievement and good conduct. The children's reasons for adhering to various classroom norms (academic, social, and moral) were coded in one of three ways: internal (i.e., I like history; so I will learn; I would feel ashamed); external (i.e., my parents will be pleased; my teacher will be cross); and empathic (i.e., my parents will be upset; someone might get hurt). With respect to actions (i.e., why is it important to get your sums right; why is it bad to cheat), the Japanese children (14%) reported less external reasoning than the American children (40%), suggesting that they were more likely to be self-motivating. On the other hand, with respect to feelings (i.e., why do you feel good when you do well in a test), the two groups of children reported the same amount of external reasons (42%). According to Hamilton et al., while Japanese children were less likely to offer external authorities, such as teacher or parents, as their reason for adhering to academic and classroom procedures, they nevertheless acknowledged that the affective motivation was more usually the wish to please important adults. This was particularly with respect to academic performance as opposed to questions about classroom procedure. A study of British children, aged 11 and 16 years (Blatchford, 1996), found that their assessments of the reasons for success and failure were similar to those of Japanese children. The British children also tended to attribute success and failure in academic work to internal factors, and very much those connected with effort, such as working hard, concentrating more, etc. These cross-cultural variations in motivation require further systematic examination, as children's attitudes towards teachers' motivating strategies are likely to be an important influence on academic outcomes.

Therefore, in addition to differences in motivation associated with age, there would appear to be other influences on children's attitudes to work and behaviour in school. While some of these cross-cultural studies have revealed differences between pupils from different cultures, this does not exclude the possibility that there are differences between schools within cultures as a consequence of variations in school ethos or organisation. For example, there may be variations in children's thinking stemming from the levels of bullying in a particular school and from the practices and strategies devised to prevent such behaviour. These variations in organisational style need further systematic exploration, so that teachers' classroom strategies can be more closely aligned with children's perceptions and expectations in order to achieve optimal performance.

PERCEPTIONS OF THE SCHOOL

While children's understanding of various aspects of school life, such as teachers, rules, and classroom matters, has been the subject of investigations, there has been much less research into children's overall observations of school. Despite children being the main users of the formal education system, there has been relatively little focused consumer research to ascertain their reactions to the school as an integral experience. However, there are undoubtedly important connections between all areas of school life, such as the links between children's understanding of rules and their perceptions of teachers' authority (see above), which require further elucidation through research into children's general perceptions of school.

British school children generally have favourable views of school, with children reporting positive attitudes towards school as an environment and towards academic work. For example, in a large sample of over 2000 secondary school children, 68% of children aged 11–12 years and 60% of children aged 13–14 years reported that they were generally happy in school (Keys & Fernandes, 1992). With respect to work, 62% of the younger group and 55% of the older group said they found their school work interesting.

However, there is some evidence that children's positive attitudes diminish with age. Another study of British school children's perspectives on school and school work took a longitudinal approach, interviewing children at 7, 11, and 16 years and found that children's evaluation of school tended to become more negative with age (Blatchford, 1996). When asked how positive they felt about going to school in the morning, the children at age 7 years (62%) and age 11 years (53%) were generally happy at the prospect, but only 35% of the children at age 16 years felt positive about going to school. This decrease in positivity may have been associated with the children's views on how interesting they found school: while over 40% of the children at both age-points 7 and 11 responded that school was mostly interesting, this declined to just 26% at age 16 years. However, there was little association between children's perceptions of school and their attainments in reading and maths, suggesting that children's evaluations of school are not simply based on their own academic progress.

These findings of general positivity, particularly in younger children, have been echoed by studies in other countries. Australian children aged 10–11 years, responding to structured questionnaires, were generally very positive about their schools, with around 85% expressing overall satis-faction with school life and with teacher–student relations in particular (Ainley & Bourke, 1992). However, the greatest positivity was reported in response to items relating to opportunities (i.e., the things I learn are important to me), suggesting an understanding of the crucial role played by schools in preparing children for the world of work and/or further edu-cation. This awareness of the wider purpose of education also emerged in the studies of Trinidadian children (Kutnick & Jules, 1993) and Dutch children (Beishuizen et al., 2001), although at an older age, possibly as a consequence of the more qualitative approach of those studies.

While such studies have produced some evidence of children's overall attitudes towards school, there has also been some criticism, as there is little attempt to probe the reasons behind children's perceptions (Lang, 1993). A notable exception to this was a study by Lee, Statuto, and Kedar-Voivodas (1983), which examined the perceptions of school life held by American children aged 7 years, 9 years, and 11 years. They used a semistructured interview to tap into children's views of the everyday conventions of schooling, asking about matters such as who decides on classroom rules, and whether school is a just place or not. However, in addition to the children's perceptions of various issues in their actual school, they were also asked about their ideal school, particularly with regard to decision-making, in order to gain further insight into the children's responses. For example, the children were first asked if they had any part in deciding how much homework they did, and then asked if they thought children should be involved in such decision-making.

The study revealed two major findings about the children's thinking. First, there was a growing divergence between children's perceptions of the actual school and the ideal, which Lee et al. suggest might cause an increase in tension as the children progress through the educational system. For example, the older children felt that they should be more actively involved in decision-making about both the curriculum (i.e., how the subject time is decided) and organisational matters (i.e., where children sit in class), while the younger children did not voice such concerns. Lee et al. suggest that the older children's expectations of their role in schools develop out of a growing belief in their autonomy and competence, as they progress up the school and become more settled into the school environment. Therefore, as the children's perception of the pupil's role appears to develop at a faster rate than teachers can accommodate, children may feel frustrated that their increasing sense of competence is not generally recognised and fostered by schools. However, the other major finding in the study would suggest that, in fact, children do not feel alienated by their developing sense of powerlessness in school. Surprisingly, the children generally reported that school is a liked (82%), responsive (93%), just (83%), and important (93%) place to be and these evaluations were greater in the older children than the younger. Therefore, despite the older children's perception that their social competence is being insufficiently appreciated, these primary school children generally acknowledged that school is a good environment for them. However, it may be that Lee et al. have correctly located in younger children the genesis of the growing overall negativity towards school reported in studies of older children, such as that by Blatchford (1996). The failure of schools to accommodate children's increasing desire to play an active part in the decision-making in their schools may be the cause of any decrease in positivity towards the school in later years.

SCHOOL COUNCILS

It would appear from Lee et al.'s study (1983) that children's perceptions of the recognition given to their views about school may be an important factor in their evaluation of school. The findings indicate that children wish to have their views about school valued and seek to be included in the decision-making processes in school. One of the ways in which this might be achieved is through school councils, which have been established in a minority of schools in the UK. School councils vary from school to school, but generally they provide a regular forum where school children, elected by their peers as representatives of their respective years, may raise issues of concern about school life. Depending on the system set up in each school, school children may actually have some power to put their decisions into practice.

Two qualitative studies have investigated British children's thinking about school councils (Alderson, 2000; Wyse, 2001). Both examined children's rights to participation in school using the United Nations 1989 Convention of the Rights of the Child as a framework. Included in the list of main civil rights drawn up by the UN are two that are directly relevant to children's participation in school decision-making: (1) the right to be heard and to have your views taken seriously in matters that affect you; and (2) the right to share in making decisions about your life. Wyse (2001), interviewing in both primary and secondary schools, found that children had very few opportunities to voice their opinions, even in schools with councils. However, a much larger qualitative survey (Alderson, 2000) that canvassed the views of over 2000 school children aged 7–17 years, of whom approximately half were in schools with councils, revealed more positive findings about school councils. The children were asked about their perceptions of everyday school life, including their views about the effectiveness of their school councils. A majority of the children whose schools did have school councils reported that their councils were allowed to raise and discuss any topic the children wanted (65%) as opposed to councils that could only talk about items proposed by teachers (20%). However, the children's evaluations of the councils' effectiveness were rather less positive; while 28% of the children reported that school councils were good at sorting out problems, 26% disagreed. More positively, 39% of the children felt that school councils helped to make the school a better place to be in, while 25% disagreed and 25% were uncertain.

Examining links between the children's evaluations of their school council and their overall perceptions of school, Alderson (2000) found that a positive view of the school council was generally associated with positive attitudes about the school's social and academic activities. On the other hand, a negative assessment of the school council was linked to more negative views of the school generally, although the direction of any influence is unclear. Alderson suggests that a council that is perceived by students to be merely a token (i.e., with minimal to no power to effect real change) might result in more negative attitudes than might be caused by the total absence of a school council, as children might be more frustrated by its ineffectiveness than its absence. Therefore, it would seem likely that a school council that is perceived by children as effective in dealing with student grievances may result in a more positive evaluation of the school in general by the children. In view of the finding of Lee et al. (1983), that children believe that their views on school life are generally not sought out or sufficiently valued, school councils may offer a way of meeting children's claims for more involvement in school decision-making.

SCHOOL AS SOCIAL SYSTEM

How do children come to understand the school as a whole community, as a microscopic society? The task of settling in to school life is probably a daunting one for the new, first-year pupil. Children enter the system of the school as relatively powerless strangers, expected to adjust to a series of strange rules without any pre-existing relationships for assistance, where success depends on rapid assessment and adoption of the pupil's role, without any clear description of exactly what is required of them. The school is clearly an extensive system, with much of its workings, structure, and power-patterns invisible and unexplained to the young pupil. It is, in microcosm, a multifaceted and multilayered society and undoubtedly presents a considerable interpretative problem for young children (Emler et al., 1987). According to Brownell (1989), it is this typical complexity of the social environment that probably makes heavy demands on the young child's developing social understanding. And yet, for successful functioning, the young pupil needs to have an understanding of the school as a whole and complex environment, with a developing grasp of the interconnected-ness of such aspects as rules, roles, power, and community. This compre-hension of the wider purpose and structure of the school both transcends and affects their understanding of particular areas within the school, such as the classroom or the playground, or of specific topics such as rule knowledge.

An examination of the understanding of the school-as-system held by young British schoolchildren (aged 5–11 years) looked at some important system concepts such as rules, community, self-system interaction, and power, and the links between them (Buchanan-Barrow & Barrett, 1996). In order to avoid the possible problems of under-reporting from Piagetian-style open-ended interviewing of children (Karmiloff-Smith, 1988), the children responded via a card-sorting task, with children selecting their responses from a series of cards presenting them with possible answers. The general picture that emerged suggested that the children's thinking begins with a simple and narrow focus on a few central features, but as they move up through the school, their understanding broadens and develops to include more complex and wider aspects of the school system. The child's first access to the system is by understanding the role of the headteacher, and even the youngest children clearly understood the position and importance of the head in the school system, supporting research by Berti (1988). Then, around the age of 7–9 years (after some 2–3 years of full-time schooling), children begin to acknowledge the next layer down in the power hierarchy, that of the teachers. Finally the oldest children (aged 9–11 years) display further changes; first, they suggest that parents have influence in school matters, and second, their responses claim an important part for children. This assertion by children of a belief in their own contribution to school decision-making reflects the findings of Lee et al. (1983) that, by the age of 11, children gain a sense of their autonomy and competence in school matters. Furthermore, the children's developing understanding of each system concept also appears to be linked to others, contributing to their overall comprehension of the system of the school.

Investigating the perceptions of parents and teachers, in addition to those of the children, in order to examine wider influences on the children's thinking about school, Buchanan-Barrow and Barrett (1998b) found indications of other influences besides those associated with age. Children from a school in a lower SES area differed in some of their responses from those given by children from a school in a higher SES area. When asked about power/authority distribution in their school, the lower SES school children perceived less involvement in the school organisation by both parents and children than was reported by the middle-class schoolchildren, suggesting a difference in organisational style between the two schools. It is not possible to ascertain whether the children's perceptions of school organisation were indeed accurate, nor if the differences perceived were unconnected with the variations associated with class between the two school populations. However, it could be argued that lower socioeconomic group parents might have less time to devote to school affairs, or that their capacity for effective intervention might be limited by lower educational attainments thus possibly diminishing their readiness to do so.

Furthermore, some indirect support was found to suggest that the two sets of parents did have different relationships with their respective schools. While there was no significant difference between the two parent populations in their overall attitude ratings of their children's schools, one specific item did show a significant variation. With respect to the parents' assessments of how welcome they felt they were in school, the parents of children in the lower SES school actually rated this more highly than the parents of children in the higher SES school. Parents with higher SES are more likely to have the necessary time to raise issues about school and may well be more assured of their ability to achieve their aims and better equipped to make their feelings known. Therefore, it might be expected that the staff in schools with a higher SES parent body might be more wary of interactions with parents and consequently less warm in their welcomes. On the other hand, the parents with lower SES, without the same sense of empowerment, may be seen by teachers as less threatening. Therefore, this difference in the way parents felt welcome in school supports the view that the children from the lower SES school were indeed correctly perceiving and reporting a more limited spread of power. The parents from the lower SES school may well have been less likely to exert real influence on the school, for a variety of reasons.

If this interpretation is indeed correct, and the children were accurately understanding and reporting the amount of power they and their parents had in their schools, then there is an important conclusion to be drawn. The children from the lower SES school may be acquiring a different sense of their own ability to exert influence in their lives and this could continue to affect other and later issues in their lives, such as employment or political matters. Furthermore, there is evidence from other studies that variations in school organisation can result in differences in children's perceptions of power and authority (Ohana, 1986). As children are believed to construct their political understanding from their comprehension of all the social groupings of which they are members (Palonsky, 1987; Stevens, 1982), their school experiences may be central to their early political understandings, as school is the paramount social environment for children, after the family. Children's comprehension of their own empowerment or powerlessness, or that of their parents, in such an important social environment as the school may set an unfortunate pattern of passivity or apathy in their political thinking, which may persist into their adult lives.

CONCLUSION

This chapter has reviewed the research literature on children's under-standing of the school. In general terms, the young school child copes well with the complex demands of the school environment, revealing an early comprehension of the more visible and pertinent aspects such as rules, power/authority, and roles. With age, children's understanding broadens to encompass less evident aspects of the school context and older school children reveal a comprehension of the system of the school and of the links between the different system concepts.

However, as will be apparent, this is an area of children's societal understanding that has been relatively underexamined. While the import-ance of the school as the context for children's intellectual development is widely acknowledged, school-based research has generally focused on academic aspects of school life, examining any aspects that are believed to influence children's performance and learning, such as teaching styles and practices, probably as a consequence of the intense preoccupation with school league tables and exam results. There has been very little research into children's own perceptions of school life, despite evidence that children do hold distinct views about their school experiences and that they wish to have them recognised and valued (Buchanan-Barrow & Barrett, 1996, 1998b; Lee et al., 1983). It would also seem potentially useful to examine both sides of the education equation, and to probe the views of pupils as well as those of teachers about the effectiveness of the teaching process. Furthermore, children's thinking about school may well be an important contributory factor in their intellectual development, as the optimal conditions for learning are likely to include children's positive evaluation of school. Thus research in this area should also assist in developing ways to improve academic performance.

The paucity of research in this area has wider implications, however. It has also diminished our understanding of the development of children's understanding of society in general. Overall, the school is a complex, multifaceted community with many of the hallmarks of a micro-society, thus presenting a considerable challenge to the understanding of the young pupil. In school the child comes into daily contact with such system concepts as power, authority rules, community, and decision-making. Children must learn to adopt the impersonal role of pupil and to interact with nonfamily adults, also taking on impersonal roles, who have considerable authority over them. They have to internalise a large body of rules, many of which may seem arbitrary, but whose transgression may result in serious consequences for the child. For a large part of their lives, school children are members of a compact and distinct community. In short, in the process of adapting and developing within this microscopic community, children may be developing their earliest understandings and beliefs about society, after the family. Therefore, the child is offered the potentiality, by membership of the school community, for acquiring some conceptions of how a social system beyond the family functions, and for experiencing the interaction between the self and system. As Minuchin and Shapiro (1983) pointed out, schools present an unrivalled possibility for mapping the child's relationship to nonparental authorities at different times and ages, as their social understanding develops, and for examining the effects of different styles of authority on the child's growing sense of responsibility, not only for their immediate circle of peers and teachers, but also for the community as a whole. Thus school children, in adapting to the system of the school, may also be constructing the basis of their thinking about other systems in society, which will eventually extend to encompass such areas as politics and the law (see chapters by Berti and by Ceci et al. in this volume). In learning how to be a pupil within the school system, they may also be piecing together an understanding of the role of the individual within the system, which may well form the basis of their future thinking about the role of the citizen. The possible links between children's understanding of the school and their future thinking about various aspects of society needs to be examined systematically.

Future research in this area, however, would also benefit from a fresh perspective. Much of the research reviewed is this chapter has been Piagetian in approach, with the characteristic use of open-ended questioning. This type of approach has drawn criticism in recent years, partly because the children's inability to access their knowledge or to articulate fully their understandings may lead the researcher to underestimate the children's thinking (Karmiloff-Smith, 1988). Thus studies such as those using children's essays to investigate the role of the teacher (Beishuizen et al., 2001; Kutnick & Jules, 1993) may be underestimating children's real comprehension in this area. Furthermore, the emphasis placed by the cognitive-developmental approach on a systematic and universal development progression in children's thinking at the expense of individual differences does not fit with the findings that children's thinking about schools may well vary as a function of the type of school they attend (Ohana, 1988) or the culture in which they are developing (Emler et al., 1987; Entwistle et al., 1989; Hamilton et al., 1989).

The more recent naïve theory approach to children's cognitive development (Wellman & Gelman, 1998) might be used productively in this area. This perspective proposes that children construct naïve theories in response to various domains of knowledge. Children draw on these naïve theories to generate domain-specific causal explanations of various phenomena, both observable and unobservable, thus constructing coherent, if immature, understanding. While children may be unable to report these theories verbally, as they are often more implicit than explicit, their existence can be tested and revealed by children's choices of proposed outcomes to various domain-specific events as presented to them in scenarios or stories. The scenarios and the possible outcomes could be based on the children's thinking as generated by the qualitative studies reviewed in this chapter. However, as the children would be selecting their responses to the scenarios from a series of possible answers, the problems associated with verbal reporting should be avoided. With respect to the school, some studies have found that children have acquired an intuitive, rather than substantive, understanding of some less visible aspects of school life, such as some parts of the role of the teacher (Emler et al., 1987) and the role of the headteacher (Buchanan-Barrow & Barrett, 1996, 1998b). The theory perspective would provide a framework for a systematic exploration of these intuitive understandings and might clarify the thinking behind the children's assertions. For example, the children's understanding of the role of the headteacher could be probed by asking children to choose between several possible actions to be taken by the headteacher in response to some event in school, and in the process some of their thinking about the headteacher's role and his authority might be revealed.

Therefore, the application of these new research approaches in examinations of children's understanding of the school should result in fresh perspectives on children's thinking about this important developmental context. Furthermore, such research may indicate some of the ways in which children construct their thinking about societal institutions beyond the school and thus contribute to our more general knowledge of children's understanding of society.

REFERENCES

Ainley, J., & Bourke, S. (1992). Student views of primary schooling. *Research Papers in Education, 7*, 107–128.

Alderson, P. (2000). School students' views on school councils and daily life at school. *Children & Society, 14*, 121–134.

Beishuizen, J. J., Hof, E., Van Putten, C. M., Bouwmeester, S., & Asscher, J. J. (2001). Students' and teachers' cognitions about good teachers. *British Journal of Educational Psychology, 71*, 185–201.

Berti, A. E. (1988). The development of political understanding in children between 6–15 years old. *Human Relations, 41*, 437–446.

Berti, A. E., & Bombi, A. S. (1985). *The child's construction of economics.* Cambridge: Cambridge University Press.

Blatchford, P. (1996). Pupils' views on school work and school from 7 to 16 years. *Research Papers in Education, 11*, 263–288.

Blumenfeld, P. C., Pintrich, P. R., & Hamilton, V. L. (1987). Teacher talk and students' reasoning about morals, conventions and achievement. *Child Development, 58*, 1389–1401.

Brownell, C. A. (1989). Socially-shared cognition: The role of social context in the construction of knowledge. In L. T. Winegar (Ed.), *Social interaction and the development of children's understanding.* Norwood, NJ: Ablex.

Buchanan-Barrow, E., & Barrett, M. (1996). Primary school children's understanding of the school. *British Journal of Educational Psychology, 66*, 33–46.

Buchanan-Barrow, E., & Barrett, M. (1998a). Children's rule discrimination within the context of the school. *British Journal of Developmental Psychology, 16*, 539–551.

Buchanan-Barrow, E., & Barrett, M. (1998b). Individual differences in children's understanding of the school. *Social Development, 7*, 25–268.

Corsaro, W. A. (1990). The underlife of the nursery school: Young children's social representations of adult rules. In G. Duveen & B. Lloyd (Eds.), *Social representations and the development of knowledge.* Cambridge: Cambridge University Press.

Dunn, J., & Munn, P. (1985). Becoming a family member: Family conflict and the development of social understanding in the second year. *Child Development, 56*, 480–492.

Emler, N., Ohana, J., & Moscovici, S. (1987). Children's beliefs about institutional roles: A cross-national study of representations of the teacher's role. *British Journal of Education Psychology, 57*, 26–37.

Entwistle, N., Kozeki, B., & Tait, H. (1989). Pupils' perceptions of school and teachers II—relationships with motivation and approaches to learning. *British Journal of Educational Psychology, 59*, 340–350.

Garner, P. (1993). What disruptive students say about the school curriculum and the way it is taught. *Therapeutic Care and Education, 2*, Winter, 404–415.

Greenstein, F. I. (1960). The benevolent leader: Children's images of political authority. *American Political Science Review, 54*, 934–943.

Hamilton, V. L., Blumenfield, P. C., Akoh, H., & Miura, K. (1989). Japanese and American children's reasons for the things they do in school. *American Journal of Educational Research, 26*, 545–571.

Houghton, S., Merrett, F., & Wheldall, K. (1988). The attitudes of British secondary school pupils to praise, rewards, punishments and reprimands: A further study. *New Zealand Journal of Educational Studies, 23*, 203–214.

Karmiloff-Smith, A. (1988). The child is a theoretician, not an inductivist. *Mind and Language, 3*, 184–195.

Keys, W., & Fernandes, C. (1992). *What do students think about school? A report for the National Commission on Education.* London: NFER.

Kutnick, P., & Jules, V. (1993). Pupils' perceptions of a good teacher: A developmental perspective from Trinidad and Tobago. *British Journal of Educational Psychology, 63,* 4000–4413.

Lang, P. (1993). Research review secondary students views on school. *Children & Society, 7,* 308–313.

Laupa, M. (1991). Children's reasoning about three authority attributes: Adult status, knowledge and social position. *Developmental Psychology, 27,* 321–329.

Laupa, M. (1995). Children's reasoning about authority in home and school contexts. *Social Development, 4,* 5–16.

Laupa, M., & Turiel, E. (1986). Children's conceptions of adult and peer authority. *Child Development, 57,* 404–412.

Laupa, M., & Turiel, E. (1993). Authority reasoning and social context. *Journal of Educational Psychology, 85,* 191–197

Lee, P. C., Statuto, C. M., & Kedar-Voivodas, G. (1983). Elementary school children's perceptions of their actual and ideal school experience: A developmental study. *Journal of Educational Psychology, 75,* 838–847.

Merrett, F., & Tang, W. (1994). The attitudes of British primary school pupils to praise, reward, punishments and reprimands. *British Journal of Educational Psychology, 64,* 91–103.

Minuchin, P. P., & Shapiro, E. K. (1983). The school as context for social development. In P. Mussen (Ed.), *Handbook of child psychology, Vol 4.* New York: John Wiley.

Nolen, S. B., & Nicholls, J. G. (1993). Elementary school pupils' beliefs about practices for motivating pupils in mathematics. *British Journal of Educational Psychology, 63,* 414–430.

Ohana, J. (1986). Educational styles and social knowledge. *Interim report to CNRS.* CNRS, France

Palonsky, S. B. (1987). Political socialization in elementary schools. *The Elementary School Journal, 87,* 493–505.

Schweder, R. A., Turiel, E., & Much, N. (1981). The moral intuitions of the child. In J. H. Flavell & L. Ross (Eds.), *Social-cognitive development: Frontiers and possible futures.* Cambridge: Cambridge University Press.

Silberman, M. L. (1971). Discussion. In M. L. Silberman (Ed.), *The experience of schooling* (pp. 362–364). New York: Holt, Rinehart & Winston.

Smetana, J. (1993). Understanding of social rules. In M. Bennett (Ed.), *The child as psychologist.* Hemel Hempstead, UK: Harvester Wheatsheaf.

Smetana, J. G., & Braeges, J. L. (1990). The development of toddlers' moral and conventional judgments. *Merrill-Palmer Quarterly, 36,* 329–346.

Smetana, J. G., Schlagman, N., & Adams, P. (1993). Preschoolers' judgments about hypothetical and actual transgressions. *Child Development, 64,* 202–214.

Stevens, O. (1982). *Children talking politics: Political learning in childhood.* Oxford: Martin Robertson.

Tisak, M. S., & Turiel, E. (1986). Children's conceptions of moral and prudential rules. *Child Development, 55,* 1030–1039.

Tisak, M. S., & Turiel, E. (1988). Variation in seriousness of transgressions and children's moral and conventional concepts. *Child Development, 55,* 1030–1039.

Turiel, E. (1983). *The development of social knowledge: Morality and convention.* New York: Cambridge University Press.

Wallace, G. (1996). Relating to teachers. In J. Rudduck, R. Chaplin, & G. Wallace (Eds.), *School improvement: What can pupils tell us?* London: David Fulton.

Wellman, H. M., & Gelman, S. A. (1998). Knowledge acquisition in foundational domains. In W. Damon (Ed.), *Handbook of Child Psychology, Vol. 2: Cognition, perception and language* (pp. 523–573). New York: Wiley.

Weston, D. R., & Turiel, E. (1980). Act–rules relations: Children's concepts of social rules. *Development Psychology, 16*, 417–424.

Wyse, D. (2001). Felt tip pens and school councils: Children's participation rights in four English schools. *Children & Society, 15*, 209–218.

CHAPTER THREE

Children's understanding of economics

Paul Webley
School of Psychology, University of Exeter, UK

INTRODUCTION: THE MEANING OF "ECONOMICS"

Economics is often used as a label for that part of the social world concerned with the acquisition, management, and distribution of assets (e.g., buying, borrowing, bargaining, banking), and for the most part this convenient approach is taken here. But it is inevitable, given that the concept of economic behaviour is culturally and historically determined, that the boundary between the economic and the noneconomic is poorly defined and rather arbitrary. Hence in this book children's understanding of social class and occupations is dealt with in Chapter 7 (by Emler & Dickinson), though aspects of this topic are clearly part of economic understanding. Agonising over definitions has never seemed to me a useful activity, but being clear about what we mean by "economics" does matter: It is important not to fall into the trap, for example, of thinking that economic behaviour must involve money. Historically, plenty of economic systems have managed without money and in the modern world there are still many areas of economic activity that are not monetised (the most notable example being the domestic sphere). What this suggests is that in considering children's understanding of economics we should not only be concerned with the cash economy but also need to consider their understanding of swapping, doing chores, and gift-giving.

So my aim in this chapter is to provide a definitive (but not exhaustive) overview of children's understanding of economics broadly conceived.

There will be a particular emphasis on the child's understanding of his or her own economic behaviour, as previous reviews (e.g., Berti & Bombi, 1988; Cram & Ng, 1999; Furnham, 1996) have concentrated almost entirely on children's understanding of the adult economy. There will also be a focus on the relative impact of indirect sources and direct experience on economic understanding and on variations in economic understanding within and across cultures.

CHILDREN'S UNDERSTANDING OF ECONOMIC CONCEPTS

There is a very substantial literature in this area. Nearly all studies are based within a cognitive interpretation of development that assumes universal stages that children have to go through in order to achieve an adult understanding of economic concepts. This is often explicitly Piagetian, though not in the earlier or more recent studies. The number of stages identified, and the detailed content, varies from concept to concept and from author to author, though there are rarely fewer than four stages or more than nine. A subsidiary theme is concerned with identifying differences in children's conceptions that can be related to the social environment.

Children's understanding of money and its origins

Children's understanding of money has been under investigation for at least 50 years. In what is probably the earliest study, Strauss and Schuessler interviewed 141 children from two social classes and from the ages of 4½ to 11½ about the meaning of money and its origins (Schuessler & Strauss, 1950; Strauss, 1952; Strauss & Schuessler, 1951). The children were each interviewed on four separate occasions, which enabled Strauss (1952) to identify nine stages through which children progress in their understanding of monetary meaning. Before the first stage (what one could label stage 0), Strauss reports that children (aged 3–4½) can distinguish between money and other objects, but can't distinguish between different coins. Their handling of coins is playful and they are only vaguely aware that money is somehow connected with buying. In stage 1, children have a notion that money can somehow buy certain commodities ("Spend it. That's what money is for") but think that any coin can buy anything. At stage 2, they recognise that some coins are more valuable than others, but believe that one must tender the exact coin—so a nickel can buy a 5-cent item but not a 2-cent item. Nonetheless, they assume that a shopkeeper always gives money back as part of the transaction. As children move through the higher stages their understanding becomes more sophisticated. So at stage 4 there is a recognition that customers have to pay the shopkeeper for goods bought in order for the shopkeeper to earn money and, by stage 9, children fully understand the notion of profit. What is missing at all stages is an understanding of the role of middlemen (wholesalers, distributors, etc.). The children were asked if it made any sense for the manufacturer to sell his goods to one person, who sold them to another, who in turn sold them to the shopkeeper. Only two children in the whole sample thought this might just make sense (the others refused to entertain the possibility), and even they believed it did not happen very often. This lack of understanding of the role of middlemen is probably a consequence of the age range of the sample, as it is evident in subsequent research that the understanding of complicated economic issues continues to develop throughout adolescence (e.g., Jahoda, 1981). It is worth noting that Strauss and Schuessler (1951) report no class or sex differences.

Berti and Bombi (1979, 1981, 1988) built on Strauss and Schuessler's work and elaborated it in two important ways. First, they explored the understanding of a younger age group, and interviewed children aged 3 to 8 about the use of money in buying and selling. Second, they investigated children's ideas about the sources of money. So as to provide a concrete starting point, Berti and Bombi used a procedure in which coins and bank notes were introduced into the interview, along with such items as sweets and comics. For the use of money in buying and selling, they identified five levels of responses (and a stage 0, in which there was almost a complete absence of knowledge about money). At stage 1, children recognise that money is used when one buys something, but do not differentiate between different notes and coins (as Strauss also found). At stage 2 children realise that not all kinds of money will buy everything, though this understanding is very broad. So a child distinguishes between coins and notes and believes that the latter would have to be used to buy higher-value items. At stage 3 children know that sometimes the money is not enough. Money cannot be used when "it is too little". What marks this stage out from stage 2 is the use of quantitative criteria. So Leo (age 5), for instance, knows that he can buy more with a 100,000 lire note than a 10,000 lire note "because there are more numbers". Stage 4 is characterised by the notion that to buy something the exact money is necessary (as in Strauss' stage 2). Berti and Bombi point out that, for some children, the idea that one must pay with the exact money alternates during the interview with the idea that one could pay more and get change, but for children at this stage the exact money notion dominates. Finally, at stage 5, children understand that change precisely compensates for any difference in value between the money tendered and the price of the goods bought.

This work goes beyond that of Strauss in interesting ways. By studying younger children, Berti and Bombi were able to see the first emergence of economic ideas. Even those children at stage 0 knew that money was somehow linked to buying, and what one can see is the gradual shift from an understanding of buying and selling as a ritual or custom to an understanding based on the relationship between money and goods. Berti and Bombi's results also give a more satisfactory picture of what happens in the early stages of the understanding of money. By interviewing the same children again a year later, they were able to confirm that the idea of being able to pay only with the exact money is an advance on the notion of being able to pay with money of a higher value. Almost all the children who had held the former view had moved on to a correct understanding a year later, whereas some of those holding the latter view had shifted, a year on, to believe that the exact sum of money was necessary.

Berti and Bombi's findings about children's ideas of the source of money are also instructive. Four categories emerged from their analysis. At level 1 (4–5 years) children had no idea of the origin of money, whilst at level 2 children saw the origin of money as independent from work; for example, the bank gives it to anyone who asks for it. At level 3, the subjects thought that the change given by shopkeepers after having bought an item was the origin of money. At level 4 (7–8 years) children associate money with work and indeed assert that money comes only from working.

The studies of Strauss and Schuessler, and Berti and Bombi, are clearly within a cognitive developmental tradition, in that their results show a progressive sequence of stages that children move through in achieving an adult understanding of money. More recent work on children's understanding of money carried out in the Czech Republic and Portugal (Morgado & Vyskocilova, 2000) and in South Africa (Bonn & Webley, 2000) has placed more emphasis on the importance of the social context, and consequently has stressed differences within samples rather than uniformity of development.

The purpose of Bonn and Webley's study, for example, was to investigate children's economic understanding in a society where there are enormous and entrenched differences in wealth based on racial grounds and where, in the past, social mobility for the poorer groups has been extremely limited. Three locations (rural, urban, semi-urban) were chosen because they provided very different social environments in which the children were gathering their "economic knowledge" about the world: Rural areas are generally extremely poor with high levels of unemployment, and such employment as there is involves migrant work; urban areas are also poor but with a greater range in the types of jobs available; and semi-urban areas are the most affluent. Over 200 children aged 7, 9, 11, and 14 years were interviewed individually in Setswana (their mother tongue) and asked, among other things, where money comes from. The answers to this question fell into clearly defined categories (Whites, God, people in general, the government, factory or mine) and tended to be brief and concrete. There were few references overall to the link between work and money. Many of the answers had a distinct South African flavour, with references being made to Nelson Mandela, the Whites, and the origins of money in the mines, the latter being a more common response among the rural children (e.g., "They dig it up, as they dig, stones of gold come out and they make money out of it"). The urban sample gave the least sophisticated answers: They notably favoured the explanations "the bank" and "God" and gave the fewest answers that referred to the government and payment. Developmental trends were not that clear, but personal references ("God", people) dropped with age and the idea that money is man-made (in a factory or in a mine) increased.

Rather than a within-country comparison, Morgado and Vyskocilova compared children from the Czech Republic (Prague) and Portugal (Coimbra). Seventy-five children from each location, with ages ranging from 7½ to 9½ years, were asked questions about the function and circulation of money. The results are quite complex, but Morgado and Vyskocilova conclude that the Czech children have a higher level of understanding than the Portuguese children do with regards to the circulation of money and goods. They also have a better knowledge of prices, but this may reflect the fact that there is still a degree of price control in the Czech Republic, whereas Portugal has a more liberal market economy. Far fewer Czech children receive regular pocket money and most believe that their father's money comes from the state (and not from his boss or manager), which again probably reflects the relatively recent transition to a market economy.

What these studies tell us is that, although there are some differences between and within countries in children's understanding of money, these are probably far less important than age differences. Morgado and Vyskocilova, for example, report quite marked developmental changes even over the relatively narrow age range that they investigated. But I suspect that some of the consistency in the findings is the result of researchers focusing on the development of the understanding of the adult use of money and the role money plays in the economy. Treating money in a broader context and asking different questions would probably be more revealing. In previous studies, children have been asked questions such as "where does money come from?", "which coin (offering a selection) will buy more?" and "If I went into a shop with this money, could I buy chocolate?". Asking children about the source of their money and why their parents give them money in the way they do might be more revealing. This might shed some light on children's understanding of the links between power and money and the tension between independence and control.

Prices, supply and demand, profits, and naïve economics

The exchange of goods, whether by bartering or, more usually, by buying and selling, is a central economic activity. But these transactions, and the wider system of which they are a part, are not easy for children to understand. A clear picture of the development of some of the basic concepts can be seen in the work of Berti and Bombi (1988) and that of Burris (1983). Burris investigated children's understanding of basic economic concepts (commodity, value, exchange) by interviewing children aged 4–5, 7–8, and 10–12. To explore their understanding of price and value they were presented with pairs of objects and asked which would cost more and why. The youngest children think that the price of a good depends upon its characteristics, especially its physical characteristics. A diamond does not cost much "because it is so tiny", while a book costs more than a wristwatch because "it is bigger". Similar reasoning is evident in this exchange, reported by Berti and Bombi (1988): "Which costs more, this lettuce or the chicken?"—"*The lettuce, because there is more of it*"—"And what if I only bought this much (removing a part of the lettuce), would I have spent more on the lettuce or the chicken?"—"*The chicken*"—"Why?"—"*because there is more of it* (he checks and sees that this is not so) *no, no, still the lettuce because there is still more of it than the chicken*". The older children (7–8) see the value (and so the price) of an object mainly in terms of its usefulness or function. So a wristwatch costs more than a book "because you can tell the time with a watch, but a book you can just read". The oldest children shift to seeing value and price as determined by the work and materials put in, a point of view expressed very succinctly by one of Berti and Bombi's 10-year-olds "Things which people work on more cost more". Very similar findings, using a rather different method, are reported by Fox and Kehret-Ward (1990). They explored conceptions of price from pre-school to adulthood by presenting people with a story about a group of friends who open a bicycle shop and need to set a price for each bicycle. The friends all have different ideas about how the bicycle should be priced: One believes that price should be based on size, another on the amount of work that went into making them, and so on. The participants are asked whether they thought each pricing scheme was a good one and why. This confirms and extends Burris' and Berti and Bombi's findings: Pre-school children thought price should be based on size, and 10-year-olds also favoured pricing by feature but recognised that the amount of work that was put in was also important. Thirteen-year-olds saw price as a function of work put in and customer preferences, with adults expressing similar views but adding ideas about supply and demand.

So young children see buying and selling as a physical act, and value (and prices) as determined by the properties of goods rather than by supply and demand. From the work of Furth (1980), Jahoda (1979), Leiser, Sevón, and Lévy (1990), and others, it is clear that children between roughly the ages of 8 and 11 have a concrete understanding of separate exchanges (e.g., between shopkeeper and buyer, between shopkeeper and factory) but do not have an integrated picture of the economic system as a whole until early adolescence. But this work tells us that children come to understand the need for the shopkeeper (and the factory owner) to make a profit, not how they come to understand pricing itself. For this we must turn to the recent work of Siegler and Thompson (1998; Thompson & Siegler, 2000).

Thompson and Siegler characterise previous work as producing "domain-general" stage theories of children's understanding of economics and point out that recent work on conceptual development has emphasised "domain-specific" knowledge. In these informal or naïve theories, understanding of domain-specific concepts is seen as crucial. Price—determined by supply and demand—is a clear instance of a theory specific to economics. So it is no surprise that Siegler and Thompson (1998) should investigate 4- to 10-year-olds' reasoning about how sales would be affected by a number of variables (supply and demand, motivation and morality of the salesperson, changes in packaging).

Siegler and Thompson carried out three experiments. In each, children were presented with stories about lemonade stands. For example, in the first experiment, the story designed to look at demand went as follows "One day it was a holiday and a lot of people were out of town, so not as many people as usual walked down Kathy's street. Do you think Kathy sold more, or the same, or less cups of lemonade than she usually did?" The supply story was equally straightforward: "Usually John's lemonade stand was the only one on the block. But one day, both kids who lived next door to John decided to run lemonade stands too. Do you think John sold more, or the same, or less?" The results of this experiment showed that by age 4 or 5 most children understand the effect of demand on sales. By age 8 they understand the impact of supply but many of the oldest (10-year-old) children did not understand the impact of motivation and morality. This was consistent with Siegler and Thompson's expectations: Demand should be the earliest variable understood as it directly causes change, does have an impact, and the impact is positive (whereas change in supply is inversely related to sales). In the second experiment, the children were presented with motivation, morality, and cup-colour stories but in this case the impact on sales was given and they had to explain why the effects (or noneffects) occurred. This showed that children were better at explaining why something had an effect than why it had no effect. In the final experiment, children were presented with stories and one of three different types of explanations. This more subtle way of revealing implicit conceptual knowledge worked well, and showed that the 8-year-old children did indeed have a good understanding of how motivation and morality can affect sales. Overall, these experiments show that economic understanding improves dramatically between ages 4 and 10, in this case mainly because of increased ability to understand indirect as well as direct causal paths, though increased experience with the economic system is probably also important.

In a second study, Thompson and Siegler (2000) looked at children's understanding of four core economic concepts: Profit seeking, competition between sellers, acquisition of desired goods, and economising (spending as little money as possible on purchases). Again, similar stories about lemonade stands were used, but in this case children's explanations were probed more deeply. Understanding of these four concepts cohered closely. The youngest children (age 6) understood that people want to acquire desired products, which derives from their general understanding of psychology, but rarely showed any understanding of the three more specifically economic concepts. But there was a marked change between 6 and 8 years, with the majority of the older children understanding all four concepts and a further gradual improvement up to age 10. Thompson and Siegler maintain that the marked improvement is probably the result of an increased ability to take unfamiliar perspectives and to understand the idea of inversely proportional relations.

This work gives an insight into how these same economic concepts are interwoven into an informal theory of economics and suggests that children have a qualitatively different informal theory of economics from age 8–9 onwards. This is congruent with recent work on children's saving (Otto & Webley, 2001), which will be considered below. Studies of children's understanding of another key economic concept (profit) suggest that there is a further qualitative change at 11–12 years. To understand profit, a child has to understand the linkages between buying (at a lower price) and selling (at a higher price) (Berti, 1992; Berti, Bombi, & De Beni, 1986; Jahoda, 1979). Jahoda investigated this with two studies of 6- to 12-year-olds' understanding of buying and selling, one consisting of a role-play, the other using a semistructured interview. The role-play involved a mock shop, with the child in the role of the shopkeeper. There was a range of simply priced goods available and, at a crucial point in the proceedings, a customer bought up all the supplies of a good, so that the shopkeeper had to phone the supplier, order fresh stock, and then pay for it. The role-play showed that only 1 of the 17 children aged 9–10 years who took part understood the idea of profit (indicated by the selling price being set higher than the buying price). By age 11–12, two thirds of the children understood profit or were at a transitional stage. The interview study showed that children's understanding progressed from having no grasp of the notion, to understanding two unconnected systems (the shop–customer relationship and the shop–supplier relationship), to an integrated system at around age 11–12 years.

Berti et al. (1986) tried to provide critical training to change children's understanding of profit so as to pinpoint what must be acquired in order to master this concept. They used two different kinds of training procedure, based on the two main kinds of experience that children will have: First that of receiving information, second that of discovering the contradictions in their own ideas. Both training procedures led to some improvement in understanding, but whilst statistically significant, the improvement was not dramatic. Berti et al. report that some children were not able to compare earnings and expenses (the very simple arithmetical calculation being beyond them) and that this hindered the acquisition of the notion of profit. Berti and De Beni (1988) showed, with a study of children aged 7–9, that there was a very strong association between children's understanding of shop profit and their ability to compare costs and income. The latter ability—according to Berti and De Beni—is probably a prerequisite for the acquisition of the notion of shop profit.

Whilst the overall picture that this research paints is fairly clear, there are some interesting variations in economic understanding that result from different types of experience. Furnham and Cleare (1988), for example, studied conceptions of economics in what has been the least-studied age group (11- to 16-year-olds). They showed that the understanding of profit continued to improve over this age range and that profit in shops and factories was understood differently. Whilst only 11% of the 11- to 12-year-olds understood profit in shops, 69% mentioned profit as a motive for starting factories. This difference probably results from profit from trading being a harder concept to grasp than profit from making. Jahoda (1983) replicated his 1979 study with Zimbabwean children, and showed that they acquired the concept of profit earlier than British children. The reason for this is that they have direct hands-on experience of trading: They are not just observers of the market but participants in it. The idea that particular kinds of experience are important is confirmed by the work of Nakhaie (1993). Nakhaie found that the mother's level of education and how often she teaches her child about the economy (money, shops, bank, etc.) at home were the best predictors of Canadian children's (age 6–11) understanding of profit. Thirty per cent of the 10- to 11-years-olds in this sample understood shop profit, which is broadly in line with the other studies discussed. Finally, Fenko (2000) was concerned with the impact of the transition to a market economy on economic socialisation. As she points out, one of the most important changes in Russia has been a shift in the role and significance of money. In the Soviet Union, money was not an important medium of exchange (in a country where there are chronic shortages of goods, bartering takes on a special role), nor was it a clear indicator of status (one's place in the bureaucratic hierarchy was more important). She studied the understanding of a variety of economic concepts (including profit) among Russian 11- and 14-year-olds and adults. What was striking was that the adolescents had a better understanding of profit than the adults—so only a minority of adults, for example, recognised that it is the aim of a businessman to make a profit on his enterprise. This clearly illustrates the crucial role played by the social context: Growing up in a centrally planned economy does not provide the experience required to understand concepts that underpin the functioning of the market.

Banks

Understanding economics is not just about mastering abstract concepts like prices, supply and demand, and profit. It is also essential to understand institutions such as banks and the government, and the role that they play in the economy. There is, in fact, a substantial literature on children's understanding of banks and banking or, to be more exact, the nature of a bank and bank profit (Berti, 1999; Berti & Bombi, 1988; Berti & Monaci, 1998; Bonn & Webley, 2000; Jahoda, 1981; Ng, 1983, 1985; Takahashi & Hatano, 1994; Wong, 1989).

The basic pattern is that children's understanding of bank profit develops from no knowledge of interest, to understanding interest on deposits, to believing that deposit interest is higher than loan interest, to believing that the interest is the same, to finally recognising that interest is higher on loans and consequently that is how banks make profits (Jahoda, 1981). At the first stage, the bank is seen as a place where money is stored safely ("It locks it up in a safe in case anybody breaks in") and children believe that you get literally the same money back as you put in. At the second stage, children are familiar with the term interest, know that a depositor gets more money back than they put in, but don't really understand why. In Jahoda's study most 11-year-olds were at either the first or second stage. When children first recognise that interest is due both on deposits and loans, they believe that deposit interest is higher and seem reluctant to concede that borrowers must pay interest ("because you've had their money for so long you really have to give them interest"). When they say that loan interest is equal to deposit interest, children are struggling with the notion that banks must make a profit—but do not understand how. Most 15-year-olds in Jahoda's study were at one of these stages. Finally there is a correct understanding of bank profit, but it should be noted that only 18 of Jahoda's 96 participants were at this level.

Subsequent studies have dealt with two interesting issues. First, researchers have considered what processes might be involved in initiating changes in economic thinking. Piagetians have stressed the importance of equilibration (Jahoda, 1984), the working out of a balance between children's understanding of the world and the world they observe.

Understanding depends partly on past experience and partly on a response to a new event: Such a response may be a search for logical consistency, which may then result in an improved level of understanding. In order to investigate equilibration, Jahoda (1981) induced cognitive conflict by asking children to explain how banks managed to pay their employees. If a child believed that deposit and loan interest were equal, such a question creates a potential conflict with their initial beliefs. Inducing cognitive conflict had a marked effect on children's understanding. Ng (1983) followed this up in a more systematic way and looked at the impact of both cognitive contrasts and cognitive conflict using a sample of Hong Kong adolescents. Contrasts were induced by presenting questions that did not involve banks (e.g., "A boy borrowed $5 from a friend to pay back later. How much money would he pay back to his friend?"). The idea here was that children would reply $5 (they all did) and then feel dissatisfied with the idea that borrowing money from the bank had the same level of obligation as borrowing from a friend. Ng found that only conflict (induced in the same way as Jahoda) significantly increased understanding. Most recently, Berti (1999; Berti & Monaci, 1998) has investigated whether the development of the understanding of banking involves accretion or restructuring. She concludes, from a series of intervention studies, that marked changes in understanding can be achieved using an appropriate curriculum (some of these were fairly substantial, involving 20 hours of lessons over a 2-month period). However, in her view, the restructuring of knowledge in this area should be regarded as the end product of incremental changes—a sequence of deleting certain rules and adding others—rather than a distinct process.

The second focus has been on cross-cultural differences in children's understanding of banks. Ng (1985) and Wong (1989) have both showed that Hong Kong children are more advanced in their understanding than their American and New Zealand counterparts. This is assumed to reflect the business ethos of Hong Kong. Takahashi and Hatano (1994), on the other hand, found that the understanding of Japanese children lagged behind both that of European and Hong Kong children. The most popular misconception in 11- to 16-year-olds in this study was that the bank was a kind of safe-deposit box. This lag in understanding was attributed to them being sheltered from economic activities. Bonn and Webley (2000) report that black South African children's conceptions were as unsophisticated as the Japanese children but argue that this reflects the impact of living in a society where economic activities are not generally flourishing. South African black children get little exposure to money, payment for work, banks, and the role of banking. There are also important within-society differences in this study, with rural children (the poorest group) having the weakest understanding. These kinds of within-society differences have been obscured in previous studies, which have based their findings on rather limited samples.

The largest body of cross-cultural data in this area is reported by Leiser et al. (1990). This study involved hundreds of children from 10 different countries. They found that their sample was split into three groups regarding the sophistication of their answers on banking. The most advanced children were the Danish and the Finnish; then came those from France, Poland, Israel, and West Germany; and the lower ones were Algeria, Yugoslavia, Norway, and Austria: This is a pattern of findings that, whilst intriguing, is impossible to interpret.

CHILDREN AS ECONOMIC AGENTS

The literature on children's understanding of economics has been overwhelmingly concerned with the understanding of the adult economic world (e.g., money, banks, unemployment)—and the legitimate economic world at that. I am not aware of any studies of children's understanding of aspects of the black economy or property crime considered as an economic act. But economic phenomena occur at home, at school, and in the playground and so children are surrounded by "economics" (although they may well not see a particular situation as economic). So whilst children may observe the functioning of the adult economy by going shopping with their parents, watching TV reports about unemployment, by reading, and by talking to teachers and others, they also participate in it and create their own autonomous economic world. Participation is through spending pocket money, and for older children, by part-time work and, in certain countries, as street traders. The autonomous economic world is the world of child–child economic relations, where possessions are swapped and the latest craze cards traded. Children's understanding of their own economic behaviour has been neglected—and is the focus of this section.

Pocket money—and other sources of money

Before children can participate in the adult economy through buying, they need to get hold of money. It is all too easy to assume that the usual arrangements in one's own country are standard throughout the Western world—but they are not. It is important to bear in mind that pocket money/ allowances (in the sense of regular fixed payments) is not an established institution in all countries. It is, for example, uncommon in Italy and Greece. The way in which money is given to children by parents reflects ideas about upbringing and the proper relationship between parents and children. So it is vital that one looks at the literature on the sources of children's income, though information is available only from a very limited range of countries. Good-quality information is available from Britain (Furnham, 1999; Furnham & Thomas, 1984; Webley & Plaisier, 1998), France (Lassare, 1996), America (Miller & Yung, 1990; Mortimer, Dennehy, Lee, & Finch,

1994), and the Netherlands (De Zwart & Warnaar, 1997; Warnaar & Van Praag, 1997).

This research shows that in these four countries parents usually introduce pocket money or allowances when a child is aged between 5 and 8 years (the mean age preferred by British parents is 6½; Furnham, 2001). The amount of pocket money is linked to age. In the UK in 1996, 8- to 10-year-olds got on average £1.69 per week, whereas 11- to 13-year-olds received £2.73 for the same period (Waterson, 1998). In the USA, in 1997 a third of 9- to 11-year-olds received no allowance and the most common amount given was $5. In the UK and France pocket money has, on average, gone up more than inflation over the last 25 years. French surveys give an indication of the extent to which different age groups rely on pocket money as a source of income. It makes up 100% of the income of French 4- to 7-year-olds but only 14% of the income of 13- to 14-year-olds, which is overall much more substantial. The rest is made up of payment for household chores (11%), part-time jobs (29%), and gifts (46%). In the UK, even for young children, pocket money is only one source of money. Webley and Plaisier (1998) identified three important sources of money for children aged from 5–12 years: Pocket money, holiday money, and birthday money. Holiday and birthday money were often quite substantial (up to £45 for holiday money and £75 for birthday money) and could make up a significant part of the child's annual income.

That children's income comes from a variety of forms matters, as money from different sources is used and thought about differently. Whilst parents tend to see pocket money as money for spending (Sonuga-Barke & Webley, 1993), quite a lot of pocket money is in fact saved. Amy (age 11) is typical "I get £2 every week . . . I pay for Guides (75p) and to go to club (45p). I save the rest of the money for Christmas and special occasions so I can buy presents". Holiday money is seen as spending money and is used for entertainment, souvenirs, and presents. As Mark (age 9) reported "My mum gave me £30. On holiday I kept this in my bedroom. If I wanted to buy something I went to the shops and bought all sorts of things. When I came home I had 1p left". Birthday money was used to buy clothes, shoes, and toys, with any money left afterwards being saved.

These different spending patterns are consistent with the idea that children, like adults, use mental accounts in thinking about their own economic activities. The term "mental accounts" was introduced by Thaler (1980, 1985, 1999). It is best understood through analogy with the behaviour of organisations. Thaler points out that most organisations have accounting systems within which there are a number of accounts. These enable spending decisions to be devolved to departments and activities to be monitored and controlled. Mental accounts function in the same way. There is a large body of evidence that adults use mental accounts (Thaler,

1999). For example, adults and 12-year-old children (but not younger children) are less willing to buy a replacement ticket if they have just lost one than they are to buy a ticket if they have lost an exactly equivalent sum of money (Tversky & Kahneman, 1981; Webley & Plaisier, 1998). The lost ticket may be seen as a loss from a mental leisure account (which is then depleted), whereas the lost money is from a mental general account, where the impact is far less.

From the perspective of parents, giving children pocket money plays an important part in developing budgeting and money-management skills (Furnham, 2001). And the evidence suggests that parents are right. Abramovitch, Freedman, and Pliner (1991), for example, studied how spending in an experimental shop was affected by children's experience of money. The children (aged 6, 8, and 10) were given money to spend in the experimental shop, either in the form of credit or cash. They could take home any money that they did not spend. Those children who received an allowance (pocket money) spent about the same amount whether they were given cash or credit, but those who did not receive an allowance spent far more when using credit.

Children's saving

A major economic problem that children (and adults, for that matter) face is adjusting the flow of their income to expenditure. Money rarely arrives in just the right amounts at just the right time. Saving is one solution to this problem, but it is important to recognise what this means. A child may spend £1.25 of the £2 pocket money she receives on Saturday and the remaining 75p on Thursday, when she goes to Guides. She may save all her pocket money for a month and then spend £8 on a computer game. Or she may save £1 a week all year to spend at Christmas. All of these involve saving, though in everyday life we might usually only use the term for the last of these patterns of behaviour. Whether something is defined as saving or not depends entirely on the accounting period we use.

As one might expect, saving does increase with age (Furnham & Thomas, 1984; Ward, Wackman, & Wartella, 1977). Older children report that they save because they have a generalised expectation that they will need money in the future. Younger children, in contrast, tend to have concrete targets, such as a game or toy. This increase in saving with age could simply be a matter of older children having higher incomes and having easier access to savings accounts. But it is more likely to be dependent on children's developing understanding of how to delay gratification, resist temptation (Sonuga-Barke & Webley, 1993), and of saving itself (Webley, Levine, & Lewis, 1991). If children are given a choice between a small immediate reward (5p now) and a larger delayed reward (10p in 5 minutes), younger children will tend to choose the immediate but smaller reward and older children will tend to wait for the bigger reward (Mischel & Metzner, 1962). This improvement in the ability to delay gratification seems to depend partly on a better comprehension of the situation and understanding helpful strategies (Mischel & Mischel, 1962; Peake, Hebl, & Mischel, 2002). These strategies include distracting oneself with another task, focusing on things other than the reward, and hiding the reward. Experiments into delay of gratification test children's ability to wait, rather than their ability to save, though clearly self-control is important in each. But in longer-term saving a child has to make a whole series of decisions (to add to savings, to withdraw) over time.

The series of studies of children's saving carried out by Webley and his colleagues (Webley, Levine, & Lewis, 1993; Sonuga-Barke & Webley, 1993; Otto & Webley, 2001) suggest that a number of processes are involved in the development of children's understanding of saving and their saving behaviour. Three of their studies involved a savings board game. Having earned tokens, the children played a game that presented them with a range of problems similar to those faced by them in everyday life. These included external threat (a rather mild-mannered robber who took just 1 token each time a child passed his hiding place) and temptation (passing a shop full of a variety of desirable sweets). The details of the board game varied between the studies but each had a shop from which the child had selected his or her preferred toy. This was the long-term target that the children were saving for. Each board game also included a bank (represented by a strong box), which was a possible strategy children could use to protect themselves from external threat or internal threat (temptation). In another study, a novel set-up was used, where the "board" gradually unrolled. This was intended to produce a situation where, as in real life, the future (including the length of the game) was unknown. Using a rather different approach, one study used a play economy where children took part and were interviewed in situ. This was situated in a suite of four rooms, in which a variety of activities that cost money (such as going to a video arcade, a sweet shop, and a café), as well as free activities (a library, a room with drawing materials), were available. Money was given out in the form of "daily" pocket money and the children had to save over a "week" to obtain their chosen toy (a day equalled a 10-minute time period). The parents of some participants were interviewed and, in one study, a questionnaire about their child's saving was completed by one parent. Participants were aged 4, 6, 9, and 12 years.

These studies give us some insight into the development of saving behaviour and children's understanding of saving. By age 6, children know that saving is a "good thing": They have learnt that self-control, patience, and thrift are virtuous. But although 6-year-olds know that saving is valued, they do not like it very much; nor do they save very well. Some see money saved as money lost (Sarah, age 6—"If I put my money in the bank I won't have any left"). In one of the board game studies, children could deposit money in the bank before encountering the robber or the temptation of the sweet shop. This would mean that they had no cash so they couldn't spend any and the robber couldn't take any. Here, as in most of the studies, the major improvements in performance occurred between the ages of 6 and 9. At age 4 the use of the bank was essentially random. This was matched with a total absence of understanding. When Patty (age 4) was asked why she used the bank she replied "because I do". Six-year-olds did save, but only because they thought they ought to. The 9- and 12-year-olds, on the other hand, understood the value of saving as a strategy to protect one's assets from threats from the inside (temptation) and outside (the robber). For example, Gail (age 9) said, "I'll put it [the money] in to make it safe from the robber". Mary (also aged 9), on landing on a square just before the toy shop, where she was able to take money out of the bank, reported "I won't take it [money] out of the bank as I don't want to be tempted". These findings were also mirrored in the play economy. Again 6-year-olds showed a limited ability to save (about half saved not at all) and many equated putting money in the bank with spending, so that money in the bank was money lost.

Most 9-year-olds and all 12-year-olds in these studies showed a functional understanding of saving. They knew what saving was for and they knew how to do it. But it is striking that children of this age had also developed other strategies for dealing with their financial affairs, most of which involved devices for getting more money out of their parents. Rather than saving being the ideal strategy, a few older children claimed that the best approach was to spend all one's money, and then emotionally blackmail parents to get more. For these older children saving is not seen as good per se, but one possible way of achieving a goal.

In some of the research on the development of children's thinking about economics described earlier, there were early stages where economic actions were explained in social terms. Similarly, in these studies of saving, the 6-year-olds said that they saved because it was a good thing and described the robber as "that naughty man". In one study children had the option of spending more tokens on something socially neutral (a ferry) or having fewer tokens robbed. Here the younger participants tended to chose the more expensive ferry (socially better but economically worse) whereas the older ones opted to brave the robber (socially worse but economically better).

These studies provide us with a fairly clear picture of children's understanding of their own saving but also leaves us with some residual puzzles. Berti (1993), in commenting on some of this work, points out that in the numerous studies of children's understanding of banks, no child, at any age, mentions that one of the functions of a bank is to help its customers resist temptation. This suggests that children's understanding of adults' saving may be rather different to their understanding of their own. What the links are between understanding of one's own economic behaviour and that of others (especially adults) is an issue that needs to be pursued.

The autonomous economic world of childhood

It is obvious that children learn to understand economics through participating in, and being taught about, the adult economic world. It is less obvious, first, that there is also an autonomous economic world of children, a world of child–child economic and social relationships, and second, that this autonomous world may play an important part in children's understanding of economics. Webley (1996) and Webley and Lea (1993) describe a number of studies of this world, which they label "the playground economy". This natural economy is surprisingly sophisticated. For example, when marbles are "in", children between the ages of 8 and 12 years play marble games in the playground. These marbles come in a wide variety of sizes and colour combinations. These cost different amounts in the shops and, what is more important, have different values and names in the playground. The unit of value is the number of "goes" that a player can have in a marble game. Thus a "bonker cats-eye" is usually valued at 10 and in the standard marble game a player would have 10 attempts at hitting the target. Marbles also have an exchange value: They can be traded as well as won and lost. In this market, the value of the different kinds of marbles (galaxies, pixies, misties, etc.) is determined by their scarcity in the school and *not* by the price of the marbles in the shops.

In one simple study (Webley, 1996), 34 children between the age of 8 and 11 were presented with two contrasting scenarios. In one, a school won a competition and every child received 100 of a new type of marble called "a metal spotted dick". In the other, at a different school, a child brought along some of the new metal spotted dicks. In the scarce condition, the children said that the new marble would be worth over twice as much as in the common condition: 31 of the children explained this in terms of the rarity of the new marble. This suggests that children may have a far better understanding of how this market works than of the adult economy, which for them is more remote.

Remarkably, as well as trading, "working" is also found in the playground economy. A child who is skilled (the "worker"), but who, on a particular day, has no marbles, may "work" for another child (the marble capitalist) who owns lots of them. If the worker wins some marbles, the proceeds are shared between the two of them. An adult researcher asking about this is told that the proceeds are shared equally. A child researcher of the same age, on the other hand, is told that the marble capitalist always gets a bigger share than the marble worker does.

Studies of swapping reveal a different side of the playground economy. Swapping is often banned in schools because teachers and parents are worried about older children exploiting younger children. But, despite sometimes being banned, swapping is widespread, particularly among 8- to 10-year-olds, and generally takes place at school. The recollections of adults and the accounts of children are very similar: Adults remember swapping pencils, stamps, beads, conkers, sweet cigarette cards, etc; children report swapping all kinds of stationery, toys, football cards, stickers, and so on. There was a consensus that items that are swapped should be of low value (partly to avoid parental disapproval). The children's accounts of why they swapped were of three kinds. First there were economic justifications ("getting rid of something you don't want any more and getting something back"), second, explanations in terms of friendship ("if we swap we become best friends"), and third, the idea of swapping as pure fun. From interviews and their responses to scenarios, it seems as if children understand swapping as an economic act with a social function. Its purpose is not really to acquire a toy, pencil, or sticker but to cement friendships. Younger children are happy to make swaps that are clearly economically a poor deal, but will always have a good reason for doing so, for example, as an overture to friendship. By approximately age 11, swapping is less popular, but is also conceived of in economic terms: It has turned into the adult act of bartering.

Although the research on children's autonomous economies is interesting, it is very limited. The data have been gathered in only one city, and it is impossible to know how significant this domain is. But I believe that, at least for some children, it is important in developing an understanding of economics that they will use later in the adult economic world.

Children from the perspective of economic theory

With a few honourable exceptions, economists have ignored children. But in recent years some experimental economists have carried out some studies that shed light both on children's economic behaviour and on their understanding of economics. Murnighan and Saxon (1998), for example, studied the development of children's ultimatum bargaining. In the ultimatum game there are two players, Albert and Ben. The rules are very simple—there is a resource (£10, a cake), Albert must decide how to divide it and Ben has to decide whether to accept Albert's division or nor. If he rejects Albert's division neither of them get anything. According to standard rationality models, Albert should divide the resource into unequal parts (£9.99 to him, 1p to Ben) and Ben should accept this division, as this way he at least gets something. If he rejected the division, he would be "cutting off his nose to spite his face". In fact, in normal ultimatum games around 15% of divisions involve equal splits and in some cases (described in detail in Güth & Tietz, 1990) the proportion of equal splits is as high as 43%. What do children do and how does their behaviour change with age?

Murnighan and Saxon set out to answer these questions and studied children aged 6–15 years and college students. The children had to divide up either money or sweets. The youngest children would accept offers of only one sweet but were also very generous, and were the only ones who in some cases gave away all the money or sweets. They showed no evidence of guile or thinking strategically. The 9-year-olds, by contrast, tended to be strategic with money (that is making lower offers when the responder— "Ben"—did not know how large a sum was being divided) but not with sweets. With sweets they acted very fairly when they were offering or responding. Twelve-year-olds—oddly—made fewer strategic offers than the 9-year-olds. Overall, the 12-year-olds' and 15-year-olds' behaviour approximated to that of the college students, though they were more generous (in economic terms "less rational") than the college students. What is interesting here is that the college students behave much more in line with economic theory, offering less but also accepting less than the children. In other words they would rather have something than nothing, whereas the children tended to reject what they saw as unfair offers.

Studies of rational choice by Harbaugh, Krause, and Berry (2001) tell a similar story. They carried out experiments to see whether children (aged 7 and 11 years) make rational choices about goods. The task they used tested a very basic requirement for rationality, namely that choices must be transitive. That is, if a person chooses A when they have a choice between A and B, and B when given a choice between B and C, if they are rational they must pick A when given a choice between A and C. Harbaugh et al.'s results show a substantial minority of the 7-year-olds act rationally, the majority of the 11-year-olds do, and the latter are just as rational in their decisions as undergraduates.

A final example looks at children's contributions in public good (social dilemma) experiments (Harbaugh & Krause, 2000). In a typical public good experiment, people have the choice between contributing to a public good (e.g., a pool of money that will be shared out equally) or acting selfishly and keeping the money for themselves. If everyone contributes, all are better off as a result—but for each individual there is a marginal gain in acting selfishly. In economic experiments on public goods, adults are more altruistic than economic theory predicts. Harbaugh and Krause found that overall the level of altruistic behaviour of children aged 6 to 12 is similar to that of adults, but that when children took part in experiments with many rounds the pattern over time is different. With adults, the standard finding is that in later rounds people contribute less than in early rounds: In other words, that, through repeated experience, they learn to free ride. This is also the case for the older children. But the contributions of younger children actually increase over rounds, which suggests that they are better at maintaining social coherence and are less driven by the need to maximise economic returns.

What all these experiments suggest is that children's understanding of economic situations is broadly comparable to that of adults by the time they are 11 or 12. At this age they may need more experience to understand the complexities of particular economic institutions, as we saw in the section on banks, but their understanding of the economic structure of particular settings is essentially adult. These experiments also allow us to draw another conclusion. In approaching particular situations, children (and adults) must decide whether it is appropriate to conceive a situation as one where economic thinking is required. In some situations, the consensus would be that economic thinking is inappropriate (not everything has its price). These experiments show—like the studies on swapping—that around age 11–12 children are shifting to an adult definition of economic situations.

CONCLUSIONS

We have covered a lot of ground in this chapter, from children's under-standing of adult economic phenomena, through children's own economic world, to children's understanding as manifest in their economic behaviour in experiments. What does it all add up to? What it is that causes the development of children's understanding of economics? Clearly domain-general cognitive changes are crucial, and underpin children's progressive understanding of economic concepts. As Siegler and Thompson (1998) spell out, the increasing ability to understand indirect as well as direct causal paths, negative correlations, and null effects are all significant factors. So too are other features of cognitive development: the ability to do complex arithmetic, to entertain multiple causation, and so on. Cognitive develop-ment is also important for children's understanding of their own economic behaviour: Making budgetary decisions about how much can be spent and when, and how to accumulate sufficient money to buy a desired toy, require a certain level mathematical reasoning ability. But there are other factors that may also be important. First there is a marked increase in economic independence and economic opportunities during childhood. Children's income typically increases considerably from age 5 to age 12 (Furnham, 1996) and there is a parallel increase in their opportunities (and freedom) to spend. From 13 years onwards, their income can increase even more, as they have the opportunity to participate (as part-time workers) in the adult economy. Active participation in the economy is surely very important in understanding aspects of economics, and may account for the superiority over European children that African children (and those from Hong Kong) show with regard to economic understanding. Second, with increasing age, children have a greater exposure to indirect sources of information and may receive formal teaching about economics. It is clear from the literature on economics education (reviewed in Lewis, Webley, & Furnham, 1995) and the intervention literature (e.g., Berti, 1999) that it is possible to teach many economic concepts to children aged 7–11. Whether or not children get formal training, they are certainly exposed to many informal forms of economics education via television, other media, schools, and parental discourse. So the marketing material that is aimed at young savers by banks presents a view of saving as a good habit that is encouraged through the "prize" for saving, namely interest. Some of this marketing material is very clearly educational. For example, in a short story in a building society brochure we read the following "As Henry's cat says 'the money is safe and what is more they pay me to save with them'. 'That sounds interesting' says Mosey Mouse. 'It is interesting, in fact it is interest and that is what they call it. When you leave your money in for a while it grows larger so you can get out more than you put in. That extra amount is called interest' replies Henry's cat" (Sonuga-Barke & Webley, 1993). There have been very few studies of socially mediated forms of communication about economics, but the likelihood is that they play an important role, particularly in acquiring more complex economic concepts.

These two factors (direct experience, indirect sources of information) are also crucial in creating variations in economic understanding, which have been rather downplayed in the literature. There are some important cross-cultural differences in economic understanding and though there is less evidence of this, within culture differences as well. These cross-cultural differences are probably most often demonstrated in the content of children's explanations and relate to the social milieu and economic structures of the society in which they live. So rural South African black children tend to have a fatalistic outlook and think God is responsible for unemployment whereas the more prosperous semi-urban children regard lack of education and individual characteristics as more important. The complexity of the explanations the children offered for these various phenomena was, by contrast, much better predicted by their age than where they lived (Bonn, Earle, Lea, & Webley, 1999).

One issue that needs to be considered is the potential of the naïve theory approach in this area. Adopting a naïve theory framework has two notable advantages. First, it ties work on the development of children's thinking about economics into a broader theory of children's conceptual development. Second, it focuses our attention on different aspects of children's understanding of economics, particularly the causal relationships between domain-specific concepts such as demand, supply, and price or, in macro-economics, taxation, government spending, and gross domestic product. One issue it leaves unresolved, however, is what determines whether an issue is defined as economic or social. An adolescent could (like a social exchange theorist) think about his or her friendships in economic terms, and regard liking and loving as forms of utility. But most do not, and would find this kind of reasoning unacceptable. A related issue is the ideological nature of theories of economics (whether formal or naïve): They do not just describe and explain the world, but also legitimate certain ways of behaving and thinking. It is no accident that economics students behave more in line with economic theory than others!

We know more about children's understanding of economics than ever before, but there are still some limitations of our current knowledge. These are worth identifying, as dealing with them provides an agenda for future research. For example, our knowledge is based on very restricted samples. Studies of children's economic thinking have been carried out in only a very limited range of cultures and within-country differences have often been ignored. That is why studies of East European children (e.g., Wosinski & Pietras, 1990), which relate children's economic thinking to changes in macro-economic structures, are so valuable. Researchers have also, in general, used a very restricted range of methods. There have been too many interview studies and not enough experimental studies, and children are very rarely used as co-researchers. There has also been a lack of collaboration with other social scientists, particularly economists. A more serious problem is that economic concepts have been treated as givens and not considered in the wider social context. Think about the core economic concept of price. This applies not only to goods but also to labour (a wage is the price an employer must pay for a person's services). Then think about gender inequalities in wages—it is clear to most of us that these are not a simple consequence of the working out of supply and demand. So a child who is thinking about this kind of issue needs to use concepts like power, take into account institutional arrangements, and place the current situation in his-torical context. Closer to home, a child may wonder how the price of school dinners relates to the price of lunch in a local café, or a student wonder how tuition fees (the price for education) are set. In other words, in order to make sense of children's understanding of economics, it needs to be placed in the broader context of children's understanding of society.

REFERENCES

Abramovitch, R., Freedman, J. L., & Pliner, P. (1991). Children and money: Getting an allowance, credit versus cash, and knowledge of pricing. *Journal of Economic Psychology*, *12*, 27–45.

Berti, A E. (1992). Acquisition of the profit concept by third-grade children. *Contemporary Educational Psychology, 17*, 293–299.

Berti, A. E. (1993). Cognitive approaches to economic development revisited. In E. J. S. Sonuga-Barke & P. Webley (Eds.), *Children's saving: A study in the development of economic behaviour* (pp. 91–104). Hove, UK: Lawrence Erlbaum Associates Ltd.

Berti, A. E. (1999). Knowledge restructuring in an economic subdomain: Banking. In W. Schnotz, S. Vosniadou, & M. Carretero (Eds.), *New perspectives on conceptual change* (pp. 113–135). Amsterdam: Pergamon.

Berti, A. E., & Bombi, A. S. (1979). Where does money come from? *Archivio di Psicologia, 40*, 53–77.

Berti, A. E., & Bombi, A. S. (1981). The development of the concept of money and its value: A longitudinal study. *Child Development, 52*, 1179–1182.

Berti, A. E., & Bombi, A. S. (1988). *The child's construction of economics.* Cambridge: Cambridge University Press.

Berti, A. E., Bombi, A. S., & De Beni, R. (1986). Acquiring economic notions: Profit. *International Journal of Behavioural Development, 9*, 15–29.

Berti, A. E., & De Beni, R. (1988). Prerequisites for the concept of shop profit: Logic and memory. *British Journal of Developmental Psychology, 6*, 361–368.

Berti, A. E., & Monaci, M. G. (1998). Third graders' acquisition of knowledge of banking: Restructuring or accretion? *British Journal of Educational Psychology, 68*, 357–371.

Bonn, M., Earle, D. C., Lea, S. E. G., & Webley, P. (1999). South African children's views of wealth, poverty, inequality and unemployment. *Journal of Economic Psychology, 20*, 593–612.

Bonn, M., & Webley, P. (2000). South African children's understanding of money and banking. *British Journal of Developmental Psychology, 18*, 269–278.

Burris, V. (1983). Stages in the development of economic concepts. *Human Relations, 36*, 791–812.

Cram, F., & Ng, S. H. (1999). Consumer socialisation. *Applied Psychology, 48*, 297–312.

De Zwart, R., & Warnaar, M. F. (1997) *Nationaal Scholierenonderzoek 1996.* Utrecht, The Netherlands: NIBUD.

Fenko, A. (2000). *Economic socialisation in post-Soviet Russia.* Paper presented at the 27th International Congress of Psychology, Stockholm, July.

Fox, K. F. A., & Kehret-Ward, T. (1990). Naïve theories of price: A developmental model. *Psychology and Marketing, 7*, 311–329.

Furnham, A. F. (1996). The economic socialization of children. In P. Lunt & A. Furnham (Eds.), *Economic socialization: The economic beliefs and behaviours of young people.* Cheltenham, UK: Edward Elgar.

Furnham, A. F. (1999). The saving and spending habits of young people. *Journal of Economic Psychology, 20*, 677–697.

Furnham, A. F. (2001). Parental attitudes towards pocket money/allowances for children. *Journal of Economic Psychology, 22*, 397–422.

Furnham, A., & Cleare, A. (1988). School children's conceptions of economics: Prices, wages, investments, and strikes. *Journal of Economic Psychology, 9*, 467–479.

Furnham, A., & Thomas, P. (1984). Adults' perception of economic socialization of children. *Journal of Adolescence, 7*, 217–231.

Furth, H. (1980). *The world of grown-ups.* New York: Elsevier.

Güth, W., & Tietz, R. (1990). Ultimatum bargaining behaviour—a survey and comparison of experimental results. *Journal of Economic Psychology, 11*, 417–449.

Harbaugh W. T., & Krause, K. (2000). Children's altruism in public good and dictator experiments. *Economic Inquiry, 38*, 95–109.

Harbaugh, W. T., Krause, K., & Berry, T. R. (2001). GARP for kids: On the development of rational choice behavior. *American Economic Review, 91,* 1539–1545.

Jahoda, G. (1979). The construction of economic reality by some Glaswegian children. *European Journal of Social Psychology, 9,* 115–127.

Jahoda, G. (1981). The development of thinking about economic institutions: The bank. *Cahiers de Psychologie Cognitive, 1,* 55–73.

Jahoda, G. (1983). European "lag" in the development of an economic concept: A study in Zimbabwe. *British Journal of Developmental Psychology, 1,* 113–120.

Jahoda, G. (1984). The development of thinking about socioeconomic systems. In H. Tajfel (Ed.), *The social dimension* (pp. 69–88). Cambridge: Cambridge University Press.

Lassare, D. (1996). Consumer education in French families and schools. In P. Lunt & A. Furnham (Eds.), *The economic beliefs and behaviours of young children* (pp. 130–148). Cheltenham, UK: Edward Elgar.

Leiser, D., Sevón, G., & Lévy, D. (1990). Children's economic socialisation: Summarizing the cross-cultural comparison of ten countries. *Journal of Economic Psychology, 11,* 591–614.

Lewis, A., Webley, P., & Furnham, A. F. (1995). *The new economic mind.* Brighton, UK: Harvester Wheatsheaf.

Miller, J., & Yung, S. (1990). The role of allowances in adolescent socialization. *Youth and Society, 22,* 137–159.

Mischel, H., & Mischel, W. (1962). The development of children's knowledge of self control strategies. *Child Development, 54,* 603–619.

Mischel, W., & Metzner, R. (1962). Preference for delayed reward as a function of age, intelligence and length of delay interval. *Journal of Abnormal and Social Psychology, 64,* 425–431.

Morgado, L., & Vyskocilova, E. (2000). La comprehension des notions économique chez les enfants Portugais et Tcheques—étude comparative [in Czech]. [Do the Czech children understand economical concepts and relations similarly to the Portuguese children?] *Ceskoslovenska Psychologie, 44,* 528–537.

Mortimer, J. T., Dennehy, K., Lee, C., & Finch, M. D. (1994). Economic socialization in the American family: The prevalence, distribution and consequences of allowance arrangements. *Family Relations, 43,* 23–29.

Murnighan, J. K., & Saxon, M. S. (1998). Ultimatum bargaining by children and adults. *Journal of Economic Psychology, 19,* 415–445.

Nakhaie, M. R. (1993). Knowledge of profit and interest among children in Canada. *Journal of Economic Psychology, 14,* 147–160.

Ng, S. H. (1983). Children's ideas about the bank and shop profit: Developmental stages and the influence of cognitive contrasts and conflict. *Journal of Economic Psychology, 4,* 209–221.

Ng, S. H. (1985). Children's ideas about the bank: A New Zealand replication. *European Journal of Social Psychology, 15,* 121–123.

Otto, A., & Webley, P. (2001). Children's saving. In A. J. Scott (Ed.), *Environment and wellbeing: Proceedings of the 26th Annual Colloquium of IAREP* (pp. 215–219). Bath, UK: University of Bath.

Peake, P. K., Hebl, M., & Mischel, W. (2002). Strategic attention deployment for delay of gratification in working and waiting situations. *Developmental Psychology, 38,* 313–326.

Schuessler, K., & Strauss, A. (1950). A study of concept learning by scale analysis. *American Sociological Review, 15,* 752–762.

Siegler, R. S., & Thompson, D. R. (1998). "Hey, would you like a nice cold cup of lemonade on this hot day?": Children's understanding of economic causation. *Developmental Psychology, 34,* 146–160.

Sonuga-Barke, E. J. S., & Webley, P. (1993). *Children's saving: A study in the development of economic behaviour*. Hove, UK: Lawrence Erlbaum Associates Ltd.

Strauss, A. L. (1952). The development and transformation of monetary meanings in the child. *American Sociological Review, 17*, 275–286.

Strauss, A., & Schuessler, K. (1951). Socialization, logical reasoning and concept development in the child. *American Sociological Review, 16*, 514–523.

Takahashi, K., & Hatano, G. (1994). Understanding of the banking business in Japan: Is economic prosperity accompanied by economic literacy? *British Journal of Developmental Psychology, 12*, 585–590.

Thaler, R. H. (1980). Towards a positive theory of consume choice. *Journal of Economic Behaviour and Organisation, 1*, 39–60.

Thaler, R. H. (1985). Mental accounting and consumer choice. *Marketing Science, 4*, 199–214.

Thaler, R. H. (1999). Mental accounting matters. *Journal of Behavioral Decision Making, 12*, 183–206.

Thompson, D. R., & Siegler, R. S. (2000). Buy low, sell high: The development of an informal theory of economics. *Child Development, 71*, 660–677.

Tversky, A., & Kahneman, D. (1981). The framing of decisions and the psychology of choice. *Science, 211*, 453–458.

Ward, S., Wackman, D. B., & Wartella, E. (1977). *How children learn to buy*. London: Sage.

Warnaar, M. F., & Van Praag, B. (1997). How Dutch teenagers spend their money. *De Economist, 145*, 367–397.

Waterson, M. J. (1998). *Marketing pocket book*. London: The Advertising Association.

Webley, P. (1996). Playing the market: The autonomous economic world of children. In P. Lunt & A. Furnham (Eds.), *The economic beliefs and behaviours of young children* (pp. 149–161). Cheltenham, UK: Edward Elgar.

Webley, P., & Lea, S. E. G. (1993). Towards a more realistic psychology of economic socialization. *Journal of Economic Psychology, 14*, 461–472.

Webley, P., Levine, R. M., & Lewis, A. (1991). A study in economic psychology: Children's saving in a play economy. *Human Relations, 44*, 127–146.

Webley, P., & Plaisier, Z. (1998). Mental accounting in childhood. *Children's Social and Economics Education, 3*, 55–64.

Wong, M. (1989). Children's acquisition of economic knowledge: Understanding banking in Hong Kong and the USA. In J. Valsiner (Ed.), *Child development in cultural context* (pp. 225–246). Lewiston, NY: Hogrefe & Huber.

Wosinski, M., & Pietras, M. (1990). Economic socialization of Polish children in different macro-economic conditions. *Journal of Economic Psychology, 11*, 515–528.

CHAPTER FOUR

Children's understanding of politics

Anna Emilia Berti
*Dipartimento di Psicologia dello Sviluppo e della Socializzazione,
Università degli Studi di Padova, Italy*

Over the last 20 years, domain-specific approaches to cognitive development have gradually supplanted domain-general Piagetian theory, stimulating a renewed interest in children's knowledge, i.e., in the content, rather than the structure, of children's thinking (Wellman & Gelman, 1998). This has led to numerous investigations of children's conceptions and naive theories about several subjects, including the social world (Bennett, 1993). Although naïve politics is one of the few naïve theories that lay adults possess, the acquisition of which can be tracked in children (Carey, 1985; Wellman, 1990), followers of the domain-specific approach have shown little interest in it. In the past too, when the leading approach was Piagetian, very few psychologists addressed this subject, and the most comprehensive studies were carried out by sociologists or political scientists (such as Connell, 1971; Moore, Lare, & Wagner, 1985) rather than psychologists.

The minimal interest in children's political understanding while the cognitive-developmental approach referring to Piaget was predominant may be explained by the fact that Piaget himself dealt with this topic only marginally (Piaget & Weil, 1951). This may have been in the belief that thinking derives from action and that children's most advanced thought is revealed by their mathematical, physical, and social concepts which, according to Piaget, are constructed through direct experience, i.e., by manipulation of the material world and through face-to-face interaction with other people. On the other hand, political knowledge is mainly acquired through verbal information, and is thus dependent on "verbal thinking" that, according to Piaget (1924), lags behind "real thinking" derived from action. The lack of interest shown by followers of the domain-specific approach in the development of political understanding may also be a Piagetian legacy. Indeed, most domain-specific investigations have focused on the same content (such as arithmetic, physics, biology, psychology, and social rules) as Piaget himself dealt with, although proposing different interpretations of phenomena originally outlined by Piaget.

Political knowledge in both adults and children has long been considered a concern of political science rather than psychology. Since the 1950s, when political science became an autonomous academic discipline, various surveys of the political knowledge of ordinary citizens have been conducted, mainly in the USA, on the assumption that, for a democratic political system to work, its citizens should have a minimum understanding of its organisation and the topics of political deliberation (e.g., Delli Carpini & Keeter, 1996; Hyman & Sheatsley, 1947).

The results of these surveys (summarised by Niemi & Junn, 1998) drew a rather alarming picture. It turned out that many Americans were not only unable to name their own State or Congress representative, but also knew little about current issues, were uncertain of how their government works, and were equally ignorant of foreign and domestic policy (Delli Carpini & Keeter, 1996). They also appeared to be ill-informed of the basic principles on which the American political system is based, or were unable to apply them to hypothetical situations, and did not know the meaning of ideological concepts such as liberalism and conservatism. What is most significant in these results, "is not so much the inability to recall isolated facts and figures, but the breadth and depth of the ignorance" (Niemi & Junn, 1998, p. 5). In addition to such basic ignorance, surveys have continued to find a consistent minority of adults with even worse knowledge, who have been labelled "chronic know-nothings" following Hyman and Sheatsley (1947), as opposed to the "know-it-alls".

In the 1950s, children's political understanding and attitudes were also widely investigated, thus giving rise to political socialisation as a distinct branch of political science (Greenstein, 1969). The assumption underlying these investigations is that cognitive and affective structures that are relevant to adults' political choices, behaviours, and attitudes emerge or develop early in childhood and adolescence. According to Easton and Hess (1962), the truly formative years of the maturing member of a political system are between the ages of 3 and 13.

The field of education has also been interested in children's and adolescents' political understanding for some time, as testified by its theoretical and empirical contributions: On the one hand, reflections on central themes such as the meaning of political education, the abilities and knowledge comprised in political literacy, and the best way to promote it (see the

Oxford Review of Education, *25*, issue 17, 1999, entirely devoted to political education); on the other, some large-scale international assessments of students' civic knowledge such as those promoted by IEA (International Association for the Evaluation of Educational Achievement) (Amadeo, Torney-Purta, Lehmann, Husfeldt, & Nikolova, 2002; Torney, Oppenheim, & Farnen, 1975; Torney-Purta, Lehmann, Oswald, & Schulz, 2001). Surveys, conducted by means of multiple-choice questionnaires and Likert scales, provide valuable information, not only about students' knowledge at certain crucial points of their education, but also about the relationships between independent variables such as gender, socioeconomic status (SES), family, race, nationality, educational attainment, pedagogical style of the school attended, and dependent variables such as political knowledge, interest in politics, and predictions of future political engagement. What are lacking are those thorough and detailed empirical analyses of students' conceptions that are currently mainstream in educational psychology with regard to other school subjects such as maths, physics, and biology.

Last, some developmental psychologists have been concerned with various aspects of political development, including political understanding. Many of their studies, similar to those carried out by political scientists and educationalists, have had the explicit purpose of contributing to the resolution of social problems, such as fostering civic identity, competence, and participation (Flanagan & Gallay, 1995; Youniss, McLellan, & Yates, 1997) or preventing the developing person from becoming a "chronic know-nothing" adult.

As a consequence of these varied approaches, research on children's understanding of politics does not fit easily into a unitary picture.

In this chapter I will first present the various waves of research within which the development of political understanding has been investigated, by outlining the purposes and theoretical framework. I will then describe the understanding of politics at various age levels. The effects of contextual variables, including what might be expected from improved teaching of politics and civics, will only be touched upon in the conclusion. Many different topics are relevant to politics, including some, such as economy, gender, and race, which are dealt with in other chapters of this book. Here I will focus on what is political in the narrow sense of the word: political institutions and their operation, political values and ideologies.

FROM POLITICAL SOCIALISATION TO POLITICAL (OR CIVIC) DEVELOPMENT

Investigations explicitly addressed to age-related changes (called socialisation, learning, or development) in political attitudes and knowledge have taken place in three distinct waves.

The first wave comprised empirical investigations into children's political attitudes carried out in the 1950s and 1960s under the label "political socialisation". These investigations (summarised in Stacey, 1978) refer mainly to system theory from political science, and psychoanalysis and learning theory from psychology. System theory stimulated the search for pre-adult antecedents of adults' loyalty towards a political system, while a belief in the long-lasting effects of early experiences as posited by these psychological theories led to a focus on childhood and adolescence. However, very little of the research conducted in those years involve children younger than 8–9 years (Moore et al., 1985). As this approach viewed the child as passive and receptive, gradually moulded by various socialisation agencies, the research typically examined such issues as the correspondence between parents' and children's political party choices, teachers' and students' attitudes towards political issues, and the influence of various socioeconomic variables such as ethnic group, socioeconomic status, and sex (Gallatin, 1980). Due to the large number of participants required to investigate these variables, the method most often used was a large survey with written questionnaires, which hampered a thorough examination of children's understanding and effectively excluded very young children.

Cognitive aspects of this research concerned knowledge about governance (such as the tasks of mayor, president, Congress, and the differences between the main parties; e.g., Greenstein, 1969). Broader topics such as children's knowledge of the class structure and prestige of occupations, and their acquisition of a sense of nationality and race (Stacey, 1978), were also considered relevant to political socialisation.

The second wave of research, which took place from the late 1960s to the 1980s, reflected the changes that occurred in those years both in political climate and in the leading theoretical frameworks in the field of psychology. Protest movements (such as those against war, for civil rights, and women's movements) shifted the attention from political stability to political change, from conventional forms of political participation (such as voting, affiliation to a party, campaigning), to forms of unconventional political activism that might involve high personal cost and a strong commitment to moral values. This stimulated researchers to concentrate on the age range most represented in the ranks of protest movements, i.e., late adolescence and early adulthood, and to regard it as a period of major change in political position and commitment.

The various theoretical frameworks that found increased support among psychologists in those years appeared to be particularly suited to interpreting these phenomena: lifespan development, with its tenets of the potential for lifelong change and the importance of the sociopolitical and historical context to psychological development; Erikson's (1968) theory regarding the development of political commitment as a fundamental component of adolescent identity formation; Kohlberg's (1976) cognitive-developmental theory of moral development, which proposes a sequence of stages of moral judgement that is also relevant to political understanding as it involves conceptions about rules, laws, and, in the most advanced stages, abstract principles that may conflict with the laws of a certain political system, thus stimulating commitment and action aimed at producing political change.

Piagetian theory, which in those years was mainstream in the study of cognitive development, also provided the framework for some studies of political understanding. Connell (1971) in Australia, and Moore et al. (1985) in the USA examined children's understanding of the political organisation of their countries. Furth (1980) tapped children's conceptions of the world of grown-ups, that is, society in its economic and political facets. Other studies focused on more specific topics such as the concepts of country and nationality (Jahoda, 1964), the workings of the judicial system (Demetriou & Charitides, 1986), and the law (Tapp & Kohlberg, 1977). Adelson and co-workers (Adelson, Green, & O'Neil, 1969; Adelson & O'Neil, 1966) interviewed pre-adolescents and adolescents about the issues facing a large group of people settling on a newly discovered island, with the purpose of tapping their political philosophy, i.e., their answers to hypothetical issues about law and justice, political processes, and the community, rather than their knowledge of current political issues.

With its methods of investigation based on individual interviews, the Piagetian approach meant that kindergarten-aged children could be assessed. In the 1960s and 1970s there was thus an extension, both upward and downward, of the age ranges involved in the study of political cognition.

In the 1980s, research on political socialisation suffered a precipitous decline (Flanagan & Gallay, 1995). However, the domain approach to social cognition proposed by Turiel and thus labelled by him and his followers addressed some politically relevant concepts, while not regarding them as political. According to Turiel (1983), reasoning about social events is structured within distinct conceptual domains, resulting from qualitatively different aspects of the individual's social interactions. Turiel distinguished two main domains of social knowledge: First, the moral domain, which stems from social actions that have an intrinsic effect on the well-being of others, and which comprises concepts of welfare, justice, rights, and the unchangeable, generalisable, and unconditionally obligatory prescriptions deriving from them. Second, the conventional domain stemming from the individual's experiences with actions whose meanings are defined by the social context (e.g., school, family, peer group) and which pertains to contextually relative, arbitrary, and changeable rules. Nucci (1981) has extended Turiel's analysis by adding a third domain, the personal domain, which comprises personal issues, i.e., actions that an individual considers to be outside the realm of societal regulation and moral concerns, thus defining the private aspects of his or her life. Neither Turiel nor Nucci recognised a distinct political domain; however, their approach has stimulated several studies of topics relevant to politics, such as the understanding of social rules, authority and its limits, personal and civil rights, and freedom in children, adolescents, and young adults.

In the 1990s the third wave of research was also affected, like the preceding ones, by an intertwining of current political problems with mainstream approaches to the study of development. The erosion of civil society in the United States (Youniss et al., 1997) and the political apathy of most young people in Western countries have stimulated a search for cognitive and affective precursors and current situational factors inductive of political commitment, and for indications of developmental risk in the direction of low political interest and political nonparticipation (Rosenthal, Feiring, & Lewis, 1998; Yates & Youniss, 1998). The explicit aim of these studies has been the development of policies and educational interventions that might help foster political and civic competence and engagement. This task is felt to be particularly urgent in the context of accelerated change and political uncertainty brought about by the end of the Cold War, the disruption of socialist governments, and increased globalisation (Youniss, Bales, Christmas-Best, Diversi, McLaughlin, & Silbereisen, 2002).

These concerns have stimulated the most recent IEA survey of political and civic knowledge in several nations (Amadeo et al., 2002; Torney-Purta et al., 2001) and also a thorough examination of experiences that might promote interest in social and political issues, help to identify an ideological perspective, and engender long lasting civic involvement in adolescents and young adults (Yates & Youniss, 1998). The term "civic" was added, or substituted, for "political" to refer not only to state and government, and conventional forms of political participation, but also to concerns regarding social issues and the skills necessary to associate freely in groups (Flanagan & Faison, 2000; Youniss et al., 2002).

This wave of studies has mainly been conducted in the framework of contextualist approaches such as those of Bronfenbrenner, Vygotsky, Erikson, and, in Europe, the theory of social representations (Doise, Staerklé, Clémence, & Savory, 1998; Emler, Ohana, & Moscovici, 1987), which all underline that children's experience of the social world is not direct and unproblematic but is mediated by the interpretations circulating in the communities in which they live. In these studies, to underline the difference in perspective from the first research wave, the term "development" is substituted for "socialisation". Researchers with a more explicit cognitive focus have looked at the domain-specific approach to cognitive development as an alternative to the approaches of Piaget and Kohlberg, which provided the framework for the previous studies of the development of political knowledge (Berti & Benesso, 1998; Torney-Purta, 1992).

Although the focus of this third research wave was mainly on adolescents and young adults, some studies on children have also been carried out (Berti & Andriolo, 2001; Berti & Vanni, 2000; Brophy & Alleman, 2002).

UNDERSTANDING POLITICAL INSTITUTIONS

The antecedents of political understanding (early childhood)

With few exceptions (e.g., Jackson, 1972), 5–6 years is the lowest age level considered in studies of political understanding. At this age children are unlikely to have heard about politically relevant current events such as Watergate or the Vietnam War in the 1970s (Moore et al., 1985). They may see national political authorities on television but, according to Connell (1971), they do not yet distinguish them from the other people appearing on TV and those whom they regard as special or important. Other political figures children may be familiar with are those in fairy tales such as kings, queens, princes, and princesses, whom they describe only by means of superficial attributes such as wearing a crown or kissing a princess, without mentioning their power or kingdom. Kingdom, in turn, is described as a castle or the place where a king lives (Berti & Benesso, 1998). This suggests that at 5–6 years children do not have the vaguest idea of a political world.

At this age children do not possess the concept of country intended as the territory of a state, nor do they have what might be considered a rudimentary version of it, that is a large territory inhabited by people who have something in common. When asked about where they live, American kindergarten children mentioned mainly the street or town. When the words "state" and "country" were explicitly introduced into the question, the most frequent answer was "don't know" (Moore et al., 1985). Many Scottish 6-year-olds described Scotland as a town or city rather than a country (Jahoda, 1963a, 1963b; see also Barrett, Chapter 10).

The first studies of children's political socialisation (reviewed by Stacey, 1978) suggested that, through the police, pre-schoolers can have direct involvement in the political system and are able to conceive of rules and decisions external to the family, and that this prepares the ground for an awareness of a political sphere of life. However, it cannot be taken for granted that children will see the police as part of the political system, that is, as people working for the government.

In Moore et al.'s (1985) study, the question "Does X work for the government?" was asked explicitly regarding the police, but also with respect to other occupations. Kindergarten children gave a majority of positive answers for the police and judges, and about 50% positive answers for the other jobs (soldier, mailman, milkman, teacher). However, the majority of children knew very little about government, believing that God or Jesus was the boss of their country, or giving "don't know" answers. It is therefore unclear if these children really differentiated between public servants and other kinds of employment or self-employment. Other data, described below, suggest that the concept of employment does not emerge before 7–8 years. Poor knowledge of the president, government, and governor was also found in American kindergarten children in a very recent study (Brophy & Alleman, 2002). Further, hardly any of these children mentioned the government or political authorities when asked how the police are paid.

These data are coherent with the belief that the first stage in children's understanding is a "prologue to politics" (Connell, 1971), or a "prepolitical stage" (Moore et al., 1985), characterised by:

> . . . an undifferentiated view of society, authority, and governance. Political symbols are recognised as *important*, but they are not clearly differentiated from religious symbols or from other nongovernmental objects. In short, there is neither differentiation between the political and the non-political nor any sense of integration or formally abstracting categories within the realm of the political. (Moore et al., 1985, p. 35).

In a study aimed at tracking children's understanding of society, and not just of politics, Furth assigned 5- to 6-year-olds to a stage called "personalistic elaborations and absence of interpretive system", which was characterised by "a confusion between personal and societal role" (Furth, 1980, p. 49); that is, a confusion between the activities people perform by personal choice or as duties related to roles such as those of parents, children, and friends, and job activities regulated by contractual obligations. Furth's view is supported by numerous data. At the age of 5–6 years children say that the police catch criminals because they want to (Berti & Benesso, 1998, Study 1); bus-drivers drive buses so that people do not have to go on foot (Berti & Bombi, 1988); that teachers can stay at home at will, or must go to school because children have to learn, and not because it is their job (Tallandini & Valentini, 1995).

From a Piagetian view, these conceptions about the political world or societal roles result from (and are expressions of) general characteristics of preoperational or "intuitive" thinking such as "seizing on odd and apparently irrelevant details and . . . the lack of synthesising power" (Connell, 1971, p. 18); or "submissive acceptance of observed experience with minimal interpretation" (Furth, 1980, p. 78). From a domain-specific view, at 5–6 years or less children do not appear to possess either a naïve theory

of politics or of economics. They are therefore bound to construe occupational and political roles in terms of their naïve theory of mind which, from
the age of 3 years, allows them to interpret people's behaviour in terms of
desires and beliefs (Leekam, 1993) or social rules that people must obey
(Turiel, 1983).

However, although young children appear to lack a conceptual political
domain, even in a very rudimentary form, they construct a set of interconnected concepts in the context of personal relations within the family,
kindergarten, and peer groups, which provide some of the threads necessary
for weaving true political concepts. These are the concepts of *rule*, *authority*, and *personal issues*, which constitute, respectively, the antecedents of
the concepts of law, political authority, and civil liberties and individual
rights, intended as limitations of government authority.

According to Piaget (1926, 1932), young children do not distinguish
between physical laws or rules governing statistical regularities on the one
hand, and prescriptive social rules (which are effective by influencing
people's intentional decisions) on the other. A further failure to differentiate occurs within social rules, as children do not distinguish between
moral and conventional rules, initially viewing both as simple commands
from authority, and then, from about 10 years, as agreements designed to
coordinate social interactions (Kohlberg, 1976; Piaget, 1932).

These views have been challenged by domain-specific studies that have
shown young children to be capable of distinguishing between natural and
social rules. From the age of 4 years children clearly state the impossibility
of physical violations, such as a child lifting a heavy sofa, while social
violations, such as having a bath with one's clothes on, may be imper-
missible but not impossible (Kalish, 1998).

The distinction between moral and conventional transgressions also
develops during pre-school years. At 3½ years, children judge the former to
be more generalisably wrong, more independent of rules and authority than
the latter (Smetana, 1993). The concept of convention is therefore interwoven with the concept of authority, whose development has been studied
mainly in children from first grade (around 6 years of age) onwards.

Understanding rules and authority paves the way for other concepts that
are at the core of politics, such as the jurisdiction and delegation of
authority. In first grade (around 6 years), children have already mastered
these concepts in the context of the authority relations in which they
participate. For instance, they say that a teacher or school principal has
authority only over certain persons and within the school, while parents
have authority within a family (Laupa & Turiel, 1993). Children also agree
that authority can be delegated from one person to another. For instance, a
parent can delegate one of his or her children to look after the others and
tell them what to do (Laupa, 1995).

Along with the idea of moral and conventional rules, and those authorities that can prescribe them, the concept of personal issues also emerges, defining a sphere that is outside the jurisdiction of any authority. Even at 3 and 4 years of age, children say that a child must comply when an adult decides about issues regarding the moral domain (e.g., hitting and stealing) and conventional domain (e.g., standing rather than sitting at dinner; not saying thank you after receiving a cookie). However, in cases of personal issues, children say that an adult should not order them what to do and a child should not comply, for example, wearing a different-coloured sweater from the one the mother wants the child to wear, or refusing to kiss an aunt the child finds unappealing (Nucci & Weber, 1995).

The understanding of societal roles and economic exchanges (6–7 years)

The confusion between personal and societal roles is resolved when children show an understanding of an institutional role for the first time, as characterised by formally defined duties and obligations that are distinct from the personal inclinations of its holders (Emler, 1992). Several studies suggest that this happens for the first time at about 6–7 years. At this age children show an awareness that teachers are not allowed to treat pupils as they like (Emler et al., 1987) and that people perform certain activities because these are their jobs, allowing them to earn a living (Berti & Bombi, 1988). At first, the jobs children know of are not represented as employment, because they believe that all, or nearly all, people—public servants included—work on their own and are paid by their customers, such as teachers by their pupils' parents or bus drivers by passengers (Berti & Bombi, 1988; Tallandini & Valentini, 1995). This not only allows children a very limited view of economic relations, but also prevents them from differentiating private from public institutions (which are nested, hierarchically organised, with governmental roles at the top).

At 6–7 years of age children have also heard of various political figures (queen, president, or premier depending on the country; Brophy & Alleman, 2002; Connell, 1971; Greenstein, 1969), but they either do not know what these figures do, or they attribute them with generic virtuous behaviours such as helping people, doing good, or performing office work such as reading, writing and having meetings. Children have not heard about elections and do not know how to access a political role, or only mention the possession of virtues or skills such as being a good person, doing well at school, or having a lot of money (Brophy & Alleman, 2002). Representation of political roles thus is very similar to the representation of other occupations. Political roles and processes therefore appear to be interpreted in terms of a rudimentary economic domain that is emerging at this age.

It is not clear if at 6–7 years children distinguish between laws and other kinds of rules. It has been found that Italian children are unable to define the word "law" or to provide any examples (Berti, Guarnaccia, & Lattuada, 1997), while American children, even at 5–6 years, define laws as rules, or provide some examples such as "don't drive fast, no stealing, no escaping" (Moore et al., 1985, p. 157). At 5–6 years, most American children say that laws are made by the police, while from 6–7 years to 9–10 years, they mention the President or other governmental authorities. However, only from the third grade (around 8 years of age) can American children spell out some differences between laws and rules, such as that rules apply only at school or home, while laws apply everywhere; or that you can break a rule, but you must obey laws (Brophy & Alleman, 2002); or that laws are enforced through sanctions (Tapp & Kohlberg, 1977). These examples provided by American children suggest that the first understanding of law is cast in terms of prohibition (Moore et al., 1985). Italian children, although unable to give a definition, say that serious infringements, such as murder or theft, are punished by imprisonment for a period of time decided by the police (Berti et al., 1997; Berti & Ugolini, 1998).

The concept of political role (7–9 years)

A turning point in children's understanding of society occurs around the age of 7–8 years, with the emergence of the idea of an elementary hierarchical structure connecting two persons, one giving orders and the other obeying. In the economic domain this leads to the appearance of two new types of actor: bosses who give orders and pay (and also, according to children, own their business), and employees. Children gradually extend this hierarchical view to an increasing number of jobs: teachers, garbage collectors, workers (Berti & Bombi, 1988), police, and soldiers (Berti & Benesso, 1998) are all seen as members of organisations with one or more chiefs. However, none of these organisations is yet embodied in a larger organisation such as the state.

The idea of chief, combined with the idea of a special or important person that children already possess, gives rise to the idea of political role (Connell, 1971). Initially children know very few political offices and do not distinguish between them according to their names, tasks, jurisdictions, or methods of appointment. Rather, by merging information about different figures (such as headmaster and other authoritative adults, queen and president) collected from various sources (ranging from family discourse to the mass media), they appear to construct an undifferentiated idea of "political role", which involves, in addition to those mentioned by younger children, the tasks of telling people what to do, building roads and organising garbage collection (Connell, 1971), giving people money, helping people, and running the country (Brophy & Alleman, 2002). Similar task descriptions, also provided by elementary school children in the early studies conducted under the label of "political socialisation", lead some authors to the conclusion that children conceive of the president and other politicians as "benevolent leaders" (Greenstein, 1960). At that time, this phenomenon was explained in psychoanalytical terms as resulting from an emotional need to see authorities as benevolent, and was viewed as the root of diffuse support for the political system during adulthood.

Various studies have testified to the presence of the notion of a hierarchical organisation and its widespread use, around the age of 7–8 years. In modified versions of Adelson and O'Neil's (1966) task about a large group of people settling on a newly discovered island, around the age of 8, children first mention the need for an organisation led by one or several chiefs (Berti 1988), or recognise the role of village leaders in making decisions about problems involving their communities (Buchanan-Barrow, 1998). In an investigation of the concept of war, some 7- to 8-year-olds attributed all decisions about starting, developing, and ending a war to the individual fighters, while others mentioned "heads" (of state, government, or president) in command of the fighters (Berti & Vanni, 2000).

Children's first ideas about how a factory boss or political leader exert their power are very concrete. Until the ages of 10–11 they represent both as personally giving orders (Berti, 1994; Connell, 1971). Up to this age, a particularly strong lack of distinction between these two figures was found in Italian children, who also believed that both the owner of a business and the mayor or president achieved their positions thanks to their wealth or career (Berti & Bombi, 1988). In other countries, children turned out to be more knowledgeable about how political offices are appointed.

In Australia, reference to voting was common from the age of 7, probably as a consequence of the fact that primary school children practice voting themselves (Connell, 1971). In America, by the end of fourth grade (around 9–10 years) most children described elections as a process that decides between competing candidates or issues (Moore et al., 1985). According to the authors, the rapid growth of knowledge about this topic followed the 1976 presidential elections. There was an increase in knowledge about elections during an election year, even in first graders (Allen, 1994). Knowledge about the subjects involved in electoral competitions, i.e., political parties, develops much later. Although from first to fourth grades (around 6–9 years), an increasing number of American children had heard the names of the two main parties, hardly any were able to say anything about them or explain what a political party is (Moore et al., 1985; see also Brophy & Alleman, 2002). In a very wide survey, elementary school children saw few differences in policy orientation between American political parties (Hess & Torney, 1967).

The concept of a hierarchical organisation is a considerable step towards the understanding of both the political and economic worlds. However, as long as it involves only two roles, that of one person giving orders and another obeying them, this concept is still too rudimentary to allow an understanding of political entities larger than a village, run by a single head or group of heads with different tasks, without any bureaucratic organisation below them. Another obstacle to understanding a hierarchical and diversified organisation is the narrow conception of the law that children still possess. During elementary school, most children still conceive of rules as prohibitions (Berti et al., 1997; Brophy & Alleman, 2002; Moore et al., 1985; Tapp & Kohlberg, 1977), thus appearing unaware of the fact that laws also establish rights, duties, how certain activities must be performed, and are the means by which the decisions of central political organs are communicated to the subordinate organisations that implement them.

During elementary school years, geopolitical knowledge grows steadily (Barrett & Farroni, 1996; Barrett, Chapter 10). In the American sample assessed by Moore et al. (1985), by fourth grade (around 9 years) most children were able to name correctly the city, state, and country in which they lived. In a Scottish sample (Jahoda, 1964) the relationship Glasgow–Scotland–Britain was correctly described by the majority of children at 10–11 years of age. However, correctly naming countries or locating them on a map does not involve an understanding of what kind of entities they are, that is, jurisdictions of central political authorities or juridical systems.

Several studies suggest that, before about 10–11 years of age, children do not know what countries (states, nations) are, or that they conceive of them as physical entities only (territories with certain natural boundaries, such as rivers or mountains) or as social but not yet political entities, that is, as large lands inhabited by certain peoples. Italian children younger than 10–11 years were either unable to define the words *state* or *nation*, or defined them as large territories with villages, towns, or cities (Berti, 1994). They stated that the areas depicted in different colours on political maps represented natural features (such as the colour of the ground or the vegetables growing there) or different "places" or "towns". Those who did know the words *state* or *nation* only mentioned language, customs (e.g., food, way of life), religion, or skin colour as differences between states, without any reference to shared law or government (Luise, 2000). In addition, before 10–11 years, children do not know what a capital city is, or describe it as a large and important city only (Berti & Benesso, 1998; Delval, 1994). They describe political union or secession only in physical terms, i.e., as the construction of a single large settlement, or the building of walls, moats, and palisades to divide a country in two parts (Berti, 1994).

According to Connell (1971), with the emergence of the concept of political role, children come to distinguish a political and governmental world from other areas of life. I think this concept, even in conjunction with the other acquisitions described above, is not sufficient for children to develop a conceptual political domain. Political leaders do not yet appear to be completely distinguished from other kinds of leader (such as the owner of a business), and the many threads emerging during this age range are still to be interwoven in the representation of an interconnected political system.

The emergence of a political domain (10–12 years)

The full emergence of a naïve political theory, with the concept of the nation-state at its core, appears to take place at about 10–11 years. At this age, while they still know very little about middle-level political and administrative roles, children distinguish between central and local political offices (such as mayor and premier) by assigning them different territories and degrees of power. They also connect these offices (although often incorrectly) in an authority hierarchy (e.g., the premier gives orders to the mayor; Connell, 1971) and represent their respective territories as one included in the other. As a result, children can conceive of the nation-state as a territory with a central power that makes laws and whose decisions affect the whole country, thanks to local authorities (erroneously represented only as mayors or local councils) and to various subordinate organisations, such as police, army, school, judicial systems, whose employees are now considered as public servants, paid by taxes (Berti & Benesso, 1998). This also affects children's view of war, which they now describe as a clash between nation-states, decided by political authorities and conducted by armies having leaders who collaborate with or are subordinate to them (Berti & Vanni, 2000).

At 10–11 years children have also developed a fairly standard conception of political parties, as connected to elections, in conflict with each other, aimed at producing leaders, and having to do with government. However, why parties are in conflict is not understood (Connell, 1971).

The main advance with respect to laws found at this age consists of an increasing awareness that they are made by parliament. However, similar to younger children, 10- to 11-year-olds still maintain that laws are made up of prohibitions and orders, that their function is to prevent disorder, and that infringement is followed by punishment such as imprisonment or fines (Berti et al., 1997; Ceci, Markle, & Chae, Chapter 5). Children do not yet know that the law regulates the most important relations between people, the working of the state, and the supply of services. Their view of the law is therefore still restrictive. According to Adelson and O'Neil (1966), a shift from a restrictive to a regulative view of the law occurs only around the age of 15. Tapp and Kohlberg (1977) found that about 50% of "middle school" children (grades 4, 6, and 8: roughly ages 9, 11, and 13) underlined the "prescriptive" or "beneficial-rational" functions of the law by describing them as general regulatory guidelines. However, how these answers were distributed across grades is not spelled out, and results from the other studies on this topic suggest that they were more likely to have been provided by the children in the highest grade.

In an Italian study (Agazzi & Berti, 1995) most 10- to 11-year-olds turned out not to know the concepts of democracy, monarchy, republic, or dictatorship. They were also unaware of the geographical and temporal contexts in which elections are the means of appointing the main political offices. They said that elections started to be used many years ago, and that they are used everywhere except for a few exceptional cases, such as countries involved in wars or represented as very primitive, for instance Amazonian America and Africa. These data suggest that when children first construct the idea of a state, they conceive of only one type of political organisation and apply it to all the countries they hear about. However, this conclusion needs to be supported by other, wider studies.

The studies conducted in a cognitive-developmental framework have underlined the relationship between the advances occurring during elementary school years and the emergence and consolidation of concrete operational thinking, A recent intervention study, conducted using a domain-specific approach, highlights the role of explicit teaching (Berti & Andriolo, 2001).

A curriculum on political concepts (law, state, the main Italian political offices, the working of the school system, and the role of the judge) was successfully implemented in a third-grade class (around 8 years). Before the intervention, participants, as expected at that grade, were unaware of most political offices and represented school and police as autonomous organisations. Children's wrong conceptions were challenged and all the necessary information was provided gradually in a supportive learning environment and through the promotion of active participation. At post- and delayed post-tests, 1 and 10 months after the intervention, children knew that a state is a territory where particular laws, made by parliament, apply and that the enforcement of these is provided for by the government using money obtained through taxes to pay the employees involved, such as teachers, police, and judges. On the whole, these children showed knowledge of the target topics similar to, or even higher than, those found in other studies of 13- to 14-year-old Italian children.

The refinement of the political domain (adolescence)

In addition to studies such as those already reviewed, adolescents' understanding of political institutions has been investigated by a few large-scale surveys. Nationally based surveys such as that of Anderson et al. (1990, cited in Niemi & Junn, 1998) in the USA, and Stradling (1977) in the UK, have dealt with particular details of government structures or policies. International surveys, such as IEA studies (Amadeo et al., 2002; Torney et al., 1975; Torney-Purta et al., 2001) could only deal with fundamental democratic principles, given the differences between the political systems of participating countries. Samples of items from some of these studies, and the age range of participants, are presented in Table 4.1.

According to Connell (1971), between 13 and 16 years there is an increased understanding of parties as representing the interests of different social groups, and as proposing different policies and views of society, or political ideologies. This allows adolescents to choose parties or candidates according to their programmes, rather than according to the preferences of their family, as is often the case for younger children. This understanding is generally rather rough, however.

In surveys carried out in the United Kingdom (Furnham & Gunter, 1983, 1987; Stradling, 1977), consistent minorities or, for some items, even

TABLE 4.1
Examples of items from large surveys of students' political knowledge

From Stradling (1977), age range 15–16 years (partly replicated by Furnham & Gunter, 1983, 1987)

True, False, Not sure questions
  The political party which gets the most votes at the general election always forms the government.
  The Prime Minister is the only person who can choose when to call general elections.

Prominent political leader (choose from among five names, four incorrect, one correct, or answer "I'm not sure", "none of these")
  Who is the Prime Minister at the moment?
  Who is the leader of the Labour Party?

Who is responsible for public services? (choose from government, local council, regional board, don't know)
  The water supply.
  Social Security.
  Hospital and clinics.
  Refuse collection.

Which party would put forward the following proposals? (choose from Conservative, Labour, Liberal, SDP)
  Taxes on both people and industries should be cut as much as possible.
  The government should take over and run more industries.
  Council tenants should be encouraged to buy their council houses and flats.

continues

TABLE 4.1

(continued)

From 1988 American NAEP (National Assessment of Educational Progress), Civic Assessment Questionnaire for 12th graders

---

Which of the following best describes the way in which the United States constitution assigns governmental power?
  A. It assigns it entirely to the states.
  B. It assigns it entirely to the national government.
  C. It divides it between the states and the national government.
  D. It divides it between the states and the federal courts.

All of the following are requirements for voting in a national election except the need to:
  A. be registered to vote.
  B. be a United States citizen.
  C. pay a poll tax.
  D. meet the age requirement.

From the 1999 IEA Civic Education Study on 14-year-olds (the instrument was later applied with some changes to 17- to 19-year-olds)

Is it good or bad for democracy . . .
  when citizens have the right to elect political leaders freely?
  when private businesses have no restriction from government?
  when newspapers are free of governmental control?
  when political leaders in power give jobs in the government to members of their family?
  (4 = very good, 3 = good, 2 = bad, 1 = very bad)

An adult who is a good citizen . . .
  obeys the law.
  takes part in activities promoting human rights.
  knows about the country's history.
  (4 = very important, 3 = somewhat important, 2 = somewhat unimportant, 1 = very unimportant)

Which of the following is most likely to happen if a large publisher buys many of the newspapers in a country?
  A. Government censorship of the news is more likely.
  B. There will be less diversity of opinion presented.
  C. The price of the country's newspapers will be lowered.
  D. The amount of advertising in the newspapers will be reduced.

---

the majority of participants, were unable to match correctly policies with political parties. For instance, about half the adolescents in all three studies recognised that cutting defence funding and at the same time increasing financing of education, building new houses, and improving the National Health Service are Labour Party policies. On the other hand, only about 30% recognised that reducing taxes for both individuals and industry as much as possible is a Conservative policy.

National surveys show the aspects and personalities of their countries' political systems about which adolescents are more knowledgeable. In the British studies (Furnham & Gunter, 1983, 1987; Stradling, 1977), nearly all participants knew who the incumbent Prime Minister was, a large majority (ranging from 97% to 65%) knew who the leaders of the Labour and Liberal parties were, and more than half answered most of the other "who is" questions correctly. Most adolescents also knew who is responsible for different kinds of public service. However, knowledge about the workings of Parliament turned out to be very poor, with most items being answered correctly by less than 50% of participants.

In the American survey, twelfth-graders (around 17–18 years) were quite well informed of criminal and civil justice and the general rights of citizens (Niemi & Junn, 1998). For instance, the great majority knew that an accused cannot be jailed indefinitely without proof of guilt, that refusing to pay tax is illegal, and that Congress cannot restrict the freedom of the Press. Their sense of what is done at each level of government was also quite good. For instance, about two thirds knew that federal government makes treaties, prints money, and regulates international trade, and that local government operates public schools. Some limits to students' knowledge were revealed by items about the structure of the state government. Although most students recognised Congress as belonging to the legislative branch, only half could correctly associate executive and legislative branches with the governor and the state assembly. According to Niemi and Junn, this suggests that students have learned discrete facts (e.g., Congress belongs to the legislative branch) rather than concepts (e.g., executive vs legislative functions). Other limits were highlighted by short essays about presidential responsibilities that a subset of the sample was asked to write. Nearly half provided an inadequate description by answering in generalities, giving a list of responsibilities that contained errors, and digressing from the topic.

After constructing the concept of political organisation, children start envisioning various types of state or government. Unlike fifth-graders (around 10 years), Italian eighth-graders (around 13 years) were able to describe (although in rough and sometimes incorrect terms) some differences between democracy, monarchy, and dictatorship (Agazzi & Berti, 1995). Their view of democracy was rather simplistic, however, consisting of the sovereignty of the people or, for 18-year-olds, respect for individual freedom. The opposite, according to eighth-graders, was a monarchy, which they defined as a state run by a king. Eighteen-year-olds mentioned the differences between absolute and parliamentary monarchy, and considered dictatorship to be the opposite of democracy. At both ages, a dictatorship was characterised as the concentration of power in a single person. Nobody mentioned the role of parties, unions, and other kinds of organisations in a democracy, and their suppression or subordination in a dictatorship.

These answers are coherent with the descriptions of democracy provided by a large sample (1000) of American twelfth-grade students (around 17–18 years) who were asked to imagine that they had to explain to a student from a nondemocratic country what makes a country democratic. The most prevalent themes were individual political freedom or people having a voice in government through elections (Siegel & Hoskin, 1981).

On the other hand, when understanding democracy is assessed by means of Likert scales (see Table 4.1), most students from Western countries, even at the age of 14, show a fairly adequate knowledge. For instance, most participants in the IEA study identified the reasons for having more than one political party, recognised the importance of basic democratic institutions such as free elections, and were aware that democracy is weakened when wealthy people have undue influence on government, politicians on the law courts, and when people are forbidden to express ideas criticising the government (Torney-Purta et al., 2001).

Other data from the same study show that at 14 years appreciation of democratic principles is often rather superficial, however. Nearly half the participants could not infer the consequences of a large publisher taking over many newspapers and even less appeared to possess the full range of concepts and skills required to perform such civic tasks as deciding between candidates based on their election leaflets, understanding newspaper editorials, and deciding whether to join a political organisation with a particular ideology. An understanding of democracy improves with age; upper secondary students are more aware of the threats to democracy represented by situations in which political or economic power is abused, and are generally likely to judge individual rights and opportunities as good for democracy (Husfeldt & Nikolova, 2002).

According to Adelson and co-workers (Adelson et al., 1969; Adelson & O'Neil, 1966), the major achievements of adolescence, occurring between the ages of 13 and 15 years, and refined between 15 and 18 years, are the acquisition of some fundamental concepts and abilities, rather than information about current political systems. These achievements comprise the following: the capacity to imagine institutions abstractly rather than in terms of specific, discrete activities; a positive view of law and government, which stresses the administrative aspect, as opposed to the negative or coercive view expressed by younger children; an appraisal of political events and laws in the light of their consequences on the collectivity rather than on individuals; a grasp of the nature and needs of the "community", by which the authors intend "not only government in its organised forms, but also the social and political collectivity more generally" (Adelson & O'Neil, 1966, p. 296).

For Adelson, these advances rely on formal operational thinking. However, some Italian data on the understanding of law suggest that the acquisition of domain-specific items of information is also involved. Unlike younger children, eighth-graders (around 13 years) and upper secondary school students provided various examples of laws, including not only prohibitions but also laws concerning constitutional rights and civil laws (such as regarding marriage and employment), which they said they had learned at school or heard about on television (Berti et al., 1997).

Last, some data indicate that during adolescence there is an increase in understanding the influence of economic organisations on policy. In an IEA study carried out in the 1970s (Torney et al., 1975), participants were asked to rate the perceived impact of ten individuals and groups on the laws made in the country. For 14-year-olds the formal political structure (e.g., prime minister and members of parliament) appeared to be primary, while 18-year-olds were more aware of the role of interest groups and the media. For instance, in Germany the wealthy were rated as being as influential as the prime minister, while the average person was ranked last. In other countries, union leaders were seen as nearly equal in policy influence as members of Parliament.

In addition to drawing a picture of the average knowledge possessed at a certain age, surveys have also outlined individual differences. According to the IEA study, in some countries there appeared to be a considerable number of students displaying knowledge "below the level that might be considered 'basic'" (Torney-Purta et al., 2001, p. 69). Individual differences at this age might have long-lasting consequences. A longitudinal study with German youth, aged 14 to 16 at the beginning, reveals high positional stability of individual differences in knowledge over a 7-year interval (Kramper, 2000). This suggests that extreme types of "chronic know-nothing" and "know-it-all", originally described for the political knowledge of American adults, may have their origins in adolescence, if not earlier. The study also found a positive correlation between political knowledge during adolescence and political activity and voting in early adulthood. This suggests that a vicious circle of low political knowledge, avoidance of political information, and no political activity might be at work rather early.

THE UNDERSTANDING OF POLITICAL VALUES AND IDEOLOGIES

In addition to knowledge of the actual working of existing political institutions, political understanding also involves mastering concepts such as justice, freedom, and other rights. These concepts refer to both political reality (e.g., provision for freedom, economic or political equality as established by constitutions or other laws of a certain nation-state) and to ideals to be affirmed through their implementation in laws (e.g., human rights). They are also values that citizens use to monitor their government and that affects their political choices. For instance, it has been found that the amount and type of perceived injustice is linked to levels of potential political protest, i.e., to the willingness to engage in or support unconventional political activity (Jenning, 1991).

Values are often embedded in belief structures that are reasonably coherent, although not necessarily involving any formal, abstract propositions about politics, such as liberal/progressive vs conservative. In the literature, these structures are referred to by a variety of terms such as *political outlook* (Connell, 1971), *ideologies* (Gross, 1996; Thoma, 1993), or *beliefs* (Raaijmakers, Verbogt, & Vollebergh, 1998). I will refer to them as "ideologies in the loose sense". Only a minority of people hold self-conscious, coherent political beliefs incorporating some abstract theory about society. Connell (1971) has called them "personal ideologies" to distinguish them from "personal outlooks" and ideologies proper, such as Marxism or Liberalism, which involve elaborated theorising. Other authors (e.g., Yates & Youniss, 1998) simply call them "ideologies". I will call them "ideologies in the strong sense".

Developmental research explicitly addressing these topics is scarce. There are few studies of ideology and of rights as stated by international political organisations, such as the UN Universal Declaration and Conventions on the Rights of the Child (United Nations General Assembly, 1989). Justice is a long-standing focus of developmental research, but it has traditionally been considered within the moral rather than political domain. Following Piaget's (1932) seminal work, studies on moral judgements have been conducted by asking participants to judge an individual's choice in an interpersonal situation (Kohlberg, 1976). Questions about hypothetical laws were asked by Turiel (1983) and followers of his domain-specific approach (e.g., "suppose there is a country where there was no law against stealing, would it be right to steal in that country?") with the purpose of identifying which issues children view as belonging to the conventional and moral domains, rather than to ascertain their constructions of justice at a societal level. In addition, children have never been asked how institutional arrangements might prevent injustice or ameliorate its consequences (Torney-Purta, 1985).

Children's conceptions of economic justice, such as rights to work, equal pay, adequate standard of living, and policies aimed at their promotion, have not been directly addressed. However, there are many investigations of children's understanding of economic inequality and its causes, which in general show an increased age-related tendency to stress individual differences in effort or merit. One study provides some hints of the links between economic and political understanding (Flanagan & Tucker, 1999). American adolescents' explanations of unemployment and poverty have been found to be correlated to their evaluations of the society they live in and economic policies. Those who endorsed individual causes were more likely to believe that the United States offers equal opportunity to all, and that government support programmes promote dependency.

Rights

In general, a person has a right when no one (individuals or institutions) ought to prevent her from doing something or refuse her some service that she needs (Plamenatz, 1968, cited in Goodwin, 1987). Some rights arise in the context of interpersonal relations, such as those deriving from promises or from participant roles (such as the rights of children to be nurtured by their parents). Other rights are ideals or means of political struggle, such as "natural rights" (e.g., to life, liberty, and property) assumed to derive from human nature by Locke, J. S. Mill, and other philosophers, or "human rights" (e.g., to education, work, fair trial) declared by international organisations such as the UN. These rights are claims to certain kinds of treatment for all human beings, made with the aim of having them translated into laws. Until they succeed, they have the status of moral statements enforceable only through conscience (Goodwin, 1987). Finally, "positive rights" are those established by laws and enforced by states and their administration.

Children have an early experience of the first type of rights (interpersonal), and knowing about them can be seen as an aspect of a naïve psychology, namely as knowledge of the expectations and obligations resulting from certain speech acts (Perner & Mant, 1988). Children also have an early experience of positive rights, to the extent that many of the duties of people they interact with (such as parents, teachers, physicians, and social workers) are established by law. However, these rights cannot be differentiated from those that only apply to interpersonal relations (such as fulfilling the promise to go to the cinema), without any comprehension, however elementary, of the state and law. Understanding them should thus be regarded as an aspect of knowledge of political institutions. Lastly, "natural" or "human" rights are usually grounded by their proponents on abstract moral principles and their increasing understanding can therefore be seen as identical to moral development. However, without an awareness of the historical circumstances in which these rights have been formulated and of the political objectives they are aimed at achieving, understanding of those rights is quite limited. Therefore, the construction of human rights should also be seen as being related to the development of the domain of political knowledge.

This was not the approach followed by studies of children's understanding of rights, however. Some studies have addressed very specific positive rights that children have in particular contexts, such as medical

(Belter & Grisso, 1984), legal (see Ceci et al., Chapter 5) and research settings (Abramovitch, Freedman, Thoden, & Nikolic, 1991). Other studies have tried to draw a more general picture of children's understanding of rights by addressing a variety of topics where interpersonal, positive, children's, and human rights were mixed and confused. Only in one study of adolescents' representations of human and children's rights, as stated by the UN, were they viewed as linked to increasing contact with various institutions and explicit teaching about rights at school (Doise et al., 1998).

The first research into children's understanding of their rights was carried out within the cognitive-development approach by Melton (1980) and identified a stage sequence parallel to the development of logical and moral thinking. According to the author, the first level (found mainly at first grade: around 6 years) is characterised by an egocentric orientation that leads children to conceive of rights as privileges bestowed or withdrawn by authority figures according to whim. At level two (from third to seventh grades: around 8–13 years) rights are seen as based on fairness, maintenance of social order, and obeying rules. At level three (achieved only by a minority of seventh-graders and college students) rights are understood in terms of abstract principles. Similar to studies on moral judgement and role-taking, an understanding of rights appears to be affected by socioeconomic background, with children from high-status families achieving higher levels earlier than others. According to Melton, this may be the result of affluent children having more opportunity to either exercise their rights or play out a variety of social roles, which fosters a respect for others that is necessary to conceptualise ethical principles.

The most recent domain-specific studies have considered children's understanding of their rights as related to the gradual acquisition of context-specific knowledge, rather than to the development of global cognitive structures. However, in only one of them has the context chosen as relevant been the political one (Del Barrio, Delval, & Espinosa, 1999), while the others have focused instead on the domain of interpersonal relations (Ruck, Keating, & Abramovitch, 1998a; Ruck, Keating, Abramovitch, & Koegl, 1998b).

When asked for an explicit definition, children up to 8 years cannot say what a right is. From the age of 10 years, most define rights as things that one wants or is allowed to do (Ruck et al., 1998b). When shown vignettes depicting conflicts between a peer and different authorities (such as parents and teacher), young children (8-, 10-, and 12-year-olds) see nurturance rights (concerning care and protection) as more salient than self-determination rights (such as expressing opinion in a school newspaper, accessing personal information from a school file), while older children (12-, 14-, and 16-year-olds) support both kinds of rights equally (Ruck et al., 1998a). According to the authors, this derives from younger children's greater familiarity with being cared for and protected, and their lesser desire for autonomy. Age differences also emerge in children's justifications for their answers. Up to 10 years, they mainly mention differences between parents and children in age, knowledge, ability, and role, while from 12 to 16 years they refer more often to parental responsibilities and duties. Younger children also tend to view their entitlement to certain rights as related to their age, whereas older children are more aware of the universal nature of various rights. In justification of some self-determination rights, several 14- and 16-year-olds explicitly mentioned issues such as freedom of expression and the right to information.

Whether older children's better understanding of parental duties and self-determination rights is related to an awareness that they are regulated by laws and enforced by political institutions is neither mentioned nor considered in the above study. However, some possible indications of this are provided by children's answers about who could revoke their rights. The number of those mentioning government, police/court, or laws and rules increases with age, reaching about 50% at 14 years, thus suggesting that the acquisition of a concept of positive rights is parallel to an understanding of the state and its institutions. A similar trend emerges in a study about children's identifying violations to their right to information (about topics such as AIDS, different religions, or drugs), and children's proposed solution to any violations (Del Barrio et al., 1999). Up to 10 years, children either justified the decision of a teacher not to provide information if some students asked for it, or they suggested personalistic solutions (trying to convince adults or obeying their decisions). From 12 years, they were increasingly aware of their right to information and of the institutional responsibility of the school to provide it.

In contrast to these studies, an early endorsement of self-determination rights was found in an investigation of freedom of speech (i.e., discussing a certain kind of music) and religion (i.e., participating in the rituals of a certain religion) regarding children and adults in the context of family, school, and their own and other countries (Helwig, 1997). Restrictions of this freedom to both children and adults were judged as wrong and outside the scope of family, school, and governmental authority in any country by more than half the 6-year-olds (however, the literature reviewed in a preceding section suggests some doubt about 6-year-olds' understanding of what country and government are). It is impossible to ascertain the extent to which the differences between these results and those described above is due to the different topics and other aspects of research procedure. Young children's dislike of restrictions were largely justified by general appeals to personal choice and the rights of agents to act in accordance with their desires, which suggests that the early construction of ideas about personal autonomy may serve as the basis for the concept of rights. By linking the concept of freedom to the personal, rather than political, domain, the author hypothesises that the development of this concept is linked to development of the idea of an agent and to the moral domain:

> These patterns suggest a progression from a view of rights in early childhood as extending from a concept of "generic agent" with individual wants, desires, and personal prerogatives to one in adolescents and young adults in which rights stem from specific properties of agents (mental competence, maturity), and are bounded by their conditions of application, including a concern with how rights should be balanced with other moral issues, such as potential harm. With development, these features of judgments become incorporated into explicitly articulated, reflective rights concepts. (Helwig, 1997, p. 493)

It is quite reasonable to expect that children's reasoning about rights reflects their views of human agents; this cannot be the whole story, however. In a study of young people in Geneva, aged 12–21 years, most said they had received instruction at school about human and children's rights (Doise et al., 1998). At all ages they were able to provide instances of these rights, but the number and kinds of examples changed with age. Older youth more often mentioned appropriate examples, referring to civil rather than concrete rights (such as eating, housing, having clothing), to enhancement of freedom or well-being, rather than prohibition (such as "it is forbidden to massacre people") and couched their definitions in terms of social categories (rights of women, children, racial groups) rather than subjective positions. These changes, according to the authors, support the hypothesis of a growing familiarity with institutionalised definitions of rights, such as those provided by the UN, which is related to educational level.

Tolerance

Closely related to freedom is tolerance, a concept originally formulated as a claim on political authorities for the freedom to hold and express dissenting and nonconformist religious, moral, and political opinions (Goodwin, 1987). Tolerance, of course, is exercised also in interpersonal and non-political situations when a person endures opinions or behaviours of which she disapproves, or even still likes people who express or perform them. Personal and political tolerance are not necessarily linked, however. One might personally dislike people with whom one disagrees, while being at the same time convinced that they must be allowed to express their views and act accordingly.

The distinction between personal and political tolerance is absent in the first studies of this concept, which were carried out within the cognitive-developmental approach. These studies focused only on the interpersonal aspect of tolerance, by asking children and young adults their opinions about a peer holding a belief different from theirs, rather than about his or her right

TABLE 4.2
Stages in development of tolerance and related cognition according to Enright &
Lapsey (1981) and Enright et al. (1984)

Tolerance	Perspective taking (Selman)	Moral (Kohlberg)
0. The child does not understand that he or she can criticise the belief of another.	0. The child lacks an understanding that the other person has a perspective.	0. The child fails to understand moral issues.
1. The child rejects the contrary belief and negatively evaluates the discrepant other.	1. One perspective at a time is taken.	1. The person takes the authority's perspective.
2. The person declines to evaluate others in relation to their beliefs or thinks that people are good regardless of their beliefs.	2. Reciprocal perspective taking.	2. Reciprocal or relativistic perspective of sharing.
3. The person realises that an evaluative judgement about disagreeing with another is possible, but only with more information about the other person and his or her beliefs.	3–4. The person develops infinite regress and system perspectives.	3–4. Moral decisions are taken from the point of view of group or society.

to express this belief (Enright & Lapsey, 1981; Enright, Lapsey, Franklin, & Steuck, 1984). However, tolerance was considered as a single, global construct, developing through a stage-like sequence, where an intolerant attitude is followed by tolerance, parallel with changes in perspective-taking and moral judgement (see Table 4.2). In all three sequences more advanced stages are characterised by an increasing number of beliefs or perspectives being taken into consideration. Sequences and their parallels are presented in detail in Table 4.2, as they provide a clear example of the cognitive-developmental approach.

The development of tolerance has recently been addressed again within Turiel's domain approach by Wainryb, Shaw, and Maianu (1998). Although this study, like those on rights and freedom, has not addressed political aspects of tolerance directly, it has at least touched upon them by asking participants to evaluate not only how good the dissenting person and her opinion is, but also if she should be allowed to say what she believes, or to act accordingly. In addition, the study assessed several dimensions of dissenting belief, such as how far they support injustice or physical and psychological harm, whether they are held by an individual or are traditionally shared in his or her country, and whether they involve moral judgements or factual knowledge.

At all age levels involved in the study (first, fourth, seventh grade and undergraduates: roughly ages 6, 9, 12, and 18+ years), patterns of tolerance and intolerance turned out to coexist. Only a few participants, mainly from the youngest group, gave all tolerant or nontolerant responses across all dimensions. At all ages, most participants made nontolerant judgements of the practices based on dissenting beliefs, underlining the unfair or harmful consequences, and taking a negative view of the person engaged in them when the practices are not part of a cultural tradition. From seventh grade (around 12 years), the majority of participants gave tolerant judgements of the person when the practice was part of a cultural tradition. With age there was also an increasing tolerance of dissenting beliefs and speech expressing them. While the majority of first-graders gave intolerant judgements, only a minority of older participants did so.

Justification of tolerant and intolerant judgements of public expression of dissenting beliefs were based on their possible influence on other people's behaviour. Whereas up to fourth grade (age 9 years) children believe it could lead others to agree with and act on such beliefs, the majority of older participants thought that speeches stimulate an exchange of opinion that might help identify inaccurate ideas and pursue the truth. In keeping with a domain-specific approach, the authors suggest that increasing tolerance for dissenting beliefs and their expression is based on age-related changes with respect to the links between beliefs and behaviour, rather than on changes in a global social-cognitive structure, as posited by the cognitive-developmental approach.

The studies on rights and tolerance have revealed interesting age-related shifts in the understanding of these topics; they have also underlined parallels with development in other conceptual domains such as the interpersonal, psychological, and moral, thus suggesting hypotheses about how advances in a domain might pave the way, or be a prerequisite for advances in other related domains. What remains to be investigated is if, and how, ideas about rights, freedom, and tolerance are linked to conceptions about international organisations, the state, the law, their functions, and about the direct and indirect consequences that laws allowing or repressing certain behaviours might have on society.

Understanding and commitment to ideologies

According to Connell (1971), a coherent outlook on political and social issues (ideology in the loose sense) starts developing between 13 and 16 years of age and is based on a growing mastery of formal operations that allows adolescents to link their views and conceptions of different topics. Adolescents also start to appreciate political ideologies as ways to characterise systems of policies or political beliefs. For instance, compared with younger children, most 13- to 16-year-olds interviewed by Connell about the Vietnam War mentioned the word "communism" while talking about the causes of the war. However, an explicit ideology is a much rarer achievement.

Ideologies in the loose sense become increasingly coherent with age. Research on adults' political choices or attitudes toward a range of political issues (such as freedom of enterprise, equality of income, tolerance of alternative lifestyles, acceptance of abortion or euthanasia, etc.) has usually found or posited one dimension—conservative or right wing vs progressive/liberal or left wing—or two factors—economic conservatism/progressiveness and cultural conservatism/progressiveness (Middendorp, 1979, 1991, cited in Raaijmakers et al., 1998). A recent longitudinal factorial study conducted on Dutch adolescents and young adults, whose ages at the first survey ranged from 15 to 24, underlines that the number of factors decreases with increasing age and education (Raaijmakers et al., 1998). Between 15 and 19 years, three factors were identified, which dealt with economic issues, personal freedom, and freedom of cultural minorities. From 20 years on, only two factors emerged, one dealing with economic issues, the other with political issues. According to the authors, this suggests that young people have a poorly articulated structure of political beliefs until the age at which they are entitled to vote. After, they demonstrate a clear two-dimensional structure of political beliefs, like adults. Last, the most integrated structure was found in highly educated young adults, whose political attitudes could all be located on one overall factor of conservatism/progressiveness.

Studies of adults and adolescents have also underlined a relationship between political ideologies and moral judgement: Conventional reasoners are more likely to endorse a conservative view, due to their focus on existing social order and laws, whereas postconventional reasoners, who are more concerned with the fit between existing social organisations and the principles of justice, are also more accepting of a liberal view (e.g., Thoma, 1993). The study by Raaijmakers et al. (1998) has also addressed this issue. The results highlight that this relationship has some qualifications. In more highly educated young adults, who had developed a single integrated view of cultural and political issues, this was also correlated with indices of moral reasoning. In adolescents and less highly educated adults, whose political beliefs were organised in two or three distinct dimensions, moral reasoning appeared to be related to dimensions dealing with freedom for individuals and cultural minorities, but not to the economic dimension.

An ideology, in the strong sense of holding explicit coherent political beliefs incorporating some abstract theory about society, is a rather rare achievement in adolescence, or even in adulthood. According to Connell (1971), it may occur from middle adolescence, because it requires the consolidation of formal operational thinking. Its acquisition cannot be considered as a regular step in the development of political thinking, however. Mastering logical operations is not sufficient; a strong stimulus from others is also required, because a personal ideology is not a personal construction, but derives from the political traditions of the groups in which the person moves. Indeed, in only one of the students participating in his study did Connell find an unequivocal expression of an ideology in the strong sense. This was a 16-year-old who expressed a coherent and recognisable pattern of opinion on national and international topics in an abstract language. He spoke of working-class, majority rule, communism, and capitalism. During the interview, the boy also referred to the militant labour background of his family. However, the family is not the only environment that may produce ideological thinking. Many youth organisations and Church groups also typically provide direct exposure to explicit ideological orientations, which their members can test and reject or assimilate into their thinking (Youniss et al., 1997).

CONCLUSION

This review has focused on age-related changes in political understanding. Age is a complex variable, however, which might be decomposed into a range of correlated processes and outcomes. Increasing age involves increasing educational attainments, role-taking opportunities, decision-making, exposure to political issues, and participation in a variety of societal institutions. It also involves the development of declarative and procedural knowledge in domains that, although distinct from politics, comprise concepts and abilities necessary for political understanding. Cognitive-developmental studies have focused on the relationship between political concepts that emerge at certain age levels and the logical and role-taking abilities that are at the core of Piaget's, Kohlberg's, and Selman's stage theories. While it is reasonable to posit the involvement of such abilities, these studies have sometimes underestimated what children can understand if they are explicitly taught or exposed to political issues and stimulated to reflect on them. Thus limited knowledge may be mistaken for deficiencies in the cognitive structures necessary for understanding or constructing that knowledge.

The domain-specific studies referring to Turiel's approach have mainly addressed the links between political concepts and conceptions about people and interpersonal relations, which can be considered part of a naïve psychology. Similar to followers of the cognitive-developmental approach, these researchers have often explicitly or implicitly suggested that political reasoning and concepts found at certain ages reflect other age-related knowledge and skills, rather than the opportunities to acquire relevant information.

Political institutions are made up of rules and nested organisations involving complex sets of roles, of which neither the totality nor significant parts are accessible to direct experience. They can only be described by a complex network of propositions, and this type of discourse is unlikely to occur unless somebody is intentionally instructing another. The effect of education on a range of political outcomes such as knowledge and skills acquisition, attitude formation, and participation in conventional and unconventional political activities has long been known, although different views have been proposed for exactly which aspects of education are responsible for the effects (Emler & Frazer, 1999), and some doubts have been raised about whether more explicit political education would yield greater political competence (Pring, 1999).

Some studies have clearly shown, however, that the explicit teaching of politics fosters political understanding in both adolescents and children. In American twelfth-graders (age 17–18 years) the length and recency of a civics course, the variety of topics studied, and the extent to which discussion of current events was incorporated into the curriculum were significantly and positively related to overall political knowledge (Niemi & Junn, 1998). Political understanding is also fostered by opportunities to confront political issues. Studies of adolescents and young adults participating in political and civil movements or voluntary service activities (e.g., teaching in schools, building houses) have shown that these experiences foster long-term engagement in political and social activities. Detailed analyses of individual essays and peer discussions about one of these experiences (volunteering in a soup kitchen for the homeless) highlights how it stimulated participants' private and public reflections about several political issues: the causes of poverty and government responsibility in preventing or coping with it, public funds, government organisation and decision-making, personal roles in enacting social changes, and limits to individual initiative (Yates & Youniss, 1998). On the whole, these studies suggest that the most effective way to foster political understanding and participation is by providing opportunities to participate in significant experiences, while at the same time providing explicit information about the issues involved and about public institutions.

The intervention study with third-graders (around 8 years) described in a preceding section (Berti & Andriolo, 2001) has shown that the misunderstandings and limited knowledge typically found in children, and usually considered as a consequence of age-related cognitive limitations, can easily be overcome by explicit teaching.

Planning effective curricula for all grades requires detailed knowledge of the cognitive structures that may constrain their understanding. These comprise the political ideas children already possess, and concepts and skills included in other conceptual domains, such as naïve psychology, economics, sociology, geography, the moral and conventional domains, and the mastery of logical and argumentative skills. While the relations between politics and other conceptual domains and skills have not been investigated sufficiently, those within the political domain have been addressed even less. There is a huge amount of work ahead for future developmental research in this field.

Most of the domains listed above overlap with disciplines taught at school, and some age differences in political concepts parallel the timing of topics within curricula. This is the case, for instance, with the increasing knowledge of civil and constitutional law found in Italian students with increasing grade. National differences may also mirror different national curricula to a certain extent. For instance, the poor knowledge of central political authorities found in Italian children below fifth-grade (under 10 years), in contrast to young American children's familiarity with the President and government, is likely to reflect the different prominence of various offices in the political systems of the two countries, as well as the fact that in Italy the state is usually taught only at fifth-grade, while in the US it is taught earlier (Brophy, personal communication). Investigating children's understanding of politics (as well as many other topics, for that matter) calls for a collaborative enterprise between developmental psychologists and educationists.

REFERENCES

Abramovitch, R., Freedman, J. L., Thoden, K., & Nikolic, C. (1991). Children's capacity to consent to participation in psychological research: Empirical findings. *Child Development*, *62*, 1100–1109.

Adelson, J., Green, B., & O'Neil, R. (1969). Growth of the idea of law in adolescence. *Developmental Psychology*, *1*, 327–332.

Adelson, J., & O'Neil, R. (1966). Growth of political ideas in adolescence: The sense of community. *Journal of Personality and Social Psychology*, *4*, 295–306.

Agazzi, A., & Berti, A. E. (1995). La conoscenza di democrazia a diversi livelli scolastici: V. elementare, Ill media el anno di università [The understanding of the concept of democracy at different educational levels: 5th and 8th grades and 1st year of university]. *Scuola e Città*, *45*, 290–301.

Allen, G. A. (1994). The growth of children's political knowledge during an election year. *Merrill-Palmer Quarterly*, *40*, 356–377.

Amadeo, J., Torney-Purta, J., Lehmann, R., Husfeldt, V., & Nikolova, R. (2002). *Civic knowledge and engagement: An IEA study of upper secondary students in sixteen countries*. Amsterdam: IEA.

Barrett, M., & Farroni, T. (1996). English and Italian children's knowledge of European geography. *British Journal of Developmental Psychology, 14,* 257–273.

Belter, R. W. G., & Grisso, T. (1984). Children's recognition of rights and violations in counselling. *Professional Psychology: Research and Practice, 15,* 899–910.

Bennett, M. (1993). *The child as psychologist: An introduction to the development of social cognition.* Hemel Hempstead, UK: Harvester Wheatsheaf.

Berti, A. E. (1988). The development of political understanding in children between 6–15 years old. *Human Relations, 41,* 437–446.

Berti, A. E. (1994). Children's understanding of the concept of the state. In M. Carretero & J. F. Voss (Eds.), *Cognitive and instructional processes in history and the social studies* (pp. 49–75). Hillsdale, NJ: Lawrence Erlbaum Associates Inc.

Berti, A. E., & Andriolo, A. (2001). Third graders understanding of core political concepts (law, nation-state, government) before and after teaching. *Genetic, Social, and General Psychology Monographs, 127,* 346–377.

Berti, A. E., & Benesso, M. (1998). The concept of nation-state in Italian elementary school children: Spontaneous concepts and effects of teaching. *Genetic, Social, and General Psychology Monographs, 120,* 121–143.

Berti, A. E., & Bombi, A. S. (1988). *The child's construction of economics.* Cambridge: Cambridge University Press.

Berti, A. E., Guarnaccia, V., & Lattuada, R. (1997). Lo sviluppo della nozione di norma giuridica [The development of the concept of law]. *Scuola e Città, 48,* 532–545.

Berti, A. E., & Ugolini, E. (1998). Developing knowledge of the judicial system: A domain-specific approach. *Journal of Genetic Psychology, 159,* 221–236.

Berti, A. E., & Vanni, E. (2000). Italian children's understanding of war: A domain-specific approach. *Social Development, 9,* 478–496.

Brophy, J., & Alleman, J. (2002). *Primary-grade student's knowledge and thinking about government as a cultural universal.* Unpublished manuscript.

Buchanan-Barrow, E. (1998). *Adelson revisited: Children's understanding of community.* Poster presented at the XV Biennial ISSBD meeting, Berne, Switzerland, July.

Carey, S. (1985). *Conceptual change in childhood.* Cambridge, MA: MIT Press.

Connell, R. W. (1971). *The child's construction of politics.* Carlton, Australia: Melbourne University Press.

Del Barrio, C., Delval, J., & Espinosa, M. A. (1999). *Children's understanding of rights: Identification of violation and coping strategies.* Paper present to Jean Piaget Society 29 Annual Symposium, June 2–5, México City.

Delli Carpini, M. X., & Keeter, S. (1996). *What Americans know about politics and why it matters.* New Haven, CT: Yale University Press.

Delval, J. (1994). Stages in the child's construction of social knowledge. In M. Carretero & J. F. Voss (Eds.), *Cognitive and instructional processes in history and the social studies.* Hillsdale, NJ: Lawrence Erlbaum Associates Inc.

Demetriou, A., & Charitides, L. (1986). The adolescent's construction of procedural justice as a function of age, formal thought and sex. *International Journal of Psychology, 21,* 333–353.

Doise, W., Staerklé, C., Clémence, A., & Savory, F. (1998). Human rights and Genevan youth: A developmental study of social representations. *Swiss Journal of Psychology, 57,* 86–100.

Easton, D., & Hess, R. D. (1961). Youth and the political system. In S. M. Lipset & L. Lowenthal (Eds.), *Culture and social character: The work of David Riesman reviewed* (pp. 336–351). Glencoe, IL: Free Press.

Easton, D., & Hess, R. D. (1962). The child's political world. *Midwest Journal of Political Science, 6,* 229–246.

Emler, N. (1992). Childhood origins of beliefs about institutional authority. In H. Haste & J.

Torney-Purta (Eds.), *The development of political understanding: A new perspective* (pp. 65–77). San Francisco: Jossey-Bass.

Emler, N., & Frazer, E. (1999). Politics: The educational effect. *Oxford Review of Education*, 25, 251–273.

Emler, N., Ohana, J., & Moscovici, S. (1987). Children's beliefs about institutional roles: A cross-national study of representations of the teacher's role. *British Journal of Educational Psychology*, 57, 26–37.

Enright, R. D., & Lapsey, D. K. (1981). Judging others who hold opposite beliefs: The development of belief-discrepancy reasoning. *Child Development*, 52, 1053–1063.

Enright, R. D., Lapsey, D. K., Franklin, C. C., & Steuck, K. (1984). Longitudinal and cross-cultural validation of belief-discrepancy reasoning construct. *Developmental Psychology*, 20, 143–149.

Erikson, E. (1968). *Identity: Youth and crisis.* New York: Norton.

Flanagan, C. A., & Faison, N. (2000). Youth civic development: Implications of research for social policy and programs, *Social Policy Report*, 15, 3–14.

Flanagan, C., & Gallay, L. S. (1995). Reframing the meaning of "political" in research on adolescence. *Perspectives on Political Science*, 24, 34–41.

Flanagan, C. A., & Tucker, C. J. (1999). Adolescents' explanations for political issues: Concordance with their view of self and society. *Developmental Psychology*, 35, 1198–1209.

Furnham, A., & Gunter, B. (1983). Political knowledge and awareness in adolescence. *Journal of Adolescence*, 6, 373–385.

Furnham, A., & Gunter, B. (1987). Young people's political knowledge. *Educational Studies*, 13, 91–104.

Furth, H. G. (1980). *The world of grown-ups.* New York: Elsevier.

Gallatin, J. (1980). Political thinking in adolescence. In J. Adelson (Ed.), *Handbook of adolescent psychology* (pp. 344–376). New York: Wiley.

Goodwin, B. (1987). *Using political ideas* (3rd ed.). New York: John Wiley.

Greenstein, F. I. (1960). The benevolent leader. *American Political Science Review*, 54, 934–943.

Greenstein, F. I. (1969). *Child and politics* (rev. ed.). New Haven, CT: Yale University Press.

Gross, M. L. (1996). Moral reasoning and ideological affiliation: A cross-national study. *Political Psychology*, 17, 317–338.

Helwig, C. C. (1997). The role of agent and social context in judgements of freedom of speech and religion. *Child Development*, 68, 484–495.

Hess, R. D., & Torney, J. V. (1967). *The development of political attitudes in children.* Chicago: Aldine.

Husfeldt, V., & Nikolova, R. (2002). *Students' concepts of democracy.* Paper presented at the Annual Meeting of the European Educational Research Association, Lisbon, September.

Hyman, H. H., & Sheatsley, P. B. (1947). Some reasons why information campaigns fail. *Public Opinion Quarterly*, 11, 412–423.

Jackson, R. (1972). The development of political concepts in young children. *Educational Research*, 14, 51–55.

Jahoda, G. (1963a). The development of children's ideas about country and nationality, Part I: The conceptual framework. *British Journal of Educational Psychology*, 33, 47–60.

Jahoda, G. (1963b). The development of children's ideas about country and nationality, Part II: National symbols and themes. *British Journal of Educational Psychology*, 33, 143–153.

Jahoda, G. (1964). Children's concepts of nationality: A critical study of Piaget's stages. *Child Development*, 35, 1081–1092.

Jenning, M. K. (1991). Thinking about injustice. *Political Psychology*, 12, 187–204.

Kalish, C. (1998). Reasons and causes: Children's understanding of conformity to social rules and physical laws. *Child Development*, 69, 706–720.

Kohlberg, L. (1976). Moral stages and moralization: The cognitive developmental point of view. In T. Lickona (Ed.), *Moral development and behavior: Theory, research and social issues* (pp. 31–53). New York: Holt.

Kramper, G. (2000). Transition of adolescent political action orientations of voting behavior in early adulthood in view of a social-cognitive action theory model of personality. *Political Psychology, 21*, 277–297.

Laupa, M. (1995). Children's reasoning about authority in home and school contexts. *Social Development, 4*, 1–16.

Laupa, M., & Turiel, E. (1993). Authority reasoning and social context. *Journal of Educational Psychology, 85*, 191–197.

Leekam, S. (1993). Children's understanding of the mind. In M. Bennett (Ed.), *The child as psychologist. An introduction to the development of social cognition.* London: Harvester Wheatsheaf.

Luise, B. (2000). *La comprensione dell'Eurdo in bambini e ragazzi dai 6 ai 13 anni* [*The understanding of the Euro in children from 6 to 13 years of age*]. Unpublished dissertation.

Melton, G. B. (1980). Children's concepts of their rights. *Journal of Clinical Child Psychology, 9*, 186–190.

Moore, S. W., Lare, J., & Wagner, K. A. (1985). *The child's political world. A longitudinal perspective.* New York: Praeger.

Niemi, R. G., & Junn, J. (1998). *Civic education: What makes students learn.* New Haven, CT: Yale University Press.

Nucci, L. (1981). Conceptions of personal issues: A domain distinct from moral or societal concepts. *Child Development, 52*, 114–121.

Nucci, L., & Weber, E. K. (1995). Social interactions in the home and the development of young children's conceptions of the personal. *Child Development, 66*, 1438–1452.

Perner, J., & Mant, C. M. (1988). The child's understanding of commitment. *Developmental Psychology, 24*, 343–351.

Piaget, J. (1924). *Le jugement et le raisonnement chez l'enfant.* Neuchatel, Switzerland: Delâchaux et Niestlé.

Piaget, J. (1926). *La représentation du monde chez l'enfant.* Neuchatel, Switzerland: Delâchaux et Niestlé.

Piaget, J. (1932). *Le jugement morale chez l'enfant.* Paris: PUF.

Piaget, J., & Weil, A. M. (1951). Le développement, chez l'enfant, de l'ideé de patrie et des relation avec l'etranger. *Bulletin International des Sciences Sociales* (pp. 605–621). Paris: UNESCO.

Pring, R. (1999). Political education: The relevance of the humanities. *Oxford Review of Education, 25*, 71–87.

Raaijmakers, Q. A. W., Verbogt, T. F. M. A., & Vollebergh, W. A. M. (1998). Moral reasoning and political beliefs of Dutch adolescents and young adults. *Journal of Social Issues, 45*, 531–546.

Rosenthal, S., Feiring, C., & Lewis, M. (1998). Political volunteering from late adolescence to young adulthood: Patterns and predictors. *Journal of Social Issues, 5*, 477–493.

Ruck, M. D., Keating, D. K., & Abramovitch, R. (1998a). Children's and adolescents' understanding of rights: Balancing nurturance and self determination. *Child Development, 69*, 404–417.

Ruck, M. D., Keating, D. K., Abramovitch, R., & Koegl, C. (1998b). Adolescents' and children's knowledge about rights: Some evidence for how young people view rights in their own lives. *Journal of Adolescence, 21*, 275–298.

Siegel, R. S., & Hoskin, M. (1981). *The political involvement of adolescents.* New Brunswick, NJ: Rutgers University Press.

Smetana, J. (1993). Understanding of social rules. In M. Bennett (Ed.), *The child as psychologist. An introduction to the development of social cognition* (pp. 111–141). London: Harvester Wheatsheaf.

Stacey, B. (1978). *Political socialization in Western society*. London: Edward Arnold.

Stradling, R. (1977). *The political awareness of the school leaver*. London: Hansard Society.

Tallandini, M. A., & Valentini, P. (1995). *La scuola è una grande casa* [*The school is a big house*]. Milano: Raffaello Cortina.

Tapp, J., & Kohlberg, L. (1977). Developing senses of law and legal justice. In J. Tapp & F. Levine (Eds.), *Law, justice, and the individual in society*. New York: Holt.

Thoma, S. J. (1993). The relation between political preference and moral judgment development in late adolescence. *Merrill-Palmer Quarterly, 39*, 359–374.

Torney, J., Oppenheim, A. N., & Farnen, R. (1975). *Civic education in ten nations: An empirical study*. New York: Wiley.

Torney-Purta, J. (1985). The development of views about the role of social institutions in redressing inequality and promoting human rights. In R. L. Leahy (Ed.), *The child's construction of social inequality*. New York: Academic Press.

Torney-Purta, J. (1992). Cognitive representations of the political system in adolescents: The continuum from pre-novice to expert. In H. Haste & J. Torney-Purta (Eds.), *The development of political understanding: A new perspective* (pp. 11–25). San Francisco: Jossey-Bass.

Torney-Purta, J., Lehmann, R., Oswald, H., & Schulz, W. (2001). *Citizenship and education in twenty-eight countries: Civic knowledge and engagement at age fourteen*. Amsterdam: IEA.

Turiel, E. (1983). *The development of social knowledge: Morality and convention*. Cambridge: Cambridge University Press.

United Nations General Assembly. (1989). *Adoption of a Convention on the Rights of the Child, UN doc. A/Res/44/25, November 1989*. New York: UN.

Wainryb, C., Shaw, L. A., & Maianu, C. (1998). Tolerance and intolerance: Children's and adolescents' judgements of dissenting beliefs, speech, persons, and conduct. *Child Development, 69*, 1541–1555.

Wellman, H. M. (1990). *The child's theory of mind*. Cambridge, MA: MIT Press.

Wellman, H. M., & Gelman, S. (1998). Knowledge acquisition in foundational domains. In D. Kuhn & R. S. Siegler (Eds.), *Handbook of child psychology, Vol. 2. Cognition, perception, and language* (5th ed., pp. 523–574). New York: Wiley.

Yates, M., & Youniss, J. (1998). Community service and political identity development in adolescence. *Journal of Social Issues, 5*, 495–512.

Youniss, J., Bales, S., Christmas-Best, V., Diversi, M., McLaughlin, M., & Silbereisen, R. (2002). Youth civic engagement in the twenty-first century. *Journal of Research on Adolescence, 12*, 121–148.

Youniss, J., McLellan, J., & Yates, M. (1997). What we know about engendering civic identity. *American Behavioral Scientist, 40*, 620–631.

CHAPTER FIVE

Children's understanding of the law and legal processes

Stephen J. Ceci, Faith A. Markle, and Yoo Jin Chae
Department of Human Development, Cornell University, Ithaca, USA

Throughout the English-speaking world, children are coming into contact with the juvenile, family, and criminal justice systems in record numbers. In part, this surge is fuelled by increases in divorce, which often result in acrimonious custody disputes in which one parent alleges abuse or neglect by the other. Typically, such allegations result in children being interviewed by social services, mental health, or law enforcement professionals, and on occasion the children may be deposed and even asked to testify in domestic relations or family court.

In addition to custody battles, there is a heightened awareness of the pervasiveness of sexual abuse of children today that did not exist in prior generations of parents. Whereas writers in the 1960s and 1970s often opined that sexual abuse of children was extremely rare[1], retrospective surveys of adults indicate that a significant proportion of the population claims to have been victims of sexual behaviour of adults when they were children[2]. In the United States, where national archives are kept for each type of

---

[1] For example, in her popular text on child behaviour problems, Elinor Verville (1968) wrote "Incestuous sexual relations are indulged in by less than one in every million people in English-speaking countries" (p. 372).

[2] Random samples of adults, asked about their childhood history, yield highly variable estimates of childhood sexual abuse, ranging, for females, from 6.8% (Siegel, Sorenson, Golding, Burnam, & Stein, 1987) to 62% (Wyatt, 1985); and for males, from 3% to 31% (see Peters, Wyatt, & Finkelhor, 1986).

maltreatment and its legal disposition, the numbers are staggering: For the 49 states reporting in NCCAN's 1998 national data system, there were 103,600 cases of *substantiated* sexual abuse (out of 315,400 reports). This represents 12.6% of all substantiated cases of abuse and neglect, including economic neglect, which is the largest category. For sexual abuse, 40.65% of all reported incidents involved children aged 7 and younger. If we add to these numbers the children who come into contact with the juvenile and criminal justice systems for other reasons (as witnesses to violence in the home, for PINS—persons in need of supervision hearings, for neglect), the numbers of young children involved in the various justice systems becomes frighteningly large.

Thus, in considering the role of children in the legal system, attention needs to be directed to the youngest children. They represent a large and growing constituency and, as we will show, they possess a special set of constraints.

Our discussion of children's understanding of the law and legal procedures will deal with two categories of information: (1) basic developmental competencies, including cognitive, social, and emotional, that may constrain children's participation, and (2) transnational differences in the way children's needs are accommodated by the legal system. In this chapter, we provide glimpses into the relevant research in each of these categories, first describing what is known about the youngest group, then discussing older children and adolescents. To adumbrate our conclusions, we argue that research has identified myriad factors that can undermine children's involvement in the legal arena; however, most national practices have failed to take these factors into consideration when dealing with child and juvenile witnesses.

BASIC DEVELOPMENTAL COMPETENCIES

In this section, we review the scientific literature dealing with the developmental trajectories of various cognitive, social, and emotional attainments that are relevant to children's ability to meaningfully participate in the legal system. We begin with the cognitive limitations that may impede children's participation, particularly their limited conceptual knowledge, memory, and language. Following this, we turn to social and emotional factors that come into play when children become enmeshed in the justice systems.

Cognitive factors

Conceptual limitations

It is a truism that knowledge accrues with experience. Children, by definition, lack knowledge. And this deficit can lead to problems with the law. Children lack substantive understanding of the aims of many legal processes, for example, the conception that witnesses give evidence related to the crime events (Saywitz, 1989; Warren-Leubecker, Tate, Hinton, & Ozbek, 1989). Thus, children are often unsure about what is required of them or what they are supposed to recount in courtroom settings, and they consequently fail to provide coherent and sufficient information (Poole & Lamb, 1998; Steward & Steward, 1996). Countless examples can be given of a child's misunderstanding of the assumptions and requirements of the legal system.

Consider a case described by Goodman (1984), in which a young boy who had been falsely accused of arson believed it was his job in court to convince the judge that the fire never occurred, rather than that he did not start it. According to Goodman, the boy's testimony lacked credibility and he was convicted for a crime he never committed. Had this boy conceptualised the legal process correctly, he might have adopted a more effective stance than the absurd one that led to his conviction.

In their handbook for attorneys and judges, Whitcomb, Shapiro, and Stellwagen (1985) surveyed attorneys and other professionals who work with child witnesses to obtain anecdotal evidence of the difficulties experienced by youthful witnesses. They found that children frequently lack basic information about the legal system. For instance, they may not appreciate why it is necessary for them to repeat their stories over and over again or that they will not be punished for misdeeds they report about others.

Peterson-Badali, Abramovitch, and Duda (1997) examined the legal understanding of children between the ages of 7 and 12 years. Half the children in this study attended a university laboratory school and were from middle to upper SES families, and the other half were from an outpatient treatment facility for children who had had police contact and were considered at-risk for delinquent behaviour. They found a number of misconceptions among pre-adolescent children in both groups. For example, children often misunderstood the role of an attorney. Fewer than half of all the children understood the attorney to be an advocate, for example, and 22% of the youngest children believed that the attorney's job was to gather information or to provide information to others. Although most children believed it was important for defendants to tell their attorneys everything, 92% of 7- to 9-year-old children believed that attorneys could divulge confidential disclosures they made to parents, and 84% believed that attorneys could share confidential information with the police. Although 10- to 12-year-old children were less likely than younger children to believe that an attorney could break confidentiality with the judge or with the police (43% and 57% respectively), 73% still believed attorneys could divulge to their parents. Other research has confirmed children's misunderstanding of the role of attorneys (e.g., Grisso, 1981; Peterson-

Badali & Abramovitch, 1992). Grisso, for example, found that about a third of his delinquent adolescent sample believed that the reason one must be honest with one's attorney was that the attorney could decide whether one was guilty or innocent. These children often believed that an attorney was not obligated to defend them if he or she thought them guilty.

In a review of the literature on children's competence to stand trial, Grisso (2000) noted that children's conception of rights differs from that of adults. For example, children under 13 tend to believe that the authorities make the laws and grant rights and that they are therefore entitled to revoke those laws and rights at any time. Grisso (1981) found that two thirds of his sample of adolescent delinquents believed that they could be punished for asserting their rights (e.g., the right to remain silent). Even 15-year-olds are not as competent as adults in comprehending their so-called "Miranda" rights (to remain silent and to be represented by counsel). Common misconceptions are that the right to remain silent means the defendant should not speak until requested to do so, or that the right to representation by an attorney means the defendant is allowed to have an attorney present, but not that an attorney must be provided if the defendant doesn't have one.

It is perhaps unsurprising that children know so little about the legal system; after all, how much direct experience are they likely to have had with it? The sources of legal information may come from children's own prior legal involvement, their family's legal involvement, and school (Tobey, Grisso, & Schwartz, 2000). Children are not routinely exposed to these sources, although no empirical studies have been done to examine the effects of such experience on children's understanding of the legal system. There is little evidence to suggest that children's experience with the law improves their understanding of legal concepts (Grisso, 2000), and one study actually found decreased understanding with increased experience among African American youth (Grisso, 1981). Few families engage their children in discussions of the purpose of courts and the nature of its procedures and personnel. However, attorneys have reported that parental sources of information are not always reliable (Tobey et al., 2000). Warren-Leubecker and her colleagues (1989) did find that nearly half of older children (adolescents) received some exposure to the legal system as part of formal classroom work on government in which they actually visited a courtroom. But such experience was rare for younger children as well as for many older children, and even for those who visit a courthouse, it is unlikely that they are tutored in legal terminology and procedures. Given their limited experiences with the legal system, children are often afraid to testify and fear not being believed in courtroom (Saywitz, 1989).

The media is another source of information to which children have ready access. This may include news coverage of prominent court cases and television court programmes. There is some evidence that children who regularly watch court programmes (actual civil trials conducted before the camera) have a slightly increased understanding of legal terminology (Saywitz, Jaenicke, & Camparo, 1990), though more information is likely to be gleaned from movies and television shows. Because these sources of information are intended primarily for entertainment rather than education, care is not taken to depict the legal system realistically. For instance, the frequency of crime is dramatically over-represented on television (Signorielli, 1991) and the types of crime represented are more violent and sensational, such as armed robbery or murder. Furthermore, the plots of most fictional shows are simplistic and formulaic in nature. In popular police television programmes, for example, the plot consists of the commitment of a crime, police investigation, and the apprehension of the criminal (Low & Durkin, 1997), but relatively little attention is paid to the judicial process. The reason so little consideration is given to courtroom scenes and to the judicial system is that, unlike the evidence in real-world crimes, the evidence in police programmes is clear-cut enough that by the end of the show the viewer is expected to have no doubt of the suspect's guilt. As a result, the information children obtain from viewing such shows is insufficient at best, and often misleading as well.

There is evidence furthermore that children's understanding of crime shows differs from that of adults, so not only are children learning about the legal system from a flawed source, but their own cognitive development limits how well such information is assimilated. For example, most adults are capable of understanding that the reason the suspect's guilt is so clear-cut is that the viewer is privy to information that the characters in the programme are not. The viewer may have seen the crime committed, or may have heard conversations that none of the fictional characters saw or heard. Young children may not have the capacity to notice or remember which characters have access to what information.

Durkin and Howarth (1997) conducted a study in which children between the ages of 5 and 9 were shown two versions of films depicting various thefts. In the first version, a witness saw the theft. The second version was identical to the first except that the witness entered the scene either before or just after the theft had been committed, so was not able to see who had done it. Even 9-year-olds sometimes made the error of thinking that the witness would know who had committed the crime when the witness had not observed it being committed. There was a linear developmental trend, with the youngest children making the most such errors and the 9-year-olds making the fewest.

The plots in these films were short and simple, portraying one unambiguous theft. The type of police show that children see on television or in movies is likely to have subplots and "red herrings", making it even more difficult to keep track of which characters have access to what information. How much of these intricacies children are able to grasp changes with maturity. When children are asked to describe what happens in a typical police programme, for example, first-graders (around 6 years old) focus on the commitment of the crime, the chase scene, and the arrest, whereas older children are able to pick up some of the subtler details, such as the canvassing of witnesses and the search for clues (Low & Durkin, 1997). Interestingly, Low and Durkin found that children in Grade 7 (early adolescence, around age 12) were more likely to mention some aspect of "due process" (evaluation of evidence, insufficient evidence, the rights of the suspect and legal hearings) than were adults, and that even when adults mentioned these aspects, they often stated that such events were rare in police programmes, as the guilt of the suspect was usually obvious. It appears, then, that children not only learn about the legal system from such shows, but also interpret these shows using their knowledge of justice and discipline gleaned from their daily lives.

Children may have conceptual impediments aside from their lack of direct contact with the justice system. Consider that prior to the age of 5, many children tend to define lying by its consequences rather than its intention. Warren-Leubecker et al. (1989) reported that in their study of 557 children aged between 3 and 13 years, response to the questions, "What would happen to you if you did something bad on purpose? What would happen if you did something bad by accident?" showed a steady linear trend to acknowledge that there should be a lesser punishment for bad things that were done by accident: 18, 32, 46, 61, 46, 51, 59, 56, 63, 67, 60% at ages 3 to 13 respectively. Similarly, younger children exhibited the belief that adults were omniscient and could tell if someone was lying by looking at them. In Warren et al.'s study, young children lacked the conceptual development necessary to render them credible as witnesses, and even many adolescents were not adult-like in their answers. Children's overestimation of adults' knowledge might derive from their experiences of everyday conversation in which adults already know the answer to the questions and subsequently tell the children whether their response was correct or incorrect. Children believe that adults are truthful, competent, cooperative, and germane (Ackerman, 1981, 1983; Demorest, Meyer, Phelps, Gardner, & Winner, 1984; Garvey, 1984). They may not even think that adults would make deceptive suggestions to confuse them. The accuracy and amount of children's testimony might be severely undermined by their mistaken belief that the communication rules of everyday life also apply in a forensic context (Saywitz & Moan-Hardie, 1994). Children believe that adults always ask them knowledgeable and logical questions that have a substantive answer (Ceci & Bruck, 1995; Saywitz, Geiselman, & Bornstein, 1992). They therefore attempt to answer even incomprehensible and bizarre questions, without knowing the response choices (Hughes & Grieve, 1980; Saywitz & Snyder, 1993). In addition, adults often encourage children to guess the answer when they are unsure. Young children are reluctant to say "I don't know", and they give more false reports to the peripheral or difficult questions (Cassel, Roebers, & Bjorklund, 1996; King & Yuille, 1987; Mulder & Vrij, 1996; Nesbitt & Markham, 1999; Parker & Carranza, 1989; Roebers & Schneider, 2000). They may try to give some response that is consistent with adults' expectations, without reporting their lack of knowledge (Ackerman, 1986, 1993; Hughes & Grieve, 1980). Thus, children possess less motivation to report accurate and true information (Seidler & Howie, 1999).

This is just one of myriad conceptual limitations of young children. A telling example in which the sort of conceptual limitations of young children can be seen is the concept of "transductive reasoning", a term applied to the type of thinking that characterises some preschoolers. Suppose that a child and her mother have often taken a bus to visit her grandmother. Then one day it is time for the child to begin school. Her mother takes her to the bus and explains that it will take her to school, and the child asks: "Is grandma the teacher?" This type of logical limitation can easily intrude into young children's legal reasoning, causing serious misconceptions.

Another limitation that is pertinent to young children's participation in the justice system is a deficit in "theory of mind". Children prior to the age of 4 years frequently fail to take the perspective of another. Suppose, for example, that a child is shown a picture of a child named *Maxi* putting his candy in a kitchen drawer; then the child is shown another picture of *Maxi*'s mother moving the candy to a different drawer after *Maxi* went out to play (Wimmer & Perner, 1983). When the child is asked: "Where will *Maxi* look for his candy when he returns from playing?" it is common for young children to claim he will look in the new drawer where *Maxi*'s mother moved it. In other words, young children lack the insight that *Maxi* has no perceptual knowledge that the candy was moved while he was outside playing. Children as old as 7 years of age still have difficulty applying theory of mind in all domains (e.g., Durkin & Howarth, 1997), and there is some evidence that even tenth-graders (15-year-olds) may not be able to use the perspectives of others in their legal decision-making (e.g., Cauffman & Steinberg, 2000). Such deficits in theory of mind become important when children attempt to differentiate their testimony based on what they assume others know. Unless one can appreciate that another's perspective differs from their own, there is ample room to overestimate the knowledge a witness or police possess.

Children may also fill in the gaps in their legal knowledge by generalising their understanding of familiar authority figures to the legal system. For example, a 12-year-old child who has stolen a car may understand that he has committed a punishable offence, but believe he will be put in lock-up for a couple weeks—the length of time for a school suspension or parental grounding (Oberlander, Goldstein, & Ho, 2001). Younger children often believe that the police have the same disciplinary role as parents in that they not only apprehend law-breakers, but also decide on and mete out punishment (e.g., "The police caught the bad guys and put them in jail") (Saywitz et al., 1990).

Older children (and even adults) who possess developmental delays behave like children, at least in terms of their deficient knowledge about the justice system and their conceptual difficulties. Recent studies show that such individuals are less likely to understand their rights when they are explained to them (e.g., to have counsel present during questioning, to remain silent), and they even reverse the meaning of important concepts such as "guilty" and "not guilty" (Ericson & Perlman, 2001; Smith & Hudson, 1995). This is important in light of the fact that adolescents with developmental delays are disproportionately represented among juvenile offenders (Grisso & Schwartz, 2000).

Memory limitations

The single most researched cognitive limitation impeding children's participation in the justice system involves their memories. Research on children's memory for witnessed events has reported age-related developmental differences, showing that older children produce more descriptions of a past experience and are less suggestible than younger children (Bruck & Ceci, 1999; Cole & Loftus, 1987; Goodman, Bottoms, Schwartz-Kenney, & Rudy, 1991a; King & Yuille, 1987; Loftus & Davies, 1984; Saywitz et al., 1992; Steward & Steward, 1996). When asked open-ended questions, preschool-aged children can recall relevant and accurate information (Bahrick, Parker, Fivush, & Levitt, 1998; Goodman, Hirschman, Hepps, & Rudy, 1991b; McCauley & Fisher, 1995; Ornstein, Gordon, & Larus, 1992; Peterson, 1999; Saywitz, 1987), but they are less responsive and provide fewer spontaneous memory reports than older children and adults (List, 1986; Marin, Holmes, Guth, & Kovac, 1979). Since young children's "free reports" of a past event are generally very brief and incomplete, they are often exposed to specific and leading questions, cues, and prompts in forensic situations (Baker-Ward, Gordon, Ornstein, Larus, & Clubb, 1993; Price & Goodman, 1990). Indeed, yes–no objective questions or multiple-choice questions are more likely to elicit children's memory for an event than mere requests for free reports, in which children are asked to remember as much as they can, in any order they wish. On the negative side, however, children are susceptible to interrogators' implied suggestions.

Thus, suggestive questions, such as "The man hurt you, didn't he?" might increase their false assents.

As briefly noted above, a great deal of research demonstrates children's heightened suggestibility, willingness to comply to gain adult approval, and failure to understand the ramifications of their statements. Suggestibility concerns the degree to which the encoding, storage, retrieval, and reporting of events can be influenced by a range of internal (developmental, cognitive, and personality) and external (social and contextual) factors (Ceci & Bruck, 1995). Children can be led to make errors when they are asked to narrate their experiences by misleading suggestions presented prior to or during a structured interview, because they tend to acquiesce to the false information embedded in an interrogator's questions (Poole & Lindsay, 1995; Quas, Goodman, Bidrose, Pipe, Craw, & Ablin, 1999).

In reviews of the 20th century's corpus of research, it is clear that children are disproportionately vulnerable to the effects of leading questions, suggestions, and pressure to conform to interviewers' wishes (Ceci & Bruck, 1993; Ceci & Friedman, 2000). This is particularly true of very young children (3- to 6-year-olds), although their greater suggestibility is a matter of degree only; even much older children and adults will succumb to suggestions and pressures[3]. Pre- and post-event suggestive information might mislead pre-school children to produce vivid and detailed reports of nonevents (Leichtman & Ceci, 1995). Moreover, some children consistently cling to their false accounts, despite efforts by parents and interviewers to dissuade them and explain that the events were false (Ceci, Huffman, Smith, & Loftus, 1994; Levine, Stein, & Liwag, 1999). Younger children are also misguided more than older children by repeated interviews employing suggestive questions (Poole & White, 1993). For example, pre-schoolers alter their responses more often than school-aged children and adults when the first leading question about a given event was followed by the stronger leading questions in the same interview (Cassel et al., 1996).

Children's vulnerability to leading questions and interviewers' suggestions has been well known for over a century. Early researchers, sometimes working within the context of a criminal investigation (e.g., Varendonck, 1911), showed that children's testimony could be influenced by the manner in which questions were posed to them (e.g., asking children if they saw the man with the red hair carry an object, when in actuality the man did

---

[3] An illuminating piece of evidence for this assertion is the work of Kassin and Kiechel (1996). They have shown that students at an elite American college will often erroneously claim they broke a computer after being told that they did by an experimenter. Moreover, they will internalise this belief, tell others they accidentally broke the computer, and sign a statement to this effect, agreeing to donate 8 hours of service to the experimenter in reparation for the alleged breakage.

not have red hair). With few exceptions, these early studies of children's suggestibility led to a jaundiced portrayal of their ability to resist an interviewer's suggestions. Beginning with the early experiments of Binet and his European colleagues (Binet, 1900; Lipmann, 1911; Stern, 1910; Varendonck, 1911), and concluding with empirical studies in the 1920s and 1930s (Messerschmidt, 1933; Otis, 1924; Sherman, 1925), early researchers viewed children as extremely susceptible to leading questions and unable to stand up to an interviewer's suggestions. A legal scholar of the day wrote: "Create, if you will, an idea of what the child is to hear or see, and the child is very likely to see or hear what you desire" (M. R. Brown, 1926, p. 133).

Modern studies of age differences in suggestibility have focused on pre-school-aged children, showing that they are especially susceptible to suggestions, although when they are appropriately questioned they are able to provide detailed lengthy reports (Ceci & Bruck, 1993). Children's suggestion-proneness can be accounted for by several cognitive (memory-based) factors.

As children grow older, their memories become more efficient because of the acquisition of strategies, knowledge, and self-insights (so-called meta-memory). Pre-school-aged children have limited capabilities of using encoding, storage, and retrieval strategies (Brainerd, 1985; Brainerd & Ornstein, 1991; Loftus & Davies, 1984). They often fail to encode new events efficiently due to their selective focus on salient or central features (Bower & Sivers, 1998), lack of knowledge about the events (Ricci & Beal, 1998), and the tendency to rely more on verbatim than gist memory (Brainerd & Reyna, 1990; Brainerd, Reyna, Howe, & Kingman, 1990; Foley & Johnson, 1985). They are also inferior to school-aged children in terms of the strength of stored representations, because use of storage strategies, such as rehearsal and organisation of stimuli, is uncommon at pre-school age. Therefore, they have weaker memory traces that are more likely to be forgotten (Baker-Ward et al., 1993). In addition, pre-school-aged children typically lack the effective retrieval strategies (e.g., use of category information) needed to search and facilitate their memories (Cox, Ornstein, Narus, Maxfield, & Zimler, 1989; Schneider & Bjorklund, 1998). Hence, they are usually dependent on external cues, such as interviewer's direction or questions, to retrieve information stored in long-term memory (Kobasigawa, 1974; Priestley, Roberts, & Pipe, 1999).

Young children have less prior knowledge that can be utilised to incorporate and organise new information (Chi, 1978; Johnson & Foley, 1984; Lindberg, 1980; Ornstein, 1990; Schneider & Bjorklund, 1998; Siegler, 1983), and they do not introspect into their memories to monitor when they need to engage in more mental work to consolidate a memory. Failure to do this often means that there is no awareness of when an event is committed to memory and when it is not—and consequently needs more mental work[4]. By failing to engage in strategies and insights, young children's memories are sometimes weaker, and therefore more susceptible to being altered or overwritten by the false suggestions of an adult (a parent, a law enforcement investigator, a social worker, etc.).

In addition, pre-schoolers lack skill at distinguishing between two or more sources of input into their memories (Gopnik & Graf, 1988; Wimmer, Hogrefe, & Perner, 1988), thus confusing things they heard with things they saw, and vice versa (Johnson & Foley, 1984; Lindsay, Johnson, & Kwon, 1991). They also exhibit the confusion between reality and fantasy that can lead at times to the belief that something was directly experienced when, in reality, it was merely dreamed or imagined (Foley & Johnson, 1985; Foley, Santini, & Sopasakis, 1989; Lindsay & Johnson, 1987; Warren-Leubecker et al., 1989). This is called "source confusion", and young children are more likely to exhibit it, such as when they misattribute an interviewer's suggestions to actual experiences (Ackil & Zaragoza, 1995).

Another limitation of pre-schoolers related to memory and suggestibility concerns so-called scripted knowledge. Scripts are temporally constructed expectations regarding typical and habitual routines of an event (Ceci & Bruck, 1993). It has been reported that young children are more susceptible to the negative effect of scripted knowledge than older children (Farrar & Goodman, 1992; Hudson, 1990; Hudson & Nelson, 1986; Powell & Thomson, 1996). For example, young children might report erroneously that a certain event occurred as it usually happens in their script, even though the event was not witnessed at that instance. Farrar and Goodman (1992) demonstrated that pre-school-aged children have more trouble recalling novel details of a single event that are inconsistent with their generalised script of the event. On four separate occasions, 4- and 7-year-olds were engaged in three standard events that were the same each time and then a novel set of deviation events. All the children possibly established script-based memory for the three standard repeated events. One week later, when asked to recall the events, 4-year-olds confused the deviation events with the standard events in such a manner that they believed nonoccurring standard events did actually occur. In contrast, 7-year-olds distinguished the memories for the two different types of events far more accurately. From this result, it can be inferred that young children's

---

[4] This lack of insight into their memories can be vividly demonstrated by asking children of various ages to memorise a long list of words. Then ask the children to raise their hands when they feel they have memorised the items, and you will discover that pre-school-aged children will raise their hands long before they have done so. They simply do not introspect into the contents of their memories the way older children and adults do.

tendency to overly rely on the scripted knowledge might lead them to be more suggestible[5].

Additionally, isolating the self from a traumatic experience, for instance sexual abuse, is especially common among preschool children. They may withhold certain types of information, such as genital touch, during the recounting of their experiences (Goodman, Quas, Batterman-Faunce, Riddlesberger, & Kuhn, 1997; Saywitz, Goodman, Nicholas, & Moan, 1991). Such isolation can lead to children's failure to report an experience (Eisen & Goodman, 1998). This is considered as a significant problem because sexual abuse is involved in most criminal trials in which children testify.

Language limitations

The issue of language is very important for several reasons. For starters, children's language ability sets limits on what they understand and what others infer from their answers to questions. The complex and unfamiliar language employed during the legal processes is developmentally inappropriate and beyond children's comprehension. Children are often exposed to lengthy questions involving embedded clauses, difficult vocabulary, double negatives, and multiple prepositional phrases in forensic settings (Brennan & Brennan, 1988; Walker, 1994). Such syntactic constructions and vocabulary used by interviewers may lead to children's misunderstanding of the questions and produce inaccurate statements (Carter, Bottoms, & Levine, 1996; Saywitz & Snyder, 1996).

Several studies have shown that pre-school-aged children are unaware of the meanings of common legal terms such as "court", "swear", "oath", "promise", and so on (Saywitz, 1987; Warren-Leubecker et al., 1989). Saywitz et al. (1990) noted that even sixth-graders (11-year-olds) do not have a complete grasp of some legal terms, such as "testify", "jury", and "attorney". They may admit to not knowing the meaning of a word, but they may also mistake the term for a more familiar, similar-sounding word (such as "jewellery" for "jury", or "the night" for "denied"). They may know a correct vernacular use of the term, but not the legal use (for example, "Charges are something you do with a credit card"), and may cling to their definition even when the term has been used in a sentence with legal context. Confusions within the legal context (e.g., defining "jury" as "a lawyer" or "judge"; or "allegations" as "evidence") tend to increase with age (Saywitz

---

[5] The other side of the scripted knowledge deficit is that often young children lack knowledge that, if they possessed it, might help cue their recollection. For instance, if they had a script for going to a restaurant that included waiting to be seated, then ordering from a menu, then being served, then ordering desert, then paying and leaving, this would provide multiple cues for them later to recall the discrete ones.

et al., 1990), which means that although older children have a better grasp of legal terminology, when they do make mistakes, they are more likely than younger children to give the impression that they understand. Furthermore, children believe they understood the term when they actually do not (Saywitz & Snyder, 1993), and thus try to answer any question without reporting their comprehension failure (Carter et al., 1996).

Children's language style is best characterised as powerless. By this, it is meant that their voices are not as audible as those of adults, they engage in powerless expressions such as "uh" and "um", greater use of hedges such as "I guess", or "kind of", they often exhibit a questioning intonation in declarative contexts, and they employ few intensifiers such as "definitely" or "certainly" (Nigro, Buckley, Hill, & Nelson, 1987). Powerless language styles are associated with juror disbelief and lower conviction rates when children testify. Thus, when a child speaks as powerfully as an adult, jurors rate that child as more credible and are as likely to convict based on the child's testimony. The problem is that children rarely speak this way. This becomes even more salient when the child is from a cultural minority or an ethnic group that routinely speaks with comparatively little power. In the United States this can be seen when children of Asian descent speak, as the custom in those cultures is to use low power styles.

Studies on the relationship between pre-school children's verbal abilities and memory performances have shown that these children's limited language skills lead to difficulties in encoding and retrieving. For example, the capability to structure narratives for recalling a past event improves with age (Mandler, 1990), and so pre-school children may have more trouble reporting even the information they remember than older children. Children's limited communication skills also contributes to the lack of spontaneous reports of stored information, and more structured questioning may be required (McCauley & Fisher, 1995; Poole & White, 1991). Sometimes, children switch the topic of conversation in the course of a forensic interview. As a result, their statements might be misinterpreted (Fivush & Hammond, 1990; Gordon & Follmer, 1994).

All of these language problems are exacerbated when the child witness or defendant does not speak English as a first language, or is bilingual. This is a special concern when one considers the disproportionate number of ethnic minorities among juvenile defendants (Woolard, Fondacaro, & Slobogin, 2001). Not only does this put such children at a greater risk of misunderstanding and being misunderstood, but they are less likely to be able to depend upon their parents for advice and information if their parents also do not speak English (Tobey et al., 2000). Furthermore, even when English is the first language of all parties, socioeconomic and ethnic variations in the use of the vernacular can cause confusion between juvenile defendants and their attorneys.

Social factors

Compliance

For the cognitively unarmed child, an interrogation by experts is no contest—children can be made to say things that are incriminating, even if they are false. In the summer of 1999, the city of Chicago witnessed a grisly murder and sexual assault of an 11-year-old girl named Ryan Harris. In the aftermath of discovering Ryan's body, two boys, aged 7 and 8, confessed to murdering her. The boys made their confessions without counsel present during a lengthy interrogation. Later, a 27-year-old ex-convict's semen was found on the dead girl's body and he now stands indicted for her murder. Why would those two boys falsely admit to things they didn't do? One possible answer lies in their eagerness to please adult authority figures. Children might respond in very compliant attitude during the interrogation, as they may be highly praised and given attention that is rare in their everyday life. The boys in the Chicago case sat around a table with two uniformed officers who held hands around the table and pledged to be on the "same team". The officers bought the boys food and explained that they could go home as soon as they helped the rest of the team clear up Ryan Harris' murder. After several hours of interrogation without the presence of an attorney or family member, each boy ended up admitting to a series of behaviours that they almost certainly could not have enacted, including raping the dead girl.

Without predicting the ramifications of their statements, children strive to avoid adults' anger and punishment by admitting to the suggested questions (Saywitz, 1989). In their daily experiences, children learn that noncompliance is met with adults' negative reaction, and so they avoid challenging adults' suggestions in courtroom situations as well (Saywitz & Moan-Hardie, 1994). Children's eagerness to please adults is easily exploitable by interrogators, as well as by defendants seeking their help.

Such sensitivity to social pressure was the earliest scientific demonstration: Small (1896) showed that children were influenced by what classmates said, and Binet (1900), the originator of the first IQ test, also showed children's tendency to be influenced by their group's behaviour. The socioemotional pressure to comply in forensic interviews seems to result from children's limited perspective-taking skill. They lack the knowledge of the interviewer's motivation, the purpose of questioning, and the forensic relevance of their responses. They sometimes acquiesce to suggestive questions in order to avoid humiliation, assuming that their lack of knowledge may be seen unfavourably (Paris, 1988).

Children's rate of compliance increases when they perceive the interviewer as authoritative or credible. It is known from experiments that children who are suggestively interviewed by a powerful adult authority figure (e.g., a police officer) will incorporate more of that adult's false suggestions into their report than will peers who are interviewed by someone possessing less authority, such as a janitor or another child (e.g., Ceci, Ross, & Toglia, 1987).

On the other hand, noncompliance with authority may interfere with communication between children and adults in a forensic setting. Juvenile defendants, for example, may be mistrustful and defiant. As mentioned earlier, they do not always completely understand their attorney's role as advocate and defender (Peterson-Badali et al., 1997), and may be wary of confiding in them. The converse can affect children's understanding of and ability to cope with the legal system: Children who have grown up in environments where adults were not trustworthy or were abusive may have a difficult time trusting any adult, including their own attorney (Tobey et al., 2000). This may affect both the amount of information these children are willing to reveal, and the veracity of their statements.

Attitudes toward the police

Researchers are in agreement that adolescents generally hold the police in lower esteem than do adults, and this is especially true of boys (e.g., Bayley & Mendelsohn, 1969; Peek, Alston & Lowe, 1978; Reasons & Wirth, 1975). In one study, junior high and high school students rated the police as friendly, hardworking, and courteous, but also considered them dishonest, rude, and prejudiced against minorities (Taylor, Turner, Esbensen, & Winfree, 2001). This study also noted that African Americans held the police in lower esteem than American Indians and Latinos, who rated the police lower than whites, a finding that seems to hold across US regions and across age from children to elderly adults (e.g., Peek et al., 1978). Hurst, Frank, and Browning (2000) discovered, however, that these racial differences disappeared after controlling for such things as whether or not the children had been victims of crimes, whether they lived in a high-crime neighbourhood, and most significantly, whether they had heard of or witnessed police misconduct directed at another person. Children who fell into one of these three categories were less likely to rate the police as competent.

Psychosocial factors

Legal decision-making

Adolescents' ability to reason is comparable to that of adults by the time children reach the age of about 15 years. Children in their mid-adolescent years are nevertheless more likely than either younger children or adults to

engage in high-risk behaviour (e.g., Fried & Reppucci, 2001). One explanation for this is that adolescents have different priorities from younger
children and adults. For example, a 14-year-old child may refuse to take a
plea bargain even though the evidence is very strong against him because he
believes his friends won't think it's cool. To this child, it is far better to
suffer a longer sentence than be humiliated in the eyes of his friends.
Research has indicated, however, that this is not the whole story (e.g.,
Cauffman & Steinberg, 2000; Grisso, 1981; Peterson-Badali et al., 1997).

Cauffman and Steinberg (2000) hypothesise that although adolescents
may be cognitively mature enough to make competent legal decisions, and
may be fully aware of the long-term consequences, they lack psychosocial
maturity. These authors define psychosocial maturity as responsibility (self-
reliance, clarity, and independence), perspective (the ability to take viewpoints other than one's own and the ability to anticipate a broad range of
consequences), and temperance (impulse control and the ability to evaluate a
situation before acting). They gave junior high and high school students
several vignettes in which they were asked to imagine themselves facing the
decision of whether or not to do something antisocial, such as shoplifting or
smoking marijuana, in response to peer pressure. They were to respond to
each vignette under each of three conditions: (1) something bad would
happen if the child committed the act, (2) nothing bad would happen, and
(3) something bad might happen. Younger children demonstrated lower
levels of psychosocial maturity but, regardless of age, those with lower levels
of psychosocial maturity were more likely than those with higher levels to
state that they would participate in antisocial behaviour, even when negative
consequences were certain.

In a legal context, this suggests that even older adolescents may make
poor choices about such crucial issues as cooperating with their attorneys,
showing up for appointments, engaging in illegal behaviour while awaiting
trial, skipping bail, or entering a plea. Peterson-Badali and Abramovitch
(1992) note that the ability to reason about whether to plead guilty
increases with age. The pre-adolescent children in their study, for example,
were more likely than young adolescents to recommend a guilty plea even
when the evidence against the defendant was weak. These children were
making a decision about a hypothetical character, however, and the choice
was simpler than the choices faced by children in court. Many factors other
than age or psychosocial maturity can affect how well children put into
practice the skills they may have.

Children with developmental delays and mental disorders are disproportionately represented among those in the juvenile justice system (e.g.,
Kazdin, 2000). Such disabilities affect how well the children are able to
comprehend their situation and the consequences, and may also affect what
choices seem more appealing to them. One of the children interviewed by

Tobey et al. (2000), for example, was so depressed that he made no independent decisions whatsoever. Another child decided to plead guilty so that he would not have to return to a dangerous neighbourhood where he had enemies waiting for him.

Racial issues affect children's decisions about how they cooperate with their attorneys and what kind of defence they are likely to make. African American and Latino children, for example, may fear that their white attorneys will not defend them or that they will not get a fair trial because of their race (Tobey et al., 2000). Being in a strange environment, sometimes hospitalised, incarcerated, or separated from their friends and family, puts a great deal of stress on these children and affects their ability to make sound decisions. Children may plead guilty just to get the process over with and get back home as quickly as possible (Tobey et al., 2000).

Orientation toward laws

Traditionally, it has been proposed that young children, at least prior to the age of 6, possess what is known as a heteronomous or unitary orientation toward laws (Kohlberg, 1981; Piaget, 1932). This is reflected in an adherence to laws even when they are viewed by adults as unjust (e.g., laws banning education for minorities), as well as rigid emphasis on punishment and obedience to authority figures.

Such emphasis on punishment and obedience may extend into adolescence. In a study on adolescents' criminal decision-making, Fried and Reppucci (2001), asked a group of high school students a number of questions regarding a film clip the children watched about some boys who stole some hotdogs and ended up seriously injuring a man. These students were recruited through an alternative high school, a detention centre, and a treatment centre for juvenile delinquents. Among this sample, the younger children (13–14 years) were more likely than older adolescents to believe the boys should be transferred to adult court and that they warranted a harsher sentence.

HOW THE LEGAL SYSTEM UNDERSTANDS CHILDREN

Children as eyewitnesses

Despite the quantity of research on children's suggestibility over the past two decades, reforms to the legal system have not, for the most part, been based on empirical findings. In fact, most attempts to make the legal system more child-friendly for young eyewitnesses have focused more on accommodating children's emotional needs than on compensating for children's immature cognitive skills, incomplete social understanding, or lack of experience with the legal system. For example, the practice of removing the defendant from the dock during a child accuser's testimony has been in practice in England for over 80 years (Spencer & Flin, 1990), and was implemented primarily because children reacted with such terror at seeing the person who had injured or threatened them that they were often unable to testify at all due to fear or shame. Children have also been allowed to testify behind a screen, to sit facing away from the defendant, and to bring a parent or other support person with them to the witness stand (Myers, 1996). Such accommodations are made at the discretion of individual judges.

The most publicised and highly criticised accommodation made for child witnesses is that of allowing them to testify via closed-circuit television (CCTV). This procedure allows for children to be questioned in a separate room while the jury watches on a screen in the courtroom. In England, this is allowed in criminal cases, but not civil cases, whereas in the US the judge makes a determination based on the unique circumstances of each case (Myers, 1996). At issue is whether protecting children from the acute trauma of testifying in front of the defendant overrides the chronic trauma of being re-abused by the defendant should the jury fail to convict in cases of actual child abuse. In the United States an additional issue is constitutional in nature; namely, the defendant's sixth Amendment right to confront an accuser. Accommodations that limit face-to-face confrontation, such as CCTV, are often challenged.

Research indicates that the CCTV is effective in reducing children's stress level (Davies, 1999) and, as mentioned previously in this chapter, children are more likely to provide accurate testimony in a relaxed and supportive atmosphere, and to provide a greater amount of information (Davies, 1999). On the other hand, juries tend to find children less credible over CCTV than live (Orcutt, Goodman, Tobey, Batterman-Faunce, & Thomas, 2001), and a number of studies have demonstrated that juries are more likely to convict when testimony is given live (e.g., Davies, 1999; Orcutt, et al., 2001). Wilson and Davies (1999) found, however, that in comparing actual cases in which this technology was used[6] with cases in which it was not, juries were no more likely to convict on evidence provided via television. This study examined all criminal trials in England that involved child witnesses over a 19-month period. A special application had to be made and approved before a child was allowed to testify via television, so that the sample was not randomly selected. Because the cases in which an application was made and approved could have been more serious

---

[6] In this study, a videotaped interview was shown to the court, followed by cross-examination via live-link television.

than in cases where an application was denied or the prosecution felt it was not necessary, this could account for the conviction rate being similar. In other words, if the CCTV defendants had committed more heinous crimes or the victims were more emotional or vulnerable, the conviction rate might have been higher than if the samples had been similar in these respects. We simply do not have sufficiently powerful evidence to draw firm conclusions regarding the effects of CCTV on convictions as yet.

When children do testify live, judges have the right to intervene during cross examination if the questioning becomes too suggestive or coercive (Myers, 1996; Spencer & Flin, 1990), but this presupposes that judges have the training, skill, and inclination to intervene effectively. Furthermore, this intervention may be too little or too late if a child has already been subjected to numerous biased interviews prior to the trial. And prosecuting attorneys are not oblivious to the fact that jurors are likely to resent an attorney who browbeats or otherwise distresses a young child in court (Brown, 1987), making intervention during cross-examination less crucial than protecting children from biased interviewing techniques during the investigation phase.

Recently, some attempts have been made to ensure that investigative interviews with young children are conducted in as unbiased a manner as possible (Myers, 1996; Spencer & Flin, 1990) although training of child interviewers has been more uniform in the UK than in the US and elsewhere (Spencer & Flin, 1990). In most US states, efforts to increase the validity of children's initial statements have generally been made by individual child protective service agencies rather than by federal legislative reforms. Procedures such as audio-recording of initial interviews with alleged child abuse victims, as well as the extent of training interviewers receive, vary from one agency to another within states, although a minority of states do have laws governing the number of interviews to which a child may be subjected (Myers, 1996). Currently, a large-scale national effort called *Finding Words* is underway to train child interviewers uniformly. It is being conducted by the American Prosecutor's Research Institute, based in the National Center for Prosecution of Child Abuse. This project is ongoing and it is too early to tell whether it will be successful in increasing the efficacy of child interviewers.

An additional issue concerns children's competence to testify. In the US system, competency means that the child is able to distinguish the truth from fantasy, that he or she understands the impact of lying (both moral and practical), and that he or she has sufficient memory of the event and can communicate effectively. As we have already pointed out, young children's cognitive limitations and their lack of experience may render them less than reliable witnesses. Nevertheless, in most US states, children are considered competent to testify without a competency hearing unless a question is raised about an individual child's competence, and the Federal Rules of Evidence favours allowing all witnesses (including children, drug addicts, mentally retarded, psychotic, etc.) to testify and allow the weight of their testimony to be assessed by the fact finder (juror or judge). In some states where children are not automatically considered competent, the competency hearing is waived for children testifying in sexual abuse cases (Myers, 1996). Furthermore, most states have modified the corroboration requirement for child abuse victims (Meyers, 1996) so that a conviction can be made solely on the basis of a child's testimony.

In the UK, competency hearings are conducted by the judge. There is no set of criteria for determining competency; it is up to the individual judge to decide what questions to ask and to determine whether the child is competent (Spencer & Flin, 1990). If it is determined that a child is not competent to take the oath, but is otherwise competent to testify, that child may be allowed to testify unsworn, a concession also available in the US. This means that the child's testimony may be heard but may not be used to convict. In other words, corroborating evidence is necessary in cases where children testify unsworn (Spencer & Flin, 1990).

Children as defendants

Despite recent research on children's legal reasoning and decision making, the juvenile justice system seemingly is becoming less adaptive to the developmental needs of children and more similar to the adult system (Ayers, 1997). The first juvenile court was founded in the US in 1899 with the goal of protecting children from the harshness of the adult legal system and "poor houses". It was to be a refuge and rehabilitation centre, not only for juvenile delinquents and troubled children, but also for child victims of abuse and neglect. The aim was to hire judges who specialised in child development and who would make individualised dispositions based on each child's background and history. As a result, dispositions varied widely from one judge to another and even from one case to another (Feld, 1998).

The shortcomings of such a system came to a head in 1967 with the case of Gerald Gault, a 15-year-old who was sentenced to 6 years in prison for making an obscene phone call. The Supreme Court overruled this child's conviction and concluded that children are entitled to due process under the law (Ayers, 1997); that is, they have the right to advance notice of charges, to a fair and impartial hearing, to assistance of counsel, and to an opportunity to confront and cross-examine witnesses. Three years later, the Supreme Court also ruled that a child's delinquency must be proven under the criminal law standard of proof beyond a reasonable doubt (Feld, 1998), rather than under the more relaxed civil law.

Although these rulings went a long way toward protecting children from false convictions and disproportionate sentencing, they also drew the juvenile system closer to the adult system. At the time of this writing, the major differences between the juvenile and adult systems are that juvenile offenders are assigned a law guardian and that the judge is still expected to look at the whole family situation and any other mitigating factors in deciding on a disposition. Dispositions are also generally less severe than sentencing in adult court and may include, from least to most restrictive, conditional discharge (the child is sent home on certain pre-determined conditions), probation, department of social services custody, group home, or residential treatment. The more restrictive dispositions are reserved for violent juvenile offenders. Runaways, children who break curfew, and other children who are out of parental control (also known as status offenders or persons in need of supervision, or PINS) are not subjected to the most restrictive dispositions.

In actual practice, the law guardian may function more as an attorney than as an advocate and protector of the child's best interests (Tobey et al., 2000). In fact, some law guardians warn juvenile offenders and their parents in advance that they will provide advice and recommendations, but in the end will act upon the child's wishes (S. Cook, personal communication, June 2002). Furthermore, judges may be willing to consider all of the juvenile offender's circumstances in making a disposition, but lack of time and resources preclude this individual attention (McGarrell, 2001). Younger offenders (under 13 years of age) are often dismissed with a conditional discharge, although research indicates that these children are at higher risk of reoffending than their older counterparts (McGarrell, 2001). Finally, despite strong evidence than adolescents even as old as 19 years are not able to reason as effectively about legal matters as adults (e.g., Cauffman & Steinberg, 2000), more and more children are being tried as adults (Woolard et al., & Slobogin, 2001).

Restorative justice

A hopeful movement that has sprung up in the past decade is the practice of restorative justice. Drawing on the justice systems of aboriginal people in New Zealand and North America, programmes have been put together in Europe, Canada, and the United States that address the needs of both victims and offenders. In Australia and New Zealand, such programmes have been used with adult offenders, but in most Western countries they are used almost exclusively with children and adolescents (M. Ray, personal communication, June 19, 2002). In its simplest form, restorative justice requires the offender to restore stolen or damaged property or to otherwise make amends in some way that satisfies the victim. Generally, the victim and offender participate in a conference with a trained mediator. In many restorative justice programmes, the victim and the offender also bring one or more support people, such as family members or close friends, who also participate in the conference. The mediator usually meets with the parties from both sides individually to listen to their stories, instruct them on the procedure, and identify any problems that could arise during the actual conference. During the conference, the victim and his or her supporters are given the opportunity to explain how the crime has impacted them and to ask questions of the offender. The offender and supporters also have an opportunity to talk about the crime and any extenuating circumstances. The discussion lasts as long as necessary to culminate in a reparation agreement. This agreement usually consists of an apology, and a require-ment that some type of restitution be made. With juvenile offenders, it often includes a requirement that the offender participate in some sort of general self-improvement as well, such as increasing school attendance, getting a job, or keeping a curfew.

Restorative justice is intuitively appealing because it holds children accountable for their misconduct. Victims report that they feel more satisfied with the outcomes and less afraid of re-victimisation than those whose cases are heard in traditional juvenile court (McGarrel, 2001). Juvenile offenders are more likely to complete their programmes than those on traditional probation. Furthermore, preliminary research indicates that recidivism is lower among juveniles who have participated in a restorative justice conference, and that re-offenders tend to commit less serious crimes than their counterparts who go through the traditional system (e.g., Bazemore & Umbreit, 2001; McGarrell, 2001).

CONCLUDING REMARKS

In closing we offer some thoughts on the best ways to handle children entering the legal system. The treatments will vary depending on whether the child comes to court as a witness, a victim-witness, or an alleged offender. Research pertinent to each of these states allows us to make some tentative suggestions.

First, in the case of child witnesses and victim-witnesses, research shows that many children, like adults, find the act of appearing in court highly stressful. Although numerous studies have documented the effects of stress of child witnesses, research indicates that, for the most part, the stress is transient, and child witnesses rebound to their pre-court conditions. In a 2-year longitudinal study of the aftermath of testifying, researchers reported that the experience of appearing in open court was often claimed by the children to be empowering—even when the jury verdict did not go their way (Goodman et al., 1998).

The situation is different when the child is accused of committing a crime. In this situation, the child is no match for the tactics that may be used against him or her. Consider the techniques sometimes used by police to interrogate children. Interrogators are permitted to deceive, promise, and threaten to obtain a confession. Investigators have no requirement to tell children the truth when they are interrogating them, and lies are frequently part of the routine. While most adults may be cognitively and socially sophisticated enough to be suspicious of such tactics and to demand their rights to counsel, children are not—until it is too late. Once it becomes clear to them that they admitted to murder, children's faces look like the proverbial cow in the corral that only now comprehends the slaughterhouse concept. They will not be permitted to go home after all, nor will they be given the rewards promised by their interrogators. Such interrogative tactics are effective in prompting confessions from the mouths of guilty children. The problem is that research amply demonstrates that the same tactics can also coerce confessions from innocent children (Ceci, 1999). Law enforcement professionals face a difficult dilemma in their efforts to protect society from truly dangerous youth. Nevertheless, court-sanctioned interviewing techniques can sabotage the search for truth when the witness is a developmentally young person.

Can high-pressure tactics be justified because they may be the most effective way to get a reluctant child to admit a heinous crime? Perhaps yes, if the child indeed committed the crime. But what if the child did not? Transcripts of children interrogated without counsel show they often do not realise what they were being asked or what they were admitting to. Like mentally ill and developmentally delayed adults, children represent a special class of defendants who require representation by counsel. It is unreasonable to expect children to withstand periods of confinement and pressurised questioning, after being told repeatedly that they are lying when they profess their innocence and that witnesses are ready to testify against them. Children actually *believe* interrogators who tell them that if they admit they murdered, they can go home. Most adults would immediately distrust such a statement. But a child desperate to go home often does not. The fear and lacerating loneliness that comes with interrogation by a highly trained professional leads to both true *and* false confessions. Children are not the equals of their adult examiners: We must not delude ourselves that a child will never admit to something he did not do.

No jurist should endorse the sentiment "Anything worth fighting for is worth fighting dirty for". But isn't that what prosecutors do when they detain young children for hours, unanchored, loosed in a world of powerful adults promising, cajoling, threatening, insulting, and intermittently touting friendship? The stakes are too high to permit children to waive the right to counsel or to remain silent. In the United States, children as young as 11 can be sentenced to life in prison in some states. Across America, 13-year-olds can be tried as adults. Children as young as 8 can be asked to waive their Miranda rights. In some American states, 16-year-olds can be sentenced to death.

All children accused of serious crimes should be represented by counsel. And all interviews—not merely the final one in which a child makes a guilty admission—should be electronically preserved. Only then can judges decide if a child's confession developed appropriately.

REFERENCES

Ackerman, B. P. (1981). Encoding specificity in the recall of pictures and words in children and adults. *Journal of Experimental Child Psychology, 31*, 193–211.

Ackerman, B. P. (1983). Speaker bias in children's evaluation of the eternal consistency of statements. *Journal of Experimental Child Psychology, 35*, 111–127.

Ackerman, B. P. (1986). Children's insensitivity to comprehension failure in interpreting a nonliteral use of an utterance. *Child Development, 57*, 485–497.

Ackerman, B. P. (1993). Children's understanding of the speaker's meaning in referential communication. *Journal of Experimental Child Psychology, 55*, 56–86.

Ackil, J. K., & Zaragoza, M. S. (1995). Developmental differences in eyewitness suggestibility and memory for source. *Journal of Experimental Child Psychology, 60*, 57–83.

Ayers, W. (1997). *A kind and just parent: The children of juvenile court.* Boston, MA: Beacon Press.

Bahrick, L., Parker, J. F., Fivush, R., & Levitt, M. (1998). The effects of stress on young children's memory for a natural disaster. *Journal of Experimental Psychology: Applied, 4*, 308–331.

Baker-Ward, L., Gordon, B. N., Ornstein, P. A., Larus, D. M., & Clubb, P. A. (1993). Young children's long-term retention of a pediatric examination. *Child Development, 64*, 1519–1533.

Bayley, D. H., & Mendelsohn, H. (1969). *Minorities and the police.* New York: Free Press.

Bazemore, G., & Unbreit, M. (2001). A comparison of four restorative conferencing models. *Juvenile Justice Bulletin, 2*, 1–7.

Binet, A. (1900). *La suggestibilité.* Paris: Schleicher Freres.

Bower, G. H., & Sivers, H. (1998). Cognitive impact of traumatic events. *Development and Psychopathology, 10*, 625–653.

Brainerd, C. J. (1985). Three-state models of memory development: A review of advances in statistical methodology. *Journal of Experimental Child Psychology, 40*, 375–394.

Brainerd, C. J., & Ornstein, P. A. (1991). Children's memory for witnessed events: The developmental backdrop. In J. Doris (Ed.), *The suggestibility of children's recollections* (pp. 10–20). Washington, DC: American Psychology Association.

Brainerd, C. J., & Reyna, V. F. (1990). Gist is the grist: Fuzzy trace theory and the new intuitionism. *Developmental Review, 10*, 3–47.

Brainerd, C. J., Reyna, V. F., Howe, M. L., & Kingman, J. (1990). The development of forgetting and reminiscence. *Monographs of the Society for Research in Child Development*, No. 55.

Brennan, M., & Brennan, R. (1988). *Strange language.* Wagga Wagga, Australia: Riverina Murry Institute of Higher Education.

Brown, M. R. (1926). *Legal psychology.* Indianapolis: Bobbs-Merrill.

Brown, P. M. (1987). *The art of questioning: Thirty maxims of cross-examination.* New York: Macmillan.

Bruck, M., & Ceci, S. J. (1999). The suggestibility of children's memory. *Annual Review of psychology, 50*, 419–439.

Carter, C. A., Bottoms, B. L., & Levine, M. (1996). Linguistic and socioemotional influences on the accuracy of children's reports. *Law and Human Behavior, 20*, 335–358.

Cassel, W. S., Roebers, C. E. M., & Bjorklund, D. F. (1996). Developmental patterns of eyewitness responses to repeated and increasingly suggestive questions. *Journal of Experimental Child Psychology, 61*, 116–133.

Cauffman, E., & Steinberg, L. (2000). (Im)maturity of judgment in adolescence: Why adolescents may be less culpable than adults. *Behavioral Sciences and the Law, 18*, 741–760.

Ceci, S. J. (1999). Why minors accused of serious crimes cannot waive counsel. *Court Review, 36*, 8–9.

Ceci, S. J., & Bruck, M. (1993). The suggestibility of children's recollections: An historical review and synthesis. *Psychological Bulletin, 113*, 403–439.

Ceci, S. J., & Bruck, M. (1995). *Jeopardy in the courtroom: A scientific analysis of children's testimony*. Washington, DC: American Psychological Association.

Ceci, S. J., & Friedman, R. D. (2000). The suggestibility of children: Scientific research and legal implications. *Cornell Law Review, 86*, 34–108.

Ceci, S. J., Huffman, M. L. C., Smith, E., & Loftus, E. F. (1994). Repeatedly thinking about a non-event: Source misattributions among preschoolers. *Consciousness and Cognition, 3*, 388–407.

Ceci, S. J., Ross, D. F., & Toglia, M. P. (1987). Suggestibility of children's memory: Psychological implications. *Journal of Experimental Psychology: General, 116*, 38–49.

Chi, M. T. H. (1978). Knowledge structures and memory development. In R. S. Siegler (Ed.), *Children's thinking: What develops?* (pp. 73–96). Hillsdale, NJ: Lawrence Erlbaum Associates Inc.

Cole, C. B., & Loftus, E. F. (1987). The memory of children. In S. J. Ceci, M. P. Toglia, & D. F. Ross (Eds.), *Children's eyewitness memory* (pp. 178–208). New York: Springer-Verlag.

Cox, B. D., Ornstein, P. A., Narus, M. J., Maxfield, D., & Zimler, J. (1989). Children's concurrent use of rehearsal and organizations strategies. *Developmental Psychology, 25*, 619–627.

Davies, G. (1999). The impact of television on the presentation and reception of children's testimony. *International Journal of Law and Psychiatry, 22*, 241–256.

Demorest, A., Meyer, C., Phelps, E., Gardner, H., & Winner, E. (1984). Words speak louder than actions: Understanding deliberately false remarks. *Child Development, 55*, 1527–1534.

Durkin, K., & Howarth, N. (1997). Mugged by the facts? Children's ability to distinguish their own and witnesses' perspectives on televised crime events. *Journal of Applied Developmental Psychology, 18*, 245–256.

Eisen, M. L., & Goodman, G. S. (1998). Trauma, memory, and suggestibility in children. *Development and Psychopathology, 10*, 717–738.

Ericson, K. L., & Perlman, N. R. (2001). Knowledge of legal terminology and court proceedings in adults with developmental disabilities. *Law and Human Behavior, 25*, 529–544.

Farrar, M. J., & Goodman, G. S. (1992). Developmental changes in event memory. *Child Development, 63*, 173–187.

Feld, B. C. (1998). The juvenile court. In M. Tonry (Ed.), *The handbook of crime and punishment*. New York: Oxford University Press.

Fivush, R., & Hammond, N. R. (1990). Autobiographical memory across the preschool years: Toward reconceptualizing childhood amnesia. In R. Fivush (Ed.), *Knowing and remembering in young children* (pp. 223–248). New York: Cambridge University Press.

Foley, M. A., & Johnson, M. K. (1985). Confusions between memories for performed and imagined actions: A developmental comparison. *Child Development, 56*, 1145–1155.

Foley, M. A., Santini, C., & Sopasakis, M. (1989). Discriminating between memories: Evidence for children's spontaneous elaborations. *Journal of Experimental Child Psychology, 48,* 146–169.

Fried, C. S., & Reppucci, N. D. (2001). Criminal decision making: The development of adolescent judgment, criminal responsibility, and culpability. *Law and Human Behavior, 25,* 45–61.

Garvey, C. (1984). *Children's talk.* Cambridge, MA: Harvard University Press.

Goodman, G. S. (1984). Children's testimony in historical perspective. *Journal of Social Issues, 40,* 9–31.

Goodman, G. S., Bottoms, B. L., Schwartz-Kenney, B. M., & Rudy, L. (1991a). Children's testimony about a stressful event: Improving children's reports. *Journal of Narrative and Life History, 1,* 69–99.

Goodman, G. S., Hirschman, J. E., Hepps, D., & Rudy, L. (1991b). Children's memory for stressful events. *Merrill-Palmer Quarterly, 37,* 109–157.

Goodman, G. S., Quas, J. A., Batterman-Faunce, J. M., Riddlesberger, M. M., & Kuhn, J. (1997). Children's reactions to and memory for a stressful event: Influences of age, anatomical dolls, knowledge and parental attachment. *Applied Developmental Science, 1,* 54–75.

Goodman, G. S., Tobey, A., Batterman-Faunce, J., Orcutt, H., Thomas, S., Shapiro, C., & Sachsenmaei, T. (1998). Face-to-face confrontation: Effects of closed-circuit technology on children's eyewitness testimony and jurors' decisions. *Law and Human Behavior, 22,* 165–203.

Gopnik, A., & Graf, P. (1988). Knowing how you know: Young children's ability to identify and remember the sources of their beliefs. *Child Development, 59,* 1366–1371.

Gordon, B. N., & Follmer, A. (1994). Developmental issues in judging the credibility of children's testimony. *Journal of Clinical Child Psychology, 23,* 283–294.

Grisso, T. (1981). *Juveniles' waiver of rights: Legal and psychological competence.* New York: Plenum Press.

Grisso, T. (2000). What we know about youths' capacities as trial defendants. In T. Grisso & R. Schwartz (Eds.), *Youth on trial.* Chicago: The University of Chicago Press.

Grisso, T., & Schwartz, R. (2000). *Youth on trial.* Chicago: The University of Chicago Press.

Hudson, J. (1990). Constructive processes in children's event memories. *Developmental Psychology, 26,* 180–187.

Hudson, J., & Nelson, K. (1986). Repeated encounters of a similar kind: Effects of familiarity on children's autobiographic memory. *Cognitive Development, 1,* 253–271.

Hughes, M., & Grieve, R. (1980). On asking children bizarre questions. *First Language, 1,* 149–160.

Hurst, Y. G., Frank, J., & Browning, S. L. (2000). The attitudes of juveniles toward the police: A comparison of black and white youth. *Policing: An International Journal of Police Strategies and Management, 23,* 37–53.

Johnson, M. K., & Foley, M. A. (1984). Differentiating fact from fantasy: The reliability of children's memory. *Journal of Social Issues, 40,* 33–50.

Kassin, S. M., & Kiechel, K. L. (1996). The social psychology of false confessions: Compliance, internalization, and confabulation. *Psychological Science, 7,* 125–128.

Kazdin, A. E. (2000). Adolescent development, mental disorders, and decision making of delinquent youths. In T. Grisso & R. Schwartz (Eds.), *Youth on trial.* Chicago: The University of Chicago Press.

King, M. A., & Yuille, J. (1987). Suggestibility and the child witness. In S. J. Ceci, M. P. Toglia, & D. F. Ross (Eds.), *Children's eyewitness memory* (pp. 24–35). New York: Springer Verlag.

Kobasigawa, A. (1974). Utilization of retrieval cues by children in recall. *Child Development*, *45*, 127–134.

Kohlberg, L. (1981). *Essays on moral development: Vol. 1*. San Francisco: Harper & Row.

Leichtman, M. D., & Ceci, S. J. (1995). The effects of stereotypes and suggestions on preschoolers' reports. *Developmental Psychology*, *31*, 568–578.

Levine, L. J., Stein, N. L., & Liwag, M. D. (1999). Remembering children's emotions: Sources of concordant and discordant counts between parents and children. *Developmental Psychology*, *35*, 790–801.

Lindberg, M. A. (1980). Is knowledge base development a necessary and sufficient condition for memory development? *Journal of Experimental Child Psychology*, *30*, 401–410.

Lindsay, S., & Johnson, M. K. (1987). Reality monitoring and suggestibility. In S. J. Ceci, M. P. Toglia, & D. F. Ross (Eds.), *Children's eyewitness memory* (pp. 92–121). New York: Springer Verlag.

Lindsay, S., Johnson, M. K., & Kwon, P. (1991). Developmental changes in memory source monitoring. *Journal of Experimental Child Psychology*, *52*, 297–318.

Lipmann, O. (1911). Pedagogical psychology of report. *Journal of Educational Psychology*, *2*, 253–261.

List, J. A. (1986). Age and schematic differences in the reliability of eyewitness testimony. *Developmental Psychology*, *22*, 50–57.

Loftus, E. F., & Davies, G. (1984). Distortions in the memory of children. *Journal of Social Issues*, *40*, 51–67.

Low, J., & Durkin, K. (1997). Children's understanding of events and criminal justice processes in police programs. *Journal of Applied Developmental Psychology*, *18*, 179–205.

Mandler, J. M. (1990). Recall and its verbal expression. In R. Fivush & J. A. Hudson (Eds.), *Knowing and remembering in young children* (pp. 317–330). New York: Cambridge University Press.

Marin, B. V., Holmes, D. L., Guth, M., & Kovac, P. (1979). The potential of children as eyewitnesses. *Law and Human Behavior*, *4*, 295–305.

McCauley, M. R., & Fisher, R. P. (1995). Facilitating children's eyewitness recall with the revised Cognitive Interview. *Journal of Applied Psychology*, *80*, 510–516.

McGarrell, E. F. (2001). Restorative justice conferences as an early response to young offenders. *Juvenile Justice Bulletin*, *8*, 1–12.

Messerschmidt, R. (1933). The suggestibility of boys and girls between the ages of six and sixteen. *Journal of Genetic Psychology*, *43*, 422–437.

Mulder, M. R., & Vrij, A. (1996). Explaining conversation rules to children: An intervention study to facilitate children's accurate responses. *Child Abuse and Neglect*, *20*, 623–631.

Myers, J. E. B. (1996). A decade of international reform to accommodate child witnesses: Steps toward a child witness code. In B. L. Bottoms & G. S. Goodman (Eds.), *International perspectives on child abuse and children's testimony: Psychological research and law*. Chicago: Sage.

Nesbitt, M., & Markham, R. (1999). Improving young children's accuracy of recall for an eyewitness event. *Journal of Applied Developmental Psychology*, *20*, 449–459.

Nigro, G. N., Buckley, M. A., Hill, D., & Nelson, J. (1987). When juries "hear" children testify: The effects of eyewitness age and speech style on jurors' perceptions of testimony. In S. J. Ceci, D. F. Ross, & M. Toglia (Eds.), *Perspectives in children's testimony* (pp. 57–70). New York: Springer-Verlag.

Oberlander, L. B., Goldstein, N., & Ho, C. N. (2001). Preadolescent adjudicative competence: Methodological considerations and recommendations for practice standards. *Behavioral Sciences and the Law*, *19*, 545–563.

Orcutt, H. K., Goodman, G. S., Tobey, A. E., Batterman-Faunce, J. M., & Thomas, S. (2001).

Detecting deception in children's testimony: Factfinders' abilities to reach the truth in open court and closed-circuit trials. *Law and Human Behavior, 25*, 339–372.

Ornstein, P. A. (1990). Knowledge and strategies: A discussion. In W. Schneider & F. E. Weinert (Eds.), *Interactions among aptitudes, strategies, and knowledge in cognitive performance* (pp. 147–156). New York: Springer-Verlag.

Ornstein, P. A., Gordon, B. N., & Larus, D. M. (1992). Children's memory for a personally experienced event: Implication for testimony. *Applied Cognitive Psychology, 6*, 49–60.

Otis, M. (1924). A study of suggestibility in children. *Archives of Psychology, 11*, 5–108.

Paris, S. (1988). Motivated remembering. In F. E. Weinert & M. Perlmutter (Eds.), *Memory development: Universal changes and individual differences* (pp. 221–242). Hillsdale, NJ: Lawrence Erlbaum Associates Inc.

Parker, J. F., & Carranza, L. E. (1989). Eyewitness testimony of children in target-present and target-absent lineups. *Law and Human Behavior, 13*, 133–149.

Peek, C. W., Alston, J. P., & Lowe, G. D. (1978). Comparative evaluation of the local police. *Public Opinion Quarterly, 42*, 370–379.

Peters, D. D., Wyatt, G. E., & Finkelhor, D. (1986). Prevalence. In D. Finkelhor (Ed.), *A sourcebook on child sexual abuse*. Beverley Hills, CA: Sage.

Peterson, C. (1999). Children' memory for medical emergences: 2 years later. *Developmental Psychology, 35*, 1493–1506.

Peterson-Badali, M., & Abramovitch, R. (1992). Children's knowledge of the legal system: Are they competent to instruct legal counsel? *Canadian Journal of Criminology, 34*, 139–160.

Peterson-Badali, M., Abramovitch, R., & Duda, J. (1997). Young children's legal knowledge and reasoning ability. *Canadian Journal of Criminology, 39*, 145–170.

Piaget, J. (1932). *The moral judgement of the child*. London: Routledge & Kegan Paul.

Poole, D. A., & Lamb, M. E. (1998). *Investigative interviews of children: A guide for helping professionals*. Washington, DC: American Psychological Association.

Poole, D. A., & Lindsay, D. S. (1995). Interviewing preschoolers: Effects of nonsuggestive techniques, parental coaching and leading questions of reports of nonexperienced events. *Journal of Experimental Child Psychology, 60*, 129–154.

Poole, D. A., & White, L. T. (1991). Effects of question repetition on the eyewitness testimony of children and adults. *Developmental Psychology, 27*, 975–986.

Poole, D. A., & White, L. T. (1993). Two years later: Effects of question repetition and retention interval on the eyewitness testimony of children and adults. *Developmental Psychology, 29*, 844–853.

Powell, M. B., & Thomson, D. M. (1996). Children's recall of an occurrence of a repeated event: Effects of age, retention interval, and question type. *Child Development, 67*, 1988–2004.

Price, D. W. W., & Goodman, G. S. (1990). Visiting the wizard: Children's memory for a recurring event. *Child Development, 61*, 644–680.

Priestley, G., Roberts, S., & Pipe, M. E. (1999). Returning to the scene: Reminders and context reinstatement enhance children's recall. *Developmental Psychology, 35*, 1006–1041.

Quas, J. A., Goodman, G. S., Bidrose, S., Pipe, M. E., Craw, S., & Ablin, D. S. (1999). Emotion and memory: Children's long-term remembering, forgetting, and suggestibility. *Journal of Experimental Child Psychology, 72*, 235–270.

Reasons, C. E., & Wirth, B. A. (1975). Police community relations units: A national survey. *Journal of Social Issues, 31*, 27–33.

Ricci, C. M., & Beal, C. R. (1998). Child witness: Effect of event knowledge on memory and suggestibility. *Journal of Applied Developmental Psychology, 19*, 305–317.

Roebers, C. M., & Schneider, W. (2000). The impact of misleading questions on eyewitness memory in children and adults. *Applied Cognitive Psychology, 14*, 509–526.

Saywitz, K. J. (1987). Children's testimony: Age-related patterns of memory errors. In S. J.

Ceci, M. P. Toglia, & D. F. Ross (Eds.), *Children's eyewitness memory* (pp. 36–52). New York: Springer Verlag.

Saywitz, K. J. (1989). Children's conceptions of the legal systems: Court is a place to play basketball. In S. J. Ceci, D. F. Ross, & M. P. Toglia (Eds.), *Perspectives on children's testimony* (pp. 131–157). New York: Springer Verlag.

Saywitz, K. J., Geiselman, R. E., & Bornstein, G. (1992). Effects of cognitive interviewing and practice on children's recall performance. *Journal of Applied Psychology, 77*, 744–756.

Saywitz, K. J., Goodman, G. S. Nicholas, G., & Moan, S. (1991). Children's memory for genital exam: Implications for child sexual abuse. *Journal of Consulting and Clinical Psychology, 59*, 682–691.

Saywitz, K., Jaenicke, C., & Camparo, L. (1990). Children's knowledge of legal terminology. *Law and Human Behavior, 14*, 523–535.

Saywitz, K. J., & Moan-Hardie, S. (1994). Reducing the potential for distortion of childhood memories. *Consciousness and Cognition, 3*, 408–425.

Saywitz, K. J., & Snyder, L. (1993). Improving children's testimony with preparation. In G. S. Goodman & B. L. Bottoms (Eds.), *Child victims, child witnesses: Understanding and improving testimony* (pp. 117–146). New York: Guilford Press.

Saywitz, K. J., & Snyder, L. (1996). Narrative elaboration: Test of a new procedure for interviewing children. *Journal of Consulting and Clinical Psychology, 64*, 1347–1357.

Schneider, W., & Bjorklund, D. F. (1998). Memory. In W. Damon (Series Ed.), D. Kuhn, & R. S. Siegler (Vol. Eds.), *Handbook of child psychology: Vol. 2. Cognition, perception, and language* (pp. 467–521). New York: Wiley.

Seidler, K. M., & Howie, P. M. (1999). Motivational factors in children's reporting of events: The influence of age and expected reinforcement contingency. *Journal of Applied Developmental Psychology, 20*, 101–118.

Sherman, I. (1925). The suggestibility of normal and mentally defective children. *Comparative Psychology Monographs, 2*.

Siegel, J. M., Sorenson, S. B., Golding, J. M., Burnam, M. A., & Stein, J. A. (1987). The prevalence of childhood sexual assault: The Los Angeles epidemiologic catchment area project. *American Journal of Epidemiology, 126*, 1141–1153.

Siegler, R. S. (1983). Five generalizations about cognitive development. *American Psychologist, 38*, 263–277.

Signorielli, N. (1991). *A sourcebook on children and television*. New York: Greenwood.

Small, M. H. (1896). The Suggestibility of Children, *Pedagogical Seminary, 4*, 172–186.

Smith, S. A., & Hudson, R. L (1995). A quick screening test of competency to stand trial for defendants with mental retardation. *Psychological Reports, 76*, 91–97.

Spencer, J. R., & Flin, R. (1990). *Evidence of children: The law and the psychology*. London: Blackstone.

Stern, W. (1910). Abstracts of lectures on the psychology of testimony and on the study of individuality. *American Journal of Psychology, 21*, 270–282.

Steward, M. S., & Steward, D. S. (1996). Interviewing young children about body touch and handling. *Monographs of the Society for Research in Child Development*, 61 (n4–5).

Taylor, T. J., Turner, K. B., Esbensen, F., & Winfree, L. T. (2001). Coppin' an attitude: Attitudinal differences among juveniles toward police. *Journal of Criminal Justice, 29*, 295–305.

Tobey, A., Grisso, T., & Schwartz, R. (2000). Youths' trial participation as seen by youths and their attorneys: An exploration of competence-based issues. In T. Grisso & R. Schwartz (Eds.), *Youth on trial*. Chicago: The University of Chicago Press.

Varendonck, J. (1911). Les temoignages d'enfants dans un proces retentissant [The testimony of children in a famous trial]. *Archives de psychologie, 11*, 129–171.

Verville, E. (1968). *Behavior problems of children*. Philadelphia: W. B. Saunders.

Walker, A. G. (1994). *Handbook of questioning children: A linguistic perspective*. Washington, DC: American Bar Association.

Warren-Leubecker, A. R., Tate, C., Hinton, I., & Ozbek, N. (1989). What do children know about the legal system and when do they know it? First steps down a less traveled path in child witness research. In S. J. Ceci, D. F. Ross, & M. P. Toglia (Eds.), *Perspectives on children's testimony* (pp. 158–183). New York: Springer-Verlag.

Whitcomb, D., Shapiro, E. R., & Stellwagen, L. D. (1985). *When the victim is a child: Issues for judges and prosecutors*. Washington, DC: National Institute of Justice.

Wilson, J. C., & Davies, G. M. (1999). An evaluation of the use of videotaped evidence for juvenile witnesses in criminal courts in England and Wales. *European Journal on Criminal Policy and Research, 7*, 81–96.

Wimmer, H., Hogrefe, G. J., & Perner, J. (1988). Children's understanding of informational access as a source of knowledge. *Child Development, 59*, 386–396.

Wimmer, H., & Perner, J. (1983). Beliefs about beliefs: Representation and constraining function of wrong beliefs in young children's understanding of deception. *Cognition, 13*, 103–128.

Woolard, J. L., Fondacaro, M. R., & Slobogin, C. (2001). Informing juvenile justice policy: Directions for behavioral science research. *Law and Human Behavior, 25*, 13–24.

Wyatt, G. E. (1985). The sexual abuse of Afro-American and white American women in childhood. *Child Abuse and Neglect, 9*, 507–519.

CHAPTER SIX

Children's understanding of gender roles in society

Kevin Durkin
Department of Psychology, University of Strathclyde, Scotland

. . . all cognition is warm, some a bit warmer

Kagan, 1989, p. 186

Researchers experienced in working with young children—say, 4- to 6-year-olds—anticipate that the occasional participant will decline to comply with the experimental procedure. In a random sample of 100, it would not be unusual to encounter a few children who refuse, perhaps because of temperament, mood, or some other reaction. Warin (2000), working with 100 children in exactly this age group, was rather unlucky: 43 participants were adamant that they would not engage in a task that she set them. The problem was not due to any lack of administrative skill or interpersonal sensitivity on the part of the experimenter; the children happily performed several other tasks and patiently answered miscellaneous questions. Recalcitrance set in when Warin wanted the children to do something that they clearly regarded as outrageous: She asked them to put on the clothes typically associated with the opposite sex. Boys were invited to wear a frilly pink dress and girls were offered army fatigues.

It is not easy for a 4- to 6-year-old to refuse the requests of an adult, especially in the school setting, but clearly, a substantial number of these children felt that this kind of thing was beyond the pale, and said so. Even among those who did as instructed, grimaces, pulled faces, and other signs of displeasure were common. One boy who did comply announced that the experience had been "yucky", made it clear that he did not like wearing

135

dresses, and later told his parents that the event had been "horrible. It made me feel like a girl" (Warin, 2000, p. 222).

These children's reactions remind us of two obvious but important considerations in respect of children and gender. The first is that, from an early age, most children have knowledge about gender categories and about the attributes and behaviours correlated with those social groupings. The second is that this knowledge is intimately associated with strong emotions, including moral emotions (about what is right and appropriate), self-presentational emotions (about what would be downright embarrassing to be seen in or to be seen doing), and feelings of group identification (about where one belongs). The acquisition of knowledge has been given high priority among researchers interested in the study of gender role development. This has led to many interesting and important findings and has been the primary focus of the dominant theoretical tradition in the field since the 1960s, namely cognitive developmental perspectives. In contrast, the emotional intensity of the domain tends to be noted only incidentally. This is despite abundant evidence that, as Fagot, Rodgers, and Leinbach (2000) observe: "the gender category system is infused with affect to an extent few other knowledge bases can match" (p. 65). The reactions of Warin's participants serve to remind us that coming to understand gender is not a dispassionate activity. Part of the purpose of this chapter will be to consider why cognition is so closely interwoven with emotion in this domain and to consider the implications for the ways in which children come to understand gender in society.

The goal is not to argue for a new or neglected factor that "explains" gender role development. One of the achievements of work in this field over the last couple of decades has been an increasingly broad consensus that gender role development cannot be explained in terms of a single factor (biology, environment, cognition). Although there are disputes and controversies, it is now widely acknowledged that gender role acquisition is multifaceted and multidetermined (Archer, 1992; Bussey & Bandura, 1992, 1999; Eckes & Trautner, 2000; Egan & Perry, 2001; Huston, 1983; Kenrick & Luce, 2000; Maccoby, 1998; Martin, Ruble, & Szkrybalo, 2002; Ruble & Martin, 1998). In this context, it would be facile to maintain that emotions somehow *cause* gender roles. Instead, the focus here is on how children come to understand gender roles as part of their broader understanding of the nature of human society. But, because the complicated processes of gender role development are multifaceted, to understand the development of understanding we need to take into account the ways in which the acquisition and organisation of knowledge is related to biological, interpersonal, and societal processes. These are highly motivating forces and, in this context, emotions provide an interweaving, organising role, albeit one that is still little understood.

The chapter is structured as follows. First, I provide a brief review of some of the recurrent themes of theory and research concerned with the development of gender roles. These include biological accounts, learning theories, especially Bussey and Bandura's (1999) social cognitive theory, and cognitive developmental theories, including Kohlberg's (1966) model and the currently influential gender schema theory of Martin (1999, 2000). Cognitive developmental approaches, not surprisingly, furnish us with substantial information on how children come to conceive of gender and its place in society, but these theories tend to be rather individualistic and "cold", in the sense that they have treated gender as another body of knowledge that the child has to come to terms with. Recent work in gender schema theory, however, has led to increasing interest in the ways in which children organise social knowledge, and these issues will be summarised. This leads in turn to a consideration of the ways in which social processes might be implicated in gender role understanding, and some examples will be considered. Understanding will be seen throughout to be linked closely to enacting behaviours, experiencing feedback, and relating to others— which is why emotions come to the fore repeatedly. Finally, because it is clear that gender role understanding is intimately associated with relating to society and its products, I consider some aspects of the ways in which children respond to one of the most pervasive sources of gender role information in contemporary societies, namely the mass media.

THEORIES OF GENDER ROLE DEVELOPMENT

Early debates about the origins and maintenance of gender roles tended to revolve around whether a "biological" or a "social" explanation best accounted for the data. Quite apart from the fact that it is futile to presume that biological and social phenomena are mutually exclusive, this dichotomy diverts attention from the dynamic and constructive facets of human development by emphasising (often vaguely defined) determinist forces. Determinist theories of these kinds do not have great appeal for child developmental psychologists, who are preoccupied with the immensely complex nature of children's emergent minds. The fundamental question for the developmentalist in almost any domain tends to be: "How can the child come to understand this?" The Piagetian heritage in particular has inoculated us against any theories that assume knowledge is attained by absorption. Because of this influence, many developmental psychologists (especially in the cognitive developmental tradition) have tended to down-play the possible contributions of both biology and society. However, this may mean that important factors influencing why gender *matters* to children have been neglected (Maccoby, 1998).

Biological accounts of gender role development

Some early biological—particularly sociobiological—accounts of human gender role differences attributed them directly to evolutionary effects (Wilson, 1978). Only a cursory overview will be provided here but the essence of these approaches is that gender roles have emerged in the course of evolution as humans have adapted to survive and reproduce in a competitive natural environment. The most efficient distribution of human capacities allegedly proved to be one in which males, as the physically stronger partner, took on responsibility for the more vigorous roles of hunting and fighting (e.g., in territorial or resource disputes) while females, having natural advantages in the abilities to give birth to and breastfeed the young, took on the greater share of domestic responsibilities. These patterns evolved and were consolidated over countless generations, gradually being written into the species' genetic code.

On a similar basis, biologically given differences in how males and females contribute to reproduction have been argued to result in different orientations towards sexual congress (Trivers, 1972). For males, this is a relatively undemanding, typically pleasurable, and easily repeated way to promote the continuity of one's genetic material, and so males should be inclined to seek frequent opportunities to procreate. For females, pregnancy and child-rearing are enduring and onerous responsibilities and so females, because they invest more in the reproductive process and in the survival of the offspring, should be inclined to caution in conferring sexual favours; they should be selective, seeking mates with good prospects of providing resources and of staying around. The developmental implications of this kind of account are that because gender differences have evolved over millennia, they should be early emerging (though this is not to preclude the contributions of later occurring biological effects, such as puberty) and robust (not critically dependent upon parental guidance, difficult for cultures to repress).

Among the problems with these kinds of theories is that they do not account very well for the enormous within- and cross-cultural variability in gender roles, nor for the radical changes in the organisation of gender roles in Western societies in the last few decades (except, perhaps, to insist that these are contrary to the laws of nature and are bound to end in unhappiness and failure). (See Berscheid, 1993; Bussey & Bandura, 1999; Sayers, 1986, for more extensive critiques.)

Geary (1998) points out that an aversion to biological determinism leads social scientists to approach issues of gender differences in humans in a markedly different way to how scientists approach these in any other species, namely sexual selection in the course of evolution. Whether social scientists should worry too much about being markedly different from biologists is perhaps a moot point—many biologists, for example, approach the study of the human species oblivious to the fact that it is uniquely endowed with minds, language, and cultures—but it is certainly hard to refute that biology is implicated in human gender role differences. Gender is a biological given, a natural dichotomy with pervasive consequences for the organisation, conduct, and phenomenology of social life (Maccoby, 1998). Even the most radical environmentalist theory has to acknowledge that the presumed social influences all focus upon a biological distinction.

The question of particular interest here is: How does biology contribute to social development and ultimately to social understanding? Current attempts to take account of biological factors in gender role development tend to be more sophisticated than early popularisations of sociobiology and they allow for complex gene–environment interactions (Geary, 1998; Kenrick & Trost, 1993; Kenrick & Luce, 2000; MacDonald, 1988). These theories still maintain that our evolutionary heritage is manifest in our behaviour but stress also that cultural processes can "oppose or exaggerate biological differences" (Kenrick & Trost, 1993, p. 168). From this perspective, culture itself is seen as the product of interdependent and dynamic interactions between human genetic predispositions and the past conditions we have experienced and, to some extent, constructed (Kenrick & Trost, 1993).

In a detailed developmental account, Geary (1998) argues that early emerging patterns of sex differences in physical and social behaviour reflect innate competencies and result in enduring biases in the ways in which females and males selectively attend to and process environmental cues and act upon the environment. For example, male infants have on average a longer forearm than do females, and this skeletal difference appears to be related to an early emerging gender difference in throwing skills. Female infants and toddlers have been found to pay greater attention to the properties and behaviour of people, and to be more sensitive to indicators of others' distress (such as crying). Geary proposes that these and other differences result in differences in play preferences, emerging early but enduring throughout childhood. Extensive cross-cultural evidence confirms, for example, that pre-school boys enjoy rough-and-tumble play and engage in it much more extensively than do girls (Smith, Smees, Pellegrini, & Menesini, 2002), while girls are much more likely to focus on doll play and interpersonal relations (Lindsey & Mize, 2001; Moller, Hymel, & Rubin, 1992). Children show preferences for sex-typed toys as early as 1 year of age (Servin, Bohlin, & Berlin, 1999).

Evidence that children's gender-stereotyped activity or toy preferences may be shared with other primate species lends some support to biological accounts. Sex differences in rough-and-tumble play emerge early in monkeys, for example (Brown & Dixson, 2000; Wallen, 1996). An imaginative study by Alexander and Hines (2002) raises the possibility that monkeys and human children may have similar, gender-linked, toy preferences. The researchers placed gender-stereotyped children's toys, one at a time, in the cages of mixed age and sex groups of monkeys. Toys were masculine (ball, police car), feminine (soft doll, cooking pot), or neutral (picture book and stuffed dog), and previous research had established human children's gender biases towards them. Male monkeys spent more time in contact with the masculine toys than did female monkeys, while female monkeys spent more time in contact with the feminine toys.

As the authors point out, it is implausible to account for these results in terms of cognition (vervet gender schemas are presumed to be negligible) or prior experience (the animals were captive and the toys were novel). Instead, Alexander and Hines favour an argument, similar to Geary's above, based on the cue-signalling potentials of the objects interacting with evolved, innate sex-specific biases in the animals. In brief, males are attracted to objects that can be propelled in space, that facilitate rough-and-tumble play (such as a ball) or hunting and navigating (such as a car), while females are attracted to objects that elicit feelings of nurturance/contact. The authors do not make clear on what cognitive basis the male monkeys would be able to represent the hunt-facilitating potentialities of a toy police car several times smaller than their own bodies, especially since they had presumably never seen a real car, nor why the female monkeys should appreciate the functions of a cooking pot when they lived in a community accustomed to a diet of raw foodstuffs. Nevertheless, it is plausible that there is an interaction between the animals' predispositions and the affordances of the objects. By extension, the authors offer the proposal that their findings of "sex-typed toy preferences in vervet monkeys suggest that perceptual features with differential adaptive significance for males and females may facilitate the formation of children's sex-typed object categories" (2002, p. 475).

In short, biological accounts range from theories of simple determinism of the "gender is destiny" type to more subtle accounts of the ways in which genetically given potentialities are likely to "feed into" children's early play behaviour. Importantly, these predispositions influence what children want to do, what they find enjoyable. This contributes to a motivational basis for participation in the social and physical world that, in the majority of cases, is likely to be met by gender-differentiated opportunities for play and other activity. One of the most reliable features of children's spontaneous social organisation from about the third year is that they segregate by gender, irrespective of parental and other adult exhortations (Glick & Hilt, 2000; Maccoby, 1998). A plausible argument is that this reflects, at least in part, biologically given predispositions towards particular types of activity, associated with emotional arousal and optimally undertaken in the company of like-minded peers (Maccoby, 1998). However, although bio-logical theories can help to explain some aspects of gender role develop-ment, including the importance of emotions from very early in the process, they do not offer a great deal in terms of explaining the development of understanding of gender in society. Thus, for example, a young monkey and a little boy may have similar interests in rough-and-tumble play but only the latter is going to go on to develop a large body of knowledge about how gender is organised, some of which knowledge he will be able to make explicit if required and from which he will be able to make inferences and predictions as well as regulate his own behaviour (see below).

Learning theories

Learning, or environmentalist, accounts are usually seen as being pitted against biological theories of gender role acquisition from the opposite end of the theoretical continuum. This is not necessarily the case, in that at least some evolutionary theories accommodate social learning and cultural processes very readily, by arguing that it is inevitable that societies will evolve means of fostering behaviours in the young that have proved adaptive for previous generations (Kenrick & Trost, 1993; MacDonald, 1988), and some learning theories accommodate evolutionary processes by pointing out that evolution itself is affected by new selection pressures as humans change the nature of their social environments (Bussey & Bandura, 1999). It is also important to note that learning theories range from strongly behaviourist positions, which attribute almost all learning to the effects of external reward and punishment (Staats, 1975), through obser-vational learning accounts (Mischel, 1966), which highlight the accelerative potency of learning by watching others, to the current social cognitive theory of Bussey and Bandura (1999), which both acknowledges a role for evolutionary factors in human adaptation and stresses the integral role of cognitive information processing in the acquisition and regulation of gender. Nevertheless, learning theorists do attribute a much more funda-mental role than do biological theorists to environmental contingencies and the broad societal context (Bussey & Bandura, 1999; Lott & Maluso, 1993).

Environmental experiences

There is good reason to emphasise the contributions of the environment. Information, expectations, models, instruction, and restrictions concerning gender are pervasive in all known societies. In Western societies, parents perceive their newborns differently according to their gender (Rubin, Provenzano, & Luria, 1974; Sweeney & Bradbard, 1988), dress them differently (Pomerleau, Bolduc, Malcuit, & Cossette, 1990; Shakin, Shakin, & Sternglanz, 1985), decorate their bedrooms differently (Rheingold &

Cook, 1975), steer them towards different activities, and provide different kinds of nonverbal feedback (Fagot, 1978; Leeb & Rejskind, 2004; Leve & Fagot, 1997). We considered above interesting evidence of early emerging gender differences in play and toy activity that have been attributed to biological potentialities, but it is also the case that parents provide infants with different toys as a function of the child's gender: Boys are given robust materials such as blocks, play hammers, and guns, while girls are handed dolls and cuddly animals (Seavey, Katz, & Zalk, 1975; Sidorowicz & Lunney, 1980). When male toddlers choose to play with blocks and female toddlers play with dolls, they receive positive verbal feedback from their parents (Fagot, 1978).

These processes are widespread and striking and it is sometimes assumed that their ubiquity explains gender role differentiation. However, the evidence is not so clear. Correlations between parental behaviour and children's early gender role behaviour tend to be weak (Huston, 1983; Maccoby, 1998), and closer analysis of parent–child interactions reveals that in many respects parents do not appear to differentiate markedly by gender (Lytton & Romney, 1991; Maccoby, 1998). In a careful review, Maccoby (1998) concludes that parental socialisation probably plays only a minor role in the emergence of the gender segregation that appears pivotal to early peer interactions. Even so, note again that these miscellaneous social circumstances often directly or indirectly contribute to the affective backdrop of the child's life: They communicate parents' feelings, they establish or consolidate preferential patterns of behaviour, and they shape the familiar, the everyday world the child comes to know and act within (see also Eccles, Freedman-Doan, Frome, Jacobs, & Yoon, 2000; McHale, Crouter, & Whiteman, 2003).

Social cognitive theory

Bussey and Bandura's (1999) exposition of social cognitive theory offers the most elaborate and ambitious application of contemporary social learning theory to the development of gender. In contrast to early learning theories, this account incorporates cognitive processes and it also accords a role to biological potential. However, it insists that whichever cognitive processes come into play and whichever biologically given potentials are realised depend considerably upon the surrounding social structures that establish possibilities and limits (e.g., different cultures foster varying patterns of gender differentiation).⁺Importantly, Bussey and Bandura maintain that gender development is the outcome of multifaceted motivational, affective, and environmental factors interacting with the individual's cognitive capacities (which are presumed to change with developmental status). One of the great potential strengths of this theory is its account of emotional engagement (especially via self-evaluative mechanisms) as a dynamic component of children's adjustment to societal structures bearing on gender differentiation.

⌐ Three major modes of influence upon gender development are proposed: modelling (observational learning), enactive experience (learning about the outcomes of one's own gender-linked behaviour, including the evaluative reactions of others), and direct tuition. Although the theory is more concerned with how children acquire and enact gender roles rather than with how they understand gender, it certainly presupposes that these processes are interdependent and that the modes of social influence affect the ways in which children construct their gender-linked knowledge. Increasing awareness of the social significance of gender is argued to guide self-regulatory processes, such that children monitor and care about how well they are performing in respect of their understanding of the culture's gender role standards. The theory also proposes that attention to gender models is selective, such that once children are capable of differentiating the sexes they begin to pay greater attention to models that they believe can provide personally relevant information, namely same-sex models.

Bussey and Bandura (1999) maintain that although some awareness of gender categories has been demonstrated as early as infancy, the achievement of the capacity to label gender prompts substantial advances in the understanding of the concept and the recognition of its many ramifications in the social world. Once children categorise themselves as boys or girls, they start to gain more knowledge about gender attributes, roles, and rules. They also begin to monitor and to evaluate how they themselves behave and the resultant emotions predict their subsequent behaviour. For example, 3- and 4-year-olds judge that they will feel "real great" about gender-consistent behaviours but will feel "real bad" about gender-inconsistent behaviours (Bussey & Bandura, 1992).

Bandura and Bussey (1999) do not address in detail how the expansion of the gender knowledge base occurs or develops; it appears to be regarded as accumulative, though the authors also stress that the environment is not homogenous or monolithic and that some social phenomena are more easily understood than others. (Other social forces are presumed to be potent, such as peers, the school, the mass media, and later, the occupational world.) Social cognitive theory does not appear to have a great deal to say, either, about why children's gender role conceptions are sometimes more extreme and more rigid than those of the social environment. (See Martin et al., 2002, for a more extensive critique.)

In sum, learning theories may initially have oversimplified the acquisition of gender role development by depicting it as a unidirectional process in which "society" somehow writes its message upon the *tabula rasa* of the innocent and ignorant child. More recent developments, particularly social cognitive theory, have greatly enriched the explanatory scope of this per-spective, especially in highlighting the motivational mechanisms that ensure that gender matters to children and that they are keen to self-regulate their behaviour to match their developing conceptions of societal requirements. However, because this theoretical perspective assumes that ultimately gender role acquisition is determined by the environment, it does not address in detail what children's concepts of gender are or how they develop and use them, other than as possible reference guides to "ideal" gender-typed behaviour.

Cognitive developmental theories of gender role development

In contrast to the then-influential biological, psychoanalytic, and social learning accounts, Kohlberg (1966), in what proved to be the seminal paper for cognitive developmentalists interested in this area, saw the origins of gender role acquisition in the child's "concepts of physical things—the bodies of himself and of others—concepts which he relates in turn to a social order that makes functional use of sex categories in quite culturally universal ways" (1966, p. 82). Kohlberg pointed out that, in order to begin to learn about gender-appropriate behaviour, the child needs first to dis-cover that she or he is a member of a particular gender. This is a cognitive achievement, though it is also a motivational one in that, because the child is presumed to be driven to achieve understanding and self-esteem, she or he will be driven to seek more gender-relevant knowledge and relate it to the self-concept. In keeping with the general tenets of Piagetian theory, Kohlberg saw the universal ways of elaborating the categories as proceeding through a predictable stage sequence.

Kohlberg's theory

Kohlberg (1966) saw the development of gender constancy (the under-standing that an individual's gender is invariant) as a key achievement in the construction of an understanding of gender. This is not a given or instantaneous achievement but one that Kohlberg proposed is attained over several years in three stages: gender labelling, gender stability, and gender consistency. These are assumed to be universal and roughly age-related and a function of broader cognitive development. They can be briefly charac-terised as follows.

Gender labelling (approximately 2 to 3½ years). The child becomes aware of gender labels, discovering that she or he is a member of a par-ticular sex (e.g., "I'm a girl"). Gradually, the child acquires other gender labels (such as *boy, woman, man*), though knowledge of gender categories is not perfect and sometimes toddlers make mistakes with basic labels.

Gender stability (approximately 3½ to 4½ years). Children gradually become aware that membership of a particular gender category is a long-term arrangement. They can predict correctly what sex they will be when they grow up. However, understanding of gender remains dependent upon the child's concept of physical things: A male is someone who looks like (e.g., dresses like) a male. Hence, children in this stage are confused if a person makes superficial changes to his or her appearance, and may conclude that a person who puts on opposite-sex clothes has now changed sex. This is very similar to children's difficulties with perceptual transformations in physical or spatial tasks, such as conservation of liquid or number tests.

Gender consistency (approximately 4½ to 7 years). Gender is now seen as consistent across time and contexts. The child understands that a person who dresses up in opposite-sex clothes or engages in opposite-sex activities remains nonetheless a member of his or her initial gender. Not surprisingly from a Piagetian perspective, this conceptual understanding is attained at around the same time the child is able to handle standard conservation tests.

Kohlberg's model: Evidence and controversy

Research inspired by Kohlberg's account provided considerable evidence to support the general characterisation. Young children's understanding of gender labels was tested by Thompson (1975). Two-year-olds performed at around chance level when asked whether they were a boy or a girl, and when asked to differentiate among everyday gender-typed objects (lipsticks, neckties) as "for mommies or for daddies". By 2½ years, children were better than chance on these tasks (though there were still many errors), but still did not appear to understand the significance of labelling an object as "for boys" or "for girls" (i.e., this did not influence their own preferences). By age 3, children could answer most of the labelling questions correctly, and showed sensitivity to the "for boys/girls" description, but still performed at only marginally above chance when asked whether they were going to be a "mommy or a daddy" when they grew up (i.e., a gender stability question). Martin and Little (1990) found that children aged 3 to 5 years showed a good knowledge based on tests of gender labels. The younger children tended not to do well on tests of temporal gender stability but this level of understanding increased during the age range tested. More recent work has shown that even toddlers have knowledge of the gender associations of everyday household activities (Poulin-Dubois, Serbin, Eichstedt, Sen, & Beissel, 2002).

One issue that has been controversial in responses to Kohlberg's theory has been the measurement and status of gender constancy. Gender constancy has been measured in various ways, but two influential initial paradigms are those of Emmerich, Goldman, Kirsh, & Sharabany, (1977) and Slaby and Frey (1975). In the Emmerich et al. procedure, the child is shown a series of pictures of a boy (or girl) who is dressed initially in gender-appropriate clothing. Once the child has confirmed the gender of the figure, the experimenter asks a series of questions designed to tap the participant's understanding of the constancy of gender, such as: "If William wants to be a girl can he be?" "If William puts on girls' clothes [illustrated by flipping to a new picture of William in a dress], what would he be? Would he be a boy or a girl?" In the Slaby and Frey procedure the child is asked similar sorts of questions, stratified to correspond to the Kohlbergian stage sequence (e.g., gender identity questions such as "Is this a girl or a boy?", gender stability questions such as "When you grow up, will you be a mommy or a daddy?", and gender constancy questions such as "If you played [opposite-sex] games, would you be a girl or a boy?"). Emmerich et al. found age-related improvements but report that even among 7-year-olds many children still find gender constancy challenging. Slaby and Frey (and subsequent researchers using their method) found only small proportions of children give responses inconsistent with the predicted stage sequence (see also Gibbons, 2000, for a review of cross-cultural applications of this paradigm).

The original Emmerich et al. and Slaby and Frey tasks may give unduly conservative indicators of this aspect of gender understanding. One limitation is that the tasks involve relatively complex syntax ("If . . . then" sentences), which are themselves difficult for children in this age range, irrespective of content. They also have a story-like aspect, and children are used to "suspending disbelief" in the course of enjoying fiction or games (Martin & Halverson, 1983). It has been shown that if the test alerts the young participant to plausible reasons for an appearance transformation (e.g., "Would you really be a boy/girl [when dressed in opposite-sex clothing] or would you just be pretending to be girl/boy?") then higher constancy scores are obtained at an earlier age (Leonard & Archer, 1989). Varying the order of questions can also lead to higher scores (Siegal & Robinson, 1987).

Notwithstanding these limitations, cognitive developmental research does in general support the assumption that children's understanding of gender and knowledge of gender stereotypes are increasing through early childhood. This much is not surprising, of course, because we know that most areas of children's understanding is expanding during this period (see other chapters in this volume). However, a large and growing body of findings has demonstrated impressive progress from the pre-school to mid-childhood years in children's acquisition of knowledge about the genders, including appearance, behaviour, and internal (psychological, personality) attributes. Initially, this knowledge tends to be consistent with, though often still more rigid than, traditional stereotypes, but during mid-childhood, with the advent of cognitive capacities that enable children to attend to individuating information and more complex associations, it becomes more flexible (Biernat, 1991; Martin, 1993; Ruble & Martin, 1998; Signorella, Bigler, & Liben, 1993).

Importantly, developmental progress in this conceptual knowledge is often interwoven with affective reactions in complex ways. For example, Stoddart and Turiel (1985), working within a neo-Kohlbergian model of moral development, elicited children's and adolescents' reactions to scenarios depicting gender-inconsistent behaviours (such as a boy wearing nail polish or a girl having a crew cut). Kindergartners, whose concepts of gender appropriateness tend to be highly concrete, rejected these physically anomalous behaviours, while primary school-aged children, who are more able to take into account the arbitrary nature of social conventions, tended to be more accepting. However, adolescents, who attach more importance to gender identity in terms of psychological orientation, found the transgression as unacceptable as kindergartners did. Thus, understanding of gender is linked to strong views about what is "right" or "wrong" at both kindergarten and adolescence but the quality of the underlying reasoning alters dramatically.

Gender schema theory

The Kohlberg (1966) account made a major contribution to the direction of gender role acquisition research by casting the fundamental question in a new light: not "What do genes or society do to the child?" but "What does the child do with the information that society makes available?" It also, as we have seen, inspired a large amount of fruitful empirical work that has enriched our understanding of the changes in the course of developing gender knowledge. However, one limitation of the account is that it attributes a great deal to the influence of gender constancy. Gender constancy is a relatively late achievement, and there is a lot of evidence that children behave in gender-specific ways from much earlier.

This led Martin and Halverson (1981, 1987; Martin, 1991) to propose a new cognitive developmental theory, gender schematic processing theory. This theory accepts Kohlberg's emphasis on the organising of the child's active cognitive processing of gender information but maintains that the process begins much earlier, as soon as children discover their own gender identity. Once this is attained, children are motivated to learn more about what gender entails and they organise this information into gender schemas.

Martin and Halverson distinguished two types of gender schemas: a superordinate structure, which contains broad information about the sexes, and an own-sex schema, which is more detailed. In common with other schema theories in cognitive psychology, the assumption is that the schemas operate to organise incoming data, to guide attention selectively, to under-pin memory for relevant facts (as well as reject irrelevant or inconsistent data), and to bias behaviour and evaluations. For example, if one expects (has a gender schema that predicts) girls to play with dolls, then one tends to notice and recall instances of girls playing with dolls but occasional observations of girls playing with dragons or fire engines are not given much attention or are forgotten; also, if one is a girl, given a choice between dolls and dragons then the former is seen as the more natural option (that is, the gender schema guides behaviour).

Martin and Halverson (1983) showed that 5- and 6-year-olds presented with sets of pictures of children performing either gender-consistent or gender-inconsistent activities subsequently recalled the pictures in line with gender stereotypes. Bradbard, Martin, Endsley, and Halverson (1986) found that 4- to 9-year-olds presented with sets of gender neutral toys that were labelled as "for girls" or "for boys" spent more time tactually exploring the toys labelled for their own sex and, 1 week later, remembered more detailed information about own-sex than other-sex objects. In an incidental exposure task, Cherney and Ryalls (1999) obtained superior memory for the identity and location of own-gender consistent objects among 3- and 6-year-olds. Levy (1999) found that children as young as 20 to 28 months showed preferential contact with own-sex toys.

Importantly, the schema perspective offers an explanation for frequently observed facts in children's gender role understanding (Martin, 1999). These include the facts that it is at some stages of development more strongly stereotyped than that of the adult community, that it does not necessarily accommodate readily available empirical data (for example, the children of mothers with out-of-home occupations often insist it is a fact that only daddies go to work and mummies stay at home), and that it is resistant to intervention (counterstereotyping; see below).

Another important feature of gender schema theory is that it incorporates a motivational dimension at its core. The acquisition of gender schemas is seen not merely as a dispassionate intellectual mapping but as one of the first in-group/out-group distinctions that the child assimilates. There are not just boys/men and girls/women, there are "us" (my gender) and "them" (the other gender). This dichotomy is seen as giving the primary impetus to the development of gender understanding.

Gender schemas and a naïve social psychology of gender

Other contributors to this volume have shown the fruitfulness of a "naïve theory" approach to the study of children's societal understanding (e.g., Webley, Chapter 3; Berti, Chapter 4; Hirschfeld, Chapter 8). In a similar vein, Martin (2000) extends gender schema theory to propose that children may also develop a naïve social psychology, a set of ideas about the nature of people in social situations, including abstract ideas about the nature of gender. Drawing also on social identity theory (Tajfel & Turner, 1979; see also Lutz & Ruble, 1995, and Barrett, Chapter 10), she suggests that fundamental among these ideas (and with developmental priority) is a "within-group similarity theory" (i.e., that all or most girls tend to have characteristics and preferences in common) and a "between-group differences theory" (i.e., that girls and boys have different attributes, interests, and behaviours).

As they emerge, these naïve theories should predict how children will interpret social data and, like all good theories, they should inform the theorists' inferences about unobservable data. For example, suppose that a child knows (a) that he is a boy, and (b) that he likes this toy: How much will the child think that other boys will like the toy? Martin and her colleagues (Martin, Eisenbud, & Rose, 1995) found that 4- to 6-year-olds make inferential generalisations from their own liking for a toy to predict the preferences of other children of the same sex but not those of children of the opposite sex. Thus, the children appeared to use within-group similarity theories: "I am a boy, we boys like the same kinds of things, I like X, and so other boys like X". It was less clear, in this study, that children also apply between-group differences theories (their own likings were unrelated to their predictions for the opposite sex), though this may be partly because young children know less about the opposite sex. Between-group differences may be more apparent in contexts that encourage choices (e.g., "Which of these two children [a boy and a girl] will also want to play with X?"). Several independent studies confirm that, from the pre-school years on, children can use gender labels to make novel inferences about the psychological attributes and preferences of unfamiliar individuals (Bauer, Liebl, & Stennes, 1998; Biernat, 1991; Gelman, Collman, & Maccoby, 1986; Heyman, 2001; Lobel, Gruber, Govrin, & Mashraki-Pedhatzur, 2001; Powlishta, 1995, 2000).

Martin (2000) sketches other lines of enquiry prompted by a naïve social psychology perspective. These include studies of the nature and development of folk beliefs about the causes of gender differences. For example, Taylor (1996) asked 4- to 10-year-olds (and adults) about the consequences of raising a boy on an island with only opposite-sex caregivers: Would the child's gender role characteristics reflect his biological category or his social experiences? Until age 9 or 10, the participants were confident that boys will be boys, and gender-stereotyped properties would develop regardless of the social context. Like Martin, Taylor proposes that young children may have an early bias to regard gender categories as predictive of essential within-group similarities; with cognitive development and social experience children come eventually to acknowledge the role of other causal mechanisms in influencing individuals' gender role attributes.

Perceptions of relative social status may also be implicated in children's naïve social psychology of gender. For example, children as young as 3 to 4 years are aware of the gender stereotypes of occupations (Emler & Dickinson, Chapter 7; Huston, 1983; Levy, Sadovsky, & Troseth, 2000). Pre-schoolers already indicate preferences for gender-stereotyped occupations and Levy et al. found that they express greater happiness at the prospect of growing up to have gender role consistent occupations. Young children are also aware of the differential statuses associated with male stereotyped and female stereotyped occupations (Huston, 1983; Levy et al., 2000; Liben, Bigler, & Krogh, 2001). Unfortunately, there is a real-world confound in that male-dominated occupations do tend to be of higher status than female-dominated occupations. Liben et al. circumvented this problem by having children rate the status of novel (fictitious) occupations, shown in pictures as being performed either by women or men. By later childhood (11 years in this study), children were more likely to rate novel jobs as of higher status if performed by males. Although Liben et al. do not couch their explanation in terms of naïve social psychology of gender, the findings are consistent with such an account. It appears that children extrapolate from some abstract understanding (naïve theory) of the relative standing of the genders to infer the standing of previously unfamiliar occupations that they have been led to believe are associated with one gender or the other.

The proposal of a naïve social psychology of gender, then, goes beyond describing the expanding contents of children's gender role knowledge (itself a worthwhile and formidable task) to indicate mechanisms by which children organise information and use it to make predictions in situations where they have only partial empirical evidence available or to interpret novel phenomena. As Martin (1999, p. 62) puts it: "One may think of children as being gender theoreticians who develop ideas about the sexes, revise them on occasion, and then apply these theories to help make sense of the social world".

How social is a naïve social psychology of gender?

Arguably, one limitation of naïve social psychology is that it subscribes to the individualistic perspective on social cognition that takes the domain of enquiry as the individual's processing of information about the social

world (in contrast to social perspectives on social cognition, which emphasise the interactive, collaborative processes by which understanding is
achieved; see Durkin, 1995; Emler & Ohana, 1993). Notice also that,
although cognitive developmental theories incorporate a strong motivational component, the motivation of greatest interest to researchers has
been the desire to acquire and master information (the cognitive motivation), while arguably at least as important to the developing person is the
social motivation, to *be* a male or female and to relate to the world in male
or female ways. Many cognitive developmental studies in this area investigate children's knowledge of male and female preferences ("If she likes
to play with X, will she like Y?", "Who will want to play football?"),
acknowledging at best implicitly that not only do children know about
likings and preferences but they also have them.

However, a naïve social psychology of gender that is sensitive to
intergroup processes, as Martin (2000) suggests, can also help illuminate the
ways in which social participation affects and reflects gender understanding
and self-knowledge (David, Grace, & Ryan, in press; Lutz & Ruble, 1995;
Powlishta, in press; Ruble et al., in press). Like Martin, these authors draw
on social identity theory/self-categorisation theory, proposing that individuals strive for a positive self-concept via a positive social identity and
that accepting a social categorisation (such as gender) "can set in motion
intergroup processes whereby the in-group is favoured, differences between
and similarities within groups are exaggerated, and the out-group is often
homogenized" (Powlishta, in press). Consistent with this perspective, intergroup biases based on gender have been demonstrated in children at least as
young as 5 years (Glick & Hilt, 2000; Yee & Brown, 1995). From a similar
theoretical perspective, David et al. and Ruble et al. emphasise that understanding of the gendered self is a social, flexible, and labile process,
influenced at any point by reference to the social context.

This kind of approach leads to a more dynamic, context-sensitive social
cognition, in that the "mere act" of invoking social categories need not be
assumed to operate continuously or invariably but is responsive to social
environments (Lutz & Ruble, 1995). Sani and Bennett (2001) provide a
concrete illustration. They asked 6- to 7-year-olds to select trait descriptions
of a member of their in-group (boys or girls) in conditions where they either
first described an out-group person distinguished by age (same sex but adult)
or by gender (same age but opposite sex). The children showed a greater
tendency to gender stereotyping in the latter condition. For example, they
were more likely to describe boys as "strong" and "brave" when the task
was preceded by having to describe girls than when it was preceded by
having to describe men. In other words, the children's stereotypes may not be
rigid cognitive structures but a more fluid "group in context" representation
(Sani & Bennett, 2001, p. 227).

Emotions, gender, and a social naïve social psychology

Note that acknowledging an emotional dimension to the development of gender understanding, which has been stressed in this chapter, does not entail a regression to an individualistic, intrapsychic account. Emotions are highly potent for the individual and have biological instantiations, but they are not simply of internal origin. At all times, they presuppose an interaction between the individual and the environment (Brothers, 2001). Emotions are shared at micro (interpersonal) and macro (community, societal) levels. Indeed, some argue that they are a primary medium through which individual–society relations are negotiated (Moore & Isen, 1990; Nussbaum, 2001; Planalp, 1999; Zajonc, 1998). Emotions are socialised through interactive processes with more knowledgeable persons (such as caregivers) who provide models, labels, interpretations, and feedback about the appropriateness of particular displays (Denham, Mitchell-Copeland, Strandberg, Auerbach, & Blair, 1997; Dunn, Bretherton, & Munn, 1987; Eisenberg, Cumberland, & Spinrad, 1998; Lagattuta & Wellman, 2002; Magai & McFadden, 1995; Ontai & Thompson, 2002).

Furthermore, these processes are differentiated by gender. Adults have stereotypes of gender differences in emotional displays and reactions. These include the beliefs that females are more demonstrative and more likely to experience feelings such as sadness and fear, while males are generally deficient in the expression of feelings but more likely to express more assertive emotions, such as anger and pride (Fabes & Martin, 1991; Fivush & Buckner, 2000; Plant, Hyde, Keltner, & Devine, 2000). Mothers direct more comments about feelings to daughters than to sons (Dunn et al., 1987), maintain greater emotional closeness to daughters (Beneson, Morash, & Petrakos, 1998), and emphasise different emotions according to the sex of the child, such as sadness in conversations with daughters (Fivush, Brotman, Buckner, & Goodman, 2000). These differences are not absolute (Maccoby, 1998) but they are widespread, subtle indicators of caregivers' expectations. Causal directions are difficult to determine (Maccoby, 1998) but it is clear that children soon come to demonstrate gender differences in the display, verbal expression, and understanding of emotions (Cervantes & Callanan, 1998; Denham et al., 1997). They develop stereotypes in interpretations of others' emotions: For example, preschoolers are more likely to associate sadness with females (Karbon, Fabes, Carlo, & Martin, 1992), pre-school boys are more likely than girls of the same age to label their anger reactions (Peterson & Biggs, 2001), and preschoolers in one study showed a bias to interpret male facial expressions in reactions to an emotional event as disgust while female expressions tended to be seen as fearful (Widen & Russell, 2002).

Children are aware of, and organise their own gender behaviour and cognitions in light of, other people's actual or anticipated emotional reactions (see Bussey & Bandura, 1992, above). Raag and Rackliff (1998) found that pre-school boys in particular were more likely to make stereotyped toy choices in a playroom if they perceived that their fathers would regard gender-incongruent play as "bad". Bannerjee and Lintern (2000) asked children (aged 4 to 9 years) to indicate their toy and gender preferences, once when alone and once when in front of a group of same-sex peers. Young boys provided the most gender-stereotyped responses in both conditions but were particularly traditional when surrounded by their peers: The authors attribute this to the boys' desire to solicit positive social evaluations: "Children are not passively shaped by peer evaluation; instead, when sufficiently motivated, they will actively use their knowledge about gender stereotypes to manipulate that evaluation" (Bannerjee & Linter, 2000, pp. 405–406). Recalling Warin's (2000) task described at the beginning of this chapter, it is reasonable to estimate that adding a peer evaluation manipulation to the request to don a frilly pink dress would have resulted in a near 100% refusal rate among little male participants.

Again, social identity theory/self-categorisation theory provide a framework for interpreting gender-related emotional responses in the context of social processes (Lutz & Ruble, 1995; Ruble, Alvarez, Bachman, & Cameron, in press). If children incorporate a social identity (a gender) in their self-concepts, then "children are more likely to view events in group-relevant terms and experience group-relevant emotions" (Lutz & Ruble, 1995, p. 148). In contexts where the genders are perceived as being in social competition, then threats or intrusions from the rival group may evoke hostile reactions, even prejudice. Lutz and Ruble suggest the example of boys' reactions to girls' attempts to play (worse still, excel in) "boys'" games: boys may experience anger at the challenge to their collective gender identity and this may lead to vigorous remedial actions.

In sum, cognitive developmental approaches have contributed a major impetus to the study of gender role development per se and to our knowledge of children's understanding of gender in particular. These are not quite the same thing, and cognitive developmentalists have been criticised for assuming they are (see Bussey & Bandura, 1999; Martin et al., 2002, for discussions). Kohlberg's (1966) model provided a valuable structure for research into early understanding; in some respects, it has been borne out but in others (most notably, gender constancy) it remains controversial (see Lutz & Ruble, 1995). Martin and Halverson's gender schema theory has advanced the field considerably by, among other contributions, highlighting the ways in which children's developing theories of gender guide their interpretation of the social environment and their inferences about it. In more recent developments, this has led to promising intersection with social psychology, in the form of Martin's (2000) sketch of a naïve social psychology of gender, related overlaps with other current work in the application of social identity theory/self-categorisation theory to developmental issues (Powlishta, in press; Ruble et al., in press), and in the study of emotional development in social context. In these ways, research in this field is beginning to ameliorate a "blind spot" of developmental research, namely social influence (Eckes & Trautner, 2000).

UNDERSTANDING GENDER ROLES IN THE MEDIA

If we admit that the development of gender role understanding is sensitive to the surrounding culture (Bussey & Bandura, 1999), then the media stand out as omnipresent and relatively quantifiable components of that culture—as well as being very attractive to young people. Self-evidently, this comment applies only to recent and contemporary cultures, and only in some parts of the world; it is worth bearing in mind that for the larger part of human history, and still today in some societies, communities have evolved differentiated patterns of gender roles, which they have maintained and transmitted to the next generation efficiently and powerfully, without any involvement of the mass media. Nevertheless, the media are important as a collective representation of what gender means and as a guide to what is valued within a society. Of course, the media do not function democratically in respect of representing the diversity of gender ideologies, nor are they faithfully reflective of the demographic structure of their societies or the capacities of individuals, but they do stand as a reflection of how gender is organised and they thereby provide children with a "window" on societal images of gender. The question of interest, then, is how might the media be related to children's understanding of gender roles in society?

Let us take as given that the popular media are highly stereotyped in the ways in which they represent gender; this has been documented in numerous content analyses of various media in various societies at various times over the last three decades (Craig, 1992; Durkin, 1985a; Furnham & Mak, 1989; Glascock, 2001; Hurtz & Durkin, 1997, in press; Leaper, Breed, Hoffman, & Perlman, 2002; Mazzella, Durkin, Cerini, & Buralli, 1992). An exhaustive review of work on the relationship between media and gender role development will not be attempted in the limited space available (see Durkin, 1985b, 1985d; Gunter, 1995). However, it is important to note that the role of the media in this respect is frequently assumed rather than demonstrated. A common account runs like this. The media are very bad (full of sexist stereotypes). Children watch a lot of media. Children acquire gender roles and, during some periods of the early lifespan, express and endorse gender role stereotypes and beliefs that may be stronger than those of their parents. Hence, the media cause, or at least contribute substantially to, the acquisition of traditional gender roles. This is, in essence, a "linear effects" or "injection" hypothesis. It follows (loosely) from this hypothesis that, if we change the media, we will change children's gender role behaviours and beliefs (inject a cure).

Parts of this rationale seem to be manifest, for example, in Bussey and Bandura's (1999) assertions that: "In social cognitive theory, . . . the mass media provides pervasive modelling of gendered roles and conduct" (p. 685) and "It is not surprising that those who have a heavy diet of the televised fare display more gender stereotypic gender role conceptions than do light viewers" (p. 701).

But it is surprising that Bussey and Bandura are not surprised. In the light of all we know, and all that we know we do not know, about the complexity of gender role development (including the sophisticated and wide-ranging theory that Bussey and Bandura themselves articulate), it would be extraordinary if we could find a simple cause–effect relationship between media content and children's gender role conceptions. Elsewhere in the same paper they insist that "people do not passively absorb gender role conceptions from whatever influences happen to impinge upon them . . . The development of gender role conceptions is a construction rather than simply a wholesale incorporation of what has been socially transmitted." (p. 689). This general comment fits much better with the evidence on children and the media than does the authors' reiteration of the linear effects assumption. Some of this evidence will be summarised, with reference to selective attention, inferential processes, reactions to counter-stereotypes, and the importance of male power.

Selective attention and preferences

Children attend selectively to their media, reflecting, among other things, their level of gender role development. Slaby and Frey (1975) provided the first evidence that the attainment of gender constancy promotes increased attention to gender-relevant information in television. Their participants were pre-schoolers (aged 2 to 5 years) who had low or high scores on their gender constancy test. The children viewed a silent film showing, on a split screen, a male actor and a female actor simultaneously carrying out a series of simple everyday activities. The dependent measure was the child's visual attention to the same-sex model. As predicted, children with high levels of gender constancy showed greater attention to the same-sex model (though the finding reached statistical significance for boys only). The researchers inferred that children were engaged in self-socialisation, actively scouring the social environment (here, the TV screen) for information about the rules governing the behaviour of the gender to which they have recently realised they will belong for life.

Further evidence of the relevance of gender constancy to the inter-pretation of social information about gender was provided by Ruble, Balaban, and Cooper (1981), also using TV stimuli. In this case, the researchers exposed 3- to 6-year-olds to a toy commercial, in which the actors (playing with the toy) were either two boys or two girls. The toy itself had been determined in pretesting not to be associated with a particular gender. Viewers who scored high on gender constancy were much more likely to spend time playing with the toy if they had seen a commercial associating it with their own sex; high scorers were also more likely to avoid the toy if it had been depicted in association with the opposite sex. These differences were not obtained among the low gender constancy children. Again, it seems that children with gender constancy take note of social data and interpret their implications for their own behaviour.

These conclusions from laboratory findings are borne out by two studies of home viewing, conducted by Luecke-Aleksa, Anderson, Collins, and Schmitt (1995). In video recordings of viewing over a 10-day period, 5-year-old boys scoring high on gender constancy were observed to view more programmes with a greater percentage of male stars than did their low gender constancy peers. Analyses of a large sample of children's diary records also showed that boys with gender constancy chose more pro-grammes intended for adults (especially sports and action programmes). Interestingly, girls with gender constancy also viewed more action pro-grammes, possibly because they were interested in how the female characters behaved or possibly because they were interested more generally in more mature TV content than preschoolers are often encouraged to watch.

As children begin to show preferences for particular programme types, they tend to demonstrate more gender-stereotypic judgements in other contexts, such as indicating their own future job preferences (Thompson & Zerbinos, 1997). Their emotional reactions to television content differ by gender (Oliver & Green, 2001). Oliver and Green found that girls were more likely than boys to express sadness in response to a sad scene from a "female" movie; this held for both self-reports and observational measures of facial affect. Of particular interest is Oliver and Green's finding that children's reported enjoyment of a "male" or "female" movie clip was associated with the gender categories they imposed on the material. Among children who perceived a movie as "for girls", girls reported greater liking than boys; correspondingly, among children who perceived a movie as "for boys", boys reported greater liking than girls. As the authors note, the "liking/gender categorisation" relationship could be interpreted in either direction: A boy might categorise a film as "for boys" because he likes it (and infers that other boys will like what he likes) or a boy might like a film because he has categorised it as "for boys" (and feels that he ought to express boy preferences). As the children's gender categories tended to be accurate (i.e., they classified the films in line with traditional gender stereotypes), the latter explanation seems more likely, but either interpretation suggests an interweaving of developing gender knowledge and emotional reactions to the media (and consistent with this interpretation, the gender differences tended to increase with age, over the period 3 to 9 years).

Similar processes obtain in relation to other media use. For example, girls tend to be less attracted to computers and computer games than do boys (Durkin & Barber, 2002; Newman, Cooper, & Ruble, 1995; Subrahmanyam, Greenfield, Kraut, & Gross, 2001). Newman et al. found that girls who had gender constancy and high levels of knowledge about gender stereotypes reported lower levels of liking for computers than did other girls or boys. Gender stereotypes and role expectations seem also to be implicated in the findings of Fitzpatrick and Hardman (2000), that among 7- to 9-year-olds, girls paired with boys in collaborative learning tasks were more likely to defer to their partner in the case of task difficulty than were girls in same-sex dyads or girls in mixed-sex dyads undertaking a non-computer task.

In short, rather than being the outcome of passive exposure to the mass media, children's developing gender role understanding guides how they select among, attend to, and process information in the media.

Active inferential processes in media use

Consistent with gender schema theory and the notion above, of a naïve social psychology of gender, children demonstrate quite early that they can make inferences that take them beyond the available information on screen. Durkin (1984) interviewed 4- to 9-year-olds about the contents of short excerpts of traditionally gender-stereotyped television material. The children were not only able to explain the stereotyped behaviours easily but also to offer plausible, gender-stereotyped, inferences about events and behaviours not actually present. For example, in a beauty commercial, children could explain (with reference to the interaction of affective and sensory processes) why a young man would give flowers to a young woman who had just applied a hair spray; more importantly, they were able to predict that the young man would not give flowers to the train driver, who they assumed—without any indicators in the material itself—would be male. The children were also able to explain the absence of women from a scene involving heroic menfolk in a mediaeval castle on the basis that the females would be in the kitchen, doing the washing-up. Durkin and Nugent (1998) found that 4- and 5-year-olds could predict the gender of not shown television actors, given only short scenes depicting the need for someone to undertake a gender-stereotyped activity (e.g., someone to do some sewing, wash clothes, fix a car, or put out a fire). These findings leave open the question of to what extent earlier TV viewing had contributed to children's stereotyped expectations and inferences but they make clear that children are not restricted to the information on-screen in constructing their theories of gender in society.

Resistance to counterstereotypes in the media

Contrary to the linear effects assumption that the media can shape children at will, young viewers prove resistant to counterstereotypes. In early attempts to persuade children via television programmes that women could be doctors and men could be nurses, Cordua, McGraw, and Drabman (1979) and Drabman, Robertson, Patterson, Jarvie, Hammer, and Cordua (1981) found that participants subsequently recalled the gender of the actors in line with traditional stereotypes. This finding is consistent with the predictions of gender schema theory, that schemas should bias information processing, such that schema-inconsistent data should be disregarded or poorly recalled (Martin, 1989). Durkin and Hutchins (1984) found that early adolescent viewers strongly and scornfully resisted nontraditional careers education programmes; the authors interpreted this as reflecting children's reluctance to abandon conceptions of societal organisation that had been constructed over several years and that were now integrated with the young people's values and personal expectations. Other experimental and field studies have yielded mixed results (see Durkin, 1985c, 1985d; Pickering & Repacholi, 2001; Johnston & Ettema, 1982) but none has resulted in a radical and enduring abandonment of traditional beliefs (see Bigler, 1999, for similar conclusions about non-media-based intervention efforts).

More generally, intervention studies have tended to focus on children's *knowledge* of gender (i.e., by providing new information to indicate that females and males can do a broader range of things than traditional stereotypes suppose) but have neglected children's *motivations.* On the one hand, children are motivated to maintain traditional beliefs because they are closely linked to their developing self-concepts and their group identifications; on the other hand, in some contexts at least, children may be motivated to control stereotypic responding (such as the reluctance to appear prejudiced; see Lutz & Ruble, 1995; Rutland, in press).

The importance of male power

Most studies find that boys are more resistant to counterstereotypes in the media than are girls, a finding that can be interpreted in relation to the more prescriptive nature and higher standing of the male role, provoking boys' emotional resistance to threats to masculine status (Durkin, 1985d; Jeffrey & Durkin, 1989; Pickering & Repacholi, 2001). Consistent with the emphasis on the attractiveness to children of social power in Bussey and Bandura's (1999) theory (see also Bussey & Bandura, 1984), with cognitive developmental theory (Kohlberg, 1966; Lutz & Ruble, 1995), as well as with theories of intergroup relations and gender (Glick & Hilt, 2000; Lutz & Ruble, 1995; Powlishta, in press), children respond differentially to counterstereotyped media if the power of the protagonists is manipulated. For example, Jeffrey and Durkin (1989) tested children's reactions to a counterstereotyped programme showing a father engaged in domestic chores during a day off work. In one condition, the father was revealed earlier in the programme to have a low-status job (low power), and in the other condition he was revealed to be a high-status executive (high power). In the low power condition, results replicated Stoddart and Turiel's (1985) findings, discussed earlier, of a U-shaped developmental curve when judging the acceptability of the nontraditional behaviour: Younger children and adolescents rejected the idea (i.e., they thought it was a bad thing for a man to do routine domestic work). In the high power condition, the pattern was reversed and children in these age groups were significantly more likely to accept the nontraditional behaviour.

In sum, there is no doubt that the media present stereotyped, if occasionally heterogenous, representations of gender roles and there is no doubt that children are avid consumers of the media, especially television. However, this correlation does not confirm a unidirectional causal relationship in respect of children's own gender role development or their understanding of gender roles in society. Instead, consistent with the broad thrust of cognitive developmental theories (and some aspects of social cognitive theory), children turn out to be discerning viewers who attend selectively to the material available and interpret it in accord with their developing naïve social psychologies of gender and their personal (though gender-linked) preferences. They also, once again, filter the information through affective processes, and are quite ready to reject ideas and images if they are incompatible with their theories and values.

CONCLUSIONS

Gender is given, grown, imposed, expected, regulated, learned, reflected upon, enacted, experienced, and shared. In this complex, multifaceted, and multidetermined minefield, children are actively engaged as thinkers and as emotional beings striving to determine who they are and how they relate to the social structure. Early attempts to explain gender role development tended to ignore or neglect the child's understanding. Cognitive developmental theories corrected this and inspired a large body of fruitful research, though these theories in turn have tended to neglect how children feel about gender. As in much cognitive developmental work, they tended to treat the child as a cognitive isolate or mini-scientist engaged in interesting epistemological quests with little reference to anyone else. Recent developments within cognitive developmental theory and at the points of intersection with social psychology have brought social processes and motivational and affective considerations more to the fore.

Two issues emerge to guide future research. First, although children's understanding of gender roles in society is, of course, subject to developmental processes, it is becoming apparent that it is misleading to conceive of it as an incremental body of knowledge that is static at a given point in development. Instead, it is fluid, context sensitive, and socially shared and may be expressed or accessed in different ways in different circumstances. Thus, the task ahead is not so much to refine our maps of what is known at different ages or stages but rather to investigate how children draw upon their developing knowledge to meet specific demands as social actors. Second, understanding gender in society is closely linked to emotional processes. Gender is motivating to children as highly personally salient information, as a fundamental organising feature of any community, and as a framework of values in relation to which feedback is received almost continuously from other people and institutions. Importantly, the cognitive engagement can be constrained by the emotional engagement. For example, increasingly sophisticated and flexible knowledge can be put aside in sufficiently motivating contexts of intergroup rivalry, where the young person may revert to simplistic, even prejudiced, stereotypes, or in contexts where gender identity might be threatened in other ways (for example, by being asked to wear frilly pink dresses, which will be declined not only by 5-year-old boys with strong gender stereotypes but by a majority of males in most other age groups). We still have much to understand about how children come to understand gender roles in society, but finding out more holds enticing prospects of improving our accounts of how developing human beings mediate the complex relations between biology and social structure.

REFERENCES

Alexander, G. M., & Hines, M. (2002). Sex differences in response to children's toys in nonhuman primates (*Cercoptihecus aethiops sabaeous*). *Evolution and Human Behavior, 23*, 467–479.

Archer, J. (1992). Childhood gender roles: Social context and organisation. In H. McGurk (Ed.), *Childhood social development: Contemporary perspectives* (pp. 31–61). Hove, UK: Lawrence Erlbaum Associates Ltd.

Bannerjee, R., & Lintern, V. (2000). Boys will be boys: The effect of social evaluation concerns on gender-typing. *Social Development, 9*, 397–408.

Bauer, P. J., Liebl, M., & Stennes, L. (1998). Pretty is to dress as brave is to suitcoat: Gender-based property-to-property inferences by 4½-year-old children. *Merrill-Palmer Quarterly*, *44*, 355–377.

Beneson, J. F., Morash, D., & Petrakos, H. (1998). Gender differences in emotional closeness between preschool children and their mothers. *Sex Roles, 38*, 975–985.

Berscheid, E. (1993). Foreword. In A. E. Beall & R. J. Sternberg (Eds.), *The psychology of gender* (pp. vii–xvi). New York: Guilford Press.

Biernat, M. (1991). Gender stereotypes and the relationship between masculinity and femininity: A developmental analysis. *Journal of Personality and Social Psychology, 61*, 351–365.

Bigler, R. S. (1999). Psychological interventions designed to counter sexism in children: Empirical limitations and theoretical foundations. In W. B. Swann, J. H. Langlois, & L. A. Gilbert (Eds.), *Sexism and stereotypes in modern society. The gender science of Janet Taylor Spence* (pp. 129–151). Washington, DC: American Psychological Association.

Bradbard, M. R., Martin, C. L. Endsley, R. C., & Halverson, C. F. (1986). Influence of sex stereotypes on children's exploration and memory: A competence versus performance distinction. *Developmental Psychology, 22*, 481–486.

Brothers, L. (2001). *Friday's footprint: How society shapes the human mind.* London: Oxford University Press.

Brown, G. R., & Dixson, A. F. (2000). The development of behavioural sex differences in infant rhesus macaques (*Macaca mulatta*). *Primates, 41*, 63–77.

Buckner, J. P., & Fivush, R. (1998). Gender and self in children's autobiographical narratives. *Applied Cognitive Psychology, 12*, 407–429.

Bussey, K., & Bandura, A. (1984). Influence of gender constancy and social power on sex-linked modeling. *Journal of Personality and Social Psychology, 47*, 1292–1302.

Bussey, K., & Bandura, A. (1992). Self-regulatory mechanisms governing gender development. *Child Development, 63*, 1236–1250.

Bussey, K., & Bandura, A. (1999). Social cognitive theory of gender development and differentiation. *Psychological Review, 106*, 676–713.

Cervantes, C. A., & Callanan, M. A. (1998). Labels and explanations in mother–child emotion talk: Age and gender differentiation. *Developmental Psychology, 34*, 88–98.

Cherney, I. D., & Ryalls, B. O. (1999). Gender-linked differences in the incidental memory of children and adults. *Journal of Experimental Child Psychology, 72*, 305–328.

Cordua, G. D., McGraw, K. O., & Drabman, R. S. (1979). Doctor or nurse: Children's perception of sex typed occupations. *Child Development, 50*, 590–593.

Craig, R. S. (1992). The effect of television day part on gender portrayals in television commercials: A content analysis. *Sex Roles, 26*, 197–211.

David, B., Grace, D., & Ryan, M. K. (in press). The gender wars: A self-categorization perspective on the development of gender identity. In M. Bennett & F. Sani (Eds.), *The development of the social self.* Hove, UK: Psychology Press.

Denham, S. A., Mitchell-Copeland, J., Strandberg, K., Auerbach, S., & Blair, K. (1997). Parental contributions to preschoolers' emotional competence: Direct and indirect effects. *Motivation and Emotion, 21*, 65–86.

Drabman, R. S., Robertson, S. J., Patterson, J. N., Jarvie, G. J., Hammer, D., & Cordua, G. (1982). Children's perception of media-portrayed sex roles. *Sex Roles, 7*, 379–389.

Dunn, J., Bretherton, I., & Munn, P. (1987). Conversations about feeling states between mothers and their young children. *Developmental Psychology, 23*, 132–139.

Durkin, K. (1984). Children's accounts of sex-role stereotypes in television. *Communication Research, 11*, 341–362.

Durkin, K. (1985a). Television and sex-role acquisition 1: Content. *British Journal of Social Psychology, 24*, 101–113.

Durkin, K. (1985b). Television and sex-role acquisition 2: Effects. *British Journal of Social Psychology*, *24*, 191–210.

Durkin, K. (1985c). Television and sex-role acquisition 3: Counter-stereotyping. *British Journal of Social Psychology*, *24*, 211–222.

Durkin, K. (1985d). *Television, sex roles and children: A developmental social psychological account.* Milton Keynes, UK & Philadelphia: Open University Press.

Durkin, K. (1995). *Developmental and social psychology: From infancy to old age.* Oxford: Blackwell.

Durkin, K., & Barber, B. (2002). Not so doomed: Computer game play and positive adolescent development. *Journal of Applied Developmental Psychology*, *23*, 373–392.

Durkin, K., & Hutchins, G. (1984). Challenging traditional sex role stereotypes in careers education broadcasts: The reactions of young secondary school pupils. *Journal of Educational Television*, *10*, 25–33.

Durkin, K., & Nugent, B. (1998). Kindergarten children's gender-role expectations for television actors. *Sex Roles*, *38*, 387–402.

Eccles, J. S., Freedman-Doan, C., Frome, P., Jacobs, J., & Yoon, K. S. (2000). Gender-role socialization in the family: A longitudinal approach. In T. Eckes & H. M. Trautner (Eds.), *The developmental social psychology of gender* (pp. 333–360). Mahwah, NJ: Lawrence Erlbaum Associates Inc.

Eckes, T., & Trautner, H. M. (2000). Developmental social psychology of gender: An integrative framework. In T. Eckes & H. M. Trautner (Eds.), *The developmental social psychology of gender* (pp. 3–31). Mahwah, NJ: Lawrence Erlbaum Associates Inc.

Egan, S. K., & Perry, D. G. (2001). Gender identity: A multidimensional analysis with implications for psychosocial adjustment. *Developmental Psychology*, *37*, 451–463.

Eisenberg, N., Cumberland, A., & Spinrad, T. L. (1998). Parental socialization of emotion. *Psychological Inquiry*, *9*, 241–273.

Emler, N., & Ohana, J. (1993). Studying social representations in children. In G. M. Breakwell & D. V. Canter (Eds.), *Empirical approaches to social representations* (pp. 63–89). Oxford: Clarendon.

Emmerich, W., Goldman, K. S., Kirsh, B., & Sharabany, R. (1977). Evidence for a transitional phase in the development of gender constancy. *Child Development*, *48*, 930–936.

Fabes, R. A., & Martin, C. L. (1991). Gender and age stereotypes of emotionality. *Personality and Social Psychology Bulletin*, *17*, 532–540.

Fagot, B. I. (1978). The influence of sex of child on parental reactions to toddler children. *Child Development*, *49*, 459–465.

Fagot, B. I. (1985). Beyond the reinforcement principle: Another step toward understanding sex role development. *Developmental Psychology*, *21*, 1097–1104.

Fagot, B. I., Rodgers, C. S., & Leinbach, M. D. (2000). Theories of gender socialization. In T. Eckes & H. M. Trautner (Eds.), *The developmental social psychology of gender* (pp. 65–89). Mahwah, NJ: Lawrence Erlbaum Associates Inc.

Fitzpatrick, H., & Hardman, M. (2000). Mediated activity in the primary classroom: Girls, boys and computers. *Learning and Instruction*, *10*, 431–446.

Fivush, R., Brotman, M. A., Buckner, J. P., & Goodman, S. H. (2000). Gender differences in parent–child emotion narratives. *Sex Roles*, *42*, 233–253.

Fivush, R., & Buckner, J. P. (2000). Gender, sadness, and depression: The development of emotional focus through gendered discourse. In A. H. Fischer (Ed.), *Gender and emotion: Social psychological perspectives. Studies in emotion and social interaction. Second series* (pp. 232–253). Cambridge: Cambridge University Press.

Furnham, A., & Mak, T. (1999). Sex-role stereotyping in television commercials: A review and comparison of fourteen studies done on five continents over 25 years. *Sex Roles*, *41*, 413–437.

Geary, D. (1998). *Male, female: The evolution of human sex differences.* Washington, DC: American Psychological Association.

Gelman, S. A., Collman, P., & Maccoby, E. E. (1986). Inferring properties from categories versus inferring categories from properties: The case of gender. *Child Development, 57,* 396–404.

Gibbons, J. L. (2000). Gender development in cross-cultural perspective. In T. Eckes & H. M. Trautner (Eds.), *The developmental social psychology of gender* (pp. 389–415). Mahwah, NJ: Lawrence Erlbaum Associates Inc.

Glascock, J. (2001). Gender roles on prime-time network television: Demographics and behaviors. *Journal of Broadcasting and Electronic Media, 45,* 656–669.

Glick, P., & Hilt, L. (2000). Combative children to ambivalent adults: The development of gender prejudice. In T. Eckes & H. M. Trautner (Eds.), *The developmental social psychology of gender* (pp. 243–272). Mahwah, NJ: Lawrence Erlbaum Associates Inc.

Gunter, B. (1995). *Television and gender representation.* London: John Libbey.

Heyman, G. D. (2001). Children's interpretation of ambiguous behavior: Evidence for a "boys are bad" bias. *Social Development, 10,* 230–247.

Hurtz, W., & Durkin, K. (1997). Gender role stereotyping in Australian radio commercials. *Sex Roles, 36,* 103–114.

Hurtz, W., & Durkin, K. (in press). The effects of gender stereotyped radio commercials. *Journal of Applied Social Psychology.*

Huston, A. C. (1983). Sex typing. In P. H. Mussen & E. M. Hetherington (Eds.), *Handbook of child psychology, Vol. 4, Socialization, personality, and social behavior* (4th ed.). New York: Wiley.

Huston, A. C. (1985). The development of sex typing: Themes from recent research. *Developmental Review, 5,* 1–17.

Jeffrey, L., & Durkin, K. (1989). Children's reactions to televised counter-stereotyped male sex role behaviour as a function of age, sex and perceived power. *Social Behaviour, 4,* 285–310.

Johnston, J., & Ettema, J. S. (1982). *Positive images: Breaking stereotypes with children's television.* Beverly Hills, CA: Sage.

Karbon, M., Fabes, R. A., Carlo, G., & Martin, C. L. (1992). Preschoolers' beliefs about sex and age differences in emotionality. *Sex Roles, 27,* 377–390.

Kenrick, D. T., & Luce, C. L. (2000). An evolutionary life-history model of gender differences and similarities. In T. Eckes & H. M. Trautner (Eds.), *The developmental social psychology of gender* (pp. 35–63). Mahwah, NJ: Lawrence Erlbaum Associates Inc.

Kenrick, D. T., & Trost, M. R. (1993). The evolutionary perspective. In A. E. Beall & R. J. Sternberg (Eds.), *The psychology of gender* (pp. 148–172). New York: Guilford Press.

Kohlberg, L. A. (1966). A cognitive-developmental analysis of children's sex role concepts and attitudes. In E. E. Maccoby (Ed.), *The development of sex differences* (pp. 82–173). Stanford, CA: Stanford University Press.

Lagattuta, K. H., & Wellman, H. M. (2002). Differences in early parent–child conversations about negative versus positive emotions: Implications for the development of psychological understanding. *Developmental Psychology, 38,* 564–580.

Leaper, C., Breed, L., Hoffman, L., & Perlman, C. A. (2002). Variations in the gender-stereotyped content of children's television cartoons across genres. *Journal of Applied Social Psychology, 32,* 1653–1662.

Leeb, R. T., & Rejskind, F. G. (2004). Here's looking at you, kid! A longitudinal study of perceived gender differences in mutual gaze behaviour in young infants. *Sex Roles, 50,* 1–14.

Leonard, S. P., & Archer, J. (1989). A naturalistic investigation of gender constancy in three- to four-year-old children. *British Journal of Developmental Psychology, 7,* 341–346.

Leve, L. D., & Fagot, B. I. (1997). Gender-role socialisation and discipline processes in one- and two-parent families. *Sex Roles, 36,* 1–21.

Levy, G. D. (1999). Gender-typed and non-gender-typed category awareness in toddlers. *Sex Roles, 41*, 851–873.

Levy, G. D., Sadovsky, A. L., & Troseth, G. L. (2000). Aspects of young children's perceptions of gender-typed occupations. *Sex Roles, 42*, 993–1006.

Liben, L. S., Bigler, R. S., & Krogh, H. R. (2001). Pink and blue collar jobs: Children's judgments of job status and job aspirations in relation to sex of worker. *Journal of Experimental Child Psychology, 79*, 346–363.

Lindsey, E. W., & Mize, J. (2001). Contextual differences in parent–child play: Implications for children's gender role development. *Sex Roles, 44*, 155–176.

Lobel, T. E., Gruber, R., Govrin, N., & Mashraki-Pedhatzur, S. (2001). Children's gender-related inferences and judgments: A cross-cultural study. *Developmental Psychology, 37*, 839–846.

Lott, B., & Maluso, D. (1993). The social learning of gender. In A. E. Beall & R. J. Sternberg (Eds.), *The psychology of gender* (pp. 99–123). New York: Guilford Press.

Luecke-Aleksa, D., Anderson, D. R., Collins, P. A., & Schmitt, K. L. (1995). Gender constancy and television viewing. *Developmental Psychology, 31*, 773–780.

Lutz, S. E., & Ruble, D. N. (1995). Children and gender prejudice: Context, motivation, and the development of gender concepts. *Annals of Child Development, 10*, 131–166.

Lytton, H., & Romney, D. M. (1991). Parents' differential socialisation of boys and girls: A meta-analysis. *Psychological Bulletin, 109*, 267–296.

Maccoby, E. E. (1998). *The two sexes: Growing up apart, coming together.* Cambridge, MA: Harvard University Press.

MacDonald, K. B. (1988). *Social and personality development: An evolutionary syntheses.* New York: Plenum Press.

Magai, C., & McFadden, S. H. (1995). *The role of emotions in social and personality development. History, theory, and research.* New York & London: Plenum Press.

Martin, C. L. (1989). Children's use of gender-related information in making social judgments. *Developmental Psychology, 25*, 80–88.

Martin, C. L. (1993). New directions for investigating children's gender knowledge. *Developmental Review, 13*, 184–204.

Martin, C. L. Martin, C. L. (1991). The role of cognition in understanding gender effects. In H. W. Reese (Ed.), *Advances in child development and behavior, Vol. 23* (pp. 113–149). San Diego, CA: Academic Press.

Martin, C. L. (1995). Stereotypes about children with traditional and nontraditional gender roles. *Sex Roles, 33*, 727–751.

Martin, C. L. (1999). A developmental perspective on gender effects and gender concepts. In W. B. Swann & J. H. Langlois (Eds.), *Sexism and stereotypes in modern society: The gender science of Janet Taylor Spence* (pp. 45–73). Washington, DC: American Psychological Association.

Martin, C. L. (2000). Cognitive theories of gender development. In T. Eckes & H. M. Trautner (Eds.), *The developmental social psychology of gender* (pp. 91–121). Mahwah, NJ: Lawrence Erlbaum Associates Inc.

Martin, C. L., Eisenbud, L., & Rose, H. (1995). Children's gender-based reasoning about toys. *Child Development, 66*, 1453–1471.

Martin, C. L., & Halverson, C. F. (1981). A schematic processing model of sex typing and stereotyping in children. *Child Development, 52*, 1119–1134.

Martin, C. L., & Halverson, C. F. (1983). Gender constancy: A methodological and theoretical analysis. *Sex Roles, 9*, 775–790.

Martin, C. L., & Halverson, C. F. (1987). The roles of cognition in sex role acquisition. In D. B. Carter (Ed.), *Current conceptions of sex roles and sex typing: Theory and research* (pp. 123–137). New York: Praeger.

Martin, C. L., & Little, J. K. (1990). The relation of gender understanding to children's sex-typed preferences and gender stereotypes. *Child Development, 61,* 1427–1439.

Martin, C. L., Ruble, D. N., & Szkrybalo, J. (2002). Cognitive theories of early gender development. *Psychological Bulletin, 128,* 903–933.

Mazzella, C., Durkin, K., Cerini, E., & Buralli, P. (1992). Sex role stereotyping in Australian television advertisements. *Sex Roles, 26,* 243–259.

McHale, S. M., Crouter, A. C., & Whiteman, S. D. (2003). The family contexts of gender development in childhood and adolescence. *Social Development, 12,* 125–148.

Mischel, W. (1966). A social-learning view of sex differences in behavior. In E. Maccoby (Ed.), *The development of sex differences* (pp. 56–81). Stanford, CA: Stanford University Press.

Moller, L. C., Hymel, S., & Rubin, K. H. (1992). Sex typing in play and popularity in middle childhood. *Sex Roles, 26,* 331–353.

Moore, B. S., & Isen, A. M. (1990). Affect and social behavior. In B. S. Moore & A. M. Isen (Eds.), *Affect and social behavior* (pp. 1–21). Cambridge: Cambridge University Press.

Newman, L. S., Cooper, J., & Ruble, D. N. (1995). Gender and computers: II. Interactive effects of knowledge and constancy on gender-stereotyped attitudes. *Sex Roles, 33,* 325–351.

Nussbaum, M. C. (2000). Emotions and social norms. In L. P. Nucci, G. B. Saxe, & E. Turiel (Eds.), *Culture, thought, and development. The Jean Piaget symposium series* (pp. 41–63). Mahwah, NJ: Lawrence Erlbaum Associates Inc.

Oliver, M. B., & Green, S. (2001). Development of gender differences in children's responses to animated entertainment. *Sex Roles, 45,* 67–88.

Ontai, L. L., & Thompson, R. A. (2002). Patterns of attachment and maternal discourse effects on children's emotion understanding from 3 to 5 years of age. *Social Development, 11,* 433–450.

Peterson, C., & Biggs, M. (2001). "I was really, really, really mad!" Children's use of evaluative devices in narratives about emotional events. *Sex Roles, 45,* 801–825.

Pickering, S., & Repacholi, B. (2001). Modifying children's gender-typed musical preferences: The effects of gender and age. *Sex Roles, 45,* 623–643.

Planalp, S. (1999). *Communicating emotion: Social, moral and cultural processes.* New York/ Paris: Cambridge University Press.

Plant, E. A., Hyde, J. S., Keltner, D., & Devine, P. G. (2000). The gender stereotyping of emotions. *Psychology of Women Quarterly, 24,* 81–92.

Pomerleau, A., Bolduc, D., Malcuit, G., & Cossette, L. (1990). Pink or blue: Environmental gender stereotypes in the first two years of life. *Sex Roles, 22,* 359–367.

Poulin-Dubois, D., Serbin, L. A., Eichstedt, J. A., Sen, M. G., & Beissel, C. F. (2002). Men don't put on make-up: Toddlers' knowledge of the gender stereotyping of household activities. *Social Development, 11,* 166–181.

Powlishta, K. K. (1995). Gender bias in children's perception of personality traits. *Sex Roles, 32,* 17–28.

Powlishta, K. K. (2000). The effects of target age on the activation of gender stereotypes. *Sex Roles, 42,* 271–282.

Powlishta, K. K. (in press). Gender as a social category: Intergroup processes and gender-role development. In M. Bennett & F. Sani (Eds.), *The development of the social self.* Hove, UK: Psychology Press.

Raag, T., & Rackliff, C. L. (1998). Preschoolers' awareness of social expectations of gender: Relationships to toy choices. *Sex Roles, 38,* 685–700.

Rheingold, H. L., & Cook, K. V. (1975). The contents of boys' and girls' rooms as an index of parents' behavior. *Child Development, 46,* 459–463.

Rubin, J. Z., Provenzano, F. J., & Luria, Z. (1974). The eye of the beholder: Parents' views on sex of newborns. *American Journal of Orthopsychiatry, 44,* 512–519.

Ruble, D. N., Alvarez, J., Bachman, M., & Cameron, J. (in press). The development of a sense of "we": The emergence and implications of children's collective identity. In M. Bennett & F. Sani (Eds.), *The development of the social self*. Hove, UK: Psychology Press.

Ruble, D. N., Balaban, T., & Cooper, J. (1981). Gender constancy and the effects of sex-typed television toy commercials. *Child Development, 52*, 667–673.

Ruble, D. N., & Martin, C. L. (1998). Gender development. In W. Damon & N. Eisenberg (Eds.), *Handbook of child psychology: Vol. 3, Social, emotional and personality development* (pp. 933–1016). New York: Wiley.

Rutland, A. (in press). The development and self-regulation of intergroup attitudes in children. In M. Bennett & F. Sani (Eds.), *The development of the social self*. Hove, UK: Psychology Press.

Sani, F., & Bennett, M. (2001). Contextual variability in young children's gender ingroup stereotype. *Social Development, 10*, 221–229.

Sayers, J. (1986). *Sexual contradictions: Psychology, psychoanalysis and feminism*. London: Tavistock.

Seavey, C. A., Katz, P. A., & Zalk, S. R. (1975). Baby X: The effect of gender labels on adult responses to infants. *Sex Roles, 1*, 103–109.

Servin, A., Bohlin, G., & Berlin, L. (1999). Sex differences in 1-, 3-, and 5-year-olds' toy-choice in a structured play-session. *Scandinavian Journal of Psychology, 40*, 43–48.

Shakin, M., Shakin, D., & Sternglanz, S. H. (1985). Infant clothing: Sex labeling for strangers. *Sex Roles, 12*, 955–964.

Siegal, M., & Robinson, J. (1987). Order effects in children's gender-constancy responses. *Developmental Psychology, 23*, 283–286.

Sidorowicz, L. S., & Lunney, G. S. (1980). Baby X revisited. *Sex Roles, 6*, 67–73.

Signorella, M. L. (1999). Multidimensionality of gender schemas: Implications for the development of gender-related characteristics. In W. B. Swan, Jr, J. H. Langlois, & L. A. Gilbert (Eds.), *Sexism and stereotypes in modern society: The gender science of Janet Taylor Spence* (pp. 107–126). Washington, DC: American Psychological Association.

Signorella, M. L., Bigler, R. S., & Liben, L. S. (1993). Developmental differences in children's gender schemata about others: A meta-analytic review. *Developmental Review, 13*, 147–183.

Slaby, R. G., & Frey, K. S. (1975). Development of gender constancy and selective attention to same-sex models. *Child Development, 46*, 849–856.

Smith, P. K., Smees, R., Pellegrini, A. D., & Menesini, E. (2002). Comparing pupil and teacher perceptions for playful fighting, serious fighting, and positive peer interaction. In J. L. Roopnarine (Ed.), *Conceptual, social-cognitive, and contextual issues in the fields of play. Play and culture studies, Vol. 4* (pp. 235–245). Westport, CT: Ablex.

Staats, A. W. (1975). *Social behaviorism*. Homewood, IL: Dorsey.

Stoddart, T., & Turiel, E. (1985). Children's concepts of cross-gender activities. *Child Development, 56*, 1241–1252.

Subrahmanyam, K., Greenfield, P., Kraut, R., & Gross, E. (2001). The impact of computer use on children's and adolescents' development. *Journal of Applied Developmental Psychology, 22*, 7–30.

Sweeney, J., & Bradbard, M. R. (1988). Mothers' and fathers' changing perceptions of their male and female infants over the course of pregnancy. *Journal of Genetic Psychology, 149*, 393–404.

Tajfel, H., & Turner, J. (1979). Social categorization, social identity and social comparison. In W. Austin & S. Worchel (Eds.), *The social psychology of intergroup relations* (pp. 33–47). Monterey, CA: Brooks/Cole.

Taylor, M. G. (1996). The development of children's beliefs about social and biological aspects of gender differences. *Child Development, 67*, 1555–1571.

Thompson, S. K. (1975). Gender labels and early sex role development. *Child Development*, *46*, 339–347.

Thompson, T. L., & Zerbinos, E. (1997). Television cartoons: Do children notice it's a boy's world? *Sex Roles*, *37*, 415–432.

Trivers, R. L. (1972). Parental investment and sexual selection. In B. Campbell (Ed.), *Sexual selection and the descent of man*. Chicago: Aldine.

Wallen, K. (1996). Nature needs nurture: The interaction of hormonal and social influences on the development of behavioral sex differences in rhesus monkeys. *Hormones and Behavior*, *30*, 364–378.

Warin, J. (2000). The attainment of self-consistency through gender in young children. *Sex Roles*, *42*, 209–231.

Widen, S. C., & Russell, J. A. (2002). Gender and preschoolers' perception of emotion. *Merrill-Palmer Quarterly*, *48*, 248–262.

Wilson, E. O. (1978). *On human nature*. Cambridge, MA: Harvard University Press.

Yee, M., & Brown, R. J. (1994). The development of gender differentiation in young children. *British Journal of Social Psychology*, *33*, 183–196.

Zajonc, R. B. (1998). Emotions. In D. T. Gilbert, S. T. Fiske, & L. Gardner (Eds.), *The handbook of social psychology, Vol. 1* (4th ed., pp. 591–632). New York: Oxford University Press.

CHAPTER SEVEN

Children's understanding of social class and occupational groupings

Nicholas Emler
Department of Psychology, University of Surrey, Guildford, UK

Julie Dickinson
Department of Organizational Psychology, Birkbeck College, London, UK

INTRODUCTION

If the title of this chapter provides an honest indication of its scope and content, it does not say why the topic, defined in this way, is worth addressing. All kinds of reasons could be given, including that the topic is interesting in its own right. For us, however, its interest lies in the light it can shed on more general questions about human societies, the forms they take, and the processes that sustain or modify these forms. We start from the proposition that societies are economic systems, which require the input of energy or "work" on the part of their members and which then allocate the fruits of these efforts in some way. There are, of course, many different ways in which the inputs could be arranged and the outcomes distributed. Indeed, one of the most striking features of human, as compared to other animal, societies is the sheer variety of arrangements that have, historically, proved viable at some level. If durability is a relevant test of viability, then the slave economies of the Roman empire, the feudal economies of mediaeval Europe, and the despotic empires of pre-revolutionary China all qualify. Our focus here is upon one such set of arrangements, those found in contemporary capitalist economies. The chapter title relates to two linked features of these arrangements; the distribution of benefits, reflected in social class divisions, and the organisation of the inputs (or work) around occupations.

There are two features of these arrangements to which we wish to draw attention. First, the allocation of resources in capitalist economies is

169

characterised by considerable inequalities of wealth. Marked inequalities in prosperity are not, of course, peculiar to societies of this kind. With the possible exception of hunter-gatherer societies, all the economic arrangements humans have so far devised have entailed an unequal distribution of the benefits of membership. Even communist regimes, both past and present, feature considerable income and other material differentials. However, the conditions that sustain these inequalities in modern capitalism are rather more distinctive. Those with the most wealth may invest in elaborate and expensive security to protect it, but this protection is not from a hostile and deprived majority. On the contrary, the majority appear to accept that some degree of inequality is entirely legitimate. In other words, these arrangements, and more specifically these inequalities, survive because they attract a measure of acceptance.

The second feature concerns the inputs. In effect there are two parallel systems of labour, one in which the work is performed in exchange for a financial reward, and one in which it is not. The former corresponds to what we are now in the habit of regarding as employment (and characteristically the exchange involved is taxed). The most significant, even if not the only, form of the latter is domestic labour. One interesting feature of this division is that these two systems are distinguished only by the motivations that sustain them and not in terms of any intrinsic differences in the content or objectives of the work involved. Also interesting is that labour as paid work in contemporary capitalist economies is specialised to an extraordinary degree, whereas the opposite is true of domestic labour. Thus, in Britain, more than 20,000 distinct occupations are now officially recognised in employment statistics. In the domestic sphere, in contrast, the trend appears to have been, if anything, in the other direction. Even the simple traditional task divisions and specialisations based on gender are becoming blurred and male as well as female household members are increasingly expected to become, however reluctantly, generalists.

SOCIAL REPRODUCTION

With respect to these two aspects of the socioeconomic system—the division of labour, and division of the spoils of labour—what happens over the course of childhood is important for two kinds of reason. First, as already noted, division of the spoils is not achieved through coerced compliance but through a degree of willing acquiescence. The foundations for this acquiescence are laid over the course of childhood and are to be found in the understandings children develop about social classes, wealth, poverty, and income differentials, and the explanations they adopt and moral judgements they make about these.

Second, divisions of labour—and more particularly, the allocation of particular individuals to particular roles within society's economic systems—depend on active participation in the process of allocation by the individuals concerned. Unlike ants, we are not born predestined for certain economic roles in our communities; indeed, the variety of and continual change in human economic arrangements reflects the almost limitless adaptability of humans to adapt to different economic roles. But neither are the specific roles we each perform assigned to us without our consent. It would, of course, be simple-minded and simply wrong to imply that each individual freely decides to do just what he or she wants. Nor should it be forgotten that the economic position any individual occupies as an adult is, in broad outline, highly predictable from the social class into which that individual is born. But this predictability remains an empirical observation in need of explanation. As to what produces it, and what in general underlies the allocation of individuals to economic roles, the answer is likely to be that opportunity structures and preferences interact to produce the patterns observed. Unpacking the processes in all their complex details is far beyond the scope of this chapter. What we can address, however, are some parts of the process. Children from working-class and middle-class backgrounds so often end up as adults in working-class and middle-class occupations respectively, in part because of choices they have previously made in childhood and adolescence. And these choices, we suggest, will, in their turn, have been moulded by beliefs and understandings that have been developed about employment and occupations.

Our aspiration in this chapter is to set out what is currently known about children's understanding of social stratification and occupational groupings. But we also wish to consider how their understanding can be explained, and this necessarily takes us into the realm of theory: What theoretical framework provides the most adequate account of development in this domain of social knowledge? In particular we shall contrast the claims of cognitive developmental theory with those of a "sociogenetic" approach (cf. Moscovici, 1976).

PERCEPTIONS OF SOCIAL CLASS AS A CONTRAST BETWEEN WEALTH AND POVERTY

Social scientists have found it difficult to agree on a single definition of social class, but in discussions of social stratification three concepts are typically distinguished, those of occupation, class, and status (e.g., Gerth & Mills, 1953). Thus, individuals may or may not have occupations—activities pursued on a regular basis as their major source of income—but a social class position is often attributed to entire families and not just to those within them who have occupations. Class positions, Gerth and Mills propose, have to do with the amount and sources of income available to families. Status refers to the relative prestige or deference individuals and families are accorded. Both the social scientist and the lay member of society expect these three attributes to be related, even if the former recognises the complications and ambiguities involved.

The classical notion of social class, was articulated by Marx but used well before him by Adam Smith (in 1776), who defined broad classes in terms of their distinctive income sources. The aristocracy or upper class derived income from inherited property—rents from land. The middle class derived income from business profits (or in Marxist terms, ownership of the means of production). The lower or working class derived income from wages. This simple, three-tiered system is still reflected in our stereotypes of class but has long ceased to be a reality. Three things have changed. Inheritance taxes and a sharp decline in the value of land rents and have destroyed the economic dominance of a land-owning class. The bourgeoisie class of business owners has largely been replaced in economic and political significance by a cadre of professional managers. Finally, the wage-earning category has expanded substantially, but of much more importance it has become highly differentiated internally. Thus, the different income *sources* barely correspond at all to differences in income *level*; the variance within the "old" categories, and particularly within the wage-earning category, is much more substantial than variance between the categories. Thus, remuneration from employment contracts at the beginning of the 1990s was on average at least 35 times greater at the top of large companies in Britain that that at the bottom (Will, 1991)[1], and the weekly salary of many premier league footballers currently exceeds the yearly salary of most university teachers.

One consequence is that although we may continue to talk of social classes, as if there really are internally homogeneous strata of people, each separated from adjacent strata by sharp discontinuities, the current reality is continuous variation along a scale of relative wealth, privilege, and prestige. And the key determinant of placement on this continuum is not the source of a person's income but the nature of their occupation. Nonetheless, we find it less easy to order our representations of the world in terms of variations along a continuous scale than in terms of discrete categories (cf. Tajfel, 1969), and the social categories of class continue to be significant.

---

[1] Will actually compares the average for CEOs of large corporations with the income of the "average worker"; using the same basis for comparison the difference is nearer 100-fold for the USA (and he notes that one major corporation had paid its CEO 1200 times as much as an employee starting at the bottom of the company).

This is particularly apparent in younger children's representations of the socioeconomic structure of society. They may not now use the language of social classes to represent this structure but they do recognise and can articulate concepts of wealth and poverty. Moreover, once children have recognised that such differences exist, they embark upon attempts to make sense of these, to explain them. The youngest children included in most of the published research have been 5- to 6-year-olds (e.g., Connell, 1977; Danziger, 1958; Furby, 1979; Jahoda, 1959), perhaps because questioning younger children has been uninformative, but perhaps more so because children are conveniently available in schools from this age. Whatever the reason, little can be said with any certainty about the views of younger children, but 5- to 6-year-olds do have some awareness of social and economic differences.

Children at this age represent economic differences in terms of what Connell (1977) aptly called dramatic contrasts. Their representations are anchored in the extremes of wealth and poverty; the oppositions in childhood literature of princes and paupers, palaces and hovels, rags and riches, reflect these extreme contrasts. Looking at the detail of children's representations, Jahoda (1959) reported awareness of differences in housing, clothing, and lifestyle among Scottish 6- to 7-year-olds, and Furby (1979) similarly noted perceptions of differences in material possessions among American 6-year-olds. At this age, however, children can give very little by way of explanation for the differences they describe. Jahoda's 6- to 7-year-olds did refer to the types of jobs people had but did not systematically make any connection to earnings. Furby's 6-year-olds did make this connection, attributing differences in possessions to earning differences as well as to having better jobs or just having more money. But they did not see any *necessary* connection between jobs and money; rather they seemed to assume that if people wanted or needed more money they were able to have it. Both Jahoda and Furby found that clearer connections were being made between types of work, income, and material wealth by age 8 to 9 years.

These age-related trends were confirmed in a larger-scale study sampling a wider range of ages (720 children aged 6, 11, 14, and 17 years) by Leahy (1981, 1983, 1990). He described three stages in the development of thinking about wealth and poverty: peripheral, central, and sociocentric. At the "peripheral" stage, which dominated the thinking of 6-year-olds, wealth and poverty were defined purely in terms of material possessions and external attributes—appearance and behaviour. These features of thinking at this age have been replicated by Bombi (1996) using a different approach. She had 6- to 11-year-olds draw rich and poor people. Not every child produced two recognisably distinct images, but this may have more to do with their drawing skills than with the absence of distinct images in mind.

The most commonly employed indicator of the two categories was clothing, followed by objects such as jewellery.

Turning to explanations, Leahy found that in the youngest group these tended towards circularity in so far as they were provided at all: Rich people are rich because they have money. Among the 11- and 14-year-olds, central descriptions and explanations became much more common, while description tended to become integrated with explanation. Thus, the differences between rich and poor now included internal and more psychological qualities such as intelligence and ability, and explanations for the differences were offered in terms of the different kinds of work done by rich and poor people respectively, work differing in the education, effort, or talents required. The final, sociocentric stage, invoking political power, prejudice and exploitation, limited opportunity structures, and life chances to explain wealth and poverty, was apparent only among the oldest members of Leahy's sample, but even at this age it remained a minority perspective.

This pattern was largely replicated by Ng and Jhaveri (1988) in New Zealand and India. However, they did find at least one difference pointing to the influence of culture. Indian children more frequently gave fatalistic explanations for differences in wealth. This does raise questions about the influence of the sociocultural environment in which a child grows up. The almost complete absence in Leahy's sample of any references to sources of wealth, or lack of it, other than occupation-based income may reflect current realities. But inheritance, rents from property, and earnings on invested capital have not entirely ceased to be consequential in their impact on wealth differences, and fate—or luck—is no more obvious an influence on the fortunes of people in India than it is in the United States or New Zealand. Thus one question raised is whether explanations are favoured because, within a given cultural context, they provide credible and easily grasped justifications for inequalities rather than because they have the virtue of being right. On the other hand, magical explanations for wealth, heavily promoted in fairy tales, are only rarely given credence even by the youngest children. The process of legitimising inequalities of wealth is evidently not straightforward, but we will later explore other options for its explanation.

THE CHILD'S THEORY OF LABOUR: OCCUPATIONS AND EARNINGS

The relationship between occupation and income—namely the manner in which work generates income—is not transparent and simple even for adults. The simplest kind of connection arises when an individual is paid directly by a customer or client for a service or a product. But though this might once have been a relatively common way of deriving income from work it is now a minority solution (and craftsmen selling the products of their labour are less common than professionals selling advice). A more complex exchange arises where the income is derived from profits running a business (though even in the case of direct payment for services or products, costs and losses must be set against earnings to determine net income). But in the case of most occupations, those pursued by at least 85% of the employed population, the income takes the form of a salary or wage. Not surprisingly, young children are most likely to conclude that the income from any occupation is the money that customers pay, for example to shop workers or bus drivers (e.g., Berti & Bombi, 1988). Understanding the concept of profit, and therefore the possibility of deriving income from profits, comes later (Berti, Bombi, & de Beni, 1986a).

Equally challenging for children is the concept of employment or the wage–labour contract made between one individual (an employee) and another (employer). We should not be greatly surprised about this given that there is nothing whatsoever natural in this arrangement. The idea that people might in effect sell their time to be used by the buyer as he or she wished was, when first introduced little more than 200 years ago, so alien a notion to the population of the time that only those in the weakest economic circumstances and without other options could be induced to accept it (Perrow, 1986). The people most likely to be in this position were paupers and criminals. Now we take it entirely for granted, but young children do not.

Children initially, which is to say prior to the age of 8 years, think of an employer or "boss" as someone who pays people for their work (Berti & Bombi, 1988; Danziger, 1958; Strauss, 1952). Such people are assumed to have the means to make the payment either because they are rich or because the government has given them money. Missing at this point is a recognition that employees are also in a subordinate relationship. An understanding of the authority relations that are a key feature of many waged occupations comes later (e.g., Furth, 1980) as does a recognition of the distinction between ownership and control of the means of production (Berti, Bombi, & Lis, 1986b).

INCOME AND PRESTIGE

As we have seen, children are increasingly likely as they grow older to link inequalities in wealth to differences in the kinds of work people do. Some appreciation that money earned varies with the nature of the job is apparent very early. Duveen and Shields (1985), for example, found that children between 3½ and 5 years would award more pay to people seen as powerful, such as police officers. However, it is not until at least 8 years that children begin to produce a crude rank ordering that approximates the realities of income inequalities (Emler & Dickinson, 1985). Representations of the rank order are progressively refined and differentiated so that by early adolescence rankings of jobs in terms of both income and prestige are similar to those of both adults and official measures of socioeconomic status (Dickinson, 1990).

As to how children are able to rank order occupations in terms of income, it seems likely that relative income is inferred from the apparent relative status or prestige of different jobs. In practice, information about status is much the more visible of the two. As Gerth and Mills (1953) observed, status is the deference shown by one person to another. Deference must by definition, therefore, be a visible feature of every social encounter. As children learn to interpret verbal and nonverbal cues, so they will be able to analyse the status order revealed through encounters between people in different occupations. To begin with, high status may be confused with place-specific authority, leading to errors of the kind made by Duveen and Shields's young subjects. But these anomalies are progressively sorted out as observations accumulate, and further visible status markers such as clothing (cf. Bombi, 1996) and accent are decoded. Moreover, television undoubtedly plays a part. Even those fortunate children who have never seen the inside of a hospital or doctor's surgery are likely to have seen dramatisations of these settings on television and to have noticed the greater deference displayed towards doctors than towards nurses or receptionists. One nice illustration of television as instructor in status differentials comes from an early study by Himmelweit, Oppenheim, and Vince (1958). They found that children without access to television associated status with locally prestigious jobs such as factory foreman, whereas children with such access were more likely to recognise the higher status of professional jobs. Television is also a far from perfect instructor given its biased sampling of the occupational spectrum. DeFleur and DeFleur (1967) compared children's knowledge of personal contact occupations (teacher, shopkeeper, etc.), TV contact occupations (lawyer, reporter), and other occupations with which children normally have no contact, such as accountant or engineer. They found that level of knowledge of occupations in the first two categories was virtually indistinguishable from 8 years onwards, but remained substantially lower into the teens for the third category.

We should also remember that relative occupational status is by no means perfectly correlated with relative incomes. So using the first to guess at the second will generate errors. Nonetheless, the relative social standing of different jobs does seem to be the main influence on estimates of relative income, a conclusion consistent with the observation that although rank orders of wage estimates can be quite accurate, the absolute sizes of wage estimates are highly inaccurate.

OCCUPATIONAL CHOICE

It seems likely that a growing awareness of social class and occupational status influences the kinds of occupations that children see as appropriate for themselves. For the most part, they learn to reject occupations that offer a much lower status and standard of living than that of their parents, but little is known about the relationship between children's developing understanding of social class and occupational groupings and their occupational aspirations. What is known is that children talk about *choosing* an occupation, and most children explain their preferences in terms of how attractive they find the job rather than how suited they are to the job in terms of their background and abilities. For instance, Dickinson (1986) found that social class predicted the occupational aspirations of adolescent boys, but almost all the boys explained their choices in terms of the intrinsic interest of the jobs. However, Bandura, Barbaranelli, Caprara, and Pastorelli (2001) have recently reported evidence that career preferences in early adolescence are also influenced by the beliefs young people have about their efficacy with respect to different kinds of work.

The process of following the appropriate routes to enter an occupation— developing the necessary competence, qualifications, attitudes and experience—is so steeped in the language of choice that it is difficult to write about this process without referring to choice. In fact, most people end up in occupations that are highly predictable on the basis of gender, parents' occupations, schooling, area of residence, and ability, and it is probably more accurate to speak of people being channeled into occupations rather than choosing occupations.

Children are aware of constraints on occupational choice but they tend to be optimistic about their own occupational chances. Simmons and Rosenberg (1971) found that working-class American teenage boys were well aware of socioeconomic and racial disadvantages and cynical about the idea of equal opportunities, and yet 97% of them still felt they had "as good or better a chance to rise in the world than most". Children recognise that different people have different opportunities and that factors like academic ability, class, and ethnicity are associated with occupational outcomes, but they seem to mould their aspirations to what they think is appropriate or achievable and continue to talk in terms of personal choice. When black university students were asked why they would not consider a particular occupation in which black people were under-represented, they were more likely to justify their rejection in terms of lack of interest in the job rather than barriers related to ethnicity or ability (Emmanuel, 2003). Part of the explanation for this paradox may lie in Jencks's observation that children know little about most jobs and change their choice of desired career often. Consequently they probably do not notice when many of their ambitions move out of their reach (Jenks, 1972).

The continuing illusion of choice is also preserved by the way in which occupational choices are gradually and subtly circumscribed. Gottfredson (1981) argued that occupational aspirations are tailored stage by stage to fit our socioeconomic characteristics, abilities, and interests. Gender is the first factor to limit occupational choice. Children start to become aware of the gender bias of many jobs just as they are developing their own gender identity and the result is the sex-typing of occupational choices. Later, awareness of class, ethnic, and educational differences in occupations orientates children towards jobs with role models similar to themselves. By the time children come to consider what occupations might match their particular interests, values, and abilities, usually after the age of 13 years, they have already limited the range of occupations by gender, class, and academic level of achievement. However, the limitation—the ruling of which jobs are applicable and which are not—has seemed like a personal choice rather than a social structural constraint on choice.

Just as there are developmental trends in children's representations of occupational income and prestige, so are there changes with age in their representations of the occupational opportunity structure. Dickinson (1999) used character vignettes that manipulated the factors of social class background, academic achievement, and personal interests to investigate 7- to 16-year-old children's understanding of the opportunity structure. She found that children aged 7 to 11 years only related personal interests to occupational outcomes. From the age of 11 years the children started to relate social class background and academic achievement as well as per- sonal interests to occupational outcomes. The general developmental trend was from picking one factor—personal interests—to predict occupational choice to using a combination of factors—personal interests, social class background, and academic achievement—to predict occupational choice. The change at around 11 years in the way the children perceived the opportunity structure fits with Leahy's (1981, 1983, 1990) observed changes at this age in the way children explained wealth and poverty. Children start to recognise that occupations produce different incomes and require different levels of education. They are beginning to represent occupations as key elements in the distribution of wealth and the organised division of labour. The increased understanding of the relationship between educa- tional achievements and occupational outcomes may also reflect the struc- ture of the educational system in Britain. At 11 years, children enter secondary school and begin preparation for the qualifications that will grade their later entry into the labour market.

Dickinson's findings provide another reason why children might be optimistic about their own occupational chances. The 11- to 16-year-olds recognised academic achievements as a constraint on occupational choice (good marks at school predicted the higher status occupation and bad marks at school predicted the lower status occupation), but they regarded social class background only as a *potential* advantage. They seemed to think that coming from a higher social class background could help people to get better jobs, either by encouraging them to pursue more prestigious careers or by providing resources to support career development. They did not relate a lower social class background to the achievement of lower status jobs. This finding fits with Evans' (1993, 1997) findings from studies of adult perceptions of the opportunity structure. Adults in these studies proposed that life chances are influenced by socioeconomic factors, but they also believed that disadvantage can be overcome by individual effort and ability. The children in Dickinson's study had yet to understand social class background as a limitation on life chances, but that might be because this kind of sociological understanding doesn't usually emerge until after 16 years of age. Certainly Leahy found that only a small proportion of the 14- to 17-year-olds in his study related socioeconomic factors to the creation of wealth and poverty.

EXPLANATIONS AND JUSTIFICATIONS

Children's explanations for income inequalities initially go little beyond describing particular jobs (Dickinson, 1986; Gunn, 1964; Weinstein, 1958), though from the age of 7 children do begin to refer to particular jobs in value-laden terms such as "important", "good", or "dirty" (Dickinson, 1986; Jahoda, 1959). From the age of 8, explicitly comparative judgements about work—working "harder" or "better"—are used more consistently (Berti & Bombi, 1988) and from 10 years onwards, elements of these descriptions are increasingly applied to distinguish and rank-order jobs. One job is seen to require more effort than another, to be more difficult, to involve longer hours, more skill, greater danger, more responsibility, or higher qualifications, or to make a more valuable contribution to society (Dickinson, 1986; Furnham & Cleare, 1988; Lauer, 1974; Leahy, 1983). By adolescence, market forces may occasionally also be invoked to explain income inequalities (Dickinson, 1986) but such references remain quite rare even in adulthood (Dickinson & Sell-Trujillo, 1998). A conspicuous feature of this trend is the increasing number of dimensions along which different jobs can be ordered and compared. Thus, no single criterion emerges as the key to explaining income inequalities.

   The development of judgements as to what are appropriate levels of income for different kinds of work takes a slightly different course. Children's first inclinations tend to be, if anything, egalitarian; they prefer income equality and judge inequalities to be unfair (e.g., Connell, 1977), even though they recognise that jobs differ in various ways. Thereafter, they shift to the view that inequalities of income are appropriate. Thus, in Connell's Australian sample, income inequality was judged unfair up to age 8 but thereafter was increasingly likely to be judged as fair. The same trend has been reported in virtually every study of children's views about inequalities of income and wealth (Baldus & Tribe, 1978; Cummings & Taebel, 1978; Emler & Dickinson, 1985; Lauer, 1974; Leahy, 1983; Siegal, 1981). Siegal found that justifications for income inequality were closer to Marxism than to capitalism; when he asked children to distribute money to different recipients, their recommended allocations primarily reflected the perceived relative needs of the recipients (see also Sevón & Weckström, 1989; Winocur & Siegal, 1982). Older children, however, offered justifications that emphasised differential inputs, not differential needs. Most other studies find only these kinds of justifications, following the earlier preference for equality. Connell's older respondents, for example, were likely to say that wealthy people had worked harder to achieve their wealth. The participants in our research (Emler & Dickinson, 1985) and in Leahy's (1983) study drew upon many of the same criteria to justify income inequalities as they had invoked to explain them, notably differential effort, social value, and educational requirements.

It is notable that justifications for income inequality are dominated throughout development by considerations of fairness. This may, of course, reflect the questions that researchers in this area have chosen to ask, and we should beware that our research findings can reflect the limitations of these choices. Research with adult populations indicates that different payment allocations for work are recommended depending on the allocator's primary goal. Stake (1983) showed that if allocators are asked to prioritise harmony within a work group they tend to ignore contribution differences and allocate equally. If they are asked to maximise fairness, they match payment to performance. But if asked to prioritise productivity they tend to link allocations to relative capabilities. Quite possibly a focus on the risk of labour shortages in strategic occupations could lead people, both adults and children, to the conclusion that in a free market certain income inequalities are going to be justified on the grounds of social need. But the fact is that such justifications rarely emerge spontaneously when young people are asked to decide whether differences in income or wealth are justified. Instead, their primary preoccupation seems to be fairness.

CHILDHOOD CONSTRUCTION OF A THEORY OF DISTRIBUTIVE SOCIAL JUSTICE

It is clear that the way that social inequalities come to be represented over the course of childhood and adolescence is closely bound up with an implicit if not explicit theory of social justice. There have been two serious attempts to explain not only why but how such a theory is developed over the course of childhood and adolescence.

According to Lerner's (1977) "just world" theory, people's beliefs and perceptions are strongly shaped by an underlying view that the world ought to be a just place, and anticipates that this "ought" frequently becomes an "is". Lerner's point is not that justice is indeed at work in society, producing deserved inequalities, but that people wish to believe this is so and consequently accord legitimacy to whatever circumstances obtain. Lerner has also explicitly located the origins of belief in a just world in early childhood, arguing that children first develop a personal contract with the world, an expectation that immediate gratifications can be deferred in exchange for longer-term benefits. The terms of the contract are that one will, in the long run, receive what one is entitled to receive. This is then supplemented by a social contract, as the child comes to recognise that others also need to operate in terms of similar personal contracts (Simmons, 1981). Lerner's theory directly addresses the issue of motivation, proposing that people need to believe that inequalities are justified, particularly those they can do little to change, and so when inequalities are encountered they are impelled to search for good reasons for these.

Cognitive constructivism (Piaget, 1954) provides an account drawing upon its more general analysis of the development of social knowledge. The central idea is that children construct their own intellectual competencies through their interactions with the environment. These competencies are essentially problem-solving instruments, progressively constructed and perfected over the first 15 years of life. The progression is in the direction of increasingly logical or internally consistent mental operations, increasingly adapted to the external world. The focus for research within this theoretical perspective has gradually expanded from an interest in the manner in which these intellectual competencies are applied to make sense of the natural world to include interest in children's representations of the social world. The underlying assumption is that what individuals think and believe, about social arrangements as well as about natural phenomena, is a function of the capacities they have developed to reason about and make sense of available evidence.

Consider next the kind of account this offers for children's developing understanding of social inequalities related to occupation. Cognitive developmental theory offers two relevant models. The first, represented in the work of Furth (1978a, 1978b, 1980) and Jahoda (1984) treats social life as presenting children with problems of social description. Social life is structured around institutions and practices that embody systems of relations. Social knowledge is therefore an understanding of these systems. The relevant systems are assumed to be objective, to the extent that knowledge about them is more or less adequate or correct. As Furth (1978a, p. 120) says:

> Societal institutions . . . present themselves to adults as objectively given, with some clear-cut rules of how they work. Adults could easily recognise a list of statements relative to business, occupational roles, government or community. To understand societal institutions means precisely to understand this framework.

For Jahoda, the relationships involved in buying and selling of commodities contain a necessary and discoverable logic. What the individual child gradually comes to recognise is this necessity. Labour markets are likewise systems of relations and likewise with a necessary structure. This model can plausibly be applied to children's developing knowledge of employment relations as a process in which children progressively construct a veridical model of this system of relationships, along the way integrating an increasingly complex and extensive set of concepts relating to money, buying and selling, and profit. Note that this model emphasises a basic parallel between the social and the material environment: The former, like the latter, has objective properties that can be objectively understood.

A second model emphasises a different kind of parallel. Just as there are properties intrinsic to matter that determine the effects of manipulations effected upon it, so there are qualities intrinsic to human nature that determine the viability of different kinds of relationships between people. One such is the exchange relationship. In this context the development of social knowledge entails construction of rational principles for the reconciliation of competing interests. These are rules or principles for achieving distributive justice, an allocation of finite resources that all parties involved can regard as fair (cf. Damon, 1977). Research does point to a clear sequence in the development of such principles, consistent with the complexity of the mental operations involved.

Piaget (1932) identified three developmentally ordered forms of thinking about distributive justice. The first or "authority" stage defines a fair outcome as whatever outcome parents or other adults decree. The second stage, appearing from 7 years onwards, defines a fair outcome as one producing strict equality of outcomes. The third stage, seldom apparent before age 10 among the children studied by Piaget, links outcomes to inputs. Thus fair outcomes are no longer necessarily equal outcomes; the relative merit of claimants is also considered. Piaget described this as the "equity" stage, but it includes consideration of relative needs as well as relative contributions.

The first authority stage did not emerge in later work by Damon (1975, 1977, 1981) but he did find the shift with age from equality to relative deservingness, albeit at an earlier age than Piaget had found. One can see that, cognitively, equality is the simpler principle; one need only match outcomes, even if this does require the capacity to count or to measure. Piagetian equity in contrast requires comparison, and some rank ordering, of claimants or inputs as well as a matching of these to rank-ordered outcomes or allocations. One can also anticipate that other developing insights will refine judgements of relative merit. So, for example, the ability to judge and compare intentions allows children to consider relative effort as a basis for relative deservingness (Weiner & Peter, 1973).

There may also be a further stage beyond the relative deservingness Piaget and Damon identified. Reviewing the literature on developmental changes in children's allocation decisions, Hook and Cook (1979) make a persuasive case for three distinct, developmentally ordered patterns. The first two are respectively the already familiar patterns of equality and equity as a rank ordering of recipients. They call this latter "ordinal" equity and find that it predominates between 6 and 12 years. It requires the ability to make ordinal comparisons on two dimensions. The further step is to make allocations directly proportional to inputs. This "proportional" equity, they argue, is unlikely to appear before the age of 13 because it requires a more complex mental operation, the computation of ratios. According to Inhelder and Piaget (1958), this ability is a part of formally operational thinking, the highest level of intellectual development.

This cognitive developmental analysis of distributive justice does quite a good job of accounting for key features in children's developing views about occupational status and income inequalities. It anticipates the observed pattern in which equality is initially preferred but is then replaced with a preference for inequalities justified on the grounds of variations in contributions. But is the job it does good enough? Do we need to look no further to explain the pattern? If it is good enough then it carries an important message about social reproduction, and more specifically the reproduction of a hierarchical socioeconomic system in which considerable inequalities of wealth attract widespread acceptance. The implication is that a commitment to rational principles of justice emerges naturally from the process of intellectual growth and that these rational principles support and indeed require these inequalities.

LIMITS TO CONSENSUS—CLASS-BASED DIFFERENCES

There are several reasons to doubt that the pattern of understanding observed is nothing other than the natural result of scrutinising social reality with increasingly well-organised intellectual resources (see also Emler & Dickinson, 1993). One problem is the disappearance of the principle of relative need. Piaget and others show that this principle begins to inform children's judgements about allocation decisions, at least in simple cases within their own direct experience, from the age of 8 to 10 years. But it is briefly and barely applied to judgements about incomes. Does this merely reflect the temporary over-generalisation of a recently learned principle beyond its proper domain of application? Does it disappear from the employment domain because children come to recognise that different domains are governed by different exchange and distribution principles? If so, is there something natural or logical about these domain differences? Is it more natural for wage–labour exchanges to be governed by free-market principles but for relative needs to be addressed through a taxation and benefits system? Or are these choices rooted in our cultural and political history as a society? We incline towards this latter answer, though explaining why it is a more satisfactory answer is not easy.

Useful steps in this direction can be made, however, by considering the implications of a larger fly in the ointment. There are limits to the consensus about socioeconomic inequalities and their legitimacy, and these limits are consistently related to individuals' own positions within this system of inequalities. Several studies point to class-related differences in children's consciousness of social differences (e.g., Coles, 1977; Connell, 1977; DeFleur & DeFleur, 1967; Stacey, 1987; Tudor, 1971); effectively, children from privileged backgrounds are more conscious of the differences than children of the same age from more disadvantaged background.

In our own research we have found three linked differences between children from different social backgrounds (Dickinson, 1990; Emler & Dickinson, 1985). First, middle-class children perceive much greater income differentials between occupations than do working-class children. The former's estimates of absolute incomes were still far from accurate in our research but estimates of differentials were more realistic. Middle-class children's greater appreciation of the scale of inequalities was also reflected in their better appreciation of some of the economic consequences of income differences, for example housing. Second, all children were inclined to view income differences as fair and, increasingly so inclined with age, but working-class children were less resistant than middle-class children to the proposition that greater equality might be fairer still. Also, by virtue of their rather different beliefs about the scale of the differences involved, their judgements of fairness were not judgements of the same outcomes; in effect, middle-class children were deciding that rather large differences were fair, and working-class children that small differences were fair. Third, middle-class children generated a greater number and range of both explanations and justifications for income inequalities. In sum, middle-class children seemed better informed about income inequalities, more committed to them, and able to offer more extensive justifications for them.

Burgard, Cheyne, and Jahoda (1989) attempted a replication of parts of the Emler and Dickinson (1985) study in West Germany (the participants in our research were Scottish). They found that income estimates were related to children's age but not to their social class background. Their different results may have arisen because social class differences are, or were, less pronounced in Germany or because class background was operationalised in different ways in the two studies. For example, we compared children in state and independent schools whereas Burgard et al.'s children were all in the same school system. Whatever the reason for this particular result, we have replicated the pattern we found earlier in studies in the United States and in France (Emler, Ohana, & Dickinson, 1990). Moreover, some similar effects of social background have been reported in other studies, including effects on explanations (Leahy, 1981) and judgements (Leiser, Sevon, & Levy, 1990).

Cognitive developmentalists, however, point out that class differences of these kinds do not represent a threat to the cognitive developmental account. Enright and colleagues (Enright, Enright, Mannheim, & Harris, 1980) reported a social class difference in children's use of equity as a principle in simple distribution tasks; middle-class children were more likely to apply this principle than working-class children. Their explanation is that "lower class children lag behind their middle class cohorts in distributive justice reasoning" (p. 561). In other words, all children are on the same developmental pathway, but at any age some have made more progress along the path than others. Jahoda (1984) makes the same point when he argues that the rate at which children develop knowledge about the socioeconomic system will depend upon how information-rich and intellectually stimulating is the social environment they inhabit. Working-class children are presumably disadvantaged in these respects.

If these explanations for the observed class differences are correct, then class differences should parallel age differences. In other words, older working-class children should resemble younger middle-class children; the same developmental milestones are passed by the two groups but at different average ages. But this is not the case. The class differences we observed were not related to age. Our view is that there is a case for a rather different account of children's development of social knowledge, including their knowledge of occupations and social differences (see Dickinson & Emler, 1996; Emler, 1987; Emler & Ohana, 1993). In the next section we set out this case and address some of the criticisms it faces from the perspective of cognitive developmental theory.

CONSTRUCTING ACCOUNTS OF SOCIAL INEQUALITIES: A SOCIOGENETIC VIEW

The essence of the sociogenetic view is that the generation of knowledge is a social process. This includes the generation of knowledge, both of the material and the social worlds, in the minds of individual children. Thus their understandings of such matters as social inequalities are constructed within and derive from the social groups to which they belong. Children do not independently construct explanations for income differences; rather the social groups to which they belong present them with explanations, which they then adopt. We also propose that different social groups may construct and disseminate different interpretations of the social world. Thus social classes may not have the same reality as clearly stratified and internally homogeneous social groups that they once did, but children whose families occupy the lower rungs of the income ladder, who live in state-owned housing in a poor area of the city, and who go to a neighbourhood school, inhabit very different social worlds from those of children growing up in wealthy families, dwelling in private housing in a prosperous area, and attending a private school. We anticipate that these different social worlds provide their inhabitants with rather different intellectual resources for making sense of their own and others' economic circumstances. We also suggest that the relevant resources will be more extensively developed in more economically advantaged social groups.

Why is this more plausible than the conclusion that when asked, for example, about the fairness of income inequalities, individuals—children and adults—will examine the relative inputs and consult a principle of distributive justice such as equity to generate an answer? One reason is that this latter alternative is so *im*plausible. When children have been shown to apply an equity or contributions rule in making payment allocations themselves this has been in response to cases in which the inputs are precise, simple, quantified, and known. For example, one "employee" may have painted 6 feet of fence while another has painted only 4 feet (cf. Leventhal & Anderson, 1970). In the case of occupations in the real world, inputs will be complex and imprecise mixes of task requirements and personal qualifications, almost impossible to quantify and only vaguely recognised by most people. But even if the inputs were known with any certainty, the relevant weight to be attached to each is undecidable on logical grounds alone. Should effort count more than job difficulty, or physical risk, or level of responsibility, or hours worked, or training required, or the social value of the work? Finally, the equity formula (cf. Hook & Cook, 1979) requires quantified inputs, yet hardly any of these inputs can be quantified in any meaningful way.

The following, we believe, is a more plausible story and more consistent with empirical observations. Different societies construct different solutions to basic problems such as the division of labour and allocations of the fruits of labour (though globalisation may be eroding these differences). Insofar as the solutions involve wage–labour systems and income differentials, societies will also construct accounts of these solutions, described by Tajfel

(1984) as social myths, which both explain and justify them. Children become familiar with the myths that are dominant in their cultures and social groups and increasingly adept at drawing upon these to justify the income inequalities they observe. In this respect Lerner's (1977) view seems apposite: The fairness of the inequalities is not a conclusion reached after comparing inputs but a motivated presumption that then prompts a search for supporting arguments. It is striking that children so frequently use clichés surrounding particular jobs to provide these arguments: "managers have a lot of responsibility", "fire officers do a dangerous job" (Dickinson, 1986). There is no logical basis for selecting these and not other standards of comparison in these instances; their use has more to do with social norms about what constitute appropriate rationalisations in particular cases.

It is also clear that children learn more than one type of justification per job. By 10 or 11 years of age they can draw on several different criteria to debate the fairness of wage differentials. For instance, a child might argue that a road sweeper is poorly paid because he doesn't need many qualifications but should be paid more for the social value of his work in keeping the streets clean and preventing disease (Dickinson, 1986). Effectively, children learn to draw on the discourses surrounding pay in a rhetorical fashion to construct the arguments they wish to make (cf. Billig, 1987). The available repertoire of arguments, however, varies between social groups. We still need to explain why the repertoire varies with social class background, and moreover varies in size, and indeed why knowledge of inequalities differs between classes. But first we should address some potential objections to this account.

THE CONSTRUCTIVIST CRITIQUE OF SOCIAL TRANSMISSION: A CRITICAL APPRAISAL

The dominant position of cognitive developmental theory as an account of the child's development of social knowledge has rested upon its critique of its principle theoretical competitors, socialisation or social transmission theories (Gibbs & Schnell, 1985). This critique can be summed up in terms of five contrasting views of the developmental process and its results (see Turiel, 1983).

First, socialisation theories accord the child a passive role in its own development; evidence and cognitive developmental theory coincide in the conclusion that the child is in reality active in constructing its knowledge of the world. Second, this active role is apparent in children's spontaneous and independent discovery of knowledge, whether this be knowledge of how social institutions work or of moral principles according to which social relations ought ideally to be regulated. Socialisation theories instead suppose that everything the child knows has been transmitted to it by its social environment. Third, what is transmitted in this way can be quite arbitrary; the success of the transmission process is unrelated to the truth value of what is transmitted. Some critics go further and argue that truths cannot be acquired in this way; children can only grasp valid truths about the world—material or social—to the extent that they have constructed these for themselves. Generally, it is asserted that only cognitive developmental theory provides a satisfactory explanation for the development of nonrelative and nonarbitrary beliefs about the world.

Fourth, socialisation theories do not predict that knowledge will be acquired or developed according to a sequence. They imply instead that children will acquire knowledge in whatever order it happens to be presented to them. In clear contradiction of this supposition, social knowledge is constructed according to a consistent, invariant sequence. Moreover, knowledge construction occurs in discrete stages, each successive stage qualitatively distinct from the preceding one. This well-established stage-like character of sociocognitive development, the critics argue, cannot be explained by social transmission. Fifth, and finally, the notion of socialisation as the social transmission of ideas predicts that different societies and social groups will transmit different ideas to the children who grow up in them. This, the critics point out, is inconsistent with the lack of any clear evidence for such differences; instead one finds the same stages in the same sequence, irrespective of the cultural background or social group membership of the children studied.

The critique succeeded so well in part because social knowledge had never been a focal concern of the theories criticised. Mainstream socialisation theories, such as those based upon psychoanalysis or learning theory, were constructed to explain the acquisition of values, motives, and habits of behaviour, not the acquisition of knowledge. Consequently, they generated no systematic programme of research that might have provided the evidence to challenge these criticisms. Nonetheless, evidence is now available from a variety of sources, pointing to two kinds of flaw in the critique. One is that the theoretical alternatives to cognitive constructivism do not reduce to the single position caricatured as socialisation theory. The other consists of factual errors in the picture of development presented.

The supposition that social transmission necessarily accords a passive role to the child confuses social influence with compliance (cf. Moscovici, 1976). Contemporary theories of social influence predict that the ability of social influence to produce a cognitive change in targets of influence will depend upon the degree to which those target actively processes the content of a persuasive message (Moscovici, 1980; Petty & Wegener, 1998). The prediction has been extensively confirmed by research. The implication is that social transmission of concepts will occur largely to the extent that the child actively engages with the content transmitted.

Research reports have often contained apparently compelling illustrations of children making spontaneous and independent discoveries of knowledge of some or other objective truth about social relations (e.g., Furth, 1978b; Jahoda, 1984; Smetana, 1993). There are two points about these illustrations. One is that illustrations are not demonstrations; in this case, the claim to be demonstrated is that this is the primary, if not the invariable, method by which knowledge is assembled. One can just ask whether this is credible. Our current conditions of life are built upon a vast stock of knowledge about how the world works and how it can be manipulated, but most of us will not in our lifetimes rediscover any of this from scratch (cf. Humphrey, 1976). If we really had to develop our knowledge of the material world in this way, our conditions of life would barely match those of our most primitive ancestors. And what is true of our knowledge of the material world is surely no less likely to be true of our knowledge of the social world (see also Emler, 1998; Emler & Ohana, 1993). In other words, even though we might occasionally make minor discoveries on our own, the primary method of knowledge acquisition is through membership of a social group within which this knowledge is disseminated.

The other point is that the illustrations reflect insights children develop either in response to others' reactions, which are in effect, therefore, influence attempts, or in response to carefully constructed prompts by an interviewer. This Socratic process is, after all, a social process; someone else has to play Socrates—the child's own mind cannot be expected to be its own Socratic foil.

The third constructivist claim, that because children's social knowledge is nonarbitrary it could not be a product of social transmission, is demonstrably wrong. It is entirely possible for children to acquire more objective representations of the material world and more logically coherent patterns of reasoning about this world through a process of social transmission. This has now been demonstrated experimentally on numerous occasions (Botvin & Murray, 1975; Russell, 1981). It has likewise been demonstrated for social knowledge and moral judgements (Leman & Duveen, 1999; Roy & Howe, 1990). There is no incompatibility between the claim that knowledge is acquired through social transmission and the observation that at least some of this knowledge is objective and nonarbitrary.

The fourth claim is much less of a problem than it might appear. We do not dispute that knowledge is structured and organised or that it is assembled in a particular order. The issue is what this implies about the means by which it is assembled. Any maths teacher knows that the subject is best taught in an orderly sequence; simple concepts need to be introduced and mastered before more complex concepts that incorporate these simpler elements. Social experience may not be such a systematic teacher but children cannot be influenced by complex ideas before they have first absorbed the less complex ideas on which these depend. Note, for example, that at the very least, equity involves putting two different kinds of rank order into correspondence. But to do this one must first grasp the idea of a rank order. Contemporary research on social influence again provides informative insights here. This reveals that adults can show all kinds of resistance to social influence. It is not an easy matter to persuade people to adopt new ideas, and there is no reason to expect children to be any different except perhaps in degree. The resistance stems from the fact that neither adult nor child will be cognitively empty in advance of any influence. Influence is hardly ever about introducing something into an empty vessel but about changing or adding to what is already there. And its impact will depend upon the initial cognitive state of the target.

The social influence research literature has highlighted four factors in particular that affect a target's response to an influence attempt. First, influence may threaten the social identity of the target and insofar as it does so it will trigger resistance (cf. Mugny & Papastamou, 1982). This factor has as yet only been touched upon in the context of children's sociocognitive development—mainly with respect to threats to gender identity—and would surely repay more attention in future research. The second factor has likewise received very little attention in this context; individuals are more likely actively to process the content of persuasive messages to the extent that the issue at stake is personally involving or relevant (Petty & Wegener, 1998). We might ask, for instance, what would make the determinants of pay levels highly involving for children.

The third and fourth factors are linked. Insofar as persuasive messages are actively processed by a target, those containing strong arguments are more persuasive than those offering weak arguments (Petty & Wegener, 1998). The research has yet to determine with any clarity what makes an argument strong or weak, but there are reasons to expect that this will be relative to the existing cognitive resources of the target. Among these reasons is that the fourth factor to determine persuasive impact concerns the level of cognitive resources a target is able to bring to bear upon a message. In effect, the target needs to possess sufficient resources to comprehend the message. This is consistent with the observation that social influence is most likely to produce sociocognitive change when the content transmitted differs only minimally from the child's initial cognitive level (Doise & Mugny, 1984; Emler & Glachan, 1985).

There is finally a point to be made here about developmental stages. Many of those who have described children's developing knowledge of society and social institutions have characterised this as a sequence of distinct stages. Arguably this terminology is misleading. The changes observed are of several kinds. They include changes from not understanding something to understanding it. They include changes that involve the addition of some concept to existing ones. They may include application of principles to new domains. And they include the combination or integration of concepts that were previously only applied separately. But they do not involve the replacement of one system of thinking with another qualitatively different system of thinking. Take for example, Leahy's three "stages" in the development of thinking about inequalities of wealth—the peripheral, central, and sociocentric. They are not stages in the strict Piagetian sense so much as a series of additions to the repertoire of ideas that can be drawn upon to make sense of inequalities.

The fifth claim, that there are no consequential cultural or social group differences in social knowledge, only age differences, is also factually wrong. That this assertion ever appeared to be plausible reflects a combination of circumstances: researchers did not systematically look for such differences, used methods that were unlikely to detect them, failed to acknowledge differences when they were found, or reinterpreted them as differences in rate of development (Emler & Ohana, 1993). A further problem is a lack of sufficient historical perspective in developmental psychology. Consequently it is vulnerable to mistaking currently widespread beliefs for human universals rendering the social processes that generated them invisible. Consider, for example, hygiene practices. Children will spontaneously remark upon a connection between lack of cleanliness and the risk of illness (cf. Calvert, 1987). Moreover, there is in reality an objective, nonarbitrary connection between the two. But it is not a self-evident connection that each child has independently discovered and verified for itself. Two hundred years ago it was not even evident to doctors (Paicheler, 1988). If children now almost universally appreciate something akin to the germ theory of disease, this is because the theory has been disseminated within the cultures into which they were born and not because they have each spontaneously constructed this insight. A similar point could be made about the historical relativity of the employee–employer relationship and our current understanding of it, though whether it is also objectively superior to any other way of organising labour is less clear.

Cultural and social group influences can also be shown, however, without recourse to history. For instance, and specifically in the domain of social cognition relevant here, children in collectivist cultures like Japan are more likely than children in Western cultures to draw on parity arguments for determining rewards (Mann, Radford, & Kanagawa, 1985). Nisan (1984) identified a similar contrast, comparing kibbutz and city children in Israel. Snarey (1985), reviewing cross-cultural research on moral reasoning, found that moral arguments emphasising the distribution of rewards according to relative merit are more common among the members of competitive industrialised societies than in more cooperative and communally oriented societies. And we have found that middle-class children are more likely than working-class children to relate pay differentials to qualifications (Dickinson, 1990).

SOME CONCLUDING OBSERVATIONS ON SOCIAL CLASS AND THE UNEQUAL DISTRIBUTION OF SOCIAL KNOWLEDGE

Why do children differing in social background differ in their knowledge and views of social inequalities? We think two distinct social processes are at work here. First, social groups collectively construct accounts of matters that are relevant to their circumstances. It may be that in all societies, privileged social groups need to construct rationalisations of their privilege, even when their position can readily be defended by force. But the need is particularly strong in societies where power is allocated by popular mandate. Arguments for privilege will need to be deployed in the contests for power represented by parliamentary elections, for example. But a particularly important audience for these arguments will be the in-group. The in-group needs to remain convinced of its virtue and must take responsibility for defending its economic position. If we are right this leads to the expectation that arguments for inequality will be most extensively developed within the social group that benefits most from this inequality. But why should children from economically advantaged backgrounds also be much more aware of the scale of inequalities than children from economically disadvantaged backgrounds?

Consistent with observations of greater class consciousness among middle-class and upper middle-class children, we suggest these children—and the social groups to which they belong—are more inclined to organise their knowledge of inequality in terms of social class categories. Tajfel's (1969) analysis of social categorisation makes two relevant points here. First, when social phenomena are categorised greater differences are perceived between categories on any dimensions on which they can be compared. So if occupations are seen as categorised into working class and middle class, manual and nonmanual, or blue collar and white collar, differences between occupations in different categories, such as differences in pay levels, will be emphasised. Second, when people compare their own social category with others they will emphasise the magnitude of any difference that favours their own and de-emphasise any that does not, but only if the difference is perceived to be legitimate. Interestingly, we found (Emler & Dickinson, 1985) that those middle-class children who regarded income differences as *un*fair also perceived the gap between the earnings of middle-class and working-class occupations to be smaller than children from the same social background who regarded such differences as fair.

It is customary to conclude reviews of past research with calls for further inquiries. Only a little of the research we have reviewed here is very recent. Research interests have moved on and elsewhere, perhaps encouraged by the perception that all the relevant questions here have been answered. We doubt that this is the case; there is, for example, still much to be understood about the manner in which social influence processes operate in childhood to construct the child's social knowledge. In the current climate it may nonetheless be difficult to stir up enthusiasm for further studies of knowledge about social inequalities. But let us mention just one significant but unresolved question.

What consequences do the beliefs apparent at the end of childhood actually have? In particular, what are the consequences of the differences observed between children from contrasting social backgrounds? We proposed in the Introduction that beliefs about inequality play a part in the reproduction of inequalities, and more particularly that children from different social backgrounds end up in different occupational strata partly because of what they respectively believe about the relative economic positions of these strata. But is this true? If it is true, it has important implications for the impact of education upon destinations in the labour market. For the present, however, it remains only a speculation.

REFERENCES

Baldus, B., & Tribe, V. (1978). The development of perceptions and evaluations of social inequality among public school children. *Canadian Review of Sociology and Anthropology*, *15*, 50–60.

Bandura, A., Barbaranelli, C., Caprara, G. V., & Pastorelli, C. (2001). Self efficancy beliefs as shapers of children's aspirations and career trajectories. *Child Development*, *72*, 187–206.

Berti, A. E., & Bombi, A. S. (1988). *The child's construction of economics*. Cambridge: Cambridge University Press.

Berti, A. E., Bombi, A. S., & De Beni, R. (1986a). Acquiring economic notions: Profit. *International Journal of Behavioral Development*, *9*, 15–29.

Berti, A. E., Bombi, A. S., & Lis, A. (1986b). The child's conceptions about means of production and their ownership. *European Journal of Social Psychology*, *12*, 221–239.

Billig, M. (1987). *Arguing and thinking: A rhetorical approach to social psychology*. Cambridge: Cambridge University Press.

Bombi, A. S. (1996). Social factors of economic socialization. In P. Lunt & A. Furnham (Eds.), *Economic socialisation: The economic beliefs and behaviours of young people*. Cheltenham, UK: Edward Elgar.

Botvin, G., & Murray, F. B. (1975). The efficacy of peer modelling and social conflict in the acquisition of conservation. *Child Development*, *46*, 796–799.

Burgard, P., Cheyne, W., & Jahoda, G. (1989). Children's representations of economic inequality: A replication. *British Journal of Developmental Psychology*, *7*, 275–287.

Calvert, S. (1987). *Children's representations of hygiene*. Unpublished Doctoral dissertation, University of Dundee, UK.

Coles, R. (1977). *Children of crisis. Vol. 5*. Boston: Little John.

Connell, R. W. (1977). *Ruling class, ruling culture*. Melbourne, Australia: Cambridge University Press.

Cummings, S., & Taebel, D. (1978). The economic socialisation of children: A neo-Marxist analysis. *Social Problems, 26*, 198–210.

Damon, W. (1975). Early conceptions of positive justice as related to the development of logical operations. *Child Development, 46*, 301–312.

Damon, W. (1977). *The social world of the child*. San Francisco: Jossey-Bass.

Damon, W. (1981). The development of justice and self interest during childhood. In M. J. Lerner & S. C. Lerner (Eds.), *The justice motive in social behavior*. New York: Plenum Press.

Danziger, K. (1958). Children's earliest conceptions of economic relationships. *Journal of Social Psychology, 47*, 231–240.

DeFleur, M. L., & DeFleur, L. B. (1967). The relative contribution of television as a learning source for children's occupational knowledge. *American Sociological Review, 32*, 777–789.

Dickinson, J. (1986). *The development of representations of social inequality*. Unpublished PhD thesis, University of Dundee, UK.

Dickinson, J. (1990). Adolescent representations of socio-economic status. *British Journal of Developmental Psychology, 8*, 351–371.

Dickinson, J. (1999). *Developing conceptions of the opportunity structure*. Birkbeck College, London: Department of Organizational Psychology Working Paper.

Dickinson, J., & Emler, N. (1996). Developing ideas about distribution of wealth. In P. Lunt & A. Furnham (Eds.), *Economic socialisation: The beliefs and behaviours of young people* (pp. 47–68). Cheltenham, UK: Edward Elgar.

Dickinson, J., & Sell-Trujillo, L. (1998). Fair pay and pay determination. In P. Taylor-Gooby (Ed.), *Choice and public policy*. Basingstoke, UK: Macmillan.

Doise, W., & Mugny, G. (1984). *The social development of the intellect*. Oxford: Pergamon.

Duveen, G., & Shields, M. (1985). Children's ideas about work, wages and social rank. *Cahiers de Psychologie Cognitif, 5*, 411–412.

Emler, N. (1987). Socio-moral development from the perspective of social representations. *Journal for the Theory of Social Behaviour, 17*, 371–388.

Emler, N. (1998). Sociomoral understanding. In A. Campbell & S. Muncer (Eds.), *The social child*. Hove, UK: Psychology Press.

Emler, N., & Dickinson, J. (1985). Children's representations of economic inequalities: The effects of social class. *British Journal of Developmental Psychology, 3*, 191–198.

Emler, N., & Dickinson, J. (1993). The child as sociologist. In M. Bennett (Ed.), *The child as psychologist: An introduction to the development of social cognition* (Ch. 7, pp. 168–190). Hemel Hempstead, UK: Harvester.

Emler, N., & Glachan, M. (1985). L'edude experimentale du developpement sociocognitif. In G. Mugny (Ed.), *Psychologie sociale du developpement de la connaissance*. Geneva: Peter Lang.

Emler, N., & Ohana, J. (1993). Studying children's social knowledge: Just old wine in new bottles? In G. Breakwell & D. Canter (Eds.), *Empirical approaches to social representations* (pp. 63–89). Oxford: Oxford University Press.

Emler, N., Ohana, J., & Dickinson, J. (1990). Children's representations of social relations. In G. Duveen & B. Lloyd (Eds.), *Social representation and the development of social knowledge* (pp. 47–69). Cambridge: Cambridge University Press.

Emmanuel, M. (2003). *An exploration of the factors influencing the decision to enter the academic labour force: The perception of black students*. MSc dissertation, Department of Organizational Psychology, Birkbeck College, University of London.

Enright, R., Enright, W., Mannheim, L., & Harris, B. E. (1980). Distributive justice and social class. *Developmental Psychology, 16*, 555–563.

Evans, G. (1993). Cognitive models of class structure and explanations of social outcomes. *European Journal of Social Psychology, 23*, 445–464.

Evans, G. (1997). Political ideology and popular beliefs about class and opportunity: Evidence from a survey experiment. *British Journal of Sociology, 48*, 450–470.

Furby, L. (1979). Inequalities in personal possessions: Explanations for and judgments about unequal distributions. *Human Development, 22*, 180–202.

Furnham, A., & Cleare, A. (1988). School children's conceptions of economics: Prices, wages, investments and strikes. *Journal of Economic Psychology, 9*, 467–479.

Furth, H. G. (1978a). Children's societal understanding and the process of equilibration. *New Directions for Child Development, 1*, 101–122.

Furth, H. G. (1978b). Young children's understanding of society. In H. McGurk (Ed.), *Issues in childhood social development*. London: Methuen.

Furth, H. G. (1980). *The world of grown ups*. New York: Elsevier.

Gerth, H., & Mills, C. W. (1953). *Character and social structure: The psychology of social institutions*. New York: Harcourt, Brace & World.

Gibbs, J. C., & Schnell, S. (1985). Moral development "versus" socialization: A critique. *American Psychologist, 40*, 1071–1080.

Gottfredson, L. S. (1981). Circumscription and compromise: A developmental theory of occupational aspirations. *Journal of Counseling Psychology Monograph, 28*, 545–579.

Gunn, B. (1964). Children's conceptions of occupational prestige. *Personnel and Guidance Journal, 42*, 558–563.

Himmelweit, H. T., Oppenheim, A. N., & Vince, P. (1958). *Television and the child: An empirical study of the effects of television on the young*. Oxford: Oxford University Press.

Hook, J., & Cook, T. (1979). Equity theory and the cognitive ability of children. *Psychological Bulletin, 86*, 429–445.

Humphrey, N. (1976). The social function of the intellect. In P. P. G. Bateson & R. A. Hinde (Eds.), *Growing points in ethology*. Cambridge: Cambridge University Press.

Inhelder, B., & Piaget, J. (1958). *The growth of logical thinking from childhood to adolescence*. London: Routledge.

Jahoda, G. (1959). Development of the perception of social differences in children from six to ten. *British Journal of Psychology, 50*, 158–196.

Jahoda, G. (1984). The development of thinking about socio-economic systems. In H. Tajfel (Ed.), *The social dimension. Vol. 1*. Cambridge: Cambridge University Press.

Jencks, C. (1972). *Inequality: A reassessment of the effect of family and schooling in America*. New York: Basic Books.

Lauer, R. H. (1974). Socialization into inequality: Children's perceptions of occupational status. *Sociology and Social Research, 58*, 176–183.

Leahy, R. L. (1981). The development of the conception of economic inequality: Descriptions and comparisons of rich and poor people. *Child Development, 52*, 523–532.

Leahy, R. L. (1983). The development of the conception of economic inequality: II. Explanations, justifications and concepts of social mobility and change. *Developmental Psychology, 19*, 111–125.

Leahy, R. L. (1990). The development of concepts of economic and social inequality. *New Directions for Child Psychology, 46*, 107–120.

Leiser, D., Sevon, G., & Levy, D. (1990). Children's economic socialization: Summarising the cross-cultural comparison of ten countries. *Journal of Economic Psychology, 4*, 209–221.

Leman, P. J., & Duveen, G. (1999). Representations of authority and children's moral reasoning. *European Journal of Social Psychology, 29*, 557–575.

Lerner, M. (1977). The justice motive in social behavior: Some hypotheses as to its origins and forms. *Journal of Personality, 45*, 1–52.

Leventhal, G., & Anderson, D. (1970). Self-interest and the maintenance of equity. *Journal of Personality and Social Psychology, 15*, 312–316.,

Mann, L., Radford, M., & Kanagawa, C. (1985). Cross-cultural differences in children's use of decision rule: A comparison between Japan and Australia. *Journal of Personality and Social Psychology, 49*, 1557–1564.

Moscovici, S. (1976). *Social influence and social change.* London Academic Press.

Moscovici, S. (1980). Towards a theory of conversion behavior. In L. Berkowitz (Ed.), *Advances in experimental social psychology, vol. 13.* New York: Academic Press.

Mugny, G., & Papastamou, S. (1982). Minority influence and psycho-social identity. *European Journal of Social Psychology, 12*, 379–394.

Ng, S. H., & Jhaveri, N. (1988). *Young people's understanding of economic inequality: An Indian-New Zealand comparison.* Paper presented at the XXIV International Congress of Psychology, Sydney, Australia.

Nisan, M. (1984). Distributive justice and social norms. *Child Development, 55*, 1020–1029.

Paicheler, G. (1988). *The psychology of social influence.* Cambridge Cambridge University Press.

Perrow, C. (1986). *Complex organizations: A critical essay* (3rd ed.). New York: Random House.

Petty, J., & Wegener, D. (1998). Attitude change: Multiple roles for persuasion variables. In D. T. Gilbert, S. T. Fiske, & G. Lindzey (Eds.), *Handbook of social psychology, vol. 1* (4th ed.). New York: McGraw-Hill.

Piaget, J. (1932). *The moral judgment of the child.* London: Routledge.

Piaget, J. (1954). *The construction of reality in the child.* New York: Basic Books.

Roy, A., & Howe, C. (1990). Effects of cognitive conflict, socio-cognitive conflict and imitation on children's socio-legal thinking. *European Journal of Social Psychology, 20*, 241–252.

Sevón, G., & Weckström, S. (1989). The development of reasoning about economic events: A study of Finnish children. *Journal of Economic Psychology, 10*, 495–514.

Siegal, M. (1981). Children's perceptions of adult economic needs. *Child Development, 52*, 379–382.

Simmons, C. (1981). Theoretical issues in the development of social justice. In M. J. Lerner & S. C. Lerner (Eds.), *The justice motive in social behavior.* New York: Plenum Press.

Simmons, R. G., & Rosenberg, M. (1971). Functions of children's perceptions of the stratification system. *American Sociological Review, 36*, 235–249.

Smetana, J. (1993). Understanding of social rules. In M. Bennett (Ed.), *The child as psychologist: An introduction to the development of social cognition.* Hemel Hempstead, UK: Harvester.

Snarey, J. (1985). Cross-cultural universality of socio-moral development: A critical review of Kohlbergian research. *Psychological Bulletin, 97*, 202–232.

Stacey, B. (1987). Economic socialization. In S. Long (Ed.), *Annual review of political science, Vol. 2.* Norwood, NJ: Ablex.

Stake, J. (1983). Factors in reward distribution: Allocator motive, gender and Protestant ethic. *Journal of Experimental Social Psychology, 44*, 410–418.

Strauss, A. (1952). The development and transformation of monetary meaning in the child. *American Sociological Review, 53*, 275–286.

Tajfel, H. (1969). Cognitive aspects of prejudice. *Journal of Social Issues, 25*, 79–97.

Tajfel, H. (1984). Intergroup relations, social myths and social justice in social psychology. In H. Tajfel (Ed.), *The social dimension, Vol. 2.* Cambridge: Cambridge University Press.

Tudor, W. (1971). The development of class awareness in children. *Social Forces, 49*, 470–476.

Turiel, E. (1983). *The development of social knowledge: Morality and convention.* Cambridge: Cambridge University Press.

Weiner, B., & Peter, N. (1973). A cognitive-developmental analysis of achievement and moral judgments. *Developmental Psychology, 9*, 290–309.

Weinstein, E. (1958). Children's conceptions of economic stratification. *Sociology and Social Research, 42*, 278–284.

Will, G. (1991, September 2). Corporate raiders. *Boston Globe*, p. 15.

Winocur, S., & Siegal, M. (1982). Adolescents' judgments of economic arrangements. *International Journal of Behavioral Development, 5*, 357–365.

CHAPTER EIGHT

Children's understanding of racial groups

Lawrence A. Hirschfeld
Departments of Anthropology and Psychology, University of Michigan, Ann Arbor, USA

Research in psychology exploring children's understanding of race is principally concerned with the development of racial prejudice, and, particularly in the last decades, with the cognitive processes (like stereotyping, illusory correlation, etc.) that give rise to it. Less effort has been invested in exploring the development of the *concept* of race—the idea that human beings can be exhaustively partitioned into natural categories grounded in inherited biological differences. Several factors have contributed. Racial prejudice plays a crucial role in the organisation of political-economic life and is central to analyses of the nature and scope of social, economic, and psychological inequity. This in itself would doubtless privilege the study of racism as a political belief system over the study of race as a cognitive category.

There is, however, a less obvious factor contributing to this division of research labour; namely, an assumption that racism poses a genuine intellectual and social problem, whereas the concept of race does not. Understanding the causes of racism is not self-evident. After all, societies are not *necessarily* racist, and there is great concern with identifying the factors that determine its emergence and maintenance. Indeed, much study of racism is explicitly concerned with understanding prejudice in order to reduce or eliminate it. In contrast, race as a concept is viewed as essentially a transparent consequence of biological diversity.

The view that racial categories are "easy" to learn follows from what might be termed a "realist" perspective on race widely held among

199

psychologists. On this view, the concept of race is directly derived from readily discernible biological variation, the recognition of which requires relatively low-level processes (a general propensity to categorise coupled with a device for recognising general patterns of perceptual similarity). Race, in short, is what the anthropologist Brent Berlin (1992) says, with reference to nonhuman biological variation, something that "cries out" to be named.

This is not to suggest that the formation of race concepts and race prejudice are considered to be independent phenomena. Since Allport's (1954) classic work, the dominant view seeks to explain racial prejudice as a function of the normal cognitive processes linked to concept or category formation. Prejudice is the regrettable precipitate of the processes of category formation when those processes are applied to person categories. Racial and other social categories are cognitively organised in the same way as object categories. People, in Allport's view (1954, p. 17), "slip so easily into ethnic prejudice" because the vagaries of "natural and common" processes of categorisation in themselves produce bias. For example, the tendency to reduce perceived differences among category members and amplify perceived differences between members of different categories applies both to chromatic colour categories (Kempton & Kay, 1984) and to social colour categories (Sporer, 2001). In short, learning about race is like learning about chairs or ducks, and the way that these categories are formed underlies the emergence of virtually all social prejudice. The overwhelming bulk of subsequent work in psychology has endorsed this domain-general cognitive framework (Hamilton & Trolier, 1986; Hilton & Von Hippel, 1996; Taylor & Fiske, 1978).

In this chapter, I will argue that none of these assumptions is warranted. Instead, I propose that the development of the concept of race is the product of a singular and specialised knowledge structure. Prejudice is less an accidental consequence of general category formation than the conceptual "politics" of this singular and specialised knowledge structure. Prejudice is tethered to race because of the very peculiar nature of racial categories.

THE PROBLEM OF COGNITIVE ARCHITECTURE

The view that racial categories emerge through lower-order cognitive processes that apply to all perceptually based categories is difficult to reconcile with recent work on cognitive architecture. Research from several traditions in cognitive science has converged on a view that the mind is not a general processing device (see Hirschfeld & Gelman, 1994, for a review). This reappraisal of cognitive architecture was in part motivated by problems with the claim that a general notion of similarity is sufficient to account for judgements of similitude (Medin, Goldstone, & Gentner, 1990). The mind is composed of an amalgam of cognitive abilities specialised to handle specific types of information that define specific kinds of similarity. Special-purpose cognitive mechanisms are triggered by specific environmental conditions, sensitive to a specific range of input, and yield a specific kind of output.

To illustrate, it is now widely accepted that common sense (or naïve) psychology and common sense (or folk) biology are special-purpose cognitive mechanisms. Much evidence indicates that the human mind is organised (and likely to be preorganised) to interpret and predict behaviour that is motivated by mental states such as beliefs and desires, which are not directly observable (e.g., that Joe carries an umbrella on a sunny day because he believes that it will in fact rain that day and he desires not to get wet) (Baron-Cohen, 1996; Leslie, 1994). Similarly, the mind is disposed to sort nonhuman living things into nested hierarchies that support inferences about, among other things, the behaviours of nonhuman living things that go far beyond the information given (e.g., that a three-legged, albino tiger is still a tiger, and hence will act like a tiger, by virtue of a hidden intrinsic nature) (Atran, 1990; Carey, 1985; Gelman, 1989; Hatano & Inagaki, 1994).

Humans also interpret behaviour in terms of aggregate-level phenomena. For example, we anticipate that an individual's action (say, choosing which public bathroom to use) is motivated by the social group to which he or she belongs (in this case, his or her gender). Curious, as self-evident as this seems, only limited research has explored the cognitive mechanisms that support this sort of expectation. Humans invest massive cognitive effort in organising and interpreting their interactions with other humans. Plausibly, people spend more time talking and thinking about other humans than any other single dimension of the world (there is, of course, considerable variation in how people interpret others' speech and actions, a piece of conventional wisdom to cultural anthropologists, but increasingly to psychologists as well: Markus & Kitayama, 1991; Nisbett, Peng, Choi, & Norenzayan, 2001).

People attend closely to others as members of groups, analyse their behaviour in relationship to the behaviour of others in the same group, and seek information about others by listening to what people *say* about social groups and their interrelationships. Indeed, these group-based interpretations are often in "competition" with mental-state-based interpretations, and they frequently trump them. A prejudiced person expects a member of one race to be incompetent in some domain in virtue of expectations about members of that race rather than expectations derived from that person's individual properties. Our expectations about how a grocery store cashier will behave is similarly based on our expectations about social roles and the behaviours that flow from them, not on expectations, say, about how that individual happens to feel that day.

Social-group-based reasoning requires proficiency in identifying which group affiliations are relevant in a given context. This is not a trivial task given the multitude of groups to which each individual belongs. In virtually all human societies, individuals are members of many groups, and these groups often have competing interests. As a consequence, in any particular situation, an individual has several groups to which an attribution of membership can be made. A major cognitive and social task is to determine which affiliations and allegiances are relevant. Unlike mental states, for which a limited but highly informative and universal facial and behavioural "vocabulary" exists (Ekman, 1984), group affiliation and allegiance are not always clearly signalled. Perceptual cues are often thought to make group affiliation blatant—particularly for those groups that are precociously grasped, like race and gender. Still, it has long been acknowledged that perceptual evidence for the social *groups* themselves (as opposed to their members) is scarce (Asch, 1952). Moreover, arguably the earliest emerging social groups recognised by the child have few if any obvious perceptual correlates, namely kinfolk (Hirschfeld, 1989) (in spite of claims that young children initially focus on groups that are perceptually easy to distinguish).

Despite this challenge, strikingly, people are able to make fairly accurate social interpretations. Admittedly, mistakes—misattributions—occur. There are at least two errors possible when parsing a social situation. The first is misidentifying the group to which an individual belongs. The second is misidentifying the particular group affiliation relevant to an individual in a particular context. Both types of error are attention-demanding, most probably because both types are infrequent. The cultural cost of misattributions seem disproportionately linked to errors of the first type. There is a major genre in American literature and film, for instance, that treats racial misattributions as particularly anxiety-provoking and of great cultural concern (Hirschfeld, 2000). The fear that a (minority) individual is mistaken for a (majority) individual has occupied Americans (actually virtually all colonial administrations) from the earliest settlements in the New World (Stoler, 1995). Indeed, there is a complex—and shifting—set of cultural rules whose purpose is precisely to unambiguously resolve cases of ambiguous racial identity (Hirschfeld, 1995).

THE DEVELOPMENT OF SOCIAL CATEGORIES

Because of the centrality of these tasks for human social life, the degree of cognitive demand required to meet them, and the prevalence of specialised cognitive capacities associated with other structurally similar tasks, I contend that it is plausible, if not likely, that reasoning about a specific range of human categories, of which race is one, is governed by a special-purpose cognitive device. The remainder of this chapter outlines this hypothesis, puts it in context of what we now know about cognitive architecture, and presents evidence supporting this possibility.

For a child to understand society she must be able to identify and reason appropriately about social entities. Clearly social knowledge accumulates with experience. Nonetheless, children begin life with significant foundational (if rudimentary) and dedicated capacities for identifying and reasoning about social entities. The concept of *person* is a cognitive primitive, and by extension a social primitive (Bonatti, Frot, Zangl, & Mehler, 2002; G. Miller & Johnson-Laird, 1976). Infants are also endowed with capacities that permit them to track specific individuals by discriminating over faces and voices. They exploit this information to draw nondemonstrative inferences about individuals (e.g., as means of identifying a person's mood, intentions, etc.) (Baron-Cohen, 1996). They can also use these skills to recognise individuals as tokens of types of relationships (Bowlby, 1958), and display rudimentary understanding of the intentions of other people (Woodward, Sommerville, & Guajardo, 2001). Further, they can use this knowledge to accrue new knowledge (as, e.g., when they use speaker's gaze to identify the reference of an unfamiliar word; Baldwin, 1991).

Infants and young children are also capable of gaining information about social aggregates. Consider early expectations about language. Neonates discriminate between mother's native language and speech in another language, even when mother's native language is spoken by an unfamiliar person (Mehler, Jusczyk, Lambertz, Halsted, Bertoncini, & Amiel-Tison, 1988), suggesting that a specific language is treated from the outset as a property of a group of people. Experience with multiple languages is not needed to trigger this expectation. Infants living in monolingual environments also give evidence of conceptualising language as an aggregate phenomenon. For example, with age, the infant's ability to discriminate between phonetic variation narrows (Grieser & Kuhl, 1989). The language-learner also needs to narrowly discriminate speech sounds to the point of recognising, and at times rejecting, information about the phonetic properties of intra-language accent. When children of non-native speaking parents, for example, develop native speaker accents, they are evidently showing sensitivity to a broader speech community rather than a local family environment. There are potentially several ways to account for this, but all turn on the language learner's capacity to attend less to frequency of input and more to the social boundaries (and social nature) of input. Somehow the language-learning child "weighs" linguistic evidence that presupposes that language is a population-based phenomena (Hirschfeld & Gelman, 1994).

Aggregates, of course, are composed of individuals. It is possible that the child's knowledge of aggregates is simply an extension of her knowledge of individuals. There is reason to be sceptical of this hypothesis. Many adult folk expectations about group membership and behaviour suggest that an adequate knowledge of aggregates cannot be adduced from knowledge of the individual persons who compose them (Hirschfeld, 2001). (Whether this represents an ontological truth—i.e., that aggregates are really greater than the sum of their parts—is beside the point of this discussion: people *believe* that there are aggregate social entities, knowledge of which is not adduceable from knowledge of individuals. Similarly there are aggregates—corporations—that are held to be responsible independent of attributions of malfeasance by identifiable individuals.) Aggregates sharing these sorts of properties with individuals (especially aggregates to which intentions are attributed) have a special kind of identity independent of their members' identities, a quality that is highlighted when they are referred to as "moral individuals".

Intention-bearing aggregates are attributed with singular physical as well as conceptual properties. Yet coming to recognise and adequately characterise these aggregations is plausibly a more difficult task than coming to recognise and characterise individuals. Unlike individuals—who are bounded in both space and time, who move as a single unit, and who are identifiable by constellations of properties that are the product of a shared genome—aggregations are seldom encountered in ways that render their membership perceptually obvious (Asch, 1952). Nonetheless, adults readily ascribe properties to groups and conceptualise them as entities (Yzerbyt, Rogier, & Fiske, 1998).

Even young children do this. In a recent unpublished study, Michael Baran, Paul Bloom, Susan Gelman and I, adapting the task used by Heider and Simmel (1944) in their classic study, showed 5-year-olds a video depicting the movement of three groups, each group composed of collections with a distinct geometric shape and distinct colour. Children were asked to describe the movements of the objects depicted, each group of which moved independently. Children readily attributed intentions to the objects depicted in the video, as had adults in an earlier study by Bloom and Veres (1999). Intriguingly, all children in our study used both plural and singular terms to refer to the objects, suggesting either very loose language or some conceptual distinction between instances in which singular referring terms versus plural referring terms were employed. We found that their use of number was associated with attributions of intentionality. Singular terms were used reliably more often when intentions were ascribed to the groups, and plural terms when nonintentional language was used. Thus, when the objects were interpreted as moving in an intentional manner, the group was conceptualised as a single entity. In contrast, when intentions were not ascribed to the objects, the individual members of each group were conceptualised as distinct entities or units. Evidently children conceptually distinguish between aggregates that are mere collections and those that they interpret as "moral individuals" with intentionality.

EMBODIED SOCIAL CATEGORIES

Not all groups are equally informative about their members, nor are all groups equally informative in parsing social situations. Individuals belong to multiple aggregations, each of which has different (and frequently competing) relevance depending on environmental conditions. At any given moment what an individual does may be contingent on the person being a friend, a colleague, or a token of an ethnic or gender type. Which of these underlies their behaviour requires considerable interpretive skills (as anyone who has participated in a faculty meeting knows). One way to manage this problem is to reduce the relative contribution that membership in different groups makes in interpreting an individual's behaviour. For instance, in a particular situation, an individual's behaviour might be interpretable as a function of that individual's membership in two different groups (say, race or occupation). If membership in one of these groups is reliably more important in governing behaviour, cognitive demand is reduced (since one membership can essentially be discounted as a causal factor underlying behaviour). Thus, for most Americans, race is unfortunately thought to be more crucial than occupation, as most minorities who have applied for a mortgage can attest.

Not all groups are conceptually equivalent. Membership in some is more constant *and* more relevant across time, place, and context. Membership in some—e.g., race and gender—carry substantial inductive potential (i.e., support a large number of inferences beyond the information immediately available), whereas membership in other groups does not—e.g., occupation or height. A parallel exists with the varied ways we conceptualise non-human living things. The same creature conceptualised as a member of a species—a dog—has more inductive potential than when it is seen as a member of an artifact category—a pet. Knowing that one dog barks is sufficient evidence for a young child to believe that all dogs bark; knowing that one dog makes a good house pet is not good evidence that all dogs make good house pets. In social categorisation, gender, race (in North America and Northern Europe), and age have great inductive potential. Knowing that someone is a woman, Asian, or elderly is informative in many circumstances and supports a broad range of inferences about how he or she behaves and or what he or she believes.

The enormous literature on stereotyping—stereotypes being by definition inferences beyond the information given—provide massive evidence of this (Hamilton & Trolier, 1986; Hilton & Von Hippel, 1996). Curiously, although this empirical support is massive, it is implicit. As noted earlier, most literature in psychology assumes that all social group categories are formed in the same way and have the same conceptual properties. I contend here that this is not the case, that social group categories have very different conceptual properties. The empirical literature supports this precisely because it almost always uses social group categories that bear great inductive potential (particularly race and gender) (Hirschfeld, 1996).

Gender and race (as well as age) are all of a type. All are embodied (or putatively so). (This varies in degree from culture to culture. Race is not relevant in South Asia, where, for example, occupation is thought to be embodied in caste. In contrast, occupation is not thought to be embodied in North America: Hirschfeld, 1995.) All three categories—all three bases for aggregation—are associated with a density of correlated properties that are a product of each group's "genome-equivalent". There is a sizeable literature on how children come to grasp embodied groups. Most researchers have assumed that race and gender are precociously grasped because children find it easy to recognise tokens of embodied types—all members supposedly share a number of physical properties. Physical properties, however, need not be embodied in a perceptually obvious way. They may be inscribed corporeally in some hidden or underlying fashion. Gender, for example, is signalled by dress, preference, and behaviour, hence it is unsurprising that children discriminate between men and women in early infancy (Leinbach & Fagot, 1993; C. L. Miller, 1983). More strikingly, young children's *reasoning* about gender seems to depend on knowledge not of noncorporeal outward appearance, but typically hidden differences in genitalia (Bem, 1989).

THE EMERGENCE OF RACIAL THINKING

Race, while perhaps not so redundantly marked as gender, is nonetheless thought to be patently obvious, literally as plain as the nose on one's face. By the time children enter school they clearly notice the race of others and use race as a basis for further inference (Aboud, 1988; Katz, 1983; Van Ausdale & Feagin, 1996). Race awareness undergoes a singular developmental pattern. Categorical discrimination appears at the same time as the predilection to socially discriminate. By early school age, children show sensitivity to racial differences, the principal evidence of which are practices of racial inclusion and exclusion. This is a singular pattern of development in that most aggregates that become targets of stereotyping and prejudice are categorically recognised before stereotypes about them crystallise. Other embodied social differences—e.g., gender, age, and even language spoken— are reliability discriminated before they become the targets of biased judgements and practices of inclusion and exclusion. Infants, for example, discriminate people by gender long before they develop gender stereotypes

(Katz, 1983). Similarly, as noted earlier, neonate can distinguish between languages long before the language someone speaks becomes the basis for prejudice.

The developmental pattern of the concept of race is actually more curious still. It is less the exception to the rule as its inverse. In proposing that the categorical discrimination of race and practices of racial social discrimination emerge simultaneously, I did not faithfully convey the developmental course of the race concept, which is based on what can be inferred from observations of the everyday lives of children. If we rely on naturalistic observation, social and categorical discrimination come to shape children's behaviour at the same time. Experimental evidence, however, indicates that children as young as 3 years of age are stridently prejudiced in the way they think about members of other races. Yet their everyday behaviour gives no evidence of this. Why this is so reveals the very specific nature of racial thinking.

The appearance of race

Race "appears" in two distinct fashions, first as a category in one putatively natural partitioning of the human population, and second as a belief *about* outward appearances linked to the system of partition. On a realist interpretation of race, these two are contingent. Thus, for example, the development of racial categories has virtually universally been attributed to the act of sorting people into categories based on the way they look (for a review of the literature, see Hirschfeld, 1996). Race as a category, on this view, is psychologically relevant because it is physically striking, and physically striking phenomena are attention-demanding.

The notion that race categories are fundamentally derived from visual information plays a central role in explaining the move from the concept of race to racial bias. Hamilton and Sherman (1996), for example, had adult subjects read statements that identified an individual with a group and described that individual as acting in a desirable or undesirable way. There were fewer vignettes about minority group members than majority group members, although the proportion of desirable and undesirable behaviours was the same for both groups. Nonetheless, when asked to match individuals to behaviours, subjects judged members of the minority group as having performed proportionately more undesirable actions than had actually been depicted in the vignettes. Hamilton explained the results in terms of information processing: Undesirable behaviours are more attention-demanding than desirable behaviours and minority individuals are more attention-demanding than majority individuals *because of their appearance, even though the stimuli were not visual*. In brief, subjects over-attribute undesirable traits to members of minority populations—that is, they exhibit prejudice—simply because they link two attention-demanding qualities, group membership and relative desirability of behaviour

If racial group membership is easily distinguishable by virtue of outward appearance, and appearance powerfully affects information processing, it seems plausible to suppose that the perceptual factors are important to category *development*. Yet the relationship between visual information, category formation, and the emergence of prejudice suggest a considerably more complex structure. First, young children are typically inconsistent in sorting people into "appropriate" racial categories. Racial misidentifications—assigning a child, frequently oneself, to an "inappropriate" racial category—are common (Clark & Clark, 1950; Cross, 1991). It is not until elementary school that children's sorting people by race becomes reliable. It is also in elementary school that race begins to play an important role in shaping everyday social interaction, closely predicting patterns of social inclusion and exclusion. In contrast, during the pre-school years race plays little role in predicting playmate choice (Williams & Morland, 1976).

Curiously, this "colour-blind" pattern of playmate choice is not accompanied by "colour-blind" attitudes toward members of other races. By 3 years of age, children display marked bias in their interpretation of hypothetical situations. The methods used to assess pre-schooler prejudice vary, from the early doll studies of the Clarks (Clark & Clark, 1950) to more recent studies of Aboud and others (Aboud, 1988). All share a common format, however: Children are told about a child or adult who performs a particular act that is either positive ("a child finds a lost wallet and returns it to the owner") or negative ("one child can't spell his name"). Subjects are then asked which of two persons, one black the other white, fits the description best. Using a fairly conservative metric, Williams and Morland (1976) propose that a child shows clear bias if his or her judgements are prejudiced on at least 17 of 24 items (i.e., they select the majority child when asked about positive events and the minority child when asked about negative events). Summarising the results of several studies, Williams and Morland found that 72% of tested children were clearly biased.

These results are surprising. If nearly three-quarters of 3- and 4-year-olds hold clearly biased racial attitudes, why don't they "act" on these attitudes? Even accepting that attitude and behaviour are only indirectly associated, during the pre-school years children are not using race as a factor in social inclusion and exclusion, as older children are (Killen, Lee Kim, McGlothlin, & Stangor, 2003). Why, then, do even young pre-schoolers appear to endorse strident racial bias? The answer, I suggest, lies in the assumption that the input modality of information relevant to attitudes and the input modality of information relevant to behaviour are the same. If, instead, children are relying on one kind of input in finding targets for prejudice and another in determining with whom they play, differences in attitude and behaviour could easily be explained.

Several years ago I put the question to test, specifically by investigating what modality of information is relevant to the formation of racial and other social categories (Hirschfeld, 1993). Three- and 4-year-old French children were assigned to one of two conditions: Half listened to a narrative in which the characters' race, occupation, body build and gender were mentioned (although none of these dimensions was important to the narrative's plot). The other half viewed a cartoon story book in which the same social attributes and same narrative plot were visually depicted. After listening to the verbal story or viewing the cartoon story book version, children were asked to recall the story. The study's logic was straightforward. Children's memory for social information should reflect the kind of input to which they attended. If children relied on the same kinds of input in their representations of race, then their retelling of the story in both conditions should be largely the same. If they relied on different kinds of input, then their recall of the story should reflect these differences. We found that there were significant differences in the verbal and visual conditions. In the verbal condition, race was a highly salient category: Both younger and older pre-schoolers recalled the race of the characters in the story. In the visual condition, in which the standard view might predict high rates of recall, the character's race was almost never mentioned. Older pre-schoolers actually remembered nonracial physical features more than they remembered racial ones. What can be inferred from these findings? First, in building mental representations of race, 3- and 4-year-olds concentrate their attention on verbal information, not information about physical appearances.

Children are clearly curious about the elements that constitute the social world. Not surprisingly, in both conditions children were able to recall a good deal of information about the gender, occupation, and mood of each character. Young children are also curious about race, as the prejudice studies demonstrate. They are, however, unsure of physical properties diagnostic of race. Instead, they attend more to verbal information in building a catalogue of relevant group differences and use this information to interpret behaviour. Knowing that someone is a member of a minority race—knowing the appropriate linguistic *term* for a minority race—warrants using that information to infer behaviour under conditions of considerable doubt, under conditions in which the *only* thing the child knows is the individual's race. This categorical information is more crucial than information about the specific physical features associated with each race. (It is important to stress that children associate race with physical differences from the outset. What is relevant here is that they appear not to be concerned with what the specific physical differences actually are. Shown pictures depicting people who exhibit embodied differences, they tether these differences to negative attitudes. This is the only physical information with which they are presented. In everyday life, however, people vary on many dimensions, and the information sufficient to link a distinctively unusual person with a racial attitude is no longer possible; at least not until children set for themselves the task of identifying the relevant physical differences associated with race, something they do toward the end of their fifth year.)

RACE AND REALITY

As I suggested earlier, it is widely believed that race is one of several embodied social categories. On this view, race captures actual and perceptually discriminable discontinuities in corporeal appearance. A developmental consequence is that children recognise these discontinuities as relying on relatively lower-order perceptual processes such as colour, shape, and texture perception. The child attends to little more than (skin and hair) colour, (nose and lips) shape, and (hair) texture in order to sort people into racial categories. Reasoning about race is initially similarly concerned with surface appearances.

Understanding how the child discovers and represents race is interesting to the extent that it is informative of a developmental process from initial states to some adult endpoint. In the overwhelming bulk of studies, the adult endpoint is assumed to be the realist view that humans are partitioned into natural groupings, readily discriminated by visual cues. It is this adult belief system that a developmental account needs to explain. Because the realist view represents the principal, if often tacit, interpretation of the phenomenon under scrutiny, it is important to be sure that this view adequately captures the adult belief system—and the phenomenon that the adult belief system is meant to reflect. As self-evident as the realist view is assumed to be among researchers in psychology, it may not in fact be the case. Indeed, I argue that the realist view is not an adequate account of the adult belief system, rather, it is a (folk) belief about the adult (folk) belief system.

Specific claims about outward appearance, in fact, are neither the only nor the most important attributes of racial thinking. For adults in North America and Northern Europe, the concept of race includes a corollary belief about unseen or inner traits as well as outward appearance. In many ways, it is this account of inner traits that makes race both a powerful concept politically and an inferentially potent one conceptually. Consider biomedical research and clinical practice. In both, race is frequently used explicitly in compiling risk factors to disease (hypertension, prostate cancer, sickle-cell anaemia, etc.) and serves implicitly to explain them. The logic of this analytic strategy rests on the frequently observed statistical association of race, presumably as a physically apparent category, and disease. Being a member of a race that *looks* a certain way is in fact linked to the way that person is internally constituted. Still, individuals whose membership in a particular race is determined genealogically rather than by induction from appearances are considered to be as susceptible to a (putatively) race-related disorder as someone whose appearance accords more closely to racial "prototypes".

This expectation can be derived from a constellation of claims that are central to the concept of race. The adult folk belief system comprises three related propositions: the belief (1) that humans can be partitioned into discrete groupings based on their physical constitution, (2) that "physical constitution" includes clusters of enduring traits in outward appearance as well as clusters of enduring nonobvious or inner traits, and (3) that these outward and inner clusters of traits are the product a single causal relation involving attribution of an inner, heritable essence specific to each racial group. Nothing in this characterisation seems self-evidently controversial. Controversy arises around which particular nonobvious traits are causally linked to race (i.e., whether the claim is that members of one race are cognitively inferior to other races versus whether the claim is that members of one race are more likely to have a genetic disposition for hypertension).

Unfortunately the characterisation misrepresents the scope and nature of population differences; ultimately this misrepresentation has important consequences for the nature and course of development of racial cognitions and, hence, any account of them. The first and most fundamental inaccuracy is that, contrary to a realist account, human biological variation is not captured by *any* known system of racial thinking. Indeed, worldwide there are almost as many systems of racial categorisation as there are cultural traditions that include them. Moreover, there are massive differences between them. A further complication is that biological variation in outward appearances diagnostic of race typically are a function of adaptations to climatic variation. Consequently these differences are literally on the surface. There simply are no consistent inner correlates to racial categories (Marks, 1995). From the viewpoint of a particular system of racial categorisation, like those found in North America and Northern Europe, the categories seem to reliably pick out differences in appearance. To some extent this is true even from a perspective outside the system of categorisation, but only if we are concerned to link racial categories to differences in appearance as opposed to biological relevant differences in type. Social factors, like marriage laws that kept members of different racial categories from *marrying*, contribute to our common sense perception of race as readily apparent. It should be noted, however, that marriage laws do not govern *mating*, so that even in societies in which social factors come to bear, they do not ensure reliable biological differences.

Why, then, do differences in susceptibility to disease seem to map onto racial categories? Surely such mappings suggest some reliable link between these categories, outward appearance, and nonobvious inner phenomena. The problem is that the apparently reliable link between biomedical conditions, such as differential risk of various diseases, reflect differences in the distribution of properties derived from populations of origin. These population differences are subsumed, typically haphazardly, under racial categories. Accordingly, because differential susceptibility to disease is linked to population of origin, and population of origin is in turn linked to particular racial categories, a statistical association between race and epidemiological consideration emerges. But the population and the racial category are virtually never coterminous. Indeed, racial categories typically (and massively) overdetermine epidemiological patterns of disease susceptibility.

Since this might seem counter-intuitive, at least from a viewpoint grounded within a system of racial thought, consider a specific case. Sickle-cell anaemia is a genetically determined malady generally described in Western medical literature as a racially varying susceptibility. Blacks are considerably more susceptible to the disease than whites. Biomedical researchers have long "recognised" that sickle-cell anaemia is higher among American blacks than American whites. However, this effect is not as direct—or causal—as biomedical researchers suggest. Rather it is largely carried by the fact that rates of sickle-cell anaemia are higher among descendants of a population originally from Central Africa that is largely subsumed under the category of American blacks. Still, most American blacks are not descendants of this population. The relationship between American blacks and higher rates of sickle-cell anaemia is, in fact, a function of a social system of classification, not of population dynamics. If a greater percentage of American whites were descendants of Sardinian immigrants, among whom rates of sickle-cell anaemia are also high, there might well be no difference in susceptibility to the disorder between American blacks and American whites. There are a proportionally higher percentage of individuals descended from Central African populations among American blacks then there are individuals descended from Sardinia among American whites. Hence the association to race in one case, and a lack of one in the other. Still, at the turn of the 20th century, Southern and Eastern Europeans were not considered white in America. Had rates of sickle-cell anaemia been compiled then, the association between race (Southern Europeans) and the distribution of this disease would have been as "reliable" as that found among blacks and sickle-cell anaemia now.

Supposed perceptual differences seem to follow from particular systems of racial thinking rather than racial thinking following from perceptible difference. Before the collapse of apartheid, the South African government maintained racial identity courts to which one could petition to change racial assignment. These courts regularly made determinations that left full siblings or parents and children no longer classified as members of the same race. Such paradoxes are not limited to the especially well-codified (and hence open to more obvious inconsistencies) South African system of racial thought. In a fascinating account, the historian Linda Gordon describes how a group of "nonwhite" Irish children left New York by train in the early decades of the 20th century, yet arrived "white" a few days later in Arizona (Gordon, 1999).

Realism and development

What developmental consequences does all this have? According to the standard view, early representations of race are driven by surface differences in appearance. These differences are interpreted as superficial; i.e., they are interpreted solely in terms of their outward, surface properties. Young children are thought to form racial categories much as they form other object categories, on the basis of like-goes-with-like. Pre-school-age children, on the standard account, would not grasp racial constancy— would not understand that a person's race does not change over time— because they would not grasp that race is a function of family biological background. Several studies have lent support to this view. In one, kindergarteners (5-year-olds) and third graders (approximately 8 years old) were asked what would happen if a familiar child were made up to look as if he had changed race (e.g., if a white child was made to look like an Inuit child). Unlike third graders, kindergartners reasoned that the person's race had changed (Aboud, 1988). Semaj (1980), using a similar protocol, found that 4-year-olds expected that a black child made up to look white had become white. These results are interpreted as evidence that children, unlike adults, do not conceive of race as embodied, as a function of biological or corporeal nature.

If this were an accurate account, it would raise an important cross-domain question. Young children, for instance, readily grasp the deep natures of the relationship between members of categories that at first blush seem much like race, such as nonhuman living things (Gelman, 1989). Why would similar adult-like beliefs be absent in a domain of knowledge at the core of children's social reasoning? After all, from the literature on young children's racial attitudes we know that children use race as a basis for going far beyond the information given, a pattern of reasoning not at all consistent with the idea that these children conceive of race as a superficial attribute. To better appreciate this conundrum, consider young children's reasoning about gender. As in the literature on race, it has been widely accepted that pre-schoolers do not grasp gender constancy. Support came from studies using manipulations similar to those used by Aboud and Semaj. More recent studies, however, have convincingly demonstrated that 4-year-olds have an adult-like grasp of gender constancy (Gelman & Taylor, 2000). Pre-schoolers' beliefs about gender are not simply derived from outward cues, but rather in a notion of embodied but hidden physical properties. Bem (1989), for example, found that those pre-schoolers who grasped gender constancy, as assessed on traditional measures, had domain-specific knowledge that the genitalia constitute the defining attributes of male and female.

Gender is not the only phenomenon in which pre-schoolers demonstrate a more adult-like understanding of constancy. Similar results obtain for species constancy. Even very young children expect that a creature's species and its inherent nature are constant and more informative of that nature than surface-level similarities (Gelman, 1988; Gelman & Coley, 1990). Gelman and Wellman (1991) found that species-typical properties are conserved even when a creature is raised among members of a species whose species-typical properties are quite different. Children also grasp that creatures that change radically in appearance during development (e.g., tadpole to frog or caterpillar to moth) remain the same kind of creature. Pre-schoolers also expect that internal bodily functions, such as digestion, are involuntary (Hatano & Inagaki, 1994).

This constellation of expectations is consistent with a more explicitly articulated adult belief that a creature's specific kind and inherent nature are causally linked to a species or gender essence that is unseen but that governs the development of and inherent nature of all tokens of the kind. Atran and his colleagues (Atran, 1990, 1995; Bailenson, Shum, Atran, Medin, & Coley, 2002) provide considerable cross-cultural evidence that this constellation of beliefs is universal in both adults' and children's thought. Other work suggests that species essence is conceived as both hidden *and* particulate, fixed at birth when it is transmitted from mother to foetus during pregnancy (Springer, 1996). Perhaps most strikingly, children's expectations about essences seem to develop largely on their own, and are not dependent on adult tuition (Gelman, Coley, Rosengren, Hartman, & Pappas, 1998).

Much of this research construes children's and adults' beliefs about embodiment, constancy, and inherent nature as part of complex knowledge structures best characterised as folk theories (sometimes called lay theories or naïve theories). Folk theories, unlike scientific theories, are resistant to change. But like scientific theories, these theories function to channel attention toward particular kinds of phenomena, to favour a particular range of causal explanation, and to recognize a set of concepts that link the phenomena to relations in the world that affect them. Standard accounts of race treat children's beliefs as limited to surface-level explanations. But increasingly, research indicates that race can also be understood in terms of a folk theory endorsed even by young children. Hamilton and Trolier (1986) define stereotype as "a knowledge structure containing a perceiver's beliefs about the characteristics and behaviors of a particular social group" (p. 137). Young pre-schoolers' racial prejudice and gender stereotypes fit this description well. The ready use of these biases and stereotypes indicate that pre-school children's representation are consistent with one aspect of the adult folk theory of race; viz. that race has great inductive potential.

Studies that I have conducted demonstrate that much of the adult racial belief system is also shared by young children. One reason that this is not revealed in earlier research is a task demand of the most common paradigm used to access children's understanding of racial constancy. Recall that in both Aboud's and Semaj's studies, children were asked about abrupt and contrived changes in a child's appearance, about which the experimenter asked counterintuitive questions. The most rudimentary form of object constancy, which even infants grasp, would predict that a person remains that person from one moment to the next under pretty much all states of affairs. If the experimenter asks a young child whether a person remains a particular person from one moment to the next, the question is arguably leading. Why would the experimenter ask it, if the answer isn't derived from deeply grounded common sense? To avoid this potential problem, when I explored young children's grasp of racial constancy, I asked about changes over time that are accompanied by other dramatic bodily changes: Specifically, changes that accompany growth and inheritance. With age, a person's body changes dramatically, although identity does not. Similarly, a child resembles his or her parents but not exactly. Would young children interpret race such that it is not constant over these changes?

I found that the answer is no. In contrast to the standard account, even 3-year-olds believe that race, unlike many other social categories, is fixed-at-birth, impervious to environmental influences, immalleable over the lifespan, inherited, and essentialised (Hirschfeld, 1996). In sum, children clearly believe that humans can be sorted into distinct types on the basis of their concrete, observable constitution. Like adults, they interpret "observable constitution" as embodied, natural, enduring, and a function of unseen and inner qualities. They also understand that race is an explanation of how observable properties in appearance and behaviour are linked to this embodied, incorrigible nature. Race is neither a catalogue of surface differences in appearances nor a catalogue of differences in behaviours. Race is a theory of difference, a theory of behaviour, that *interprets* differences in appearance and behaviour.

I am proposing here that race and gender are singular social categories by virtue of the inherent underlying natures that children and adults attribute to them. There is an alternate explanation of the pattern of racial and gender reasoning I've described. It is possible that children attribute nonobviously derived inherent natures to *all* social categories. Admittedly this would stand the standard view on its head, suggesting that pre-schoolers are not mistaken in thinking that all social categories are a function of surface-level phenomena; rather, they are mistaken in thinking that all social categories have underlying essential natures. Young children's reasoning would thus not reflect a naïve nurture strategy, as the standard view holds, but a naïve nativist one.

This possibility can be ruled out by earlier studies that I conducted. In them I found that pre-schoolers do not treat all social categories alike either in terms of how they are encoded or how they are reasoned about. For example, in one story-recall study, 3- and 4-year-olds revealed good memory for visually marked social categories like gender and occupation but not for race, an equally visually marked social category (Hirschfeld, 1993). In a switched-at-birth study exploring children's reasoning, 4-year-olds expected a black couple's child to be black even if he were raised by a white couple. Another group of 3- and 4-year-olds similarly expected a hefty couple's child to be hefty even if he were raised by wiry adoptive parents. Thus, pre-schoolers endorse a nativist interpretation of race and physique. However, when a third group of children were given a task in which race and physique were crossed, and asked to choose between a hefty white child and a wiry black child, even 3-year-olds reasoned that a hefty, black couple's child would be black and wiry, not white and hefty (Hirschfeld, 1995). This implies that even if children are nativist about other social categories, they distinguish the extent to which different embodied social categories are malleable.

CONCLUSION

Each chapter in this volume examines how children come to understand different aspects of different social entities. This chapter's goal is to expli-cate how children's concept of race develops. A good deal of effort was devoted to explicating the peculiar and typically unappreciated nature of the adult concept of race, in particular to the mistakenly realist perspective that has predominated in the vast psychological literature on race and racism. By doing this, I hope to have shown that the task of acquiring an understanding of the adult concept is a major cognitive challenge. Children could come to understand race via processes of empirical generalisation, in which they use a strategy of identifying similarities in outward appearance and assigning certain patterns of appearance to racial categories. I have tried to show that there is little evidence to support this view. Children do not learn about race because it is so evident; they learn that it is supposed to be so evident because it is governed by hidden but crucial processes.

I have further suggested that the young child's expectations about race, virtually from the outset, are surprisingly theory-like and adult-like. Like adults, they see race as emerging from hidden essences that govern development, conserve identity across substantial perceptual transformations, across important variation in conditions of the environment, and across generations. This cluster of beliefs is the product of elaborate knowledge structure. Clearly this knowledge structure changes over time; this is a developmental process. Importantly, however, the development is not, as is typically believed, from simple to complex, from fragmentary to consolidated, from immature to mature. Like several domains of thought—naïve psychology and naive mechanics being uncontroversial examples—children's understanding of race seems to be shaped by a preorganised and special-purpose programme of learning (Carey & Spelke, 1994).

I propose that there is a dedicated cognitive device that identifies and treats some social categories in a very specific way: It construes them as embodied and natural (more accurately controlled by natural processes). Race, I contend, is a product of a core domain-specific competency, which elsewhere I have described as folk sociology (Hirschfeld, 1996). The race concept is not the only expression of this competency: Categories of kinship, gender, caste, age-grades, and certain construals of class are all expressions of a folk sociology device. Interested readers can consult other material to learn more about folk sociology, but one of its further properties is that it is a programme to acquire knowledge. This acquisition process is not independent of the environment in which it operates. Race is not an inevitable "discovery" of the mind any more than it is an inevitable "discovery" of biology. The race concept is acquired in cultural environments in which race is an ambient belief. In other cultural environments, other concepts are ambient, and hence acquired (expressed through folk sociology). In South Asia race is not a relevant (nor recognised) embodied and natural dimension of the social world, but "occupation", in the guise of caste, is. I would argue, however, that cultural variation in social categories types is far from unlimited. Race and caste are very "easy" to learn in that they resonate with domain-specific susceptibilities. They are, in Sperber's (1990) sense, "catchy".

How so? Let me close by citing another recent, unpublished study. In earlier work I found that 3-year-olds are as willing to naturalise occupation as race, whereas 4-year-olds are not (Hirschfeld, 1995). I concluded that 3-year-olds are still in the throes of "parsing" the social environment for embodied and natural categories. Because this parsing is fragmentary and tentative, occupation is not yet "ruled out" as a relevant embodied and natural category. Still, as South Asia reminds us, occupation is eminently naturaliseable when provided with the necessary cultural support.

Susan Gelman and I wondered if there were other cultural possibilities that young children might be open to that were not supported by environment and hence were endorsed only briefly. Several cultural traditions, including Renaissance and later late-colonial Europe, held that children could develop embodied properties naturally but not through procreation. Specifically, it has been claimed that children can develop physical and behavioural qualities as a result of being wet-nursed. Gelman and I presented American pre-schoolers with a task that assessed whether they too might entertain this notion, even though it is obviously not supported by contemporary American culture. We used a switched-at-birth task with two conditions: In the first, children were told about an adoptive mother who bottle-fed her adopted child, and in the second, about an adoptive mother who breast-fed her adopted child. We found that 4-year-old children in the breast-fed condition were more likely to reason that the adopted child would share physical properties with the adoptive mother than were children in the bottle-fed condition, suggesting that they were open to endorsing a theory of natural reproduction unsupported by their particular culture but supported by others. In contrast, there was no condition effect among 5-year-olds, suggesting that this cultural possibility was foreclosed.

In sum, I suggest that asking about how children come to understand race may not be the optimal question. Rather, it may be more informative to ask how children come to understand the class of social entities of which race is one culturally specific token.

REFERENCES

Aboud, F. E. (1980). A test of ethnocentrism with young children. *Canadian Journal of Behavioural Science, 12*, 195–209.

Aboud, F. E. (1988). *Children and prejudice*. New York: Blackwell.

Allport, G. (1954). *The nature of prejudice*. Cambridge: Addison-Wesley.

Asch, S. (1952). *Social psychology*. Englewood Cliffs, NJ: Prentice-Hall.

Atran, S. (1990). *Cognitive foundations of natural history: Towards an anthropology of science*. New York: Cambridge University Press.

Atran, S. (1995). Classifying nature across cultures. In E. E. Smith & D. N. Osherson (Eds.), *Thinking: An invitation to cognitive science, Vol. 3* (2nd ed., pp. 131–174). Cambridge, MA: MIT Press.

Bailenson, J. N., Shum, M. S., Atran, S., Medin, D. L., & Coley, J. D. (2002). A bird's eye view: Biological categorization and reasoning within and across cultures. *Cognition, 84*, 1–53.

Baldwin, D. A. (1991). Infants' contribution to the achievement of joint reference. *Child Development, 62*, 875–890.

Baron-Cohen, S. (1996). *Mindblindness: An essay on autism and theory of mind*. Cambridge, MA: MIT Press.

Bem, S. L. (1989). Genital knowledge and gender constancy in preschool children. *Child Development, 60*, 649–662.

Berlin, B. (1992). *Ethnobiological classification: Principles of categorization of plants and animals in traditional societies*. Princeton, NJ: Princeton University Press.

Bloom, P., & Veres, C. (1999). The perceived intentionality of groups. *Cognition, 71*, B1–B9.

Bonatti, L., Frot, E., Zangl, R., & Mehler, J. (2002). The human first hypothesis: Identification of conspecifics and individuation of objects in the young infant. *Cognitive Psychology, 44*, 388–426.

Bowlby, J. (1958). The nature of the child's tie to his mother. *International Journal of Psycho-Analysis, 39*, 350–373.

Carey, S. (1985). *Conceptual change in childhood*. Cambridge, MA: MIT Press.

Carey, S., & Spelke, E. (1994). Domain-specific knowledge and conceptual change. In L. Hirschfeld & S. Gelman (Eds.), *Mapping the mind: Domain specificity in cognition and culture* (pp. 169–200). New York: Cambridge University Press.

Clark, K. B., & Clark, M. P. (1950). Emotional factors in racial identification and preference in Negro children. *Journal of Negro Education, 19*, 341–350.

Cross, W. E., Jr (1991). *Shades of black: Diversity in African-American identity*. Philadelphia, PA: Temple University Press.

Ekman, P. (1984). Expression and the nature of emotion. In K. Scherer & P. Ekman (Eds.), *Approaches to emotion*. Hillsdale, NJ: Lawrence Erlbaum Associates Inc.

Gelman, S. A. (1988). The development of induction within natural kind and artifact categories. *Cognitive Psychology, 20*, 65–95.

Gelman, S. A. (1989). Children's use of categories to guide biological inferences. *Human Development, 32*, 65–71.

Gelman, S. A., & Coley, J. D. (1990). The importance of knowing a dodo is a bird: Categories and inferences in 2-year-old children. *Developmental Psychology, 26*, 796–804.

Gelman, S. A., Coley, J. D., Rosengren, K. S., Hartman, E., & Pappas, A. (1998). Beyond labeling: The role of maternal input in the acquisition of richly structured categories. *Monographs of the Society for Research in Child Development, 63*, 1–148.

Gelman, S. A., & Taylor, M. G. (2000). Gender essentialism in cognitive development. In P. H. Miller & E. K. Scholnick (Eds.), *Toward a feminist developmental psychology* (pp. 169–190). Florence, KY: Taylor & Francis/Routledge.

Gelman, S. A., & Wellman, H. M. (1991). Insides and essence: Early understandings of the non-obvious. *Cognition, 38*, 213–244.

Gordon, L. (1999). *The great Arizona orphan abduction*. Cambridge, MA: Harvard University Press.

Grieser, D., & Kuhl, P. K. (1989). Categorization of speech by infants: Support for speech-sound prototypes. *Developmental Psychology, 25*, 577–588.

Hamilton, D. L., & Sherman, S. J. (1996). Perceiving persons and groups. *Psychological Review, 103*, 336–355.

Hamilton, D. L., & Trolier, T. K. (1986). Stereotypes and stereotyping: An overview of the cognitive approach. In J. F. Dovidio & S. L. Gaertner (Eds.), *Prejudice, discrimination, and racism* (pp. 127–163). San Diego, CA: Academic Press.

Hatano, G., & Inagaki, K. (1994). Young children's naive theory of biology. *Cognition, 50*, 171–188.

Heider, F., & Simmel, M. (1944). An experimental study of apparent behavior. *American Journal of Psychology, 57*, 243–259.

Hilton, J. L., & Von Hippel, W. (1996). Stereotypes. *Annual Review of Psychology, 47*, 237–271.

Hirschfeld, L. A. (1989). Rethinking the acquisition of kinship terms. *International Journal of Behavioral Development, 12*, 541–568.

Hirschfeld, L. A. (1993). Discovering social difference: The role of appearance in the development of racial awareness. *Cognitive Psychology, 25*, 317–350.

Hirschfeld, L. A. (1995). Do children have a theory of race? *Cognition, 54*, 209–252.

Hirschfeld, L. A. (1996). *Race in the making: Cognition, culture, and the child's construction of human kinds.* Cambridge, MA: MIT Press.

Hirschfeld, L. A. (2000). Making racial culture: Children and the mental life of a social concept. In J. Terwal & M. Verkuyten (Eds.), *Comparative perspectives on racism* (pp. 23–45). Aldershot, UK: Ashgate.

Hirschfeld, L. A. (2001). On a folk theory of society: Children, evolution, and mental representations of social groups. *Personality and Social Psychology Review: Special Issue, 5*, 107–117.

Hirschfeld, L. A., & Gelman, S. A. (Eds.) (1994). *Mapping the mind: Domain specificity in cognition and culture.* New York: Cambridge University Press.

Katz, P. (1983). Developmental foundations of gender and racial attitudes. In R. Leahy (Ed.), *The child's construction of social inequality.* New York: Academic Press.

Kempton, W., & Kay, P. (1984). What is the Sapir-Whorf hypothesis? *American Anthropologist, 86*, 65–79.

Killen, M., Lee Kim, J., McGlothlin, H., & Stangor, C. (2003). How children and adolescents evaluate gender and racial exclusion. *Monographs of the Society for Research in Child Development, 67*, No. 4, Serial No. 271.

Leinbach, M. D., & Fagot, B. I. (1993). Categorical habituation to male and female faces: Gender schematic processing in infancy. *Infant Behavior and Development, 16*, 317–332.

Leslie, A. M. (1994). ToMM, ToBy, and Agency: Core architecture and domain specificity. In L. Hirschfeld & S. Gelman (Eds.), *Mapping the mind: Domain specificity in cognition and culture* (pp. 119–148). New York: Cambridge University Press.

Marks, J. (1995). *Human biodiversity: Genes, race, and history.* New York: Aldine de Gruyter.

Markus, H. R., & Kitayama, S. (1991). Culture and the self: Implications for cognition, emotion, and motivation. *Psychological Review, 98*, 224–253.

Medin, D. L., Goldstone, R. L., & Gentner, D. (1990). Similarity involving attributes and relations: Judgments of similarity and difference are not inverses. *Psychological Science, 1*, 64–69.

Mehler, J., Jusczyk, P., Lambertz, G., Halsted, N., Bertoncini, J., & Amiel-Tison, C. (1988). A precursor of language acquisition in young infants. *Cognition, 29*, 143–178.

Miller, C. L. (1983). Developmental changes in male/female voice classification by infants. *Infant Behavior and Development, 6*, 313–330.

Miller, G., & Johnson-Laird, P. (1976). *Language and perception.* New York: Cambridge University Press.

Nisbett, R. E., Peng, K., Choi, I., & Norenzayan, A. (2001). Culture and systems of thought: Holistic versus analytic cognition. *Psychological Review: Special Issue, 108*, 291–310.

Semaj, L. (1980). The development of racial evaluation and preference: A cognitive approach. *Journal of Black Psychology, 6*, 59–79.

Sperber, D. (1990). The epidemiology of beliefs. In *The social psychological study of widespread beliefs* (pp. 25–44). New York: Clarendon Press/Oxford University Press.

Sporer, S. (2001). The cross-race effect: Beyond recognition of faces in the laboratory. *Psychology, Public Policy, and the Law, 7*, 170–200.

Springer, K. (1996). Young children's understanding of a biological basis for parent-offspring relations. *Child Development, 67*, 2841–2856.

Stoler, A. (1995). *Race and the education of desire.* Durham, NC: Duke University Press.

Taylor, S., & Fiske, S. (1978). Salience, attention, and attribution: Top of the head phenomena. In L. Berkowitz (Ed.), *Advances in experimental social psychology, Vol. 11* (pp. 249–288). New York: Academic Press.

Van Ausdale, D., & Feagin, J. R. (1996). Using racial and ethnic concepts: The critical case of very young children. *American Sociological Review, 61,* 779–793.

Williams, J. E., & Morland, J. K. (1976). *Race, color, and the young child.* Chapel Hill, NC: University of North Carolina Press.

Woodward, A. L., Sommerville, J. A., & Guajardo, J. J. (2001). How infants make sense of intentional action. In B. F. Malle, L. J. Moses, & D. A. Baldwin (Eds.), *Intentions and intentionality: Foundations of social cognition* (pp. 149–169). Cambridge, MA: MIT Press.

Yzerbyt, V. Y., Rogier, A., & Fiske, S. T. (1998). Group entitativity and social attribution: On translating situational constraints into stereotypes. *Personality and Social Psychology Bulletin, 24,* 1089–1103.

CHAPTER NINE

Children's understanding of ethnic belonging and the development of ethnic attitudes

Alida Lo Coco, Cristiano Inguglia, and Ugo Pace
Dipartimento di Psicologia, Università degli Studi di Palermo, Italy

ETHNIC IDENTITY FROM CHILDHOOD TO ADOLESCENCE

The last decades have witnessed a consistent migratory flow from less economically developed countries to more highly developed countries. Leaving one's native nation and settling in another place has inevitably produced extensive societal shifts, which have impacted not only upon economic, political, and social dynamics but also upon psychological dynamics. Contacts between people and cultures, as a consequence of these migrations, underline the need to take into account the psychological processes and relations between majority and minority groups in nonhomogeneous societies. In other words, intergroup interactions offer the opportunity to investigate the way in which various ethnic groups identify and perceive themselves and others, the value they attribute to their history, and the feelings they mutually develop when sharing the same living space.

To explain the complex connections ruling the relationships between both individuals and groups in multiethnic societies, researchers have often used the term "ethnic identity", which has been defined as the feeling of belonging to an ethnic group or as that part of one's thoughts, beliefs, behaviours, attitudes, and values that result from membership of such a group (Phinney, 1990; Phinney, Ferguson, & Tate, 1997; Phinney, Horenczyk, Liebkind, & Vedder, 2001).

A focus on this feeling of belonging to an ethnic group has emphasised the importance that the relationship between the individual and the group has for psychosocial adjustment. From this point of view, the group should not be considered simply as a gathering of people, but as a cognitive entity that assumes a particular significance at a particular moment for individuals (Tajfel, 1976). In this sense, the ethnic group is a group of individuals who consider themselves to belong to the same social category and who share, at the same time, the same social identification.

One of the modalities employed by individuals for self-definition is social membership of a group, the other members of which share certain characteristics with the self. In this way, one can describe oneself as male or female, student or worker, young or adult. Quoting Tajfel (1981), the result of our participation in a great variety of social situations is the acquisition of many different social identities. Belonging to different social categories, indeed, characterises each individual's life as a social being. Among the various categories employed by individuals to represent themselves, especially in multicultural societies, ethnic identity holds an important place and may be considered to be crucial to psychological functioning both through the development of self-esteem and the structure of adaptive interpersonal relationships. As a multidimensional construction, ethnic identity consists of different components by means of which individuals are able to recognise their appropriate ethnic group membership and establish the role that their own culture plays in their individual development. The different components, in a sequential and integrated way, contribute to the generation of a feeling of belonging to a social group (Phinney, 1990; Phinney et al., 1997, 2001).

According to Weinreich (1988), ethnic identity is not an entity but a complex process through which individuals actively form their own ethnicity, take decisions, and evaluate the importance of their own culture in their life. During childhood, one develops simple knowledge about one's ethnicity. This knowledge is, above all, about children's ability to choose a correct label for themselves, to identify themselves with their own group, and to adopt the specific habits and behaviours of that ethnic group. During the course of development, individuals acquire a wider and more appropriate awareness. They realise, for instance, that their own ethnicity is constant across time and that some of their beliefs, their value systems, and their daily habits emanate from their ethnic group. During adolescence, besides the achievement of a personal identity, all knowledge about the "ethnic self" becomes part of a generalised representation of the self and enables the formation of a mature kind of ethnic identity (Lo Coco & Pace, 2001; Lo Coco, Pace, & Zappulla, 2000).

In other words, children's ability to self-label or to recognise typical traditions are, initially, the result of family influences. For instance, a 4-

year-old Tamil child knows he is Tamil because, probably, his parents told him; only later does he grasp the meaning linked to the description of himself as part of a specific ethnic group. Moreover, a 5-year-old Tunisian child could probably answer "yes" to the question "Do you ever eat couscous?" but, probably, in response to the question "Why?", she would answer "Because I like it" or "Because my mum cooks it"; only later in development, when she can think in more abstract ways, will she be able to understand that some differences, for example in food habits, indicate her ethnic group.

Theoretical explanation of children's ethnic identity

According to Phinney (1990), studies on ethnic identity have been carried out within theoretical perspectives that have influenced not only their theoretical and methodological structure but also the interpretation of the results.

Early studies

Early studies on ethnic identity were carried out in the first half of the last century: They were characterised by cognitive-developmental frameworks and focused on the development of the abilities needed by children in order to gain an awareness of being part of an ethnic group (see Brand, Ruiz, & Padilla, 1974). Among the basic components of ethnic identity, the development of categorisation and identification were the most studied.

Categorisation can be defined as the child's ability to understand that individuals can be categorised and distinguished on the basis of ethnic and racial characteristics (Bernal, Knight, Garza, Ocampo, & Cota, 1990; see also Hirschfeld, Chapter 8). By contrast, ethnic identification refers to the acquisition of a precise and conscious use of an ethnic label for the self, based on the perception of being part of an ethnic group (Rotheram & Phinney, 1987). Researchers have commonly considered identification to be the starting point for the study of ethnic identity and to be one of the most significant aspects of the feeling of belonging to an ethnic group. Aboud (1987) has stated that categorisation, in comparison to identification, has a more restricted meaning. While the former only needs the simple ability to define oneself as part of an ethnic group, the latter requires the internalisation of this ability.

Early research on identification highlighted how children belonging to minority ethnic groups, either in terms of number or status, show some sense of rejection or devaluation of their own race and ethnicity (K. B. Clark & Clark, 1939; Horowitz, 1936). Using drawings, dolls, or photographs representing subjects of different races as stimuli, researchers have observed how a very high percentage of children of minority ethnic groups identified themselves with children belonging to the numerically and socially stronger ethnic groups. On the other hand, children from ethnic majority groups correctly identified themselves with their own group. This misidentification phenomenon has been well known since the pioneering studies were carried out. Even if the development of individuals' categorisation is a product of children's cognitive abilities, these findings indicate that identification cannot merely be interpreted as a result of cognitive development per se. Studies carried out in different contexts (K. B. Clark & Clark, 1947; Stevenson & Stewart, 1958; Vaughan, 1963, 1964) have sometimes supported the view that children of minority groups exhibit a tendency to identify themselves with majority group children of the same age, indicating that factors other than just cognitive development must be at play.

In the early 1970s, Porter (1971) drew attention to the particular role played by the identification test for minority ethnic group children, emphasising that Afro-American children, by identifying themselves with the white majority, are choosing to reject their own ethnic group. According to Porter, this choice is voluntary and dictated by an awareness of social, economic, and cultural differences, which characterise the cohabitation of ethnic groups in every multicultural society.

According to Vaughan (1987), the identification task can be considered as a preference test based on emotional processes, determining not how children see themselves but rather how they would like to be, depending on their experiences as members of a minority group in their first years of life. From this perspective, the responses to ethnic identification tests relate not to the child's cognitive level but to the awareness of the existence of social hierarchies, privileges, and differences among ethnic groups in multicultural societies.

Ethnic identity and social identity theory

The role played by emotional components, together with social perceptions, in the ethnic identification of minority children has been seen as central by some researchers into ethnic group membership (Tajfel, 1981; Ullah, 1985; Vaughan, 1987). Following social identity theory, this perspective assumes that the development of social structures that result from the acceptance or the rejection of one's own ethnic group plays an essential role in the ethnic identification process. According to this theoretical perspective, being part of a group gives the individual a feeling of belonging, which contributes to a positive idea about him- or herself (Phinney, 1990; Tajfel, 1981). But belonging to an ethnic group exposes the child to the development of an ethnic identity that is, inevitably, affected by the awareness of the existence of a social structure that the child cannot, in any way, influence.

Therefore, in the case of belonging to a low social status ethnic group, the child can acquire a negative social identity.

Does the development of a low self-concept represent an inevitable consequence for those who belong to low social status ethnic groups? According to some researchers (Bourhis, Giles, & Tajfel, 1973), there are different ways to escape from this outcome. One way is to try and leave one's minority group and gain entry to the majority group: however, this is not possible when visible physical characteristics mark one's membership of the minority group. A second possibility is represented by the commitment to improve the social status of one's own ethnic group: in this case, positive feelings, satisfaction, and pride towards one's own group can represent the key factors through which one can positively re-interpret one's own identity. Moreover, the development of negative social identities related to ethnic appearance is not an inevitable consequence, because this is not the hierarchical structure governing the relationship between majority and minority ethnic groups. Vaughan (1987), indeed, has emphasised that social structures are not static but always-evolving entities. In this sense, social changes can influence the way children build their social hierarchies, which govern multiethnic cohabitation. Therefore, social and political changes can positively or negatively modify the status of an ethnic group: This will influence the sense of belonging among children of that ethnic group.

In the USA, the social and political revaluation of minority groups, after the battles for the achievement of civil rights in the 1960s and 1970s, for example, has affected the outcomes of ethnic identification tests (Phinney, 1990; Rotheram & Phinney, 1987): since that period, children belonging to the Afro-American ethnic groups have exhibited a strong tendency to identify themselves with their own ethnic group. Changes in attitudes towards two of the most numerous ethnic communities in Europe, namely the Jewish and the Muslim communities, could have similar consequences, but in the opposite direction: in the case of the former group, for the stance taken over the Palestinian question, and in the case of the latter group, for the attacks on September 11 2001, both of which have been the object of discriminating attitudes in different countries. Belonging to these communities, nowadays, could in principle lead to the development of negative social identities: growing up within discriminated groups, as Tajfel (1981) stated more than 20 years ago, can result in the internalisation of discriminatory actions and can expose children to the development of a negative social identity.

Development and ethnic identity

As previously stated, ethnic identity has also been explored from a developmental perspective. In this respect, the individual's particular stage in life becomes relevant: from a stage where ethnicity is not a factor in one's identity, to later stages where the awareness of being part of an ethnic group does affect behaviours, values, and beliefs. One interpretative framework that can be used to represent the developmental process of acquiring a sense of one's ethnicity has been proposed by Erikson (1968) and Marcia (1980) in their theories about the formation of ego-identity.

According to Erikson, the achievement of identity is the result of a period of exploration and experimentation taking place during adolescence, and it leads the individual to take up an option or to commit him- or herself in several areas, such as employment, religion, and politics. For Marcia, the individual achieves individuation through four stages based on the different modalities used to explore reality and to take decisions. Neither being committed to exploration nor taking a decision imply a *diffused* identity; a commitment made without exploration, usually on the basis of the values passed on by parents or family, represents *foreclosure*; an exploration without making a commitment means that the individual is in the *moratorium* period; a precise and firm commitment after a moratorium represents the *achievement* of a fully-formed ego-identity. The formation of ethnic identity can be conceived as requiring a process similar to the one just described, which takes place when the individual explores and takes decisions about the role of ethnicity in his/her life.

Cross (1971, 1978) was the first to elaborate a developmental model of racial identity, positing a sequence of stages through which Black American people form their identity, based on their experiences of belonging to a minority group by both number and status. According to this model, the ethnic identity of minority ethnic group adolescents is inevitably affected by the visibility of their ethnic groups within the social context, with their acceptance of their own visibility being an index of the feeling of belonging. During pre-adolescence, individuals have not yet developed those critical abilities necessary to evaluate the importance of different ethnic groups. Only during adolescence, with the beginning of the identity crisis (Erikson, 1968), do these differences begin to hold an important place among the areas of exploration. Cross (1978) has considered the pre-adolescence stage as a preparation for the encounter with differences (*pre-encounter*), while adolescence is the time of life when there is a real *encounter* with the psychological dimensions under review. Subsequently, the adolescent develops new and different ways of gaining knowledge and understanding of his/her roots (*immersion-emersion*) and, after this, acquires the *internalisation* of the values and meaning of his/her own ethnic group (Atkinson, Morten, & Sue, 1983). According to Cross, this is the path that adolescents follow to reach their identity (*identity achievement*). This path, however, may fail to start or could be blocked during any of the described stages: in this case, minority adolescents will probably maintain the values and preferences similar to those of the majority ethnic groups.

Phinney (1989) has proposed a three-stage progression, which consists of a continuum that ranges from a feeling of ethnic identity not yet explored or examined through to a feeling of ethnic belonging made up of commitments and decisions. According to this model, pre-adolescents—and sometimes even adults—who do not live in multiethnic societies and are therefore not exposed to situations in which ethnicity is an evident and visible fact, are at the first stage: they have not undertaken an examination of ethnic identity. At this stage, those who belong to minority groups, both adolescents and adults, are attracted by the dominant culture, or are not interested in ethnicity, or have never thought about it. As an alternative, they can display attitudes emanating from their parents or from other significant adults about the importance of ethnicity and the relationships between cultures. The second stage is characterised by the exploration of one's own ethnicity. It can be the result of important experiences that force an awareness of the importance and value of ethnicity in one's life. This awareness, in its turn, implies an immersion in one's own ethnic group culture, habits, and traditions through daily activities. For some people, such a daily practice can mean a rejection of the dominant culture. At the end of this long and laborious process, individuals acquire a deep under-standing and appreciation of their own ethnicity, which is then internalised. For minority groups, the achievement of ethnic identity leads to two different kinds of problem: the first is to understand the difference between one's own culture and the majority one; the second concerns the awareness that differences between majority and minority groups often reflect social inequalities, economic disadvantages, and hardships.

Measurement of children's ethnic identification

From an operational viewpoint, we can infer children's ethnic identification from criteria such as the type of self-description and the understanding of ethnic constancy across time and situations (Aboud, 1987).

Self-description

This can be defined as the ability to select an attribute defining the membership of an ethnic group in a particular manner. In discourse about ethnic identification, the critical attributes are descent or kinship, nationality, religion, language, skin colour, or group name. Aboud (1987) empha-sised that the use of only one of these crucial attributes to define oneself in ethnic terms can be considered the first criterion signalling the achievement of ethnic identification.

Recognition based on visual resemblance develops around 3–4 years of age. Research has shown that, by that age, white and black children are already able to distinguish the characteristics of their own ethnic group.

The recognition of other minority ethnic groups, such as the Hispanic and the Native American in the North American context, comes later, around 8–9 years of age (Rice, Ruiz, & Padilla, 1974). The typical method of measuring ethnic identification, by means of self-descriptions based on critical attributes, uses visual stimuli, which are considered to be good indicators of the ability to make ethnic identification because they allow an immediate perception of resemblance. Generally, the procedure consists of asking the child if she perceives herself to be similar to some visual stimuli (K. B. Clark & Clark, 1947). These stimuli, differing in their ethnic characteristics, can be of various types: dolls, drawings, or photographs. The child is asked to choose among several dolls (or drawings, or photographs) the one "most similar" to herself. The answer is correct if the child points to a doll (or drawing, or photograph) presenting an attribute thought to be critical for her own ethnic group (for children, the ethnic group is considered to be their parents' ethnic group).

Self-description can involve more advanced cognitive processes than those tapped in the perception-based tests. As the latter tests evoke precise answers based on the importance of external characteristics, the former tests require abilities of classification and categorisation including the employment of cognitive inferences. This is the case with tests of categorisation and labelling.

Categorisation concerns the child's ability to recognise the existence of different ethnic groups and the characteristics used by the child to make the categorisation. This ability precedes that of identification (Bernal et al., 1990; Lo Coco et al., 2000). From a developmental point of view, categorisation is based, at first, on the ability to differentiate physical characteristics: indeed, in the case of the pre-school child, approximately between 3 and 4 years of age, children use evident morphological differences, such as skin colour (for example, whites from blacks) (K. B. Clark & Clark, 1947; Hraba & Grant, 1970). Later, at around 8–9 years of age, children are able to recognise less evident physical differences, such as eye colour or face shape (Fox & Jordan, 1973; George & Hoppe, 1979). Only at around 12 years of age do adolescents reach the awareness that the difference among ethnic groups is not just in the different somatic types, but presupposes a symbolic aspect linked to the acquisition of values and typical behaviours of ethnic groups. The procedure used to assess categorisation consists of showing the child photographs of peers belonging to different ethnic groups. The child is asked to group the photographs in some boxes, "putting them together as you like". After grouping, the child is asked to explain the criteria according to which he made the categorisation (skin colour, eye colour, face shape, typical clothes, or other).

Ethnic labelling refers to the child's ability to define him- or herself through the attribution of an ethnic label (Bernal et al., 1990). It is based on the recognition of those characteristics that make the difference between the various ethnic groups, and the contemporaneous perception of having common attributes with the other members of one's own ethnic group. The ability to use one's own ethnic label correctly is considered to be a reliable index of ethnic identification (Aboud, 1987). The development of ethnic labelling ability has been studied since the late 1950s (Spencer, 1982; Stevenson & Stewart, 1958; Vaughan, 1963). Research has shown how this ability is linked to children's age: indeed, only at around 7–8 years of age are children able to self-label correctly. The measurement of the ability to give the correct ethnic label follows a standard procedure: the child is shown a series of ethnic terms written on coloured cards. Then, he is asked to choose the term that best describes himself. If the child chooses the correct ethnic term (usually coinciding with his family one), the labelling ability is considered to be acquired. In a different version of this technique, the child is asked to describe herself. If she uses the correct ethnic label, the ability to make the identification is presumed to have been acquired (McGuire, McGuire, Child, & Fjioka, 1978).

Understanding of constancy

This concerns the awareness that one's own ethnic identity is constant across time and situations despite external changes. From a developmental viewpoint, by the time that they reach 7 years of age, children realise that ethnic identity is a characteristic unchanging in time (Aboud, 1984) and, by the time they are 8–9 years old, they acquire the awareness that every individual's characteristics remain unaffected, even in the event of external changes (Aboud & Skerry, 1983). The exploration of ethnic constancy can be achieved through the use of two different procedures. The first verifies if the child is able to notice the persistence of ethnic characteristics despite superficial changes in appearance. It consists of the presentation of a visual stimulus with ethnic characteristics. The stimulus is a photograph of a same-aged child or a doll. Then, the same stimulus is presented with a slight alteration to the clothes, wigs, and make-up. The child is asked if the ethnicity of the dolls or photographs remains the same, despite the changes (Aboud, 1984). The second procedure analyses the child's awareness that the ethnic group's attributes remain unchanged over time (Aboud, 1987; Aboud & Skerry, 1983; Semaj, 1980). It involves asking questions regarding the constancy over time of ethnic attributes. For example: "Will you be Arab in 10 years time?" or "Were your parents Arab when they were your age?" (Lo Coco et al., 2000).

Rather than using separate procedures for the different criteria, some researchers have preferred to apply a single test to examine them simultaneously. The test consists of a preliminary phase, which investigates if the child recognises the members of the different ethnic groups. The child is shown some photographs of same-aged children of different ethnic groups and asked, for example, who is white, who is black, who is Chinese, etc. After this first section, the real test begins. The child is shown some photographs of same-aged children with different ethnic attributes, and asked appropriate questions to explore the perceived resemblance, the labelling, and appreciation of constancy (Aboud, 1987).

ETHNIC BELONGING AND ETHNIC ATTITUDES

One of the most important requirements of multicultural and multiethnic societies is the analysis of the quality of feelings and attitudes mutually developed by different ethnic-cultural groups sharing the same living space. From this perspective, the social sciences, especially psychology, must give empirical support to the strategic reorganisation of social policies for ethnic integration and to answer such questions as: What are the factors mediating encounters between different ethnic-cultural groups? How do these factors operate? What role does ethnic identity play in multicultural integration? How does ethnic identity relate to attitudes and prejudices towards out-groups? In particular, it is important to adopt a developmental viewpoint exploring how, over a lifetime, feelings of ethnicity influence the individual's identity, attitudes, and social relationships. Especially in those countries where the migration flows have recently increased, and where there are many second-generation immigrant children, analysis must focus on the ways in which children acquire the behaviours, values, and attitudes of their own group, how they start considering themselves and others as members of different ethnic groups, and the factors influencing their encounters with other groups. At the same time, research must also include majority group children, who are also involved in these social changes and face new social realities.

To explain the centrality of ethnic identity as an interpersonal dimension, psychologists use the expression "ethnic attitudes". Rotheram and Phinney (1987) define ethnic attitudes as characteristic ways of reacting to one's own and others' ethnicity: these reactions can have a positive or negative meaning and different levels of intensity. Ethnic attitudes imply two fundamental elements (Aboud, 1987): (1) judgements towards one's own ethnic group (ethnic preference); (2) attitudes towards other ethnic groups (ethnic prejudice). The first dimension refers to the individual's attitudes, generally positive, towards the ethnic in-group; the second regards the individual's attitudes, generally negative, towards other ethnic groups. These two dimensions are independent and are not at the opposite ends of a continuum where preference for the in-group has, as its automatic consequence, prejudice towards out-groups (Nesdale, 2004).

Aboud (1987, 1988) has focused on prejudice, defining it as an organised predisposition to react in an unfavourable way towards people of another ethnic group because of their ethnicity. Within this general definition we can distinguish three components. The first is represented by a negative, unfavourable evaluation that can lead to rejecting behaviours towards an entire category of people or to a description of this group in exclusively negative terms[1]. The second component is that the evaluation must arise from the individual's ethnicity and not from his or her personal qualities. Judgements, even when they are expressed in relation to an individual, must refer to ethnic identity: we can talk of prejudice only if the negative evaluation is extended to many members of an ethnic group. Finally, prejudice refers to an organised predisposition to react negatively to people's ethnicity. This presupposes a stable tendency across time and situations to react to some ethnic stimuli in a negative way: prejudice is present at all times, even if not displayed.

Operationalisation and measurement of ethnic attitudes

A complex definition, such as the one proposed by Aboud presents different theoretical and methodological problems, especially regarding the operationalisation of ethnic attitudes and its assessment during childhood.

Theoretical problems include, above all, that of whether the attitude is an organised predisposition in childhood. Some researchers have emphasised the different value that this concept has for adults and children (Aboud, 1988; Phinney, 1990). Referring to children, indeed, it is pointless to talk about an organised predisposition using the same parameters adopted for adults, such as stability across time and contexts. The influence that concrete facts exercise on children's cognitive organisation, the consequent tendency to categorise on the basis of the immediate perception, the incapability of considering information from multiple perspectives, make the predisposition less stable and structured and, at the same time, dependent on social realities and on levels of cognitive development. The fact that children generally show lower organisation levels in their behaviour might suggest that children's prejudices are less organised and with a lower internal consistency than those of adults. This does not mean that children show lower prejudice levels than adults, but that these rudimentary attitudes have a simpler

---

[1] Aboud (1988) has distinguished between prejudice and a stereotype: The former refers to a generalised negative attitude; the latter consists of a rigid and overgeneralised belief about the attributes of an ethnic group. In other words, prejudice belongs to the field of evaluation, as a stereotype belongs to the field of description: two people who hold the same stereotype can show different attitudes.

structure because of cognitive and social differences. For these reasons, Aboud (1987, 1988) has suggested a focus on rudimentary and simple forms of self- and other-perception during childhood.

Methodological problems include the procedures typically used to assess ethnic attitudes. In the literature, studies on ethnic attitudes are often linked to, or even combined with, those on preference and ethnic identification. The same measures have been used to evaluate both areas. Although Aboud (1987) has underlined how ethnic attitudes and identity must not be confused, and how the preference towards an ethnic group must not be considered an index of identification with that ethnic group, many researchers have asserted that ethnic attitudes and identity are so related that they represent the two sides, a psychological one and a social one, of the same phenomenon (Berry, 1984; Cross, 1991; Helms, 1990). Therefore, tests to evaluate children's ethnic attitudes generally assess, at the same time, their ethnic identification.

The techniques used to evaluate children's ethnic attitudes can be divided into three categories. The first category includes techniques using forced-choice questions on the model of the Doll Test, developed by K. B. Clark and Clark (1947) to study racial awareness, identification, and attitudes towards one's own and other ethnic groups, in American children, white and black, aged 3–6 years. The procedure consists of the presentation of four dolls of the same dimensions, but differing in sex, skin colour, and hair colour. The child is asked seven questions: the first four assess ethnic attitudes, through the choice of a playmate ("Which doll would you like to play with?"), the preference of somatic types ("Which doll looks nice/ugly?") and the preference for the skin colour ("Which doll has a nice colour?"). For each item children have to choose a particular doll rather than another. This procedure has several limitations. First, using forced-choice answers, the acceptance of one group is confounded with the rejection of the other, and vice versa. For example, if a child prefers a same-aged playmate of his ethnic group, it is assumed that he rejects all the others. Moreover, ethnic attitudes are evaluated by a limited number of questions. Attitudes, however, can vary depending on the context: for instance, a child can prefer to study with a peer from one ethnic group but to play with someone from another group. Finally, children are not asked to express their level of preference/rejection towards the dolls: as Aboud (1988) has pointed out, within the rejection or the preference there may be different degrees of intensity that this measurement does not attempt to evaluate. For example, two children can show a negative attitude towards group X, but the intensity of their attitudes could be significantly different.

The second category of techniques includes multiple-item tests, such as the PRAM (Preschool Racial Attitude Measure) developed by Williams,

Best, and Boswell (1975) or the Katz–Zalk Projective Prejudice Test (1978). These tests have been developed to deal with some of the limits of the Doll Test and consist of presenting the child with a series of photographs representing peers of different ethnic groups, and asking her to point out the photograph closer to the description, which is given item by item. For instance, the PRAM consists of 36 items (24 racial ones and 12 gender ones), each describing a positive or negative individual quality (for example, kindness or aggressiveness). For each item, the child is shown two photographs representing a white person and a black one, and is asked to choose the one closer to the given description. The intensity of the child's attitudes is evaluated by adding "pro-white" choices to "anti-black" ones, and vice versa. The merit of this kind of procedure is that it unites various kinds of evaluation in relation to different qualities. However, it is always a forced-choice test and so, in this case also, the acceptance of one group is confounded with the rejection of the other. Moreover, when the children have to describe both ethnic groups, their approach is directly proportional to their age (Davey, 1983; Doyle, Beaudet, & Aboud, 1987). Finally, in spite of its name, the PRAM proves to be reliable only when used with pre-adolescents aged 10–12 or more (Aboud, 1988).

The third type of measurement uses continuous scales (Aboud, 1981; Aboud & Mitchell, 1977; Genesee, Tucker, & Lambert, 1978; Verna, 1981). This procedure offers several alternative responses on a continuum from positive to negative: children are asked to express their preference for each ethnic group separately, on a continuous scale ranged from "*I like it very much*" to "*I don't like it at all*". An example has been given by Aboud and Mitchell (1977)[2], who asked children to put some photographs representing same-aged children of a different ethnic group on a "liking board" and to express the ethnic preference in relation to the distance from themselves: the farthest-placed children were those they disliked, while the nearest ones were those they liked. The advantage of this kind of measure is that each ethnic group is evaluated separately, so that preference for one is not confounded with rejection of the other. Moreover, more members of the same group are assessed and therefore the level of attitude generalisation can be measured in relation to several exemplars. The limitations are that this method generally uses just one item such as "Put next to you the photographs of children you like and far from you the photographs of those you do not like"; furthermore, the contexts do not vary and so the evaluations cannot be generalised to several situations.

---

[2] Another example has been given by the "social distance scale" by Verna (1981), which requires children to mark on the paper how close they would want to sit to each of several own- and other-group members drawn on one side of the paper.

Regarding the operational definition of ethnic attitude, all three kinds of measure deal with and fulfil the first component: that is, they all measure evaluations. With regard to the second component, that is, whether the evaluations derive from the individual's ethnicity or from personal characteristics, this is provided by the measures using continuous scales and—in a limited way—by multiple-item tests. Finally, with respect to the third component, namely the evaluation of stability and consistency across time, multiple-item tests would seem to be the most appropriate. However, given the inherent limitations of each measure, the combined use of multiple-item tests and continuous scales would respect all three components that are used to define prejudice (Aboud, 1988).

Theoretical models of ethnic attitudes

The study of ethnic attitudes generates not only problems with their definition, operationalisation, and measurement, but also significant theoretical problems. Indeed, there is no consistent agreement among the theories as to how ethnic attitudes are acquired and developed. From a historical point of view, research has been dominated by two principal theoretical approaches (Aboud, 1988), namely inner state theory and social reflection theory. Neither theory deals directly with ethnic attitudes from a developmental viewpoint; however, the predictions they make about the processes involved in the development of prejudice may also be extrapolated to children

According to the inner state approach, prejudice reflects an internal disposition; a range of motivations, beliefs, and emotions that lead the individual to hold a negative attitude towards others (Adorno, Frenkel-Brunswick, Levinson, & Sanford, 1950). In the studies examining prejudice and authoritarian personality that were carried out on adults through retrospective analysis, researchers found that people who are without prejudices report having parents who accepted their individual qualities and helped them to express aggressiveness openly in controlled ways. On the other hand, those showing high prejudice levels described their parents as authoritarian people, who imposed rigid conventional rules, especially regarding the expression of aggressiveness. Because of their parents' authoritarian behaviour, these individuals never learnt to express the hostility towards their parents or other authoritarian figures, and shifted their aggressiveness to the powerless and to those without authority, such as members of minority groups. In other words, these people would not accept their antisocial and hostile impulses, denying them and projecting them on to weaker individuals. From this perspective, the interpretative model is the Freudian psychoanalytic one that puts the parent–child relationship at the centre of personality development: prejudice comes from child-rearing practices that interfere with the normal processes of conflict resolution. One of the strengths of this theory is that it can explain individual differences in prejudice levels: different educational practices will result in differences in impulse control. Furthermore, it offers a good explanation for the stability of prejudice levels. However, one of its limitations is that it does not explain how prejudice target groups are chosen: each minority group—ethnic or other—is considered equal. Additionally, no difference of prejudice between childhood and adulthood is considered.

The social reflection approach has focused on the influence that social factors have on prejudice development: attitudes and beliefs about ethnic groups reflect, in an exclusive way, the stratified structure of society. Social groups are perceived in different ways because of their different social status and power (Morland & Suthers, 1980) and the differences among groups are stressed, above all, on the basis of social or material competition (Sherif & Sherif, 1969; Tajfel, 1978). From this viewpoint, people are the product of their sociocultural environment, which in turn shapes their behaviours and attitudes. Attitudes and stereotypes related to cultural and ethnic groups develop only after the awareness of the stratification of the social structure, and so prejudice does not appear before 12 years of age, when children can understand the complexity of society. According to Allport (1954), children adopt the ethnic attitudes shown by their parents and by other significant figures, because of the influence of both educational practices and of imitation and observation processes. Initially, very young children use the same ethnic attitudes and labels as their parents without a real understanding of ethnicity's nature and meaning. With increasing ethnic awareness, there is an increase in the negative emotions associated with the ethnic labels of their parents, which crystallise into a negative attitude and a total rejection of specific groups. Later, these attitudes become part of the individual's personality, stable and difficult to modify. Allport draws a developmental path in prejudice formation. At an early age, prejudice will be absent, even though 3- to 4-year-old children are often interested in racial differences and appear to recognise them. Manifestations of prejudice come later, under the action of the socialisation process, and they will be due exclusively to the influence of the social environment.

Empirical research, however, has not supported these hypotheses: very young children show ethnic prejudice, and it reduces rather than increases with age (Aboud, 1988). From a developmental point of view, therefore, social reflection theory seems to contain several limitations because it does not explain the reason for the changes taking place during development.

To overcome the limitations of previous research, two theoretical-methodological approaches have appeared in recent years: a sociocognitive approach, examining ethnic attitude as a result of social and cognitive developmental changes (Aboud, 1988; Katz, 1976; Rotheram, & Phinney,

1987), and an approach based on a theoretical integration of social identity theory (SIT; Tajfel & Turner, 1979; Turner, 1982) and self-categorisation theory (SCT; Turner, Hogg, Oakes, Reicher, & Wetherell, 1987), which links ethnic attitude development to identification and self-categorisation processes.

The first perspective has considered prejudice to be "inevitable but not lasting" during development (Aboud, 1988), because it is based on particular aspects of children's thinking that are later abandoned (Katz, 1976; Piaget & Weil, 1951). Cognitive functioning, indeed, influences the ethnic socialisation process and determines the quality of the attitudes towards cultural and ethnic groups: at each developmental stage, qualitatively different prejudices and attitudes may be observed. At the same time, social factors, especially those inputs coming from the child's everyday social environment, play a relevant role: information coming from the child's social network or from the mass media influences the content of attitudes. However, the major role is always played by cognitive processes, which determine the attitudes' structure and can modify their content by filtering and distorting external inputs.

Most researchers have considered that the reduction in childhood egocentrism is a fundamental factor in prejudice development. For example, Piaget and Weil (1951) argued that prejudice develops according to a three-stage developmental sequence. In the first stage, between 4 and 7 years of age, children are egocentric and unaware of the existence of ethnic or national groups: every form of preference towards these groups is based on personal considerations. From 7 to 10 years of age—the second stage—children are able to decentre themselves, but they become "sociocentric", that is, they focus on the in-group and other groups are considered only in opposition to their own. In this phase, previous attitudes are rejected and the child shows a preference for the in-group and a prejudice towards outgroups. In the third stage, from 10 to 15 years, children acquire an even greater degree of decentration and integration of information. This brings them to perceive ethnic and cultural groups in a more realistic way, acknowledging the existence of intragroup differences and intergroup similarities. This model, however, does not explain how prejudice develops during subsequent phases.

A more complex model of prejudice development has been proposed by Aboud (1988), who has explained the formation of ethnic attitudes as the product of two overlapping developmental sequences, each one of them composed of three stages. One sequence consists of the processes influencing the way children's experiences are organised. At first, affective processes are dominant, and children's preferences are based on emotional states. In particular, attitudes are based on two fundamental feelings: fear and happiness. For example, children seem to prefer those people who can satisfy their needs and make them happy: they show a marked preference towards peers who give them a present, regardless of their ethnicity (Gottfried & Gottfried, 1974). In the second stage of this sequence, perceptual processes acquire a predominant role. This change reflects the quality of attitudes, which are now based on the perceived similarity with the other figures: there is a preference for similar people and a prejudice against different people. This similarity perception is exclusively based on observable and external characteristics, such as skin colour or clothes, rather than internal qualities (Aboud, 1977; Ramsey, 1982, 1983). The third stage is characterised by the dominance of cognitive judgements. Gradually, the child's experience is organised into a complex unit of thoughts based on logical and objective criteria. This change allows a more developed understanding of ethnicity as an internal quality, based on enduring criteria, which are linked by a common identity (Semaj, 1980). At the beginning of the pre-operational period, therefore, there is an increasing ethnic awareness leading to a higher evaluation of racial and ethnic criteria in the construction of social categories. Later, between 8 and 10 years of age, there is a progressive rejection of these criteria because children now rely more and more on individual qualities to perceive and evaluate others (Katz, 1976; Vaughan, 1963).

The other sequence consists of a shift in children's focus, with age, from themselves to others. The first stage of this sequence lasts until 7 years of age and it is characterised by egocentrism: children focus on their own preferences and perceptions. For example, they think their viewpoints and attitudes are the same as those of other people. The second stage is similar to Piaget's "sociocentric" stage (Piaget & Weil, 1951): children shift their attention to others, who are exclusively seen according to their ethnic categories and social groups. Differences between groups are exaggerated and prejudice is the product of this exaggeration. When children acquire a certain cognitive flexibility, categories tend to become less rigid and attention shifts from groups to individuals, who are then judged according to internal characteristics. As a consequence, prejudice decreases, even if this does not totally eliminate the use of ethnic stereotypes in the absence of personal information.

Following this model, Aboud (1988) has emphasised that ethnic preference and prejudice reach their peak between 5 and 7 years: after this age, there is a decline in both in-group preference and out-group prejudice (Katz, Sohn, & Zalk, 1975). The reason for this decline lies in the combination of two important developmental changes: the acquisition of operational thinking and of interest in other individuals. These changes allow a greater flexibility in using social categories, which slowly lose their importance in favour of individual characteristics. These conclusions have been confirmed by several studies (Doyle & Aboud, 1995; Doyle et al.,

1987), which have shown how some abilities linked to operational thinking, such as conservation, are related to a decrease in evident levels of prejudice.

Recently, several researchers (Milner, 1996; Nesdale, 2000; Nesdale & Flesser, 1999; Vaughan, 1987) have tried to study ethnic attitude development using a theoretical framework consisting of an integration between SIT (Tajfel & Turner, 1979, 1986; Turner, 1982) and SCT (Turner et al., 1987). From this perspective, ethnic preference is explained as a function of self-categorisation and identification processes with one's own social group (Bigler, Jones, & Lobliner, 1997; Brown, 1995; Powlishta, 1995). Prejudice is linked to motivational factors, because individuals tend to evaluate their own group positively and other groups negatively in order to increase their own self-esteem. Ethnic preference, developing since 4 years of age and growing side by side with ethnic awareness, is seen as a consequence of belonging to a particular group. According to these researchers, even at a very early age, children's emotional reactions towards their own and other ethnic groups reflect an attitude typical in their sociocultural environment (Morland, 1962). Indeed, children are surrounded by images and representations of other social groups, passed on by parents, neighbours, relatives, teachers, and media; in this way they learn from their own group to assume specific social behaviours and expectations towards those groups. From this perspective, attitude development does not come exclusively from the influence of social factors, but is subject to developmental constraints: the ways in which attitudes are expressed and identified vary as a function of children's cognitive, sociocognitive, and linguistic abilities (Nesdale, 2000).

Contrary to the sociocognitive approach, however, SIT does not propose that prejudice and in-group preference decline during development. Given the motivational nature of ethnic attitudes, they would be unlikely to be abandoned even with the acquisition of particular cognitive abilities. Many studies have shown that age does not in fact have a consistent effect on children's attitudes; on the contrary, preference for the in-group can sometimes increase over time (Nesdale, 2000; Rice et al., 1974). The error in the predictions of the sociocognitive approach, according to these researchers, is linked to the assessment measures, which are direct and transparent and cannot avoid social desirability effects: the decline in prejudice that is commonly observed after 7 years of age is therefore attributable to the fact that children are more aware that social discrimination is socially undesirable, and they duly react accordingly. Research using less direct procedures, such as the minimal group paradigm, has shown that prejudice may not decrease with age and may remain constant over time; a continuing preference for the in-group can also be observed in children who have an understanding of conservation (Vaughan, 1987; Vaughan, Tajfel, & Williams, 1981).

In view of the problems linked to both approaches, the aim of researchers has been to integrate the various contributions they can make: the sociocognitive approach provides the most useful theoretical and methodological support for examining the relationship between cognitive development and ethnic attitude development, while the most recent versions of SIT help to clarify the intergroup dynamics relating to ethnic attitudes.

Ethnic attitudes and status differences

According to many studies, the social status of an ethnic group is an extremely important variable in the process of ethnic socialisation: belonging to a majority or minority group significantly influences feelings, beliefs, and attitudes towards one's own and other ethnic groups. From this perspective, the study of ethnic attitudes must take into consideration, separately, minority and majority groups within a specific social system.

This idea has strengthened since the 1970s, and is based on findings from early research on ethnic attitudes and identity, carried out in previous decades on American children belonging to minority groups. These studies revealed that, from a very early age, significant differences in ethnic attitudes and identification depend on the status of the in-group (Asher & Allen, 1969; Brand et al., 1974; Cantor, 1972; A. Clark, Hocevar, & Dembo, 1980; K. B. Clark & Clark, 1947; Driedger, 1976; Porter, 1971). In particular, it was found that children from ethnic minorities negatively perceived their own ethnic group and attributed many positive adjectives to the majority group. Most majority children, on the contrary, attributed negative traits to all minority ethnic groups. This result conflicts with SIT expectations, according to which, in a context with several ethnic groups, minority status should increase the salience of race, thus promoting an ethnocentric attitude with a greater identification and preference for the ethnic in-group (Tajfel, 1981).

The social discrimination experienced by minority groups has stimulated ethnic self-assertion: the claims of minority groups are based on their right to choose to be "different", according to their own self-definition and not to implicit or explicit terms dictated by the majority (Tajfel, 1981, p. 406). In this sense, identification and preference for one's own group become strategies of adaptation to a social system based on differences and inequalities. However, according to Tajfel, when social mobility is possible, the situation can be reversed, and the minority group's members could abandon the entire system of rules, values, and prescriptions of their own ethnic community: acceptance and rejection of the minority status, and consequently of one's ethnic group, become the two opposite ends of a continuum along which individuals from minorities place their social behaviour. The most evident consequence of the rejection by minority group members of their own ethnic groups is a positive attitude towards the majority group, a phenomenon called out-group preference (Tajfel, 1981). The preference for the out-group has also been observed in several studies carried out with children from minority groups, in countries other than the USA (Jahoda, Thomson, & Bhatt, 1972; Milner, 1973; Vaughan, 1987).

The social behaviour of minority groups, therefore, cannot be evaluated in absolute and generalised terms, but must be examined through a consideration of the specific and particular political and social factors characterising the country in which they live: psychological and social relationships between minority and majority groups are constantly changing as a consequence of variations in social conditions and in the social system to which the groups belong.

In recent years, research on these topics has demonstrated an interesting reversal: 4- to 7-year-old children of minority ethnic groups now display, more than in the past, a clear preference towards peers from their own ethnic group; only between 8 and 10 years of age, when the influence of the dominating culture plays a major role, do they start giving their preference both to peers of their own ethnic group and to peers of the majority group (Aboud, 1987; Lo Coco et al., 2000, 2002; Verkuyten, 1991, 1992; Verkuyten, Masson, & Elffers, 1995). For instance, Verkuyten (1991, 1992) has shown that preference for the in-group can also be observed in children and adolescents of minority groups, although it is slightly less marked than that shown by majority groups. Laosa (1984) has provided an explanation for this change: the "misidentification" and "out-group preference" phenomena should indeed be diminished as a result of the political and social revaluation of minority groups, following the struggle to achieve civil rights. In a political and cultural situation promoting only the dominating ethnic group values—such as the one that characterised the USA up to the middle of the last century—the preference for the dominant ethnic group and for its lifestyle was an effective strategy to avoid feelings of inferiority, linked to one's ethnic group. In present-day multiethnic societies, however, ethnicity is no longer only a source of discrimination. On the contrary, for many groups, it has become an important instrument with which to access social and political resources: rejection of one's ethnic group is no longer the most effective strategy in the new social context, and there are now new forms of expression, such as biculturalism.

This idea that research findings on the attitudes held by minority group children must be considered in the light of the particular social, political, and economic conditions characterising each ethnic group history, and in each specific context, has strengthened in recent years. To make predictions regarding the development of children's attitudes, it is less important to know if they belong to a minority rather than a majority group, than to analyse the close network of social relationships of the group within a specific historical-cultural context. Only in this way can we fully understand such a complex phenomenon.

To explain this relationship, we can take into consideration the results of some research carried out in Italy. Generally, in societies such as Italy, where the multiethnic composition has only just begun, children from minority ethnic groups face negative attitudes and stereotypes regarding their ethnic origin daily. This situation can lead them to reject their own ethnicity and to develop positive attitudes towards the majority group, which is perceived as being stronger. For example, Lo Coco et al. (2000) observed in Tunisian and Asian children living in Sicily (in the south of Italy) a marked positive attitude towards Italian/white majority group members: they were perceived in a more favourable way, were described with a higher number of positive traits, and were often chosen as partners for several activities. However, some differences occurred between the various minority ethnic groups, probably due to the different historical-cultural relationships with the majority Italian group. In particular, the Tunisian children showed a significant positive attitude towards their own ethnic group: they often chose Tunisian children to share social activities and gave a high number of positive adjectives to both Tunisian and Italian children (Lo Coco et al., 2000, 2002). The favourable attitude of Tunisians towards both groups can be related to the history between the two populations. Tunisia and Italy are linked by a long tradition of economic, cultural, and social exchanges; in particular Sicily has been involved, since the 1960s, with massive migration flows from Tunisia (Giacomarra, 1994). The Tunisian community is well integrated from an economic, cultural, and social point of view, and it does not suffer either highly discriminating conditions or low ethnic visibility. This situation is reflected in the children's attitudes, who maintained a positive attitude towards their ethnicity in spite of their minority status.

RELATIONS BETWEEN ETHNIC IDENTIFICATION AND ETHNIC ATTITUDES

Another significant topic in this field concerns the relationship between ethnic identification and ethnic attitudes. SIT explicitly links prejudice to identification with the in-group and to self-categorisation: the stronger the identification with the in-group, the greater the preference for the in-group and the greater the negative attitude towards the out-group (Billig & Tajfel, 1973; Bornman, 1999; Brown, 1995; Tajfel, 1981; Verkuyten & Neukee, 1999). This is because prejudice towards the out-group and preference for the in-group are conceptualised by SIT as a means of creating a positive social identity. Re-evaluation of the in-group—and the consequent devaluation of other groups—depends on the fact that we link our social identity to our in-group: the strength of the in-group becomes our strength and what distinguishes us in our continuous social relationships.

From a developmental viewpoint, social categorisation and identification with a group become essential prerequisites of social attitudes: to show phenomena of prejudice and preference towards some social groups, the child must be able, at the same time, to identify the groups within society, and to identify with one of them. Martin and Halverson (1981), for example, have proposed a developmental sequence regarding gender identity: first, children must learn to categorise social groups by gender; then they must be able to correctly identify themselves and others according to these attributes; and finally, depending on the chosen identification, they display preference towards the in-group and prejudice towards the out-group.

Research examining the relationship between identification with cultural and ethnic groups and the formation of social preferences of children and adolescents in multiethnic societies has produced contradictory results (Bennett, Lyons, Sani, & Barrett, 1998; Duckitt & Mphuthing, 1998; Verkuyten, 1992). On the one hand, some studies have found that national or ethnic identification can be related to the preference for one's own group and to a less favourable attitude towards other groups (Aboud, 1980, 1988; Berry, Kalin, & Taylor, 1977; Davey, 1983; Fu & Fogel, 1982; Lambert & Klineberg, 1967; Piaget & Weil, 1951; Verkuyten, 1992, 1998); on the other hand, other studies have found that identification with one's own social group is not always related to children's attitudes towards their own or other groups (Bennett et al., 1998; Hraba & Grant, 1970; see also Chapter 10 by Barrett).

Some researchers have affirmed that the development of ethnic attitudes is partly independent of ethnic identification: we can also observe prejudice and preference phenomena in the absence of children's correct identification (Aboud, 1980, 1988; Fu & Fogel, 1982). For instance, Aboud (1980) has observed that some children can show, simultaneously, low identification and a marked preference towards the in-group, or strong identification and a low level of prejudice towards out-groups. Aboud has used these discrepancies as evidence for the view that, at least between 4 and 7 years of age, attitudes are not entirely determined by the perceptual and cognitive processes that form the basis of identification.

Bennett et al. (1998) provide a possible explanation for these discrepancies regarding national identity. In the early phases of development, emotional processes seem to prevail over cognitive ones, and so children can show preference behaviour for some national groups long before they develop any knowledge of those groups (Barrett & Short, 1992; Johnson, Middleton, & Tajfel, 1970). Moreover, preference for the in-group can also be observed when the child does not yet categorise him- or herself as belonging to that group. Bennett et al. (1998; see also Barrett, Chapter 10) interpret this finding as follows. Children have access daily to socially shared information regarding social groups. The nature of this information is not neutral, but may contain evaluations and judgements regarding their own and other groups. Therefore, in this way, children's cognitions and attitudes toward social groups have, to some degree, a social origin, and result from social influence processes (D'Andrade, 1981; Emler & Dickinson, 1993). Information received from significant members of one's own group is assimilated via interpersonal relationships, through participation in social practices, and through the mass media, thus influencing the contents of attitudes. However, the role played by cognitive and perceptual factors must not be overlooked; their action intertwines with social factors to contribute to the determination of social perceptions and categories (Barrett, Chapter 10; Ramsey, 1987).

Therefore, research needs to consider the interplay between different types of factor influencing ethnic attitudes and self-identification, with particular attention being paid to the role played by the social factors that moderate the relationship between the two. On the one hand, self-categorisation may influence ethnic attitudes directly, particularly with regard to in-group preference, when very important categories for children are involved such as ethnic group or gender (Bennett et al., 1998; Verkuyten, 1995). On the other hand, social factors can also significantly influence attitudes towards cultural and ethnic groups, and contribute to the relationship between prejudice and ethnic identity (Barrett, Chapter 10). For instance, Lo Coco et al. (2000) found that many Italian children, even though they identified themselves correctly, showed different attitudes towards different ethnic out-groups. In particular, while a negative attitude towards Tunisian and Asian groups was observed, many children showed a positive attitude towards black African children. On the basis of these results, Lo Coco et al. hypothesised that the antiprejudice culture, widespread in recent years in Italy, has influenced the attitudes of Italian children towards those particular minority children whose groups were involved in the social campaigns. The awareness that racial discrimination is a socially undesirable feeling, however, does not generalise to those other ethnic groups—such as Tunisians—whose level of visibility is not sufficient to justify their inclusion within the anti-racist campaign.

REFERENCES

Aboud, F. E. (1977). Interest in ethnic information: A cross-cultural developmental study. *Canadian Journal of Behavioural Science*, 9, 134–146.
Aboud, F. E. (1980). A test of ethnocentrism with young children. *Canadian Journal of Behavioural Science*, 12, 195–209.

Aboud, F. E. (1981). Egocentrism, conformity, and agreeing to disagree. *Developmental Psychology, 17,* 791–799.

Aboud, F. E. (1984). Social and cognitive bases of the identity constancy. *Journal of Genetic Psychology, 145,* 227–229.

Aboud, F. E. (1987). The development of ethnic self-identification and attitudes. In J. S. Phinney & M. J. Rotheram (Eds.), *Children's ethnic socialization.* Newbury Park, CA: Sage.

Aboud, F. E. (1988). *Children and prejudice.* Oxford: Basil Blackwell.

Aboud, F. E., & Mitchell, F. G. (1977). Ethnic role taking: The effects of preference and self-identification. *International Journal of Psychology, 12,* 1–17.

Aboud, F. E., & Skerry, S. A. (1983). Self and ethnic concepts in relation to ethnic constancy. *Canadian Journal of Behavioral Science, 15,* 14–26.

Adorno, T. W., Frenkel-Brunswick, E., Levinson, D. J., & Sanford, R. N. (1950). *The authoritarian personality.* New York: Harper & Row.

Allport, G. W. (1954). *The nature of prejudice.* Cambridge, MA: Addison-Wesley.

Asher, S. R., & Allen, V. L. (1969). Racial preference and social comparison processes. *Journal of Social Issues, 25,* 157–167.

Atkinson, D., Morten, G., & Sue, D. (1983). *Counselling American minorities.* Dubuque, IA: C. Brown.

Barrett, M. D., & Short, J. (1992). Images of European people in a group of 5–10-year-old English schoolchildren. *British Journal of Developmental Psychology, 10,* 339–363.

Bennett, M., Lyons, E., Sani, F., & Barrett, M. D. (1998). Children's subjective identification with the group and in-group favouritism. *Developmental Psychology, 35,* 905–909.

Bernal, M. E., Knight, G. P., Garza, C. A., Ocampo, K. A., & Cota, M. K. (1990). The development of ethnic identity in Mexican-American children. *Hispanic Journal of Behavioral Science, 12,* 3–24.

Berry, J. W. (1984). Cultural relations in plural societies: Alternatives to segregation and their socio-psychological implications. In N. Miller & M. Brewer (Eds.), *Groups in contact: The psychology of desegregation.* Orlando, FL: Academic Press.

Berry, J. W., Kalin, R., & Taylor, D. M. (1977). *Multiculturalism and ethnic attitudes in Canada.* Ottawa: Supply & Services.

Bigler, R. S., Jones, L. C., & Lobliner, D. B. (1997). Social categorization and the formation of intergroup attitudes in children. *Child Development, 68,* 530–543.

Billig, M. G., & Tajfel, H. (1973). Social categorization and similarity in intergroup behaviour. *European Journal of Sociology, 3,* 27–52.

Bornman, E. (1999). Self-image and ethnic identification in South-Africa. *The Journal of Social Psychology, 139,* 411–425.

Bourhis, R. Y., Giles, H., & Tajfel, H. (1973). Language as determinant of Welsh identity. *European Journal of Social Psychology, 3,* 447–460.

Brand, E., Ruiz, R., & Padilla, A. (1974). Ethnic identification and preference: A review. *Psychological Bulletin, 86,* 860–890.

Brown, R. (1995). *Prejudice: Its social psychology.* Oxford: Blackwell.

Cantor, G. N. (1972). Use of a conflict paradigm to study race awareness in children. *Child Development, 43,* 1437–1442.

Clark, A., Hocevar, D., & Dembo, M. H. (1980). The role of cognitive development in children's explanations and preferences for skin colour. *Developmental Psychology, 16,* 332–339.

Clark, K. B., & Clark, M. P. (1939). The development of consciousness of self and the emergence of racial identification in Negro pre-school children. *Journal of Social Psychology, 10,* 591–599.

Clark, K. B., & Clark, M. P. (1947). Racial identification and preference in Negro children. In T. Newcomb & E. Hartley (Eds.), *Readings in social psychology.* New York: Holt.

Cross, W. (1971). The negro to black conversion experience. *Black World, 20*, 13–27.
Cross, W. (1978). The Thomas and Cross models of psychological nigrescence: A literature review. *Journal of Black Psychology, 4*, 13–31.
Cross, W. (1991). *Shades of black: Diversity in African-American identity*. Philadelphia, PA: Temple University Press.
D'Andrade, R. G. (1981). The cultural part of cognition. *Cognitive Science, 5*, 179–195.
Davey, A. G. (1983). *Learning to be prejudiced: Growing up in multiethnic Britain*. London: Edward Arnold.
Doyle, A. B., & Aboud, F. E. (1995). A longitudinal study of white children's' racial prejudice as a social-cognitive development. *Merrill-Palmer Quarterly, 41*, 209–228.
Doyle, A. B., Beaudet, J., & Aboud, F. E. (1987). Developmental patterns in the flexibility of children's ethnic attitudes. *Journal of Cross-Cultural Psychology, 19*, 3–18.
Driedger, L. (1976). Ethnic self-identity: A comparison of in-group evaluations. *Sociometry, 39*, 131–141.
Duckitt, J., & Mphuthing, T. (1998). Group identification and intergroup attitudes: A longitudinal analysis in South Africa. *Journal of Personality and Social Psychology, 74*, 80–85.
Emler, N. P., & Dickinson, J. (1993). The child as a sociologist. In M. Bennett (Ed.), *The development of social cognition*. New York: Guilford Press.
Erikson, E. (1968). *Identity: Youth and crisis*. New York: Norton.
Fox, D. J., & Jordan, V. D. (1973). Racial preference and identification of Black, American Chinese and White children. *Genetic Psychology Monographs, 88*, 229–286.
Fu, V. R., & Fogel, S. W. (1982). Prowhite/antiblack bias among southern pre-school children. *Psychological Reports, 51*, 1003–1006.
Genesee, F., Tucker, G. R., & Lambert, W. E. (1978). The development of ethnic identity and ethnic role-taking skills in children from different school settings. *International Journal of Psychology, 13*, 39–57.
George, D. M., & Hoppe, R. A. (1979). Racial identification, preference and self-concept. *Journal of Cross-cultural Psychology, 10*, 85–100.
Giacomarra, M. (1994). *Immigrati e minoranze. Percorsi di integrazione sociale in Sicilia* (*Immigrants and minorities. Pathways of social integration in Sicily*). Palermo, Sicily: La Zisa Editore.
Gottfried, A. W., & Gottfried, A. E. (1974). Influence of social power vs. status envy modelled behaviours on children's preferences for models. *Psychological Reports, 34*, 1147–1150.
Helms, J. (1990). *Black and white racial identity. Theory, research and practice*. Westport, CT: Greenwood Press.
Horowitz, R. E. (1936). The development of attitudes toward the negro. *Archives of Psychology, 194*.
Hraba, J., & Grant, G. (1970). Black is beautiful: A re-examination of racial preference and identification. *Journal of Personality and Social Psychology, 16*, 398–402.
Jahoda, G., Thomson, S. S., & Bhatt, S. (1972). Ethnic identity and preferences among Asian immigrant children in Glasgow: A replicated study. *European Journal of Social Psychology, 2*, 19–32.
Johnson, N., Middleton, D., & Tajfel, H. (1970). The relationship between children's preferences for and knowledge about other nations. *British Journal of Social and Clinical Psychology, 9*, 232–240.
Katz, P. A. (1976). The acquisition of racial attitudes in children. In P. A. Katz (Ed.), *Towards the elimination of racism*. New York: Pergamon.
Katz, P. A., Sohn, M., & Zalk, S. R. (1975). Perceptual concomitants of racial attitudes in urban grade-school children. *Developmental Psychology, 11*, 135–144.

Katz, P. A., & Zalk, S. R. (1974). Modification of children's racial attitudes. *Developmental Psychology, 14*, 447–461.

Lambert, W. E., & Klineberg, O. (1967). *Children's views of foreign peoples.* New York: Appleton-Century-Crofts.

Laosa, L. (1984). Social policies toward children of diverse ethnic racial and language groups in the United States. In H. Stevenson & A. Siegel (Eds.), *Child development research and social policy.* Chicago: University of Chicago Press.

Lo Coco, A., & Pace, U. (2001). Strumenti e metodi d'indagine nell'esplorazione dell'identità etnica [Methods and assessment instruments in ethnic identity exploration]. In P. Bastianoni (Ed.), *Scuola e immigrazione. Uno scenario comune per nuove appartenenze* [School and immigration: A common scenario for new belongings] (pp. 99–139). Milano: Unicopli.

Lo Coco, A., Pace, U., & Zappulla, C. (2000). I precursori dell'identità etnica in età infantile [Ethnic identity precursors in childhood]. *Età Evolutiva, 66*, 77–85.

Lo Coco, A., Pace, U., & Zappulla, C. (2002). I percorsi dell'identità etnica nei bambini tunisini in Sicilia [Pathways of ethnic identity in Tunisian children in Sicily]. In F. Di Maria & A. Lo Coco (Eds.), *Psicologia della solidarietà. Condividere nelle società multiculturali* [Psychology of solidarity. Sharing in multiethnic societies] (pp. 60–88). Milano: Franco Angeli.

Marcia, J. (1980). Identity in adolescence. In J. Adelson (Ed.), *Handbook of adolescent psychology.* New York: Wiley.

Martin, C. L., & Halverson, C. F. (1981). A schematic processing model of sex-typing and stereotyping in children. *Child Development, 49*, 434–444.

McGuire, W. J., McGuire, C. V., Child, P., & Fjioka, T. (1978). Salience of ethnicity in the spontaneous self-concept as a function of one's ethnic distinctiveness in the social environment. *Journal of Personality and Social Psychology, 36*, 511–520.

Milner, D. (1973). Racial identification and preference in "black" British children. *European Journal of Social Psychology, 3*, 281–295.

Milner, D. (1996). Children and racism: Beyond the valley of dolls . . . In W. P. Robinson (Ed.), *Social groups and identities. Developing the legacy of Henry Tajfel.* Oxford: Butterworth Heinemann.

Morland, J. K., & Suthers, E. (1980). Racial attitudes of children: Perspectives on the structural-normative theory of prejudice. *Phylon, 41*, 267–275.

Morland, J. K. (1962). Racial acceptance and preference of nursery school children in a southern city. *Merrill-Palmer Quarterly, 8*, 271–280.

Nesdale, A. R. (2000). Developmental changes in children's ethnic preferences and social cognitions. *Journal of Applied Developmental Psychology, 20*, 501–519.

Nesdale, D. (2004). Social identity processes and children's ethnic prejudice. In M. Bennett & F. Sani (Eds.), *The development of the social self.* Hove, UK: Psychology Press.

Nesdale, A. R., & Flesser, D. (1999). *Social identity and the development of children's intergroup attitudes.* Unpublished manuscript, Griffith University.

Phinney, J. S. (1989). Stages of ethnic identity in minority group adolescents. *Journal of Early Adolescence, 9*, 34–49.

Phinney, J. S. (1990). Ethnic identity in adolescents and adults: Review of research. *Psychological Bulletin, 108*, 499–514.

Phinney, J. S., Ferguson, D. L., & Tate, J. D. (1997). Intergroup attitudes among ethnic minority adolescents: A causal model. *Child Development, 68*, 955–969.

Phinney, J. S., Horenczyk, G., Liebkind, K., & Vedder, P. (2001). Ethnic identity, immigration and well-being: An interactional perspective. *Journal of Social Issues, 57*, 493–510.

Piaget, J. E., & Weil, A. (1951). The development in children of the idea of the homeland and of relations with other countries. *International Science Bulletin, 3*, 561–576.

Porter, J. D. R. (1971). *Black child, white child: The development of racial attitudes.* Cambridge, MA: Harvard University.

Powlishta, K. K. (1995). Intergroup processes in childhood: Social categorization and sex role development. *Developmental Psychology, 30*, 526–536.

Ramsey, P. G. (1982). *Racial difference in young children's descriptions and contacts with peers.* Paper presented at the annual meeting of the American Psychological Association, Washington, DC.

Ramsey, P. G. (1983). *Young children's responses to racial differences: sociocultural perspectives.* Paper presented at the biennial meeting of the Society for Research in Child Development, Detroit.

Ramsey, P. G. (1987). Young children's thinking about ethnic differences. In J. S. Phinney & M. J. Rotheram (Eds.), *Children's ethnic socialisation.* Newbury Park, CA: Sage.

Rice, A. S., Ruiz, R. A., & Padilla, A. M. (1974). Person perception, self-identity, and ethnic group preference in Anglo, black and Chicano pre-school and third-grade children. *Journal of Cross-Cultural Psychology, 5*, 100–108.

Rotheram, M. J., & Phinney, J. S. (1987). Introduction: Definitions and perspectives in the study of children's ethnic socialization. In J. S. Phinney & M. J. Rotheram (Eds.), *Children's ethnic socialization.* Newbury Park, CA: Sage.

Semaj, L. (1980). The development of racial-classification abilities. *Journal of Negro Education, 50*, 41–47.

Sherif, M., & Sherif, C. W. (1969). *Social psychology.* New York: Harper & Row.

Spencer, M. B. (1982). Preschool children's social cognition and cultural cognition: A cognitive developmental interpretation of race dissonance findings. *Journal of Psychology, 112*, 275–296.

Stevenson, H. W., & Stewart, E. C. (1958). A developmental study of social awareness in young children. *Child Development, 29*, 399–409.

Tajfel, H. (1976). Psicologia sociale e processi sociali [Social psychology and social processes]. In A. Palmonari (Ed.), *Problemi attuali della psicologia sociale* [Present issues of social psychology]. Bologna, Italy: Il Mulino.

Tajfel, H. (1978). *Differentiation between social groups: Studies in the social psychology of intergroup relations.* London: Academic Press.

Tajfel, H. (1981). *Human groups and social categories: Studies in social categories.* London: Cambridge University Press.

Tajfel, H., & Turner, J. (1979). An integrative theory of intergroup conflict. In W. Austin & S. Worchel (Eds.), *The social psychology of intergroup relations.* Monterey, CA: Brooks/Cole.

Tajfel, H., & Turner, J. (1986). The social identity theory of intergroup behaviour. In S. Worchel & W. Austin (Eds.), *Psychology of intergroup relations.* Chicago: Nelson-Hall.

Turner, J. C. (1982). Towards a cognitive redefinition of the social group. In H. Tajfel (Ed.), *Social identity and intergroup relations* (pp. 15–40). Cambridge: Cambridge University Press.

Turner, J. C., Hogg, M. A., Oakes, P. J., Reicher, S. D., & Wetherell M. S. (1987). *Rediscovering the social group: A self-categorization theory.* Oxford: Basic Blackwell.

Ullah, P. (1985). Second generation Irish Youth: Identity and ethnicity. *New Community, 12*, 310–320.

Vaughan, G. (1963). Concept formation and the development of ethnic awareness. *Journal of Genetic Psychology, 103*, 93–103.

Vaughan, G. (1964). The development of ethnic attitudes in New Zealand school children. *Genetic Psychology Monographs, 70*, 135–175.

Vaughan, G. (1987). A social psychological model of ethnic identity development. In J. S. Phinney & M. J. Rotheram (Eds.), *Children's ethnic socialization.* Newbury Park, CA: Sage.

Vaughan, G. M., Tajfel, H., & Williams, J. A. (1981). Bias in reward allocation in an intergroup and an interpersonal context. *Social Psychology Quarterly, 44,* 37–42.

Verkuyten, M. (1991). Self-definition and ingroup formation among ethnic minorities in the Netherlands. *Social Psychology Quarterly, 54,* 280–286.

Verkuyten, M. (1992). Ethnic group preferences and the evaluation of ethnic identity among adolescents in the Netherlands. *Journal of Social Psychology, 132,* 741–750.

Verkuyten, M. (1995). Self-esteem, self-concept stability, and aspects of ethnic identity among minority and majority youth in the Netherlands. *Journal of Youth and Adolescence, 24,* 155–175.

Verkuyten, M. (1998). Self-categorization and the explanation of ethnic discrimination. *Journal of Community and Applied Social Psychology, 8,* 395–407.

Verkuyten, M., Masson, K., & Elffers, H. (1995). Racial categorization and preference among older children in The Netherlands. *European Journal of Social Psychology, 25,* 637–656.

Verkuyten, M., & Neukee, S. (1999). Subjective well-being, discrimination and cultural conflict: Iranians living in the Netherlands. *Social Indicators Research, 47,* 281–306.

Verna, G. B. (1981). Use of a free-response task to measure children's race preferences. *Journal of Genetic Psychology, 138,* 87–93.

Weinreich, J. (1988). The operalization of ethnic identity. In J. Berry & R. Annis (Eds.), *Ethnic psychology. Research and practice with immigrants, refugees, native peoples, ethnic groups, and sojourners.* Amsterdam: Swets & Zeitlinger.

Williams, J. E., Best, D. L., & Boswell, D. A. (1975). The measurement of children's racial attitudes in early school years. *Child Development, 46,* 494–500.

CHAPTER TEN

Children's understanding of, and feelings about, countries and national groups

Martyn Barrett
Department of Psychology, University of Surrey, Guildford, UK

This chapter reviews current knowledge about the development of children's understanding of, and feelings about, countries and national groups. The emphasis of this review will be upon empirical findings rather than theoretical explanations, mainly because existing research on this topic has failed to provide support for *any* of the available theories. The underlying argument will be that it is necessary to adopt a more inclusive and multi-layered theoretical framework than has been proposed hitherto, if the goal is to formulate an empirically adequate theoretical account of children's development in this domain.

Empirical research in this field was initiated by Piaget (1928; Piaget & Weil, 1951). Piaget's early investigations were followed by a flurry of further studies in the 1960s and early 1970s (e.g., Jahoda, 1962, 1963a, 1963b, 1964; Jaspers, Van de Geer, Tajfel, & Johnson, 1972; Johnson, 1966, 1973; Johnson, Middleton, & Tajfel, 1970; Lambert & Klineberg, 1967; Middleton, Tajfel, & Johnson, 1970; Tajfel & Jahoda, 1966; Tajfel, Jahoda, Nemeth, Campbell, & Johnson, 1970; Tajfel, Jahoda, Nemeth, Rim, & Johnson, 1972). However, this initial line of research came to an end round about 1973. The topic then vanished from the research agenda of developmental psychologists for approximately 20 years. During the 1990s, there was a resurgence of interest in this area (e.g., Axia, Bremner, Deluca, & Andreasen, 1998; Barrett, 1996; Barrett & Farroni, 1996; Barrett & Short, 1992; Cutts Dougherty, Eisenhart, & Webley, 1992; Rutland, 1998, 1999). Studies have now been conducted in a number of different national contexts including England and Scotland (e.g., Barrett, Lyons, & del Valle, 2004; Barrett, Wilson, & Lyons, 1999b, 2003; Bennett, Lyons, Sani, & Barrett, 1998), Ireland (Nugent, 1994), Holland (Verkuyten, 2001), Germany (Wilberg, 2002), Spain (Giménez, Canto, Fernández, & Barrett, 1999; Reizábal, Valencia, & Barrett, 2004; Vila, del Valle, Perera, Monreal, & Barrett, 1998), Italy (Castelli, Cadinu, & Barrett, in press; de Rosa & Bombi, 1999), Russia, Ukraine, Georgia, and Azerbaijan (Barrett, Riazanova, & Volovikova, 2001; Bennett et al., 2004).

Six principal issues have been investigated in these studies. First, some studies have investigated children's geographical knowledge of their own country and other countries. Second, some studies have examined children's feelings about countries, including their emotional attachment to their own country. Third, a handful of studies have explored children's knowledge of national emblems such as national flags, anthems, costumes, historical figures, and historical events, and the significance that children attribute to these emblems. Fourth, various studies have examined children's knowledge of, and beliefs about, the people who make up different national groups, and the development of national stereotypes. Fifth, a number of studies have investigated children's feelings towards the people who make up different national groups. Finally, several studies have explored children's national self-categorisations, and the development of children's subjective identification with their own national in-group. The following review summarises the principal findings that have been obtained within each of these six areas in turn. The chapter will conclude with some reflections concerning the inadequacies of the currently available theoretical frameworks for explaining these findings.

CHILDREN'S GEOGRAPHICAL KNOWLEDGE OF THEIR OWN COUNTRY AND OTHER COUNTRIES

It is now clear from numerous studies that, before 5 years of age, children often have very little geographical knowledge of either their own country or other countries and, indeed, may even be unable to state the name of their own country (Jahoda, 1962; Piaget & Weil, 1951). However, from about 5 or 6 years of age onwards, children do usually know the name of their own country. For example, Jahoda (1963a, 1964) interviewed 6- to 11-year-old Scottish (Glaswegian) children. He found that even the youngest children were familiar with the word *Scotland*. But some of the younger children exhibited a poor understanding of what Scotland actually was. So, when he asked questions such as "What is Scotland?", the replies included statements such as "Scotland is the capital of Edinburgh. It's in Glasgow" and "I was born in it—it's the name of the town. It's just outside Glasgow". These confusions usually diminished in subsequent years. However, even at

10 or 11 years of age, some of the children were still exhibiting confusion over what Scotland actually was. Social class differences in knowledge were also found: middle-class children exhibited higher levels of knowledge than working-class children. Although factual geographical knowledge increased significantly with age, such knowledge was *not* linked rigidly to either age or cognitive-developmental stage. For example, there were some 6-year-olds in Jahoda's sample who understood the full spatial inclusion relationship between Glasgow, Scotland, and Britain, but there were also some 10- to 11-year-olds who did not even understand that Glasgow was located within Scotland. Although Jahoda's findings show that children's geographical knowledge of their home country is not related to Piagetian stages of development (contrary to previous claims made by Piaget & Weil, 1951), more recently Wilberg (2002) has found that children's understanding of the geography of their own homeland *is* related to their understanding of part–whole relations (as assessed using a Piagetian task of class inclusion) between 4 and 7 years of age.

In another study, Barrett (1996) asked 6-, 10-, and 14-year-old English children for the name of the country in which they lived. Eighty-three per cent of the 6-year-olds (and all of the 10- and 14-year-olds) answered the question correctly (with the vast majority referring to the country as *England*, and just a small handful of children at each age calling it *Britain*: This pattern of response is also characteristic of English adults; cf. Condor, 1996). The majority of the children at each age also knew that their country was smaller than Europe (73%, 83%, and 95%, respectively). However, unlike the two older groups of children, the 6-year-olds were typically unable to name any other European countries; by contrast, the 10-year-olds could name 4–5 other European countries on average, while the 14-year-olds could name 6–7 European countries. Finally, when the children were asked whether their country was a part of Europe, only a small minority of the 6-year-olds replied in the affirmative, whereas the majority of the older children did so (20%, 85%, and 93%, respectively). The study additionally revealed that, at all ages, the boys tended to display higher levels of geographical knowledge than the girls.

Jahoda (1962) also found a significant increase in the number of foreign countries that could be named by Scottish children round about 7–8 years of age. Axia and Bremner (1992) explored 8- and 10-year-old Italian and English children's geographical knowledge of other countries by asking the children to draw a map of Europe (instead of using verbal interviewing). They found that the 10-year-olds produced more accurate and detailed maps than the 8-year-olds, and the Italian children produced more accurate and detailed drawings than the English children. Barrett and Farroni (1996) used a much larger battery of different methods (which included verbal questioning, a construction task, an outline map task, and a satellite photo interpretation task) to assess 7- to 11-year-old English and Italian children's geographical knowledge of Europe. The aim was to avoid the possible limitations that may be inherent in the use of any individual method (such as map drawing). They found that the different measures converged with one another. They too found differences associated with age, nationality, and gender, with greater knowledge being exhibited by older children, Italian children, and boys, than by younger children, English children, and girls, respectively.

Subsequent studies (e.g., Barrett, Lyons, Purkhardt, & Bourchier, 1996; Bourchier, Barrett, & Lyons, 2002; Bourchier, Barrett, Lyons, & Purkhardt, 1996; Rutland, 1998) have confirmed that children's geographical knowledge of countries does indeed vary as a function of social class, geographical location, and gender, with middle-class children tending to have more knowledge than working-class children, urban children tending to have more knowledge than rural children, and boys exhibiting higher levels of geographical knowledge than girls. In addition, Wiegand (1991) has reported evidence suggesting that differences may also occur as a function of ethnicity: He found that Indian and Pakistani 7- to 11-year-old children living in England had more geographical knowledge of the Indian sub-continent, and less knowledge of western Europe, compared with their English white majority group peers. Axia et al. (1998) confirmed that children growing up in different countries, as well as in different regions of the same country, can exhibit different levels of geographical knowledge; they found that northern Italian children are more knowledgeable about other countries than both southern Italian and English children. Finally, Jahoda and Woerdenbagch (1982) found that 11- to 16-year-old Dutch children are more knowledgeable about other countries than same-aged English children, although both groups of children exhibited very low levels of knowledge of supranational groupings such as the EU and the former Eastern Bloc.

It is possible that knowledge about other countries is at least partially derived from children's personal experiences of travelling to, or living in, those countries. This possibility was examined by Moss and Blades (1994). They tested 8- and 11-year-old British children living in Britain, and 8- and 11-year-old British children living in Germany on British army bases. The latter group of children had not only lived in but had also visited more European countries than the former group. However, when the children's geographical knowledge of Europe was examined, it was found that the latter group of children did *not* possess more knowledge than the former group overall. Similarly, Barrett (1996), Barrett and Farroni (1996), Barrett et al. (1997), and Bourchier et al. (2002) all failed to find a relationship between geographical knowledge of foreign countries and children's personal travel experience to other countries. However, Barrett et al. (1996;

Bourchier et al., 1996) and Rutland (1998) *did* find a relationship between children's knowledge of foreign countries and their general levels of travel experience. It may be the case that the discrepancy between the findings of the different studies in this area stems from the different measures of travel experience that have been used.

As far as effects of schooling are concerned, the study by Axia et al. (1998) showed that there is an effect of educational input upon children's national geographical knowledge: 10-year-olds who received formal teaching about Europe exhibited greater knowledge than 10-year-olds who did not. However, children do not only acquire their geographical knowledge from formal curricular input at school. Stillwell and Spencer (1973) looked at 9-year-old children's uptake of information about other countries from classroom posters and wall charts. They assessed children's knowledge about other countries, using interviewing, before and after mounting displays of information about other countries on classroom walls for a period of 1 week. The children acquired factual information from this source without any explicit teaching.

Most of the preceding research examined children's knowledge of the geography of their own country and other countries. A rather different kind of study was conducted by Nugent (1994). He asked 10-, 12-, 14-, and 16-year-old Irish children to write down their thoughts and feelings about Ireland. The children's written narratives were then content-analysed. The 10-, 12- and many 14-year-olds produced descriptions of Ireland largely in terms of its man-made places, its natural physical geography, and its flora and fauna. Interestingly, the 16-year-olds instead produced descriptions in terms of Ireland's history, culture, traditions, and the Irish "personality" and way of life. This study suggests that there may be an important shift in the way in which children spontaneously think about their own country at about 15 years of age.

Thus, these studies indicate that: (a) children's geographical knowledge about their own country begins to develop from about 5 or 6 years of age onwards; (b) children's knowledge about other countries begins to develop a year or two later; (c) geographical knowledge about both one's own country and other countries expands significantly through the course of middle childhood and early adolescence; (d) however, even in early adolescence, some children may still exhibit considerable geographical confusion; (e) differences in geographical knowledge can occur as a function of children's social class, gender, location, and ethnicity; (f) there may be a shift in how children think about their own country at about 15 years of age, away from thinking about it in terms of its physical geography, and towards thinking about it in terms of its distinctive history and culture; (g) children acquire information about other countries not only from formal teaching but also from incidental sources such as posters and wall charts;

(h) children may also acquire geographical knowledge about foreign countries as a consequence of foreign travel, although the actual evidence on this point is rather mixed.

CHILDREN'S FEELINGS ABOUT COUNTRIES, AND THEIR EMOTIONAL ATTACHMENT TO THEIR OWN COUNTRY

Children's acquisition of factual geographical knowledge about countries is often accompanied by the acquisition of strong feelings about those countries. The studies which have investigated this issue have employed a variety of measures to assess children's feelings, including verbal interviewing, paired comparisons, card sorts, and rating scales. Using interviewing, Piaget and Weil (1951) found rather haphazard and idiosyncratic likes and dislikes about countries being expressed by Swiss children up until about 7–8 years of age. At 7–8, an affective preference for Switzerland over all other countries emerged.

Jahoda (1962) also used interviewing to investigate Scottish children's feelings about countries. He found that before about 8 years of age, these children expressed positive feelings for distant countries that were picturesque and exotic, but otherwise tended to express random likes and dislikes based upon isolated and haphazardly acquired items of information about particular countries. By contrast, from 8 years of age onwards, the children's feelings about other countries tended to be based upon either stereotyped images of the distinctive physical features of particular countries (e.g., sun, snow, skyscrapers, etc.) or stereotypes of the people who lived in those countries. Jahoda also found that, at *all* ages, these Scottish children exhibited negative feelings towards Germany, and used references to past wars to justify these feelings. This finding, that children tend to view traditional enemy countries more negatively than other countries, was also obtained by Johnson (1966, 1973), who used rating scales rather than interviewing to assess 8- to 10-year-old English children's feelings about other countries. He found that the children held negative feelings towards Germany, Japan, and Russia. He also found that children who were regular readers of war comics liked the "enemy" countries of Germany, Japan, and Italy less, but liked the allied countries of England, America, Australia and France more, than children who did not read these comics.

Johnson et al. (1970; Middleton et al., 1970) used a rating scale to assess the feelings of English 7-, 9-, and 11-year-olds towards a number of countries. They found that, when mean ratings were considered, at all ages the children rated their own home country, England, more positively than any other country; furthermore, this preference for England strengthened with age. A mean preference for the home country at all ages was also found by Jaspers et al. (1972), who used a method of paired comparisons to assess 7- to 11-year-old Dutch children's relative degree of liking of different countries. These children also showed a significant increase in the degree of their preference for their own home country with age. However, conducting a more fine-grained analysis of the English data, Middleton et al. (1970) found that only 22% of the 7-year-olds, 44% of the 9-year-olds, and 56% of the 11-year-olds individually rated England higher than *all* other countries. In other words, while there often appears to be an overall mean preference for the home country over other countries from 7 years of age onwards, and this preference seems to strengthen through middle childhood, many individual children may nevertheless continue to rate some other countries just as positively, if not more positively, than their own home country.

The degree of liking of foreign countries is sometimes related to whether or not the child has visited those countries. Bourchier et al. (2002) used both rating scales and sorting tasks to assess 6- to 13-year-old English children's affect towards five foreign countries: France, Germany, Ireland, Italy and Spain. They found that children who had visited France, Ireland, and Spain exhibited more positive affect for these three countries than children who had not visited them. However, this relationship was not present in the case of Germany and Italy, where other factors—such as the traditional national enemy factor—may have been more powerful determinants of the children's feelings instead.

The fact that children can exhibit strong emotional responses to other countries at the same time as they are acquiring factual knowledge about those countries raises the possibility that there may be a relationship between children's affect and their knowledge acquisition in this domain. For example, strong positive affect for a country might motivate the child to seek out factual information about that country, while strong negative affect might motivate the child to avoid such information. Alternatively, the causality might run in the opposite direction: children might come to like some countries more than others because they know more about them.

Early studies (e.g., Tajfel, 1966) suggested that children sometimes have very little knowledge of those countries about which they express negative feelings. Stillwell and Spencer (1973) also found a linear relationship between knowledge and affect in a group of 9-year-old English children. Using a test of factual knowledge, and a rating scale to measure affect, they found that children knew the most about countries which they liked, knew less about neutral countries, and knew least of all about disliked countries. However, Johnson et al. (1970), who investigated this issue using similar methods to Stillwell and Spencer, obtained different results with a group of 7- to 11-year-old English children. They found a curvilinear rather than a linear relationship between knowledge and affect: the children knew most about the countries they liked, and less about countries they disliked; however, the children knew least of all about the countries about which they felt neutral.

Three more recent studies have also investigated this issue. In one study, Giménez, Belmonte, Garcia-Claros, Suarez, and Barrett (1997) failed to find any consistent relationship between affect for individual countries and geographical knowledge about those countries in a sample of 6- to 15-year-old Spanish children. In a larger cross-national study involving 1700 British, Spanish, and Italian 6- to 15-year-olds, Barrett et al. (1997) found, in the sample as a whole, small but statistically significant linear (not curvilinear) relationships between children's liking of, and geographical knowledge about, Britain, Spain and Italy (correlations ranged from .12 to .17), but found no significant relationship between affect towards and geographical knowledge about either Germany or France. However, in the most detailed study of this issue to date, Bourchier et al. (2002) failed to find any relationships at all between knowledge of, and affect towards, foreign countries. A notable feature of this study was that it employed multiple regression rather than differences in mean knowledge for liked vs neutral vs disliked countries (used by Johnson et al., 1970, and Stillwell & Spencer, 1973) or simple bivariate analysis (used by Barrett et al., 1997). Bourchier et al. found that, although significant bivariate correlations sometimes occurred between affect and factual geographical knowledge in the case of some specific countries, these correlations disappeared when these variables' covariance with other variables was controlled. Thus, this study suggests that there is no direct relationship between the amount of factual knowledge that children acquire about particular countries and the affect that those children display towards those countries.

A somewhat different line of approach was used by Barrett and Davey (2001), who focused specifically upon the relationship between English children's ability to differentiate between photographs of typically English vs non-English landscapes (as rated by English adults), and their emotional attachment to those landscapes. Attachment was measured by asking the 5- to 10-year-old children to indicate on a 5-point scale (running from *very happy* to *very unhappy*) "How would you feel about living in this place when you grow up?". It was found that the ability to sort the photographs into English vs non-English groups improved with age (increasing from 64% correct at 5–6 years, to 89% correct at 7–8 years, to 93% correct at 9–10 years). Attachment to the English landscapes also increased with age, while attachment to the non-English landscapes decreased with age. However, neither of the two attachment scores was correlated with the photograph differentiation scores when age was partialled out. Thus, once again, the evidence suggests that there is no relationship between the child's knowledge (in this case, of the landscapes that characterise the child's homeland) and the child's emotional attachment to the homeland.

Nugent (1994) also examined the types of emotional attachments to their own country that were expressed by 10- to 16-year-old Irish children in open-ended narratives about Ireland. He found that the 10-year-olds tended to display unilaterally positive and unqualified attachments to Ireland. However, the 12- and 14-year-olds were more defensive in their attitudes, tending to compare Ireland with other countries and arguing for its comparative superiority; the 14-year-olds also began to express some antagonism towards other countries. The 16-year-olds, by contrast, tended to recognise the value of Ireland being unique as opposed to being the "best". Note that the emergence of this different perspective occurred at the same age as the shift in the content of the children's descriptions of Ireland (see the preceding section).

To conclude, this body of research indicates that: (a) children's preferences for other countries tend to be rather haphazard and idiosyncratic before about 7–8 years of age; (b) an exception occurs in the case of the countries of traditional national enemies, which are often disliked from an earlier age; (c) children sometimes exhibit more positive affect towards countries they have visited; (d) from 7–8 years of age onwards, there is a mean preference for the child's own country over other countries, and this preference strengthens still further through middle childhood; (e) nevertheless, certain other countries may still be very positively liked, and may even be preferred to their own country, by individual children; (f) there does not appear to be any direct relationship between the amount of factual knowledge that children acquire about countries and the way they feel about those countries; (g) through middle childhood, children exhibit an increasing emotional attachment to the typical landscapes that characterise their own homeland; (h) through adolescence, attachment to the homeland becomes more qualified, initially being based upon a perceived comparative superiority to other countries, but by 16 years of age, these perceptions of superiority may be diminished.

CHILDREN'S KNOWLEDGE OF NATIONAL EMBLEMS, AND THE SIGNIFICANCE THAT THEY ATTRIBUTE TO THESE EMBLEMS

Sociological and social-psychological theorists (e.g., Billig, 1995; Boswell & Evans, 1999; Gellner, 1983; Smith, 1991, 1998) attribute considerable importance to the role of national emblems (such as national flags, anthems, costumes, historical icons, etc.) in mediating and sustaining adults' awareness of national groups. It is argued that these emblems are critical, because they provide concrete representations of the individual's own national group, which in itself is an imagined (rather than a personally experienced) community (Anderson, 1983). Thus, national emblems provide perceptible salient entities with which group members can identify in the course of their everyday lives, with these emblems functioning to objectify and concretise something (i.e., the nation) that is, in fact, a highly abstract political, social, and psychological construction. These emblems also serve to differentiate the individual's own nation from other nations. National historical icons (i.e., the people, places, and events that are associated with the origins and history of the nation) have been hypothesised to be especially important in this respect, due to the fact that they are claimed to embody the national group's collective memories, and serve as a reminder to group members of what they share, their common heritage and cultural kinship, differentiating them from other groups, and providing them with a sense of cohesion and group belonging that might otherwise be lacking (Devine-Wright & Lyons, 1997; Lyons, 1996; Smith, 1991, 1998; Tanaka, 1994).

To date, children's knowledge of national emblems has been investigated in only a small handful of studies. Jahoda (1963b) explored 6- to 11-year-old Scottish children's knowledge of national anthems, songs, flags, costumes, historical figures, historical buildings, etc., while Barrett et al. (1997; de Rosa & Bombi, 1999) examined 6- to 15-year-old British, Spanish, and Italian children's ability to recognise the national flags, currencies, monuments, landscapes, foods, drinks and ceremonies of Britain, France, Germany, Spain, and Italy. Not surprisingly, both studies found an increase in knowledge with age. The latter study also revealed that, although the children tended to exhibit the most knowledge of the emblems of their home country, there were some exceptions (e.g., Italian children recognised the Eiffel Tower more frequently than the Tower of Pisa). In other words, emblems of the child's own home country are not always better known than those of other countries.

Two studies have focused in greater qualitative detail upon children's understanding of national flags. Weinstein (1957) examined 5- to 12-year-old American children's understanding of the American flag. He found that, across this age range, there was a shift away from a conceptualisation of flags in terms of their physical characteristics (e.g., their colour, the fact that they are made of cloth, etc.) and simple functional utility (i.e., to differentiate "us" from "them", or to show who owns a particular country, building, ship, etc.) to an understanding of flags as conventionally agreed emblems representing countries that contain people sharing common allegiances and goals, and which can be used for the symbolic function of signifying national loyalty.

More recently, Helwig and Prencipe (1999) examined 6-, 8-, and 10-year-old Canadian children's understanding of flags and the act of flag-burning.

They found that the children at all ages viewed flags as social conventions that could be altered by consensus or shared agreement. However, the older children were more likely to recognise flag-burning as a symbolic expression of disrespect. Although younger children were just as likely to recognise that flag-burning was offensive, they focused more upon the loss of the flag's functional utility rather than upon the symbolic transgression and the wilful disrespect to the nation that flag-burning entails, which was the aspect emphasised by the older children. Hence, the younger children actually viewed the burning of a map of a country as a more serious offence than the burning of its flag, unlike the older children. Also, older children showed an awareness of possible contextual influences, whereas the younger children did not. For example, the older children were more likely to acknowledge that if a country was "unfair" (whether it be Canada or elsewhere), then it might be more acceptable to burn that country's flag.

There is some evidence that different types of national emblem have differential salience or significance for members of different national and ethnic groups. In a study of 7- to 17-year-old English and Argentinian children, Cutts Dougherty et al. (1992) found that national territorial ownership was a more important national emblem for Argentinian children than for similarly aged English children, with English children instead attributing greater importance to the Queen and to abstract political principles (i.e., democratic values and freedoms). In addition, Moodie (1980) found that 6- to 13-year-old Afrikaans-speaking children in (late 1970s) South Africa exhibited a stronger preference for the South African flag and national anthem than English-speaking South-African children of the same age. In other words, within an individual country, emotional responses to particular national emblems may well vary as a function of children's language group.

Forrest and Barrett (2001) explored children's national historical emblems. They asked 11- to 15-year-old English children to name two people, two places, and two events from history that they thought were "very English". The children cited *Henry VIII*, *Buckingham Palace*, and the *Battle of Hastings* with high frequency. However, there were also differences in the children's responses as a function of their age and gender. For example, the older children cited *Winston Churchill* and *William Shakespeare* more frequently than the younger children, whereas the younger children cited *Queen Elizabeth I* more frequently than the older children. These differences appeared to be a consequence of recent educational input to the children via the school curriculum. In addition, the boys cited *Wembley* (the location of the national soccer stadium) as a historical place, and *England Winning the Soccer World Cup in 1966* as a historical event, more frequently than the girls, while the younger girls cited *Princess Diana* (a figure who had received major news and media coverage within these children's own lifetimes) as a historical figure more frequently. These sex differences are explicable in terms of boys' greater interest in sport (Beal, 1994) and children's heightened attention to same-sex role models in the mass media (Durkin, 1985; Eckes & Trautner, 2000; Gunter & McAleer, 1997; Ruble & Martin, 1998).

Wills (1994) also studied children's national historical knowledge but using a rather different perspective. He investigated the educational presentation and uptake of historical information about America amongst eighth-grade American children (i.e., 13-year-olds, approximately). He found that there were biases and stereotypes in the presentation of information about Native Americans in the textbooks that were being used in the classroom. He also found that these biases had impacted upon the children's understanding of the origins of their own nation, especially their narrative constructions and moral justifications of the European conquest of North America (in which the role and experiences of racial and ethnic minorities were marginalised).

In summary, the evidence indicates that: (a) children already know some national emblems by 5–6 years of age, but their emblematic knowledge continues to develop up to at least 15 years of age; (b) emblems of the child's own home country are not always better known than those of other countries; (c) children's understanding of national flags shifts from a functional to a symbolic conceptualisation during the course of middle childhood; (d) there are differences in the significance attributed to particular national emblems as a function of children's nationality, language group, gender, and age; (e) the national historical emblems and representations that are acquired by children and adolescents are probably influenced by both the mass media and formal educational input.

CHILDREN'S KNOWLEDGE OF, AND BELIEFS ABOUT, NATIONAL GROUPS, AND THE DEVELOPMENT OF NATIONAL STEREOTYPES

A number of interview studies have examined the development of national stereotypes. These studies have consistently revealed that at least some national stereotypes are acquired by 5–6 years of age and that, during subsequent years, children's knowledge of and beliefs about the people who belong to different national groups expands considerably (Barrett & Short, 1992; Jahoda, 1962; Lambert & Klineberg, 1967; Piaget & Weil, 1951). Initially, at 5 or 6 years of age, children usually express consensual judgements about the characteristics of just a few salient national groups, attributing distinctive characteristics to the members of those groups. At this early age, these characteristics primarily concern the typical physical features, appearance, clothing, and behavioural habits of the people.

However, by 10 or 11 years of age, children produce much more detailed consensual descriptions of the distinctive characteristics that are exhibited by the members of a large number of different national groups; these characteristics include not only typical physical features, clothing, language, and habits, but also psychological traits and sometimes political and religious beliefs as well (Lambert & Klineberg, 1967; Piaget & Weil, 1951). This shift across middle childhood in the types of attributions that are made to national groups parallels the concurrent shift from external-peripheral to internal-psychological characteristics, which occurs in the development of children's descriptions of the self and other people who are personally known to the child (Damon & Hart, 1988; Livesley & Bromley, 1973). There is some evidence that children may begin to attribute internal-psychological characteristics to their own national group at a slightly earlier age than they do to other national groups (Lambert & Klineberg, 1967).

However, the amount of individual variation that is acknowledged to exist within populations around these national stereotypes also increases significantly through middle childhood. Barrett and Short (1992) elicited national stereotypes from 5- to 10-year-old children, and then asked the children whether *all*, *most*, or *just some* of the people in that national group were like that. There was a significant shift with age from *most* to *just some* responses. Barrett et al. (1999b, 2003) asked 5- to 10-year-old English children to attribute traits to English, German, and American people. The younger children tended to attribute univalent characteristics (e.g., *friendly*, *clean*, etc.) to all three national groups, whereas the older children tended to attribute multivalent characteristics (i.e., both *friendly* and *unfriendly*, or both *clean* and *dirty*) to the groups. Deriving a quantitative measure of perceived variability from these attributed traits, Barrett et al. (1999b) found a significant increase in the amount of variability attributed to all three national groups with age, and no significant difference between the degree of variability attributed to the national in-group and the two national out-groups. Buchanan-Barrow, Barrett, and Lyons (2001) similarly found an increase with age in the amount of variability that was attributed to seven different national groups (English, British, Scottish, French, German, Spanish, and Italian people) by English 6-, 9-, 12-, and 15-year-old children; the significant increase in the perceived variability of the groups occurred between the ages of 9 and 12 years. In this case, however, greater variability was attributed to the English and British in-groups than to the five national out-groups, at all ages. In other words, there was evidence of an out-group homogeneity effect amongst these children.

Barrett et al. (1999b, 2003) asked the 5- to 10-year-olds to attribute the traits to English people (i.e., to their own national in-group) under three different conditions: the traits were attributed by the child either to just

English people on their own, or while the child was simultaneously attributing traits to either German or American people. It was found that the
children attributed exactly the same characteristics (and the same degree of
variability) to English people irrespective of the comparative context. It had
been expected that the manipulation of the comparative frame of reference
would influence the children's attributions. For example, English children
typically view German people as being aggressive and Americans as being
friendly; hence, it had been expected that, when they were describing
English people alongside German people, they would be more likely to
describe them as being peaceful, but when describing them alongside
American people, they would be less likely to describe them as being
friendly. However, no such effects occurred in these 5- to 10-year-old
children. It is well established that national stereotype content is adjusted in
this way as a function of the prevailing comparative context in university
students (Haslam, Oakes, Turner, & McGarty, 1995; Hopkins, Regan, &
Abell, 1997). It is not known when these effects first emerge, as comparable
studies with 11- to 17-year-olds have not been conducted to date.

Penny, Barrett, and Lyons (2001) examined the criteria that children use
to predict the nationality of people. They devised a set of minimal
statements about people (e.g., this person speaks X, this person lives in X,
this person is white, etc.), and presented these statements in pairs to English
and Scottish 6- to 12-year-old children. The children were asked to make a
forced-choice prediction about which person within each pair was more
likely to be English (in the case of the English children) or Scottish (in the
case of the Scottish children). A large degree of consensus occurred in the
children's responses, irrespective of the children's age or their own national
group. The order in which the characteristics were used by the children to
predict people's nationality was: born in X > speaks X > parents are X >
lives in X ≫ is Christian > is white. In other words, for these English and
Scottish children, the first four criteria clearly dominated over both religion
and race in determining predictions about the national group membership
of people, and were themselves ordered systematically in the priority that
was accorded to them. This study therefore shows that children as young as
6 years can make coherent and systematic predictions about people's
nationality, and may have already constructed a naïve theory about the
factors that determine people's national group membership.

That said, children's reasoning about people's nationality may be limited
initially by a failure to understand nested group memberships. This issue was
originally examined by Piaget (1928; Piaget & Weil, 1951), who found that
Swiss children younger than 10–11 years denied that they themselves
simultaneously belonged to both a local geographical group (e.g., Genevese)
and to a superordinate national group (Swiss). Piaget reports a similar
failure in children's understanding of foreign national group memberships;

thus, before 10–11 years of age, these Swiss children also failed to understand the relationship between being Parisian and being French.

Jahoda (1963a, 1964) examined this issue in greater detail, using the data he had collected from his Glaswegian 6- to 11-year-olds. We have already seen that, in Jahoda's sample, there were some 6- to 7-year-olds who understood the geographical inclusion relationship between Glasgow, Scotland, and Britain, but also some 10- to 11-year-olds who did not even understand that Glasgow was located within Scotland. In this additional analysis, Jahoda found that 31% of the 6- to 7-year-olds, 56% of the 8- to 9-year-olds, and 90% of the 10- to 11-year-olds affirmed that they were simultaneously both Scottish and British. In other words, these children's understanding of their own nested multiple group memberships (just like their geographical understanding) emerged across the full range of middle childhood (and not just at 10–11 years of age, as Piaget had claimed). Jahoda also found that the geographical inclusion relationships were not always mastered prior to the nested category relationships (also contrary to Piaget's claims): 26% of the children understood the nested category relationship *before* they understood the geographical relationship.

Children appear to derive their knowledge and beliefs about national groups from a range of different sources. In their multination study, Lambert and Klineberg (1967) found that 6-year-olds reported that they had learnt about foreign groups from their parents, direct contact with foreigners, television, and movies, while 10- and 14-year-olds reported that they had acquired their information primarily from television, movies, books, school course work, textbooks, and magazines. Television was an especially prominent source cited by the 5- to 10-year-old English children interviewed by Barrett and Short (1992), with parents, holidays, and books also being mentioned by these children as their other principal information sources.

Evidence that television can indeed impact upon children's understanding in this domain is reported by Himmelweit, Oppenheim, and Vince (1958). They found that 10- to 14-year-old children who had watched television programmes about other national groups over a period of a year exhibited greater objectivity (i.e., were more factual and less value-laden) in their views of foreign peoples, and their own beliefs matched the way that these national groups were being portrayed in television programmes to a greater extent, than children who did not watch such programmes. In addition, Roberts et al. (1974) examined the impact of an American series, *The Big Blue Marble*, which had been designed specifically to influence children's beliefs about other countries and cultures. It was found that, after just four episodes, 9- to 11-year-olds began to view foreign people as being healthier, happier, and more affluent than they had previously been thought to be; the children had also begun to question the previously assumed superiority of Americans. Finally, it is noteworthy that, when the child's own nation is either currently, or has historically been, in conflict with another nation, then the mass media within that country tend to present negative images of the enemy people (Bar-Tal, 1988, 1993, 1997; Bialer, 1985; English & Halperin, 1987; Hesse & Mack, 1991; Johnson, 1966). If television does indeed impact upon children's representations in this domain, then it is perhaps not surprising that children themselves often acquire negative beliefs about enemy countries and national groups (Barrett & Short, 1992; Buchanan-Barrow, Bayraktar, Papadopoulou, Short, Lyons, & Barrett, 1999; Jahoda, 1962; Johnson, 1966, 1973).

To conclude, the evidence indicates that: (a) at least some national stereotypes are acquired by 5–6 years of age and that, during subsequent years, children's national stereotypes become much more elaborate and detailed; (b) however, through the course of middle childhood, the amount of individual variation that is acknowledged to exist within national populations around these stereotypes also increases (i.e., the degree of stereotyping decreases); (c) 5- to 10-year-old children do not vary the characteristics that they attribute to the national in-group as a function of the other national groups that are present in the prevailing context; (d) 6- to 12-year-old children use a person's place of birth, language, parentage, and current place of living (in that order) to predict their nationality, rather than a person's religion or race; (e) understanding of the relationship between people's more local and national group memberships (i.e., of nested group memberships) emerges during middle childhood, but the acquisition of this understanding is not tied closely to either age or cognitive-developmental stage; (f) children probably derive their knowledge and beliefs about national groups from a range of different sources, including television, movies, parents, and holidays in other countries.

CHILDREN'S FEELINGS TOWARDS THE PEOPLE WHO BELONG TO THEIR OWN NATIONAL IN-GROUP AND TO NATIONAL OUT-GROUPS

Children's feelings towards national groups have been investigated using a number of different measures. First, some studies have measured how much the child likes or dislikes particular named national groups, using either direct questioning or rating scales running from *like a lot* to *dislike a lot* (e.g., Barrett & Short, 1992; de Rosa & Bombi, 1999; Giménez et al., 1999; Lambert & Klineberg, 1967). Second, some studies have used tasks in which children are asked to attribute positive and negative traits to national groups; an overall trait attribution score is then computed for each national group based upon the relative proportion of positive to negative traits that have been attributed to that group (e.g., Barrett et al., 1999b, 2003). A number of studies have utilised both a *like/dislike* affect measure and a trait attribution measure (e.g., Barrett, Lyons, & del Valle, 2004; Bennett et al., 1998, 2004; Buchanan-Barrow et al., 1999, 2001; Reizábal, Valencia, & Barrett, 2004). Third, some studies have employed a measure of social distance, in which the child is asked "What do or would you think about having X friends" (where X is the name of a particular national group); the child's response is then measured using a rating scale running from *very happy* to *very sad* (e.g., Verkuyten, 2001). Fourth, some studies have asked children to rate photographs of individual people on a scale running from *like very much* to *dislike very much*, and also to classify those same photographs according to whether they show a member of the child's own national in-group or a member of a national out-group; mean liking ratings for in-group and out-group members are then calculated (e.g., Jaspers et al., 1972; Tajfel et al., 1970, 1972). Finally, a variant of the photograph task involves comparing children's affect ratings of photographs of individual people when they are unlabelled with their affect ratings of the same photographs when they have been labelled with the name of a particular national group (Rutland, 1999).

These studies have found that, irrespective of the particular method that is used, children often display a systematic preference for members of their own national in-group. This in-group bias is usually present already at 6 years of age and appears to persist until at least 15 years of age. Furthermore, it occurs in most countries in which children have been tested, including England, Scotland, The Netherlands, Belgium, Austria, Spain, Italy, Russia, Ukraine, Georgia, Azerbaijan, and the USA (Barrett, 2001; Barrett et al., 2001, 2003; Bennett et al., 1998, 2004; Buchanan-Barrow et al., 2001; Castelli et al., in press; de Rosa & Bombi, 1999; Giménez et al., 1999; Jaspers et al., 1972; Lambert & Klineberg, 1967; Tajfel et al., 1970; Verkuyten, 2001).

However, some exceptions have been reported in the literature. For example, Barrett et al. (2004) found that English, Scottish, Spanish, and Italian 6-, 9-, 12-, and 15-year-old children exhibited in-group favouritism at all ages when they were assessed using an affect measure. However, in-group favouritism was far less prevalent when the same children were assessed using a trait attribution measure. Furthermore, the latter measure yielded different developmental patterns in different countries: Italian children exhibited in-group favouritism at 6 years of age but did not do so at later ages, while Scottish children did not exhibit in-group favouritism at 6 years of age but did do so by 15 years of age. In fact, only Spanish children consistently displayed in-group favouritism at all ages on the trait attribution measure. Similarly, Tajfel et al. (1970, 1972), using the photograph rating measure, found that in-group favouritism was absent amongst 6- to 12-year-old Scottish children in the early 1970s (although the same study showed that it was exhibited by English, Dutch, Austrian, and Italian children at that time). Lambert and Klineberg (1967) found that Japanese 6-, 10-, and 14-year-olds attributed negative characteristics (e.g., *poor* and *bad*) to their own national group (in the early 1960s). Finally, Rutland (1999), using a photograph-based method, found that English children only exhibited in-group favouritism from 10 years of age onwards. This last finding is possibly due to the fact that the term *British* was used in this study as the in-group label rather than *English*: relatively few English children and adults spontaneously use the term *British* to denote their own national in-group (Barrett, 1996; Condor, 1996). Some caution, therefore, needs to be exercised in making claims concerning the prevalence of national in-group favouritism, as different findings have been obtained depending upon the particular measure that is used, the particular national population that is under study, and the particular term that is used to denote the in-group category.

These same studies have also found that many national out-groups are nevertheless positively liked and evaluated at all ages, although usually to a lesser extent than the in-group (see, for example, Barrett et al., 2003; Bennett et al., 2004; Buchanan-Barrow et al., 2001; Lambert & Klineberg, 1967). Indeed, actual out-group denigration (i.e., overall *negative* affect or trait attributions) is comparatively rare amongst children in relationship to national groups (Barrett & Short, 1992; Bennett et al., in press; de Rosa & Bombi, 1999). For example, although 5- to 11-year-old English children are usually significantly less positive towards Germans than towards any other national group (Barrett & Short, 1992; Buchanan-Barrow et al., 1999), Barrett et al. (2003) found, using a trait attribution measure, that these children did *not* attribute more negative than positive characteristics to Germans overall.

Bennett et al. (2004) also found that out-group denigration was comparatively rare amongst 6-year-olds living in England, Scotland, Russia, Ukraine, Georgia, and Azerbaijan. This study further revealed that, at 6 years of age, feelings towards the in-group are not systematically related to children's feelings towards out-groups. The children's feelings towards in-groups and out-groups were assessed independently, using both affect and trait attribution measures. Overall, there were very few significant correlations between in-group and out-group attitudes. This finding is consistent with the results of other studies that have employed factor analytic methods. Reizábal et al. (2004) assessed 6- to 15-year-old Basque children's feelings towards Basque, Spanish, French, Italian, British, and German people, again using both affect and trait attribution measures; de Rosa and Bombi (1999) assessed 6- to 15-year-old Italian children's feelings towards Italian, French, Spanish, British, and German people using an affect measure; while Verkuyten (2001) assessed 10- to 12-year-old Dutch children's feelings towards the Dutch in-group and to Americans, Germans, and Turks using a social distance measure. All three studies found that feelings towards the in-group loaded onto one factor, while feelings towards all the out-groups loaded onto a separate factor. Thus, in both children and adolescents, national in-group and out-group attitudes appear to be independent.

Although Barrett et al. (2003) found that 5- to 11-year-old English children did not attribute more negative than positive characteristics to Germans overall, this study did suggest that national groups which are the traditional enemies of the child's own nation receive trait attributions that are less positive than those made to other national out-groups. The same finding has been found in other studies, which have examined English children's feelings towards Germans (e.g., Barrett & Short, 1992; Buchanan-Barrow et al., 1999, 2001), Greek children's feelings towards Turks (Buchanan-Barrow et al., 1999), Turkish children's feelings towards Greeks (Buchanan-Barrow et al., 1999), and Azeri children's feelings towards Russians (Bennett et al., 2004). Interestingly, in the specific case of traditional national enemies, attitudes towards the in-group *are* sometimes negatively correlated with attitudes towards the enemy out-group: For example, Bennett et al. (2004) found that those 6-year-old English and Scottish children who expressed the most positive attitudes towards their own national group expressed the least positive attitudes towards Germans, and 6-year-old Azeri children exhibited exactly the same phenomenon in their attitudes towards Azeri vs Russian people.

As far as overall developmental trends in levels of affect and prejudice are concerned, once a relative order of liking for different national out-groups has been established, this order tends to remain stable and consistent across the remaining childhood years. For example, Barrett and Short (1992) found that English 5- to 7-year-olds liked French and Spanish people more than Italian people, and liked Italian people more than German people. Exactly the same relative order of liking was exhibited at 8–10 years of age.

In addition, although in-group favouritism typically persists through childhood and adolescence, it does tend to become less pronounced across the course of middle childhood. This is partly because attitudes towards the national in-group tend to become less positive between 5 and 11 years of age (Barrett et al., 2003; Castelli et al., in press; Tajfel et al., 1970), and partly because attitudes towards *all* national out-groups tend to become *more* positive across this age range (Barrett & Short, 1992; Buchanan-Barrow et al., 1999, 2001; Lambert & Klineberg, 1967). Examining this trend using a trait attribution task, Barrett et al. (2003) found that there was an increase in the number of negative characteristics that were attributed to the in-group, and an increase in the number of positive characteristics attributed to out-groups, between 5 and 11 years of age. The overall effect was a significant reduction in the degree of in-group favouritism across this age range.

Thus, feelings towards other national groups tend to become more positive through the course of middle childhood. After 11 years of age, this general increase in positive regard for other national groups typically levels out, and there are indications that there may even be a slight reduction in positive regard for national out-groups in early adolescence (Lambert & Klineberg, 1967). However, although this is the general pattern that occurs in many groups of children, once again, there are exceptions reported in the literature. For example, Lambert and Klineberg found that, unlike the other groups of children whom they tested, South African Bantu children showed no significant differences in their feelings towards national out-groups from 6 to 14 years of age. Reizábal et al. (2004) also found no changes in Basque children's national feelings as a function of age between 6 and 15 years, while Barrett (2002) found that one group of English children actually became more (rather than less) negative towards Germans between 5 and 10 years of age.

Finally, within individual countries, there are differences in feelings about national groups according to children's social class, sociolinguistic position, and ethnicity. For example, Lambert and Klineberg (1967) found that middle-class children exhibited more positive feelings towards national out-groups than working-class children. Reizábal et al. (2004) found that 6- to 15-year-old children living in the Basque Country who spoke only Basque with their parents at home exhibited systematically different national attitudes from children who only spoke Spanish in their homes; Barrett, del Valle, Lyons, Vila, Monreal, and Perera (1999a) found a parallel pattern amongst 6- to 15-year-old Catalan children according to their use of Catalan or Spanish in their homes. Pavlenko, Kryazh, Ivanova, and Barrett (2001), in the Ukraine, found systematic differences in the national attitudes exhibited by children of Russian vs Ukrainian ethnic origin. And in Georgia, Kipiani (2001) found systematic differences in national attitudes between children of Georgian vs Russian vs. Armenian ethnic origin.

To conclude, studies have revealed that: (a) children usually display a systematic preference for members of their own national in-group over members of national out-groups, particularly when affect measures are used; (b) however, in-group favouritism is not universal, and may be noticeably absent when trait attribution tasks are used; (c) national out-groups are nevertheless often positively liked, although usually to a lesser degree than the in-group; (d) out-group denigration is a comparatively rare phenomenon in children; (e) national in-group and out-group attitudes are not systematically related to each other; (f) however, national groups that are traditional national enemies of the child's own nation are usually liked significantly less than other national out-groups, and in-group attitudes are sometimes negatively correlated with attitudes towards national enemies; (g) once a relative order of liking for different national out-groups has been established, this order tends to remain stable and consistent across the remaining childhood years; (h) feelings towards, and trait attributions to, the child's own national in-group tend to become less positive between 5 and 11 years of age; (i) feelings towards, and trait attributions to, national out-groups tend to become more positive between 5 and 11 years of age; (j) however, cases have been reported in the literature in which there are no changes in national attitudes as a function of age; (k) within individual countries, there are differences in children's national attitudes as a function of social class, sociolinguistic position, and ethnicity.

CHILDREN'S NATIONAL SELF-CATEGORISATION AND THE DEVELOPMENT OF SUBJECTIVE IDENTIFICATION WITH THE NATIONAL IN-GROUP

A number of studies have investigated the age at which young children spontaneously categorise themselves as members of their own national group. Using open-ended interviewing, Lambert and Klineberg (1967) found that, occasionally, some 6- to 7-year-old children talk about members of their own national group using words such as *"they"* and *"them"* in ways that suggest they do not yet fully include themselves as members of their own national group (e.g., "they dress as we do", "they are like us", etc.). Piaget and Weil (1951) also used open-ended interviewing, and they too found that some young Swiss children, even though they knew the name of their own country, denied that they themselves were Swiss.

Another method that has been used to examine this issue involves presenting the child with a large number of cards containing various terms that can be used to describe people (e.g., *6 years old*, *9 years old*, *boy*, *girl*, *Londoner*, etc.), including nationality terms (e.g., *English*) and supra-national terms (e.g., *European*). The child is asked to select all the terms that describe him- or herself. This method has now been used in studies with 6- to 15-year-old children living in England, Scotland, Spain, Italy, Russia, Ukraine, Georgia, and Azerbaijan (Bennett et al., 1998; de Rosa & Bombi, 1999; Giménez et al., 1999; Karakozov & Kadirova, 2001; Kipiani, 2001; Pavlenko et al., 2001; Reizábal et al., 2004; Riazanova, Sergienko, Grenkova-Dikevich, Gorodetschnaya, & Barrett, 2001; Vila, del Valle, Perera, Monreal, & Barrett, 1998). These studies have found that, from the age of 6 years onwards, the majority of children in all of these countries do usually select the appropriate nationality term as a self-descriptor.

These studies have also explored how subjectively important the nationality term is to the child, by immediately following up the selection of self-descriptors with a second task in which the child is asked to rank the chosen cards in order of their importance to the child ("If you had to choose just one of these terms because it was the most important to you, which one would you choose?"; the chosen card is then removed and the question is repeated, until a rank ordering of all the selected self-descriptors is obtained). Here, two different patterns of findings have been obtained. In the first (and most commonly occurring) pattern, although nationality is typically chosen as a self-descriptor at the age of 6, it is not ranked as being very important by the child. Instead, many young children attribute greater importance to their age, gender, and city identities. However, between 6 and 12 years of age, nationality increases significantly in its importance to the child (and may even become more important to the child than either gender or age: see Barrett et al., 2003). At 12 and 15 years of age, the appropriate supranational term also begins to be chosen as a self-descriptor, and this term also begins to increase in its perceived importance; however, even by 15 years of age, greater importance is usually still attributed to national, gender, age, and city identities than to the supranational identity.

The second pattern found with this task involves high importance being attributed to national identity already at the age of 6. To date, this pattern has been obtained most notably within Spain where, at 6 years of age, Catalan-speaking children living in Catalonia attribute very high importance to their Catalan identity (Barrett et al., 1999a; Vila et al., 1998), Basque-speaking children living in the Basque Country attribute very high importance to their Basque identity (Reizábal et al., 2004), and children living in Andalusia attribute very high importance to their Spanish identity (Barrett, 2001; Giménez et al., 1999). This high level of importance is maintained at subsequent ages amongst all these groups of children.

Differences in levels of national identification have also been found to occur as a function of several further factors. First, there are differences in levels of identification between children who live in the capital city vs other locations within the nation. For example, in Russia, children growing up in Moscow attribute significantly higher importance to their Russian identity than children growing up in Smolensk (Riazanova et al., 2001), while in England, children living in London exhibit higher levels of national identification than children living outside London (Barrett, 2002).

Second, there are differences in levels of national identification between children who live in the same geographical location but who belong to different ethnic groups. For example, in Tbilisi, the capital of Georgia, there are widespread differences in the patterns of identification exhibited by ethnic majority Georgian children and ethnic minority Armenian children: In particular, levels of identification with being Georgian are much higher in the Georgian children (Kipiani, 2001). Similarly, in London, second- and third-generation Indian, Pakistani, Bangladeshi, and Black African children identify with being British at significantly lower levels than white English children (Barrett, 2002).

Third, there are differences in the national identifications of children who live in the same geographical location and belong to the same ethnic group but who differ in their sociolinguistic position. For example, in Baku (the capital of Azerbaijan), Azeri children attending schools using Azeri as the language of education exhibit higher levels of identification with being Azeri than Azeri children who attend Russian-language schools (Karakozov & Kadirova, 2001). Similarly, in Tbilisi, Georgian children attending Georgian-language schools attribute higher importance to their Georgian identity than Georgian children attending Russian-language schools (Kipiani, 2001). And within Catalonia, children's levels of identification with being Catalan and with being Spanish vary systematically as a function of whether the child speaks only Catalan in their home, both Catalan and Spanish in the home, or only Spanish in the home: higher levels of Catalan identification are exhibited by children who speak only Catalan at home, whereas higher levels of Spanish identification are exhibited by children who speak only Spanish at home (Barrett et al., 1999a; Vila et al., 1998). Analogous findings have been obtained in the Basque Country with respect to the use of the Basque and Spanish languages in the home (Reizábal et al., 2004).

Children's levels of national identification are also linked to their knowledge of national geography. Barrett and Whennell (1998) found that the degree of identification with being British and English (i.e., whether the child felt *very British/English, a little bit British/English*, or *not at all British/ English*) was correlated with factual geographical knowledge of the UK in 5- to 11-year-old English children: the greater the level of factual knowledge, the more British and English the children felt. Barrett and Davey (2001) also found that the degree of identification with being English, and the importance that was attributed to being English, were both correlated with the ability to differentiate between photographs of typically English vs non-English landscapes in English 5- to 10-year-olds. Again, greater knowledge was linked to a stronger sense of national identification.

An interesting issue is whether the strength of national identification predicts children's feelings and attitudes towards national groups; that is, whether children with the strongest national identifications are also the most biased in favour of the in-group or the most prejudiced against out-groups. In the largest and most systematic study of this issue to date, Barrett et al. (2004) used two different measures of national identification (the degree of national identification, and the importance of national identity to the child), and two different measures of children's attitudes to national in-groups and out-groups (a degree of liking measure, and a trait attribution measure). Data from 1700 6-, 9-, 12-, and 15-year-old British, Spanish, and Italian children were examined. It was found that, first, there was no relationship between levels of national identification and either liking of, or trait attributions to, national out-groups. Second, the strength of national identification tended to be positively correlated with the degree of liking of the national in-group at all ages (although, even here, this relationship was absent in the case of the English and Scottish children as far as their English and Scottish identities were concerned, and was instead only present for their British identity). Third, the strength of national identification was not correlated with the trait attributions to the in-group at any age, except in the case of the Spanish children (where the stronger the child's identification with being Spanish, the more positive were the child's attributions to Spanish people, at all ages).

Barrett et al. also examined whether the strength of national identification was related to the perceived variability of national groups; that is, whether children with stronger national identifications engage in a greater degree of stereotyping than children with weaker national identifications. They found that, in the case of Spanish 6- and 12-year-olds, children with strong national identifications stereotyped their own in-group to a greater extent than children with weak national identifications; these high-identifying children also stereotyped the British, Italian, and French out-groups to a greater extent. However, no such patterns were exhibited by the children who were growing up in either Britain or Italy, nor (rather curiously) by the Spanish children at 9 and 15 years of age.

In conclusion, studies reveal that: (a) the majority of children spontaneously categorise themselves as members of their own national group from the age of 6; (b) the importance that is attributed to national identity usually increases between 6 and 12 years of age, although there are some groups where levels of national identification are already high at the age of 6; (c) levels of national identification may differ between children who are growing up in the capital city vs other locations within the nation, between children who belong to different ethnic groups, and between children according to their sociolinguistic situation; (d) children's levels of national identification are correlated with geographical knowledge of the homeland; (e) the strength of national identification tends to be positively correlated with the degree of liking of the national in-group; (f) however, the strength of national identification is not consistently related to trait attributions to the national in-group (except in the case of Spanish children), trait attributions to national out-groups, feelings towards national out-groups, or the degree of stereotyping of national groups (except in the case of some Spanish children).

THEORETICAL FRAMEWORKS

There are four main theoretical frameworks that have been applied to children's development in this domain: cognitive-developmental theory (CDT), social identity theory (SIT), self-categorisation theory (SCT), and social identity development theory (SIDT). None of these theories is able to explain satisfactorily the empirical findings reviewed in this chapter.

CDT has been advocated by Aboud and colleagues (Aboud, 1988; Aboud & Amato, 2001; Doyle & Aboud, 1995; Doyle, Beaudet, & Aboud, 1988). They argue that, at about 5–6 years of age, children exhibit maximum positive bias in favour of their own national and ethnic in-groups, and maximum negative prejudice against national and ethnic out-groups. This polarisation in the child's attitudes towards in-groups and out-groups is hypothesised to decline after the age of 6, so that by the age of about 10, there are significant decreases in both in-group favouritism and out-group prejudice. In her own studies (which have tended to focus upon ethnic rather than national groups), Aboud has found that, at the age of 6, children attribute mainly positive characteristics to members of their own group, and mainly negative characteristics to members of other groups. After the age of 6, this polarisation in the attribution of traits to in-groups and out-groups decreases, as children gradually come to attribute more negative characteristics to the in-group, and more positive characteristics to out-groups. The net result of this process is a reduction in in-group favouritism, a reduction in out-group prejudice, and an increase in the perceived variability of national and ethnic groups. Aboud further argues that these changes are driven by the development of certain key cognitive capabilities, including conservation, the ability to use multiple classifications, the ability to judge the deeper similarities between superficially different groups, and the ability to attend to individual differences within groups. Aboud argues that these cognitive capabilities develop between 6 and 10 years of age. Hence, the developmental changes in this domain that can be observed as occurring during middle childhood are a consequence of underlying domain-general cognitive changes.

CDT can indeed explain why many children show a reduction in national in-group favouritism, an increase in positive regard for national out-groups, and an increase in the perceived variability of national groups, through middle childhood. However, there are many additional phenomena that this framework cannot explain. For example, it does not explain why children who have visited particular countries should exhibit more positive affect towards these countries than children who have not visited them; why, within individual countries, there are differences in the development of national attitudes as a function of children's social class, ethnicity, and sociolinguistic position; why television influences children's understanding of national groups; and why national groups that are the traditional national enemies of the child's own nation are evaluated significantly more negatively than other national out-groups. Even more problematically, there are several findings that run directly counter to the predictions of CDT: national in-group favouritism at the age of 6 is *not* universal (Lambert & Klineberg, 1967; Tajfel et al., 1970, 1972); some children do *not* exhibit changes in national attitudes between 6 and 10 years of age (Lambert & Klineberg, 1967; Reizábal et al., 2004); and attitudes to enemy out-groups sometimes become *more* (rather than less) negative between 6 and 10 years of age (Barrett, 2002).

Although SIT (Tajfel, 1978; Tajfel & Turner, 1986) and SCT (Oakes, Haslam, & Turner, 1994; Turner, Hogg, Oakes, Reicher, & Wetherell, 1987) were not formulated to explain developmental phenomena, attempts have been made to apply these theoretical frameworks to children's development in this domain (see, for example, Barrett et al., 2003, 2004; Rutland, 1999). SIT and SCT both postulate that in-group favouritism, out-group prejudice, and the stereotyping of in-groups and out-groups occur as psychological consequences of knowing that one belongs to a particular social group. These theories posit that these effects are most pronounced either when a particular social group membership is subjectively important to the individual (SIT) or when the prevailing social context renders a particular social group membership especially salient to the individual (SCT).

SIT predicts that feelings and attitudes towards the national in-group and/or national out-groups will be a function of the strength of subjective identification with the in-group (Hinkle & Brown, 1990; Mummendey, Klink, & Brown, 2001). However, this prediction is not supported by the available evidence on children's national attitudes. As we have seen, Barrett et al. (2004) found that, in 6- to 15-year-old British, Spanish, and Italian children, no relationship existed between levels of national identification and feelings and attitudes towards national out-groups. It was also found that, although the strength of national identification did tend to be positively correlated with the degree of liking of the national in-group, this correlation was not consistently present, and there was no consistent relationship between the strength of national identification and trait attributions to the in-group.

By contrast, SCT predicts that when the prevailing social context renders the child's own national group membership salient to the child, then he or she will stereotype the members of the national in-group to a greater degree than when national group membership is not rendered salient by the context. However, once again, there is no evidence from children's representations of national groups to support this prediction. For example, Barrett et al. (1999b) experimentally manipulated the prevailing context in order to influence the salience of the national in-group category. However, the degree of stereotyping of the national in-group did not vary in the predicted manner amongst 5- to 10-year-olds (instead, perceived variability simply increased as a function of age). SCT also predicts that the contents of the national in-group stereotype will alter, depending upon the comparative frame of reference present when the stereotype is being elicited. However, Barrett et al. (2003) found that, in 5- to 10-year-old children, the national in-group stereotype did not change as a function of the comparison national out-group that was present. An extended discussion of the empirical problems that confront the application of SIT and SCT to the development of children's representations of, and attitudes to, national groups is given in Barrett et al. (2004).

Finally, SIDT (Nesdale, 1999, 2004; Nesdale, Maass, Griffiths, & Durkin, 2003) proposes that particular national and ethnic identities develop through a sequence of four phases. In the first undifferentiated phase, national and ethnic cues are not yet salient to the young child. In the second phase, which starts at perhaps 3 years of age, awareness of such cues begins to emerge, and children gradually become able to identify and distinguish members of different groups (a process that can continue up to and beyond 10 or 11 years of age). Crucially, at this second phase, self-identification as a member of particular in-groups occurs. In the third phase, which begins at about 4 years of age as a consequence of self-identification, a particular focus upon, and preference for, the in-group emerges. During this third phase, out-groups are not actually disliked or conceptualised in negative terms as such; instead, the in-group is simply preferred over all other groups. Finally, in the fourth phase, which begins at around 7 years of age (although not all children may enter this final phase), the focus shifts from the in-group to out-groups, and instead of merely preferring the in-group, the child begins to actively dislike out-groups. Hence, between the third and fourth phases, there is a shift away from in-group preference towards out-group prejudice. This shift involves children internalising the negative attitudes towards out-groups that prevail within their own social group. The probability of such internalisation occurring is hypothesised to increase as a function of three factors: the child's level of identification with the in-group; the extent to which the negative attitudes are shared by the members of the in-group; and the extent to which the members of the in-group feel that their status or well-being is under threat.

However, SIDT fares little better than the other theories in relationship to the evidence on children's national representations and attitudes. First, as we have seen, national groups that are the traditional national enemies of the child's own nation are often liked significantly less than other national out-groups, and this phenomenon can already be present at the age of 5 or 6 (Barrett & Short, 1992; Bennett et al., 2004; Buchanan-Barrow et al.,

1999, 2001); SIDT is unable to explain the presence of this difference within the child's out-group attitudes at such an early age (when the focus is hypothesised to be upon the in-group rather than out-groups). Second, the child's feelings towards, and trait attributions to, the national in-group often become *less* positive between 5 and 11 years of age, while feelings towards, and trait attributions to, national out-groups often become *more* positive between 5 and 11 years of age (Barrett & Short, 1992; Barrett et al., 2003; Buchanan-Barrow et al., 1999, 2001; Castelli et al., in press; Lambert & Klineberg, 1967; Tajfel et al., 1970). Both of these developmental trends run counter to those predicted by SIDT. Third, there are some cases reported in the literature in which there are no changes in national attitudes as a function of age (Lambert & Klineberg, 1967; Reizábal et al., 2004). Fourth, levels of identification with the in-group only predict affect towards the in-group; they do not generally predict trait attributions to the in-group, affect towards out-groups, or trait attributions to out-groups (Barrett et al., 2004).

Hence, none of the existing theories is able to account for the various phenomena that have been identified in this domain. Instead, a more complex theoretical framework appears to be required. As we have seen, this framework needs to explain a large number of diverse phenomena, phenomena which indicate that societal influences, familial influences, personal experiences, and cognitive-motivational factors can all, under appropriate circumstances, impact upon children's understanding of, and feelings about, countries and national groups.

As far as societal influences are concerned, both the mass media and the school appear to be potentially key influences upon children's development in this domain. The mass media (i.e., television, movies, books, magazines, comics, posters, etc.) have been noted throughout this chapter as important influences upon children's national representations and attitudes. As Billig (1995) has shown, the mass media serve to transmit representations of nations to their audiences in an inconspicuous yet pervasive manner that permeates people's everyday lives. The school has also been identified throughout this chapter as another key influence on children's knowledge and beliefs about nations and national groups. Over the years, many authors have argued that nation-states often harness the state-regulated educational system in order to transmit culturally dominant representations of nations to children (Gellner, 1983; Smith, 1991, 1998; Tanaka, 1994; Wertsch, 1994, 1998; Wills, 1994). Hence, in the case of children who are exposed to a common educational system, the contents of which are tightly constrained by a prescribed national curriculum (particularly in school subjects such as history, geography and languages), common representations of both the national in-group and national out-groups could be acquired as a consequence of formal educational input.

However, family practices also have a significant impact upon children's representations and attitudes in this domain. As we have seen, children's patterns of national identification, as well as their attitudes to national in-groups and out-groups, vary systematically either according to the language(s) spoken in the family home or according to the child's language of education at school. It is unlikely that these effects are a consequence of language use per se. Instead, it is much more plausible that both language use within the home, and the language of education, are chosen by children's parents either as an ideological or cultural commitment (in the case of Spain) or to obtain the socioeconomic advantages that schooling in a politically and economically dominant language (i.e., Russian in Ukraine, Georgia and Azerbaijan) can confer upon the child. In other words, the child's own sociolinguistic situation is itself likely to be a product of parental positionings and aspirations, which in turn will be a product of parents' own national identifications and attitudes (Azurmendi, Garcia, & Gonzalez, 1998; Elejabarrieta, 1994; Valencia et al., in press). Hence, the varying patterns of national identification and attitudes that occur within children as a function of their sociolinguistic situation are almost certainly a product of their parents' attitudes and practices (with the use of language itself merely being a salient marker of those parental attitudes and practices).

In addition, children's personal experiences (which themselves are also largely a product of parental characteristics and family practices) can impact upon their national representations and attitudes. These personal experiences are likely to vary according to children's social class, ethnicity, and geographical location. For example, family trips to national museums and national monuments, family holidays to other countries, the uptake of opportunities to travel to other countries (e.g., via school trips), and personal contacts or kinship relations with people living in other countries, will all vary as a function of children's social class, ethnicity and/or geographical location. Children may also experience differential exposure to national representations in the mass media as a function of their gender and ethnicity. For example, boys are likely to have greater interest in viewing international sporting fixtures than girls, while members of minority but not majority groups will be able to access minority language radio and television stations and minority community newspapers. In other words, even though children might be exposed at school to a uniform national curriculum, there will nevertheless still be considerable variability in the national representations that are acquired by children as a consequence of variability in the information received from other familial and personal experiences.

However, children's national representations and attitudes are not solely a product of exogenous influences; they are also, at least partially, a product of endogenous cognitive and motivational factors. First, children's uptake of information and attitudes from the various exogenous sources will be affected by intraindividual cognitive factors, including the child's own attentional, retentional, and cognitive-representational processes. Second, these cognitive processes themselves are likely to be influenced by the affective valence and salience of the presented information for the individual child, by the child's own perceptual set, cognitive capabilities, and motivational state, and by the child's pre-existing cognitive representations and affective preferences. Thus, the child's level of national identification could play an important motivational role here. For example, the early emerging high levels of national identification that occur within Spain could be the crucial factor driving the distinctive developmental patterns displayed by children living within Spain; however, in other national contexts, factors extrinsic to the child may override or mediate the impact of levels of national identification.

Hence, media, educational, familial, experiential, cognitive, and motivational factors are *all* likely to play an important role in shaping children's understanding of, and feelings about, countries and national groups. The balance between these different types of factors almost certainly varies from nation to nation, and from social group to social group within a nation. The argument being put forward here is that we will only be able to explain the multifarious findings been described in this chapter when theorising finally shifts away from the narrow cognitive-developmental and social identity perspectives that have been proposed hitherto to a much broader, more inclusive, perspective that subsumes societal influences, familial influences, personal experiences, and cognitive-motivational factors.

REFERENCES

Aboud, F. (1988). *Children and prejudice.* Oxford: Blackwell.
Aboud, F., & Amato, M. (2001). Developmental and socialization influences on intergroup bias. In R. Brown & S. L. Gaertner (Eds.), *Blackwell handbook of social psychology: Intergroup processes* (pp. 65–85). Oxford: Blackwell.
Anderson, B. (1983). *Imagined communities.* London: Verso.
Axia, G., & Bremner, J. G. (1992). *Children's understanding of Europe: British and Italian points of view.* Paper presented at the Fifth European Conference on Developmental Psychology, Seville, Spain, September 1992.
Axia, G., Bremner, J. G., Deluca, P., & Andreasen, G. (1998). Children drawing Europe: The effects of nationality, age and teaching. *British Journal of Developmental Psychology, 16,* 423–437.
Azurmendi, M. J., Garcia, I., & Gonzalez, J. L. (1998). Influencia del uso de las lenguas en contacto con la identidad social en la Comunidad Autónoma Vasca. *Revista de Psicología Social, 13,* 3–10.
Barrett, M. (1996). English children's acquisition of a European identity. In G. Breakwell & E. Lyons (Eds.), *Changing European identities: Social psychological analyses of social change* (pp. 349–369). Oxford: Butterworth-Heinemann.
Barrett, M. (2001). The development of national identity: A conceptual analysis and some data

from Western European studies. In M. Barrett, T. Riazanova, & M. Volovikova (Eds.), *Development of national, ethnolinguistic and religious identities in children and adolescents* (pp. 16–58). Moscow: Institute of Psychology, Russian Academy of Sciences (IPRAS).

Barrett, M. (2002). *Children's views of Britain and Britishness in 2001.* Keynote address presented to the Annual Conference of the Developmental Psychology Section of the British Psychological Society, University of Sussex, September 2002.

Barrett, M., & Davey, K. (2001). *English children's sense of national identity and their attachment to national geography.* Unpublished paper, Department of Psychology, University of Surrey.

Barrett, M., Del Valle, A., Lyons, E., Vila, I., Monreal, P., & Perera, S. (1999a). *Bilingual children and the sense of national identity: The case of children living in Catalonia.* Paper presented at VIIIth International Congress for the Study of Child Language, San Sebastian, Spain.

Barrett, M., & Farroni, T. (1996). English and Italian children's knowledge of European geography. *British Journal of Developmental Psychology, 14,* 257–273.

Barrett, M., Lyons, E., Bennett, M., Vila, I., Giménez, A., Arcuri, L., & de Rosa, A. S. (1997). *Children's beliefs and feelings about their own and other national groups in Europe.* Final Report to the Commission of the European Communities, Directorate-General XII for Science, Research and Development, Human Capital and Mobility (HCM) Programme, Research Network No. CHRX-CT94-0687.

Barrett, M., Lyons, E., & del Valle, A. (2004). The development of national identity and social identity processes: Do social identity theory and self-categorisation theory provide useful heuristic frameworks for developmental research? In M. Bennett & F. Sani (Eds.), *The development of the social self.* Hove, UK: Psychology Press (pp. 159–188).

Barrett, M., Lyons, E., Purkhardt, C., & Bourchier, A. (1996). *English children's representations of European geography.* End of Award Report to ESRC, Research Grant No. R000235753. Guildford, UK: University of Surrey.

Barrett, M., Riazanova, T., & Volovikova, M. (Eds.) (2001). *Development of national, ethnolinguistic and religious identities in children and adolescents.* Moscow: Institute of Psychology, Russian Academy of Sciences (IPRAS).

Barrett, M., & Short, J. (1992). Images of European people in a group of 5–10-year-old English school children. *British Journal of Developmental Psychology, 10,* 339–363.

Barrett, M., & Whennell, S. (1998). *The relationship between national identity and geographical knowledge in English children.* Poster presented at XVth Biennial Meeting of ISSBD, Berne, Switzerland.

Barrett, M., Wilson, H., & Lyons, E. (1999b). *Self-categorization theory and the development of national identity in English children.* Poster presented at the Biennial Meeting of the Society for Research in Child Development, Albuquerque, New Mexico, USA.

Barrett, M., Wilson, H., & Lyons, E. (2003). The development of national in-group bias: English children's attributions of characteristics to English, American and German people. *British Journal of Developmental Psychology, 21,* 193–220.

Bar-Tal, D. (1988). Delegitimizing relations between Israeli Jews and Palestinians: A social psychological analysis. In J. Hofman (Ed.), *Arab-Jewish relations in Israel: A quest in human understanding* (pp. 217–248). Bristol, IN: Wyndham Hall Press.

Bar-Tal, D. (1993). American convictions about conflictive USA-USSR relations: A case of group beliefs. In S. Worchel & J. Simpson (Eds.), *Conflict between people and peoples* (pp. 193–213). Chicago: Nelson Hall.

Bar-Tal, D. (1997). Formation and change of ethnic and national stereotypes: An integrative model. *International Journal of Intercultural Relations, 21,* 491–523.

Beal, C. R. (1994). *Boys and girls: The development of gender roles.* New York: McGraw-Hill.

Bennett, M., Barrett, M., Karakozov, R., Kipiani, G., Lyons, E., Pavlenko, V., & Riazanova,

T. (2004). Young children's evaluations of the in-group and of out-groups: a multi-national study. *Social Development, 13*, 124–141.

Bennett, M., Lyons, E., Sani, F., & Barrett, M. (1998). Children's subjective identification with the group and in-group favoritism. *Developmental Psychology, 34*, 902–909.

Bialer, S. (1985). The psychology of US–Soviet relations. *Political Psychology, 6*, 263–273.

Billig, M. (1995). *Banal nationalism.* London: Sage.

Boswell, D., & Evans, J. (1999). *Representing the nation: A reader. Histories, heritage and museums.* London: Routledge.

Bourchier, A., Barrett, M., & Lyons, E. (2002). The predictors of children's geographical knowledge of other countries. *Journal of Environmental Psychology, 22*, 79–94.

Bourchier, A., Barrett, M., Lyons, E., & Purkhardt, C. (1996). *English children's representations of European geography.* Paper presented at the Annual Conference of the Developmental Section of the British Psychological Society, Oxford, September 1996.

Buchanan-Barrow, E., Barrett, M., & Lyons, E. (2001). *English children's representations of national groups.* Poster presented at the 10th European Conference on Developmental Psychology, Uppsala, Sweden, August 2001.

Buchanan-Barrow, E., Bayraktar, R., Papadopoulou, A., Short, J., Lyons, E., & Barrett, M. (1999). *Children's representations of foreigners.* Poster presented at the 9th European Conference on Developmental Psychology, Spetses, Greece, September, 1999.

Castelli, L., Cadinu, M., & Barrett, M. (in press). Lo sviluppo degli atteggiamenti nazionali in soggetti in eta scolare. *Rassegna di Psicologia.*

Condor, S. (1996). Unimagined community? Some social psychological issues concerning English national identity. In G. M. Breakwell & E. Lyons (Eds.), *Changing European identities: Social psychological analyses of social change.* Oxford: Butterworth Heinemann (pp. 41–68).

Cutts Dougherty, K., Eisenhart, M., & Webley, P. (1992). The role of social representations and national identities in the development of territorial knowledge: A study of political socialization in Argentina and England. *American Educational Research Journal, 29*, 809–835.

Damon, W., & Hart, D. (1988). *Self-understanding in childhood and adolescence.* Cambridge: Cambridge University Press.

de Rosa, A. S., & Bombi, A. S. (1999). Se sentir heureux d'être Italiens? La construction de l'identité nationale et supranationale dans les représentations sociales de son propre pays ou du pays d'autrui chez des enfants et chez des adolescents. In M. L. Rouquette & C. Garnier (Eds.), *La genèse des représentations sociales.* Montreal: Editions Nouvelles.

Devine-Wright, P., & Lyons, E. (1997). Remembering pasts and representing places: The construction of national identities in Ireland. *Journal of Environmental Psychology, 17*, 33–45.

Doyle, A. B., & Aboud, F. E. (1995). A longitudinal study of white children's racial prejudice as a social-cognitive development. *Merrill-Palmer Quarterly, 41*, 209–228.

Doyle, A. B., Beaudet, J., & Aboud, F. E. (1988). Developmental patterns in the flexibility of children's ethnic attitudes. *Journal of Cross-Cultural Psychology, 19*, 3–18.

Durkin, K. (1985). *Television, sex roles and children.* Milton Keynes, UK: Open University Press.

Eckes, T., & Trautner, H. M. (Eds.) (2000). *The developmental social psychology of gender.* Mahwah, NJ: Lawrence Erlbaum Associates Inc.

Elejabarrieta, F. (1994). Social positioning: A way to link social identity and social representations. *Social Science Information, 33*, 241–253.

English, R., & Halperin, J. J. (1987). *The other side: How oviets and Americans perceive each other.* New Brunswick, NJ: Transaction Books.

Forrest, L., & Barrett, M. (2001). *English adolescents' sense of national identity, identity motivations and national historical icons.* Unpublished paper, Department of Psychology, University of Surrey.

Gellner, E. (1983). *Nations and nationalism*. Oxford: Blackwell.

Giménez, A., Belmonte, L., Garcia-Claros, E., Suarez, E., & Barrett, M. (1997). *Acquisition of geographical knowledge*. Poster presented at the 7th European Conference for Research on Learning and Instruction, Athens, Greece, August 1997.

Giménez, A., Canto, J. M., Fernández, P., & Barrett, M. (1999). La identificacion social como regulador del estereotipo lo que piensan los ninos Andaluces. *Boletin de Psicologia, 64*, 81–99.

Gunter, B., & McAleer, J. (1997). *Children and television* (2nd ed.). London: Routledge.

Haslam, S. A., Oakes, P. J., Turner, J. C., & McGarty, C. (1995). Social categorization and group homogeneity: Changes in the perceived applicability of stereotype content as a function of comparative context and trait favourableness. *British Journal of Social Psychology, 34*, 139–160.

Helwig, C. C., & Prencipe, A. (1999). Children's judgments of flags and flag-burning. *Child Development, 70*, 132–143.

Hesse, P., & Mack, J. E. (1991). The world is a dangerous place: Images of the enemy on children's television. In R. W. Rieber (Ed.), *The psychology of war and peace: The image of the enemy* (pp. 131–151). New York: Plenum Press.

Himmelweit, H. T., Oppenheim, A. N., & Vince, P. (1958). *Television and the child: An empirical study of the effect of television on the young*. Oxford: Oxford University Press.

Hinkle, S., & Brown, R. (1990). Intergroup comparisons and social identity: Some links and lacunae. In D. Abrams & M. A. Hogg (Eds.), *Social identity theory: Constructive and critical advances*. Hemel Hempstead, UK: Harvester Wheatsheaf (pp. 48–70).

Hopkins, N., Regan, M., & Abell, J. (1997). On the context-dependence of national stereotypes: Some Scottish data. *British Journal of Social Psychology, 36*, 553–563.

Jahoda, G. (1962). Development of Scottish children's ideas and attitudes about other countries. *Journal of Social Psychology, 58*, 91–108.

Jahoda, G. (1963a). The development of children's ideas about country and nationality, Part I: The conceptual framework. *British Journal of Educational Psychology, 33*, 47–60.

Jahoda, G. (1963b). The development of children's ideas about country and nationality, Part II: National symbols and themes. *British Journal of Educational Psychology, 33*, 143–153.

Jahoda, G. (1964). Children's concepts of nationality: A critical study of Piaget's stages. *Child Development, 35*, 1081–1092.

Jahoda, G., & Woerdenbagch, A. (1982). Awareness of supra-national groupings among Dutch and Scottish children and adolescents. *European Journal of Political Research, 10*, 305–312.

Jaspers, J. M. F., Van de Geer, J. P., Tajfel, H., & Johnson, N. (1972). On the development of national attitudes in children. *European Journal of Social Psychology, 2*, 347–369.

Johnson, N. (1966). What do children learn from war comics? *New Society, 8*, 7–12.

Johnson, N. (1973). Development of English children's concept of Germany. *Journal of Social Psychology, 90*, 259–267.

Johnson, N., Middleton, M., & Tajfel, H. (1970). The relationship between children's preferences for and knowledge about other nations. *British Journal of Social and Clinical Psychology, 9*, 232–240.

Karakozov, R., & Kadirova, R. (2001). Sociocultural and cognitive factors in Azeri children and adolescents' identity formation. In M. Barrett, T. Riazanova, & M. Volovikova (Eds.), *Development of national, ethnolinguistic and religious identities in children and adolescents* (pp. 59–83). Moscow: Institute of Psychology, Russian Academy of Sciences (IPRAS).

Kipiani, G. (2001). Ethnic identification in the structure of personal identifications and socio-cultural conditions of development. In M. Barrett, T. Riazanova, & M. Volovikova (Eds.), *Development of national, ethnolinguistic and religious identities in children and adolescents* (pp. 84–104). Moscow: Institute of Psychology, Russian Academy of Sciences (IPRAS).

Lambert, W. E., & Klineberg, O. (1967). *Children's views of foreign peoples: A cross-national study*. New York: Appleton-Century-Crofts.

Livesley, W. J., & Bromley, D. B. (1973). *Person perception in childhood and adolescence*. London: Wiley.

Lyons, E. (1996). Coping with social change: Processes of social memory in the reconstruction of identities. In G. M. Breakwell & E. Lyons (Eds.), *Changing European identities: Social psychological analyses of social change* (pp. 31–39). Oxford: Butterworth Heinemann.

Middleton, M., Tajfel, H., & Johnson, N. (1970). Cognitive and affective aspects of children's national attitudes. *British Journal of Social and Clinical Psychology, 9*, 122–134.

Moodie, M. A. (1980). The development of national identity in white South African schoolchildren. *Journal of Social Psychology, 111*, 169–180.

Moss, N., & Blades, M. (1994). *Travel doesn't broaden the mind*. Poster presented at the Annual Conference of the Developmental Section of the British Psychological Society, Portsmouth, September 1994.

Mummendey, A., Klink, A., & Brown, R. (2001). Nationalism and patriotism: National identification and out-group rejection. *British Journal of Social Psychology, 40*, 159–172.

Nesdale, D. (1999). Social identity and ethnic prejudice in children. In P. Martin & W. Noble (Eds.), *Psychology and society* (pp. 92–110). Brisbane: Australian Academic Press.

Nesdale, D. (2004). Social identity processes and children's ethnic prejudice. In M. Bennett & F. Sani (Eds.), *The development of the social self*. Hove, UK: Psychology Press (pp. 219–245).

Nesdale, D., Maass, A., Griffiths, J., & Durkin, K. (2003). Effects of in-group and out-group ethnicity on children's attitudes towards members of the in-group and out-group. *British Journal of Developmental Psychology, 21*, 177–192.

Nugent, J. K. (1994). The development of children's relationships with their country. *Children's Environments, 11*, 281–291.

Oakes, P. J., Haslam, S. A., & Turner, J. C. (1994). *Stereotyping and social reality*. Oxford: Blackwell.

Pavlenko, V., Kryazh, I., Ivanova, O., & Barrett, M. (2001). Age characteristics of social identifications and ethno-national beliefs in Ukraine. In M. Barrett, T. Riazanova, & M. Volovikova (Eds.), *Development of national, ethnolinguistic and religious identities in children and adolescents* (pp. 105–131). Moscow: Institute of Psychology, Russian Academy of Sciences (IPRAS).

Penny, R., Barrett, M., & Lyons, E. (2001). *Children's naïve theories of nationality: A study of Scottish and English children's national inclusion criteria*. Poster presented at the 10th European Conference on Developmental Psychology, Uppsala University, Uppsala, Sweden, August 2001.

Piaget, J. (1928). *Judgment and reasoning in the child*. London: Routledge & Kegan Paul.

Piaget, J., & Weil, A. M. (1951). The development in children of the idea of the homeland and of relations to other countries. *International Social Science Journal, 3*, 561–578.

Reizábal, L., Valencia, J., & Barrett, M. (2004). National identifications and attitudes to national in-groups and out-groups amongst children living in the Basque Country. *Infant and Child Development, 13*, 1–20.

Riazanova, T., Sergienko, E., Grenkova-Dikevitch, L., Gorodetschnaya, N., & Barrett, M. (2001). Cognitive aspects of ethno-national identity development in Russian children and adolescents. In M. Barrett, T. Riazanova, & M. Volovikova (Eds.), *Development of national, ethnolinguistic and religious identities in children and adolescents* (pp. 164–196). Moscow: Institute of Psychology, Russian Academy of Sciences (IPRAS).

Roberts, D. F., Herold, C., Hornby, K., King, S., Sterne, D., Whitely, S., & Silverman, T. (1974). *Earth's a Big Blue Marble: A report of the impact of a children's television series on children's opinions*. Unpublished paper, Stanford University, CA.

Ruble, D. N., & Martin, C. L. (1998). Gender development. In W. Damon & N. Eisenberg (Eds.), *Handbook of child psychology, Volume 3: Social, emotional and personality development* (5th ed., pp. 933–1016). New York: Wiley.

Rutland, A. (1998). English children's geo-political knowledge of Europe. *British Journal of Developmental Psychology, 16*, 439–445.

Rutland, A. (1999). The development of national prejudice, in-group favouritism and self stereotypes in British children. *British Journal of Social Psychology, 38*, 55–70.

Smith, A. D. (1991). *National identity*. Harmondsworth, UK: Penguin.

Smith, A. D. (1998). *Nationalism and modernism*. London: Routledge.

Stillwell, R., & Spencer, C. (1973). Children's early preferences for other nations and their subsequent acquisition of knowledge about those nations. *European Journal of Social Psychology, 3*, 345–349.

Tajfel, H. (1966). Children and foreigners. *New Society, 7*, 9–11.

Tajfel, H. (1978). *Differentiation between social groups: Studies in the social psychology of intergroup relations*. London: Academic Press.

Tajfel, H., & Jahoda, G. (1966). Development in children of concepts and attitudes about their own and other nations: A cross-national study. *Proceedings of the XVIIIth International Congress in Psychology, Moscow, Symposium 36*, 17–33.

Tajfel, H., Jahoda, G., Nemeth, C., Campbell, J., & Johnson, N. (1970). The development of children's preference for their own country: A cross-national study. *International Journal of Psychology, 5*, 245–253.

Tajfel, H., Jahoda, G., Nemeth, C., Rim, Y., & Johnson, N. (1972). The devaluation by children of their own national and ethnic group: Two case studies. *British Journal of Social and Clinical Psychology, 11*, 235–243.

Tajfel, H., & Turner, J. C. (1986). The social identity theory of intergroup behaviour. In S. Worchel & W. G. Austin (Eds.), *Psychology of intergroup relations* (2nd ed., pp. 7–24). Chicago: Nelson-Hall.

Tanaka, S. (1994). History—consuming pasts. *Journal of Narrative and Life History, 4*, 257–275.

Turner, J. C., Hogg, M. A., Oakes, P. J., Reicher, S. D., & Wetherell, M. S. (1987). *Rediscovering the social group: A self-categorization theory*. Oxford: Blackwell.

Valencia, J., Elejabarrieta, F., Perera, S., Reizábal, L., Barrett, M., Vila, I., Gil de Montes, L., Ortiz, G., & Larrañaga, M. (in press). Conflictual national identities and linguistic strategies as positioning tools in children and adolescents. *Proceedings of the 5th International Conference on Social Representations, "New Constructions"*, Montreal, Canada.

Verkuyten, M. (2001). National identification and intergroup evaluation in Dutch children. *British Journal of Developmental Psychology, 19*, 559–571.

Vila, I., del Valle, A., Perera, S., Monreal, P., & Barrett, M. (1998). Autocategorizacion, identidad nacional y contexto linguistico. *Estudios de Psicologia, 60*, 3–14.

Weinstein, E. A. (1957). Development of the concept of flag and the sense of national identity. *Child Development, 28*, 167–174.

Wertsch, J. V. (1994). Introduction: Historical representation. *Journal of Narrative and Life History, 4*, 247–255.

Wertsch, J. V. (1998). *Mind as action*. New York: Oxford University Press.

Wiegand, P. (1991). The "known" world of primary school children. *Geography, 76*, 143–149.

Wilberg, S. (2002). Preschoolers' cognitive representations of their homeland. *British Journal of Developmental Psychology, 20*, 157–169.

Wills, J. S. (1994). Popular culture, curriculum, and historical representation: the situation of Native Americans in American history and the perpetuation of stereotypes. *Journal of Narrative and Life History, 4*, 277–294.

CHAPTER ELEVEN

The development of societal cognition: A commentary

Giyoo Hatano
Human Development and Education Program, The University of the Air, Japan

Keiko Takahashi
Department of Psychology, University of the Sacred Heart, Tokyo, Japan

Like many other topics in conceptual development, children's "understanding of societal institutions, structures, and groups" (Barrett & Buchanan-Barrow, Chapter 1, hereafter "societal cognition"), or conceptions of society, was first investigated by Piaget (Berti, Chapter 4) and studied further by Piagetians such as Furth (1980) and Berti and Bombi (1988). Children's understanding of their society has been considered to be as important as their understanding of the physical and biological world as a topic for research. However, it has not been a popular topic in developmental research. In terms of sheer number, far fewer studies on children's conceptions of society have been accumulated than on their understanding of the natural world. More importantly, whereas children's biological and physical understanding have both been historically central to major theories of children's thinking (Carey, 1985; Keil, 1992; Piaget, 1929, 1930; Siegler, 1978), societal cognition has never been the focus of intensive discussion.

We can readily offer a few possible reasons why societal cognition has not been liked by developmentalists. First, societal entities are variable cross-culturally. For example, as Buchanan-Barrow (Chapter 2) points out, after the family, the school is the first societal system children experience in industrialized countries, and thus children's experience there certainly serves as a basis for constructing their understanding of other social systems in society; but not all children in the world go to school, even nowadays. Thus, it is difficult to yield generalisations that are universally valid. Second, developmental researchers do not always have access to clear criteria by which children's responses about societal entities can be evaluated. As far as societal cognition is concerned, beliefs shared by educated adults are not always correct, as Hirschfeld (Chapter 8) aptly points out, because they may reflect prejudices and stereotypes. Needless to say, it is possible to develop scoring or coding criteria for children's responses that reflect the extent of their societal understanding, but this requires additional effort. Unless one is particularly interested in societal cognition, it is simpler to investigate physical or biological cognition for which the correct answer is obvious. Third, and last, experimental materials for societal cognition are harder to construct than for physical or biological cognition, because societal entities cannot be represented readily by pictures or toys. In short, many developmental researchers have chosen to study physical and biological cognition, not societal cognition, because it is more straightforward to do so, and because, in the Piagetian tradition, patterns of development from the stage of no understanding through the intermediate stage to the stage of full understanding were assumed to be invariant everywhere, and the stage-to-stage transitions were expected to occur at approximately the same ages.

It is now time to direct greater attention to the study of societal cognition—we hope that this belief is shared not only by all the contributors to this volume but also by many others who have yet to start their research on it. Theoretically, from domain-specific perspectives and approaches, investigations into children's societal understanding have special significance to the extent to which societal cognition has unique features. And practically, helping youngsters to become respectable citizens is no less important than developing their mathematical and scientific competence, and this seems possible only if we base our practices on our understanding of children's societal understanding.

This edited volume offers, for the first time, a comprehensive overview of the research that has been conducted on the development of societal cognition. Its contributors are all distinguished specialists themselves on the topic(s) that have been assigned to them. Interestingly, they are quite varied in their theoretical orientations as well as their nationalities; as a whole, this volume represents a variety of the current perspectives on, and approaches to, the study of societal cognition. It is especially informative because each chapter not only reviews relevant studies, but also evaluates them, and suggests future directions for research.

In this commentary, we discuss four issues based on the preceding chapters. The first two issues concern the nature of societal cognition. We are particularly interested in the advantages and the limitations of the domain-specific approach to societal cognition. The third issue concerns pathways of development, and we wish to emphasise the agency of developing individuals in addition to the list of the experiential factors that are suggested by the other contributors. Finally, we discuss the significance of societal cognition research, and indicate some additional issues not covered elsewhere in this otherwise comprehensive volume.

IS SOCIETAL COGNITION UNIQUE?

We have witnessed some marked changes in research on conceptual development, or the growth of children's knowledge systems, in the last few decades (see Hatano & Inagaki, 1999). The Piagetian theory of cognitive development that dominated the research area in the 1960s and early 1970s had two separable aspects. On the one hand, it posited that knowledge is constructed through the interaction between children and their environment, via the complementary processes of assimilation and accommodation. On the other hand, it indicated that children's competence depends on their stages, in other words, on logico-mathematical structures, which are applicable across domains. Recent trends in conceptual development research, which became more and more notable during the last quarter of the 20th century, emphasised domain-specificity instead of domain-general stages, but preserved the Piagetian constructivist view of cognitive development (Wellman & Gelman, 1998).

In current approaches, knowledge is divided into domains, without assigning special status to logico-mathematical knowledge. Recent studies have demonstrated, moreover, that individual competence varies considerably from domain to domain, irrespective of how domains are defined. The Piagetian stage theory, which posited that an individual's competence depends on his or her logico-mathematical structures, which are applicable across domains, has been challenged or even rejected by many current researchers. This implies that pieces of prior knowledge of the target domain serve as the critical constraints on problem-solving and learning in the domain, possibly except for the earliest phases of development. It also implies that there are sociocultural constraints (e.g., culturally organised practices) that enhance the acquisition of the domain knowledge. We believe, as the editors do, that societal cognition constitutes a domain of knowledge, or, to put it differently, children and lay adults have a distinguishable set of pieces of knowledge about behaviours, structures, and functions of societal entities. This must be so, for the sake of cognitive economy and coherence, in our society where pieces of information about the social world are clustered together and separated from those about individual persons or the natural world.

The knowledge in each domain is often supposed to constitute a naïve or intuitive theory, that is, a body of coherent pieces of knowledge involving characteristic causal devices. Also, a variety of innate or very early domain-specific constraints, which facilitate the acquisition and direct the elaboration of the theory, have been proposed. However, two cautionary notes are needed here. First, there have been strong alternatives to the naïve theory view even among the researchers emphasising the domain-specificity of children's knowledge. Not a few investigators claim that children's domain-specific knowledge system does not deserve the label of "theory", because it consists of a collection of situation-specific or fragmentary pieces of knowledge (sometimes called mental models) and/or lacks characteristic causal devices (e.g., diSessa, 1983; Yates, Bassman, Dunne, Jertson, Sly, & Wendelboe, 1988). They aptly point out that "naïve theories" do not cover all phenomena they could, and their implications are not fully extended nor exploited (Inagaki & Hatano, 2002). Second, although a majority of proponents of the naïve theory view hold versions of "core-knowledge theories" (Siegler, DeLoache, & Eisenberg, 2003), they do not necessarily assume that all naïve theories possess direct genetic bases or genetically given core knowledge for the theories. Most lay adults have a form of folk pedagogy, but its acquisition may be based on their experience of guided learning, although this may be assisted by the theory of mind to some extent. We use the term "naïve theory" here to mean that each domain-specific knowledge system is loosely regulated by a framework theory that has a characteristic causal principle, under which a number of specific theories and models are included (Wellman, 1990). Children's and lay adults' predictions and explanations are often constrained strongly by the relevant specific theory or model but only weakly by the framework theory.

The shift from the Piagetian approach to the naïve theory approach is related to the methodology of assessment, as pointed out by Barrett and Buchanan-Barrow (Chapter 1). Sometimes, though, posing many similar interview questions to the Piagetian ones with children and lay adults, the new approach proposes different interpretations (Berti, Chapter 4). However, at other times, in contrast to the characteristic use of open-ended questioning by the Piagetians, children's choices from a set of proposed consequences or antecedents about the typical phenomenon or event in the domain characterise the new approach. Implicit understanding is considered here, and as a result, "preoperational" children according to the Piagetian method may be attributed with some understanding.

The emphasis on domain-specificity, and the characterisation of societal cognition as a domain, produces a new research question, which is: How is the development of societal cognition similar to, or distinctly different from, the development of understanding of other aspects of the world? We speculate about this issue in the remaining part of this section, although any firm conclusions must wait for future research.

Let us start by briefly comparing societal understanding with "natural" cognition, that is, understanding of the physical and biological world. Unlike the latter, societal cognition of "how the entity is" is almost always associated with "how it should be". This probably reflects the moralistic nature of the social sciences. Webley (Chapter 3, p. 118) points out that theories in the social sciences almost always "do not just describe and explain the world but also legitimate certain ways of behaving and thinking". Is it thus nearly impossible, and probably undesirable, to eliminate moral considerations from societal understanding? We discuss this issue in the final section of this commentary. A related characterization of societal cognition is that it sometimes induces self- and other-related emotions (Durkin, Chapter 6; Lo Coco, Inguglia, & Pace, Chapter 9; Barrett, Chapter 10). For instance, even though the behaviours of one's forefathers are clearly beyond one's own control, one feels pride or shame depending upon the nature of those behaviours. Whether societal entities are always conceived as an extension of the self or of others is an interesting issue, and we will also return to this issue in the final section. Here we just claim that societal understanding is a very good domain to investigate cognition that is accompanied by moral and emotional components.

How unique societal cognition is depends, among other factors, on its causality—how do children and lay adults predict and explain behaviours and properties of societal entities as a whole or their constituents (e.g., a teacher working at school)? Because most societal entities are artifacts, their understanding must be related to understanding of "material" artifacts. How material artifacts such as machines operate can be explained in terms of mechanisms and functions (Miyake, 1986), but in everyday cognition functional or teleological explanations are expectedly more dominant than mechanistic ones. In fact, when lay adults classify artifacts, they rely much more heavily on functions than forms (Diesendruck, Hammer, & Catz, 2003). Therefore, are behaviours of societal entities also explained in terms of teleology?

We have to consider, however, that because most societal entities include the people who work for them, a version of the theory of mind may also be applied to behaviours and properties of societal entities. Relationships between societal cognition and individual person cognition seem complicated. It has been confirmed repeatedly that confusion between personal and societal roles occurs frequently among young children (Furth, 1980; Berti, Chapter 4). Does this mean that young children do not understand at all that people act differently when they are fulfilling roles in their institutions from when they behave in "private" situations? We believe they do—even young children can differentiate, to some extent, what they want to do from what they have to do, and thus recognise that societal minds are expected to operate based on teleology, that is, for the societal entities to fulfil their functions. In contrast, children usually attribute human psychosocial behaviours or the operations of individual minds under no societal duties to such proximal factors as desires, beliefs, and emotions. The theory of mind concerning how individual minds operate may sometimes intrude into societal cognition because it is acquired early, easily, and universally; in other words, it constitutes a privileged domain.

However, teleological explanations may differ between material artifacts and societal entities. Let us divide teleology into two subtypes, intrinsic (parts or properties are for the sake of their owners) and extrinsic (parts, properties, or even the whole entities are for the sake of others, most often for humans). It can be assumed that, whereas extrinsic teleology is promiscuous (Kelemen, 1999), intrinsic teleology is limited to living things in the minds of children and lay adults (Inagaki & Hatano, 2002). Unlike living things, including individual humans, and also unlike artifacts, behaviours and properties of societal entities and their constituent parts may be given both intrinsic and extrinsic teleological explanations. For example, the bank's behaviours may be predicted and explained based on its intrinsic and/or extrinsic functions, such as its profit making, the role of money circulation in the society, etc.

It will be much more intriguing to understand children's understandings of various entities or different aspects of the world in a comparative and integrated fashion than to study them separately. In this sense, progress in research on conceptual development has prepared a stage on which findings of societal cognition can be highlighted.

IS SOCIETAL COGNITION A PRIVILEGED DOMAIN?

Human development is constrained both by innate capabilities and predispositions on the one hand, and by sociocultural contexts and constructions on the other. These two types of constraint always contribute jointly to the development of mind (Cole, 1996), but may take different forms and/or operate differently from domain to domain.

There are some domains in which almost all people, often in their immaturity, acquire knowledge rapidly and easily; in contrast, in other domains the acquisition takes a long time and requires laborious effort. The former domains, which are called privileged or core domains (Siegler & Crowley, 1994; Wellman & Inagaki, 1997), concern naïve theories or coherent bodies of knowledge, the acquisition of which has been vital for the survival of our species. It has generally been agreed among developmentalists that naïve physics, theory of mind, and intuitive biology are not only the core domains of thought (Wellman & Gelman, 1992) but also privileged domains (Siegler & Crowley, 1994). In other words, these knowledge systems that deal with aspects of the world that are important for the survival of the human species are shared by most adults, both within and between cultures, and are acquired by children early and without difficulty because humans are endowed with domain-specific constraints, principles, and tendencies for them.

The latter domains, called nonprivileged or peripheral domains, represent organised bodies of knowledge (and sets of skills for using the knowledge) that an individual acquires through his or her profession or hobby. These domains may be subdivided into smaller, and more specialised, domains. Thus people often vary widely in the extent of mastery in these domains. Chess, cooking, making diagnoses by reading X-ray films, as well as raising particular animals and selling particular goods, exemplify these domains.

What about the status, then, of societal cognition or "naïve sociology"? It may be another core and privileged domain, because knowledge about people's own society must be very important for them to live in it as mature members. It may not be, however, because societal entities and how they are organised vary greatly from culture to culture and from historical time to historical time, so there can be no domain-specific innate constraints helping humans acquire knowledge about them.

Most of the contributors to this book are neutral or eclectic regarding innate bases of societal cognition, even when they refer to the naïve theory approach. Hirschfeld (Chapter 8) is a clear exception, because he seems to believe that racial phenomena and underlying thinking are strongly constrained by the human mind's scheme for collectivities, which is universal and is genetically endowed. Although he never claims that racial thinking is a product of a universal human endowment, he claims that it is a product of folk sociology, a special-purpose faculty for understanding the world of human kinds (coupled with cultural, historical conditions that make race a prominent human kind).

We are sceptical, however, about whether humans possess domain-specific innate constraints for all aspects of the world to be dealt with by societal cognition or, using Hirschfeld's terminology, folk sociology. Although to provide a set of expectations about human intrinsic kinds including race is a major task of a theory of society, it is not the theory's only major task. We would propose that it should cover understanding of culturally constructed institutions as well, which are arranged differently in different societies. If so, is this understanding, too, based on human endowment? Can children thus acquire knowledge needed for it early and easily? We cannot give an affirmative answer to these questions for empirical and theoretical reasons. Empirically, our own study on children's understanding of the banking business (Takahashi & Hatano, 1994), as well as the studies reviewed by Webley (Chapter 3), for example, have shown that, although most children were familiar with the depository function of a bank, and many of them also knew its loan function, a majority of the elementary and junior-high participants lacked ideas about how money circulates in the bank, especially the relationship between deposited money and money for loan, and how banks make profit. Some of them even considered interest as "a token of appreciation"; they were not aware of a bank's profit-producing nature, and thought that a bank was a nonprofit organisation. Many of them revealed kinds of alternative conceptions of the bank.

Such findings are not limited to naïve economics. A number of the authors of the preceding chapters mention difficulties in societal cognition. Let us offer just two more examples: The labour contract is often interpreted as voluntary because power relations between employers and employees are hard to understand (Emler & Dickinson, Chapter 7); and a careful consideration is needed of how to manage children entering the legal system of the adult society because of their cognitive limitations (Ceci, Markle, & Chae, Chapter 5).

Theoretically, it has been too recent evolutionarily that humans started to live in a fairly large society containing prototypes of institutions and structures to acquire conceptual devices for understanding these societal entities. This forces us to believe that folk sociology as a whole, which has to deal with new cultural constructions, cannot be a core and privileged domain to the same extent as naïve physics, theory of mind, and intuitive biology.

Again, a number of the contributors to this volume suggest that societal cognition is acquired through domain-general learning mechanisms, the operations of which require much time and effort. It is thus not surprising that there are a number of cognitive limitations that may impede children's participation in the adult legal system (Ceci et al., Chapter 5), and that "domain-general cognitive changes are crucial" (Webley, Chapter 3, p. 115) in the development of children's understanding of economics, if their understanding is not enhanced by domain-specific innate constraints.

However, we do not assume that no domain-specific innate constraints operate in the development of societal cognition. In other words, it is hard to simply conclude that societal cognition is a purely nonprivileged domain that is similar to chess, cooking, and making diagnoses by reading X-ray films. Several forms of social interaction, such as the division of labour, sharing the fruits of a joint endeavour, and barter, may be so basic to the life of the human species that their significance must be understood readily and universally. We fully agree with Emler and Dickinson (Chapter 7) that children incorporate explanations for economic inequalities that are offered by their social groups, but they do so with those that make sense to them— principles of equality, equity, or their mixture.

Based on the above discussion, we would like to propose our own answer to the question, "Is societal cognition a privileged domain?" We assume that, whereas its core or primitive part is privileged, its extended part is nonprivileged. This characterisation may be applied to a few other domains as well. In physical cognition, for example, even infants possess some expectations about how objects move and interact, but even college students have great difficulty in fully understanding Newtonian physics. In naïve biology, whereas even young children have some rudimentary understanding that living things take in vital power from food/water and grow using that power, understanding the Darwinian notion of evolution in terms of mutation and natural selection takes many years. As Harris (1990) suggests, we might assume that domains as a whole are not privileged nor nonprivileged; only some components are privileged.

HOW DOES SOCIETAL COGNITION DEVELOP?

Although children's development in societal cognition is slow and incomplete, it is clearly enhanced by experiential factors in sociocultural contexts. Studies reviewed by the contributors to this volume suggest that there are three major pathways through which societal cognition develops: participation in cultural practices; educational intervention; and exposure to mass media. We will discuss each of them.

Participation in cultural practices

There is a consensus that, through repeated participation in the relevant practices, children and lay adults tend to develop the skills and beliefs needed for these practices (Goodnow, Miller, & Kessel, 1995). By "practice" we mean a culturally organised sequence of activities to produce significant outcomes (e.g., products to sell), in which artifacts and other people are embedded. Even beginners in a domain can successfully participate in those practices and contribute to them (as an apprentice working with his/her master).

Many studies show that everyday practices in family environments are very effective for the development of children's societal understanding. An early study by Yoshida (1959) showed that Japanese school children from families of merchants were superior to their counterparts from salaried employees regarding the understanding of the profit-making mechanism of retail shops and of money circulation. Jahoda (1981) found that being active in trading made African children in Harare in Zimbabwe superior to European children in understanding the profit-making mechanism of a retail shop. Studies reviewed by Webley (Chapter 3) also revealed that children living in active commercial districts have a better understanding of the profit-making mechanism than others. Thus, engaging in commercial activities and observing parents' economic behaviour seem to be informative for children.

Another example of the effectiveness of engaging in familial practices is given by Weisner and his colleagues (Weisner, Garnier, & Loucky, 1994). They showed that children in nonconventional families (i.e., avant garde and countercultural families) tend to be more gender egalitarian than those in conventional families. By participating in nontraditional labour-sharing activities, children, especially girls, obtain gender-free ideas of living.

Practices are not limited to household jobs. As a classic study by Piaget (1932) indicates, through social practice (e.g., marble games) children come to understand the essential meaning of the social rules, and why and when they can change the rules if needed. Webley and his colleagues describe how children construct and use sophisticated rules through participating in their own playground "economic" activities (Webley, Chapter 3). It is an interesting question whether we can expect children, who are experts in playground politics or economics, to comprehend adult societal systems and/or can be competent citizens in the future.

Educational intervention

For the acquisition of advanced societal knowledge, it is reasonably assumed that educational and other interventions are needed. As both Berti (Chapter 4) and Barrett (Chapter 10) show, educational practices do indeed impact upon children's societal cognition. Here, we offer a few further remarkable exemplars of educational intervention for societal cognition.

Some conscientious Japanese schoolteachers (e.g., Chiba, 1993; Ohtsu, 1987; Yasui, 1986) have tried very hard to construct programmes for societal cognition and implement them. Ohtsu organised a series of programmes to help high school students understand how multinational big enterprises exploit banana farmers of the Philippine Islands, based on an elaborated analysis by a Japanese sociologist, Yoshiyuki Tsurumi (1982). She started her lesson with a question about why people in Japan could always eat a banana at a bargain rate. In the course of learning involving lectures, examining materials, and discussions, students came to understand the sophisticated but antihumanistic profit-making mechanism of the enterprises. At the final stage of the programme, the students were motivated to help the farmers with writing a letter of protest to the president of the enterprises. Another teacher from an elementary school constructed a programme for understanding what the essential nature of the recycling of aluminum cans is (Chiba, 1993), and a junior-high schoolteacher constructed a programme for understanding human rights, focusing on unfair customs for women in work places (Yasui, 1986).

There are some excellent educational programmes for the development of citizenship in youth in Europe and the United States (e.g., Holden & Clough, 1998; Yates & Youniss, 1996, 1999; Youniss & Yates, 1997).

Youniss and Yates (1996, 1997) investigated how a class of high-school students of both genders, mostly from urban middle-class African-American families, developed their civic responsibilities during a school year through being given lectures on social justice by an enthusiastic teacher and serving at a "soup-kitchen" for homeless people. Their research indicated that knowledge acquired from lectures and experiences in the soup-kitchen together deepened the students' understanding of the root questions of homelessness and elevated awareness of their social responsibilities.

These successful educational practices seem to have three characteristics. First, the teachers selected concrete examples that were familiar to students as a meaningful window to observe the society, such as a banana, a juice can, and homeless people. Second, they were based on theories and analyses by experts and used materials such as figures, pictures, and documents that persuasively explained societal mechanisms. Third, they enhanced social interactions with others (not only their classmates but also people outside the classroom, such as farmers in Philippines, a president of a big enterprise, and homeless people).

Exposure to mass media

The effects of the mass media, and particularly television, upon children's societal cognition are discussed in several of the chapters of this book; see, for example, Ceci et al. (Chapter 5), Durkin (Chapter 6), Emler and Dickinson (Chapter 7), and Barrett (Chapter 10). Information conveyed through the mass media can have two contrasting effects on the development of societal cognition. On the one hand, such information is indispensable for understanding societal entities, especially those with which individuals have little direct contact. On the other hand, however, this information often misleads children's and lay adults' societal cognition because it is erroneous or too superficial. Because the latter aspect of mass media information is not intensively discussed in the preceding chapters, we will present two impressive cases here.

First, it has been well documented that the mass media tend to increase, rather than reduce, cultural biases, stereotypes, and prejudices. For example, content analyses of television commercials, magazines, and children's books reveal that gender-biased messages are often included, and suggest their transmission of the traditional gender roles to the audience (e.g., Bartsch, Burnett, Diller, & Rankin-Williams, 2000).

Second, the mass media sometimes mislead the audience by providing true but superficial information about the target societal phenomenon. Since the Japanese bubble economy, with artificially high land and stock values, collapsed in 1990, the Japanese economy has been in a state of recession, bordering on depression, and many negative facts about the economy have been reported by the mass media. Almost every day, there is news of banks suffering bankruptcies, heavy debts, etc. It is assumed that even ordinary Japanese people are acutely aware of the Japanese economic and monetary crises. In fact, a number of surveys reported that negative images of the banking business gradually penetrated into young and middle-aged working people. However, our study of college students' folk economics of the banking business toward the end of the 20th century (Takahashi & Hatano, 2000) showed that a large majority of them applied "humanistic rules" when they predicted the bank's behaviours, such as assuming a bank's goodwill, bargains in interest rates, and the extension of loan periods with a sympathetic consideration of borrowers' economic circumstances. In other words, through watching news of the recession through the mass media, people became aware that the banking business was not in a good shape but failed to predict the bank's behaviours in terms of its profit-making mechanisms. Lo Coco et al. also indicate that the anti-racism campaign through mass media had only limited effects (Chapter 9).

Children as active agents of development

As Furth (1980) put it, children are not only socialised, but also construct societal cognition. This emphasis on the active, constructive role of developing individuals in cognitive development is one of the most significant of Piaget's legacies. As some of the contributors to this volume suggest, the active tendency among children is especially important in the development of societal cognition. Analyses of children's narratives and behaviours in the educational programmes that we referred to in the previous section clearly indicate how strongly children and adolescents are motivated to seek appropriate evidence and arguments for understanding mechanisms of societal systems.

For instance, essays written by students after performing voluntary activities (Youniss & Yates, 1997) indicate that the students, step by step, constructed their own knowledge using information that they had been provided with in previous lectures and other sources. That is, high-school students wrote: "Social Justice class definitely changed me for the better. I used to argue constantly with Mr. Siwek (a teacher) about issues such as homelessness, gun control, defense spending, etc. Those arguments served to give me a new sense of responsibility and awareness"; "Working at the soup kitchen taught me there are people who are less fortune than me. Before going there, I always thought of homeless people as being dumb, uneducated, dirty individuals. After meeting with them, I realized that most of them did not want to be homeless or come to kitchen. Most of them I talked with were college graduate, young mothers, and everyday people just like everybody else" (Youniss & Yates, 1997, p. 124). We need elaborate analyses to show how children and young people construct their own societal knowledge, and what kind of programmes are helpful for their own construction of societal cognition.

Moreover, in societal understanding, as Buchanan-Barrow (Chapter 2) suggests, it is very important for citizens to realise that they can change societal systems if they need. According to her, in the school, because it is a microsociety in which children can participate as real members, they have the opportunity to experience directly democracy and decision-making. In this vein, the democratic attitude of school councils and teachers are very important for the growth of these future citizens. We need studies that focus on children as active protagonists in school life.

WHY DO WE HAVE TO STUDY SOCIETAL COGNITION?

Our answer to this question is twofold, as suggested at the beginning of this commentary. From the theoretical perspective, societal cognition research should have special significance to the extent to which this domain has characteristic features. Thus, we may assert, for example, that investigating societal cognition is needed to clarify environmental or experiential influences on the developing individuals' naïve theories, because it is expected to reveal clearer and wider variations due to historical and cultural contexts than its neighbours such as naïve physics or theory of mind – societal cognition research may serve to "socialise" conceptual development researchers who tend to assume that children's naïve theories develop monotonously with their age or the amount of general experience. However, we would like to emphasise here that societal cognition is a particularly good domain to investigate the understanding that is accompanied by moral and self-related emotional components.

We also give an answer from the practical point of view: We have to study societal cognition to make the world a place where every human being can live happily and can be treated with respect, care, and fairness, a goal that can be achieved only when all children become economically and politically literate and responsible citizens. We can educate such responsible citizens only when we understand the pathways and mechanisms of the development of societal cognition.

These theoretical and practical contributions are not independent. We learn much about the roles played by morality and emotion in societal cognition when we try to facilitate it. When we succeed in developing children's societal cognition, we almost inevitably observe that the achieved deep societal understanding is accompanied by emotion and morality.

Understanding and morality in societal cognition

When we discuss the inseparable, mutually facilitating relationships between societal understanding and morality, we should keep in our mind that some societal systems are based on conventional or convenient customs and rules, while others are constructed to actualise morality. According to Turiel (2002), conventions are shared behaviours and meanings that are defined by societal systems, whereas morality is not determined by existing uniformities, specific customs of a given society, or personal preferences (p. 110). Thus, morality may be a source of conflict because it exposes injustices and inequalities embedded in the existing societal systems (p. 2). Ideas of fairness, social welfare, human rights, and justice are essential in modern societal cognition. In order to put these moral ideas into practice, the existing societal systems are often radically modified or rearranged, and people are encouraged to assume responsibility and spare expense.

An epoch-making study by Gilligan (1982/1993) exemplifies how humans continuously refine morality, and suggests how morality and societal understanding go together. She successfully indicated that the European male-centred culture highly evaluated the independent nature of human tendencies but regarded the interdependent aspect of the human mind as weak and inferior, and assigned the latter to the secondary citizens, women. She claimed that, though these cultural and artificial assignments produced a different morality among each gender, the inclusion of both aspects of morality was indispensable for understanding human morality (p. 105). Nowadays, most researchers in human development agree that humans of both genders have both mental tendencies, i.e., autonomy and harmony, detachment and attachment, and that an androgynous mentality is the most healthy for humans (Bem, 1975). Such a Zeitgeist actually influences societal systems as well as societal understanding: This reinterpretation of genders unties people from the traditional concept of gender and gender-roles. In retrospect, we may wonder whether Kohlberg's (1976) stage theory view almost equated the development of morality with socialisation into the idealised convention. As a result, his research programme did not have the power to induce insight into social inequalities or to reform society.

The necessity of morality for societal cognition to develop may be observed at levels of ordinary people, too. For example, children and young people are often motivated to understand societal forces and mechanisms when they encounter states of affairs that they feel are unfair or inhumane. In this sense, we may claim, attempts at societal understanding are triggered by moral sensitivity and substantiated by personal experience of morality.

When intervention succeeds

As several contributors to this volume suggest, emotions, especially self-related emotions, play an important role in societal cognition. This can be seen not only in typical developmental or social-psychological studies but also in intervention studies.

Young people's utterances in successful educational programmes surely indicate that they are moved emotionally. With knowledge and direct experiences, students are often emotionally concerned with their societal experiences. The students of the Social Justice class (Youniss & Yates, 1997) reported that "I worked so hard. I wasn't happy. I was just MAD. Not at the people there or workers. . . ., I began to think why doesn't the government give food . . ." (p. 60); "I mean not just with homeless people. It happens with everybody" (p. 102); "As a result of my experience in the junior year, I am much more compassionate toward people . . ., this class forces you to think about important issues and to evaluate yourself and what you're made of" (p. 130).

These narratives suggest that deep understandings are accompanied by self-related emotions and self-reflection. With warm concerns for others, even for people who are invisible or for people with whom they have no chance to interact, children and young people might feel responsibility and involvement in societal systems. We see "hot" societal cognition as well as economic and political literacy in the successful programmes.

CONCLUSION

As a number of the preceding chapters suggest, investigating children's societal cognition is rewarding both theoretically and practically. In particular, as reviewed in this commentary, societal cognition is a fascinating domain to investigate the understanding that is accompanied by moral, emotional, and teleological components. It is now time for energetic study of development in the domain of societal cognition. We sincerely hope that this volume will be the first step, both towards a collective attempt to produce autonomous citizens who have sufficient knowledge and warm concerns for others, and towards the establishment of comprehensive theories of conceptual development.

REFERENCES

Bartsch, A. R., & Burnett, T., Diller, R. T., & Rankin-Williams, E. (2000). Gender representation in television communication: Updating and update. *Sex Roles, 43*, 735–743.
Bem, S. (1975). Sex role adaptability: One consequence of psychological androgyny. *Journal of Personality and Social Psychology, 42*, 155–162.
Berti, A. E., & Bombi, A. S. (1988). *The child's construction of economics*. Cambridge: Cambridge University Press.

Carey, S. (1985). *Conceptual change in childhood.* Cambridge, MA: MIT Press.

Chiba, T. (1993). Which coke is delicious? In M. Satomi (Ed.), *Where is the Earth going to?* [in Japanese] (pp. 96–124). Tokyo: Taro-Jiro-sha.

Cole, M. (1996). *Cultural psychology: A once and future discipline.* Cambridge, MA: Harvard University Press.

Diesendruck, G., Hammer, R., & Catz, O. (2003). Mapping the similarity space of children and adults' artifact categories. *Cognitive Development, 18,* 217–231.

diSessa, A. A. (1983). Phenomenology and the evolution of intuition. In D. Gentner & A. L. Stevens (Eds.), *Mental models* (pp. 15–33). Hillsdale, NJ: Lawrence Erlbaum Associates Inc.

Furth, H. G. (1980). *The worlds of grown-ups: Children's conceptions of society.* New York: Elsevier.

Gilligan, C. (1993). *In a different voice: Psychological theory and women's development.* Cambridge, MA: Harvard University Press. (First published 1982.)

Goodnow, J., Miller, P., & Kessel, F. (1995). *Cultural practices as contexts for human development.* San Francisco: Jossey-Bass.

Harris, P. L. (1990). The nature of everyday science: A commentary. *British Journal of Developmental Psychology, 8,* 299–303.

Hatano, G., & Inagaki, K. (1999). Domain-specific constraints of conceptual development. *International Journal of Behavioral Development, 24,* 267–275.

Holden, C., & Clough, N. (Eds.) (1998). *Children as citizens: Education for participation.* London: Jessica Kingsley Publishers.

Inagaki, K., & Hatano, G. (2002). *Young children's naive thinking about the biological world.* New York: Psychology Press.

Jahoda, G. (1981). European "lag" in the development of economic concept: A study in Zimbabwe. *British Journal of Developmental Psychology, 1,* 110–120.

Keil, F. C. (1992). The origins of an autonomous biology. In M. R. Gunnar & M. Maratsos (Eds.), *Modularity and constraints in language and cognition. The Minnesota Symposia on Child Psychology, Vol. 25* (pp. 103–137). Hillsdale, NJ: Lawrence Erlbaum Associates Inc.

Kelemen, D. (1999). Function, goals and intention: Children's teleological reasoning about objects. *Trends in Cognitive Sciences, 3,* 461–468.

Kohlberg, L. (1976). Moral stages and moralization: The cognitive-developmental approach. In J. Lickona (Ed.), *Moral development and behavior: Theory, research and social issues.* New York: Holt, Rinehart & Winston.

Miyake, N. (1986). Constructive interaction and the iterative process of understanding. *Cognitive Science, 10,* 151–177.

Ohtsu, K. (1987). *Social studies: Viewed from a piece of banana* [In Japanese]. Tokyo: Kokudo-sya.

Piaget, J. (1929). *The child's conception of the world.* London: Routledge & Kegan Paul.

Piaget, J. (1930). *The child's conception of physical causality.* London: Routledge & Kegan Paul.

Piaget, J. (1932). *The moral judgment of the child.* London: Routledge & Kegan Paul.

Siegler, R. S. (Ed.) (1978). *Children's thinking: What develops?* Hillsdale, NJ: Lawrence Erlbaum Associates Inc.

Siegler, R. S., & Crowley, K. (1994). Constraints on learning in nonprivileged domains. *Cognitive Psychology, 27,* 194–226.

Siegler, R. S., DeLoache, J., & Eisenberg, N. (2003). *Handbook of child development.* New York: Worth.

Takahashi, K., & Hatano, G. (1994). Understanding of the banking business in Japan: Is economic property accompanied by economic literacy? *British Journal of Developmental Psychology, 12,* 585–590.

Takahashi, K., & Hatano, G. (2000). *Does economic depression affect on naive theories of banking business among Japanese college students?* Paper presented at the Meeting of International Society for the Study of Behavioural Development. Beijing, China.

Tsurumi, Y. (1982). *Bananas and the Japanese* [in Japanese]. Tokyo: Iwanami-syoten.

Turiel, E. (2002). *The culture of morality: Social development, context, and conflict.* Cambridge: Cambridge University Press.

Weisner, T. S., Garnier, H., & Loucky, J. (1994). Domestic tasks, gender egalitarian values and children's gender typing in conventional and nonconventional families. *Sex Roles, 30,* 23–54.

Wellman, H. M. (1990). *The child's theory of mind.* Cambridge, MA: MIT Press.

Wellman, H. M., & Gelman, S. A. (1992). Cognitive development: Foundational theories of core domains. *Annual Review of Psychology, 43,* 337–375.

Wellman, H. M., & Gelman, S. A. (1998). Knowledge acquisition in foundational domains. In W. Damon (Series Ed.), D. Kuhn & R. Siegler (Eds.), *Handbook of child psychology, Vol. 2, Cognition, perception and language* (5th ed., pp. 523–573). New York: Wiley.

Wellman, H. M., & Inagaki, K. (Eds.) (1997). *The emergence of core domains of thought: Children's reasoning about physical, psychological, and biological phenomena.* San Francisco: Jossey-Bass.

Yasui, T. (1986). *Teaching students to understand civic rights* [in Japanese]. Tokyo: Ayumi-shuppan.

Yates, J., Bassman, M., Dunne, M., Jertson, D., Sly, K., & Wendelboe, B. (1988). Are conceptions of motion based on a naive theory or on prototypes? *Cognition, 29,* 251–275.

Yates, M., & Youniss, J. (1996). Community service and political-moral identity in adolescents. *Journal of Research on Adolescence, 6,* 271–284.

Yates, M., & Youniss, J. (Eds.) (1999). *Roots of civic identity: International perspectives on community service and activism in youth.* New York: Cambridge University Press.

Yoshida, N. (1959). Development of concepts with relation in usage of terms in social studies [In Japanese]. *Japanese Journal of Educational Psychology, 4,* 238–243.

Youniss, J., & Yates, M. (1997). *Community service and social responsibility in youth.* Chicago: University of Chicago Press.

Author index

Abell, J. 264
Aboud, F.E. 206, 208, 213, 215, 225, 229, 231–239, 242, 244, 275
Ablin, S.S. 113
Abramovitch, R. 56, 91, 107, 108, 119, 120
Ackerman, B.P. 110–111
Ackil, J.K. 115
Adams, P. 20
Adelson, J. 2, 73, 80, 82, 87
Adorno, T.W. 236
Agazzi, A. 83, 86
Ainley, J. 30
Akoh, H. 29, 38
Alderson, P. 32, 33
Alexander, G.M. 140
Alleman, J. 75–76, 78–81
Allen, G.A. 80
Allen, V.L. 241
Allport, G. 200
Allport, G.W. 237
Alston, J.P. 119
Alvarex, J. 151, 153–154
Amadeo, J. 71, 74, 84
Amato, M. 275
Amiel-Tison, C. 203
Anderson, B. 260

Anderson, D. 186
Anderson, D.R. 156
Andreasen, G. 251, 254–255
Andriolo, A. 75, 83, 98
Archer, J. 136, 146
Arcuri, L. 254, 258, 260
Asch, S. 202, 204
Asher, S.R. 241
Asscher, J.J. 26, 28, 31, 37
Atkinson, D. 228
Atran, S. 201, 214
Auerbach, S. 152
Axia, G. 251, 253–255
Ayers, W. 124
Azurmendi, M.J. 279

Bachman, M. 151, 153–154
Bahrick, L. 112
Bailenson, J.N. 214
Baker-Ward, L. 112, 114
Balaban, T. 156
Baldus, B. 180
Baldwin, D.A. 203
Bales, S. 74
Bandura, A. 136–138, 141–143, 153–155, 159, 177
Bannerjee, R. 153

305

Barbaranelli, C. 177
Barber, B. 157
Baron-Cohen, S. 201, 203
Barrett, M. 20, 21, 23, 27, 34–36, 38, 81, 244–245, 251–255, 257–258, 260–274, 276–279
Bar-Tal, D. 266
Bartsch, A.R. 297
Bassman, M. 290
Batterman-Faunce, J.M. 116, 122, 126
Bauer, P.J. 149
Bayley, D.H. 119
Bayraktar, R. 266–269, 277–278
Bazemore, G. 126
Beal, C.R. 114, 262
Beaudet, J. 235, 239, 275
Beishuizen, J.J. 26, 28, 31, 37
Beissel, C.F. 146
Belmonte, L. 258, 272
Belter, R.W.G. 91
Bem, S. 300
Bem, S.L. 206, 214
Beneson, J.F. 152
Benesso, M. 75, 76, 79, 81–82
Bennett, M. 69, 151, 244–245, 252, 254, 258, 260, 267–269, 271, 277
Berlin, B. 200
Berlin, L. 139
Bernal, M.E. 225, 230
Berry, J.W. 234, 244
Berry, T.R. 61
Berscheid, E. 138
Berti, A.E. 2, 27, 34, 44–46, 48, 50–53, 58, 63, 75–76, 78–83, 86, 88, 98, 175, 179, 287
Bertoncini, J. 203
Best, D.L. 235
Bhatt, S. 242
Bialer, S. 266
Bidrose, S. 113
Biernat, M. 147, 149
Biggs, M. 152
Bigler, R.S. 147, 150, 158, 240
Billig, M. 187, 243, 259, 278
Binet, A. 114, 118
Bjorkland, D.F. 111, 113–114
Blades, M. 254
Blair, K. 152
Blatchford, P. 29–30, 32
Bloom, P. 204

Blumenfeld, P.C. 19–21, 29, 38
Bohlin, G. 139
Bolduc, D. 141
Bombi, A.S. 2, 27, 44–46, 48, 50–52, 76, 78–80, 173, 175–176, 179, 252, 260, 266–268, 271, 287
Bonatti, L. 203
Bonn, M. 46, 52–53, 63
Bornman, E. 243
Bornstein, G. 110, 112
Boswell, D. 259
Boswell, D.A. 235
Bottoms, B.L. 112, 116–117
Botvin, G. 189
Bourchier, A. 254–255, 257–258
Bourhis, R.Y. 227
Bourke, S. 31
Bouwmeester, S. 26, 28, 31, 37
Bower, G.H. 114
Bowlby, J. 203
Bradbard, M.R. 141, 148
Braeges, J.L. 20
Brainerd, C.J. 114
Brand, E. 225, 241
Breed, L. 154
Bremner, J.G. 251, 253–255
Brennan, M. 116
Brennan, R. 116
Bretherton, I. 152
Bromley, D.B. 263
Brophy, J. 75–76, 78–81
Brothers, L. 152
Brotman, M.A. 152
Brown, G.R. 139
Brown, M.R. 114
Brown, P.M. 123
Brown, R. 240, 243, 276
Brown, R.J. 151
Brownell, C.A. 34
Browning, S.L. 119
Bruck, M. 110, 112–115
Buchanan-Barrow, E. 20–21, 23, 27, 34–36, 38, 80, 263, 266–269, 277–278
Buckley, M.A. 117
Buckner, J.P. 152
Buralli, P. 154
Burgard, P. 184–185
Burnam, M.A. 105
Burnett, T. 297
Burris, V. 2, 48

Bussey, K. 136–138, 141–143, 153–155, 159

Cadinu, M. 252, 267, 269, 278
Callanan, M.A. 152
Calvert, S. 191
Cameron, J. 151, 153, 154
Camparo, L. 109, 112, 116
Campbell, J. 251, 267, 269, 276, 278
Canto, J.M. 252, 266–267, 271
Cantor, G.N. 241
Caprara, G.V. 177
Carey, S. 69, 201, 217, 287
Carlo, G. 152
Carranza, L.E. 111
Carter, C.A. 116–117
Cassel, W.S. 111, 113
Castelli, L. 252, 267, 269, 278
Catz, O. 291
Cauffman, E. 111, 120, 125
Ceci, S.J. 110, 112–115, 119, 126
Cerini, E. 154
Cervantes, C.A. 152
Charitides, L. 73
Cherney, I.D. 148
Cheyne, W. 184–185
Chi, M.T.H. 114
Chiba, T. 296
Child, P. 231
Choi, I. 201
Christmas-Best, V. 74
Clark, A. 241
Clark, K.B. 208, 225–226, 230, 234, 241
Clark, M.P. 208, 225–226, 230, 234, 241
Cleare, A. 51, 179
Clémence, A. 74, 91, 93
Clough, N. 296
Clubb, P.A. 112, 114
Cole, C.B. 112
Cole, M. 292
Coles, R. 184
Coley, J.D. 214
Collins, P.A. 156
Collman, P. 149
Condor, S. 253, 268
Connell, R.W. 2, 69, 73, 75–76, 78–82, 84, 89, 95–97, 173, 179–180, 184
Cook, K.V. 142
Cook, T. 183, 186
Coley, J.D. 214
Cooper, J. 156–157

Cordua, G. 158
Cordua, G.D.
Corsaro, W.A. 22
Cosette, L. 141
Cota, M.K. 225, 230
Cox, B.D. 114
Craig, R.S. 154
Cram, F. 44
Craw, S. 113
Cross, W. 228, 234
Cross, W.E. 208
Crouter, A.C. 142
Crowley, K. 292
Cumberland, A. 152
Cummings, S. 180
Cutts Dougherty, K. 251, 260

Damon, W. 182–183, 263
D'Andrade, R.G. 245
Danziger, K. 2, 173, 175
Davey, A.G. 235, 244
Davey, K. 258, 273
David, B. 151
Davies, G. 112, 114, 122
Davies, G.M. 122
De Beni, R. 50, 51, 175
DeFleur, L.B. 176, 184
DeFleur, M.L. 176, 184
Del Barrio, C. 91–92
Delli Carpini, M.X. 70
DeLoache, J. 290
Deluca, P. 251, 254–255
Delval, J. 81, 91–92
del Valle, A. 252, 263, 267, 270–274, 276–278
Dembo, M.H. 241
Demetriou, A. 73
Demorest, A. 110
Denham, S.A. 152
Dennehy, K. 54
de Rosa, A.S. 252, 254, 258, 260, 266–268, 271
Devine, P.G. 152
Devine-Wright, P. 260
De Zwart, R. 55
Dickinson, J. 176–180, 183, 184–185, 187, 192, 245
Diesendruck, G. 291
Diller, R.T. 297
diSessa, A.A. 290
Dixson, A.F. 139

Diversi, M. 74
Doise, W. 74, 91, 93, 189
Doyle, A.B. 235, 239, 275
Drabman, R.S. 158
Driedger, L. 241
Duckitt, J. 244
Duda, J. 107, 119, 120
Dunn, J. 20, 152
Dunne, M. 290
Durkin, K. 109–111, 151, 154, 157–159, 262, 277
Duveen, G. 175, 176, 189

Earle, D.C. 63
Easton, D. 70
Eccles, J.S. 142
Eckes, T. 136, 154, 262
Egan, S.K. 136
Eichstedt, J.A. 146
Eisen, M.L. 116
Eisenberg, N. 152, 290
Eisenbud, L. 149
Eisenhart, M. 251, 261
Ekman, P. 202
Elejabarrieta, F. 279
Elffers, H. 242
Emler, N. 18, 22, 24–25, 27–28, 34, 38, 74, 78, 98, 151, 176, 180, 183–185, 189–192, 245
Emmanuel, M. 177
Emmerich, W. 146
Endsley, R.C. 148
English, R. 266
Enright, R. 185
Enright, R.D. 94
Enright, W. 185
Entwistle, N. 24, 26, 28, 38
Ericson, K.L. 112
Erikson, E. 72, 228
Esbensen, F. 119
Espinosa, M.A. 91–92
Ettema, J.S. 158
Evans, G. 179
Evans, J. 259

Fabes, R.A. 152
Fagot, B.I. 136, 142, 206
Faison, N. 74
Farnen, R. 71, 84, 88
Farrar, M.J. 115
Farroni, T. 81, 251, 253–254

Feagin, J.R. 206
Feiring, C. 74
Feld, B.C. 124
Fenko, A. 51
Ferguson, D.L. 223–224
Fernandes, C. 30
Fernández, P. 252, 266–267, 271
Finch, M.D. 54
Finkelhor, D. 105
Fisher, R.P. 112, 117
Fiske, S. 200
Fiske, S.T. 204
Fitzpatrick, H. 157
Fivush, R. 112, 117, 152
Fjioka, T. 231
Flanagan, C.A. 71, 73–74, 89
Flesser, D. 240
Flin, R. 122–124
Fogel, S.W. 244
Foley, M.A. 114–115
Follmer, A. 117
Fondacaro, M.R. 117, 125
Forrest, L. 261
Fox, D.J. 230
Fox, K.F.A. 48
Frank, J. 119
Franklin, C.C. 94
Frazer, E. 98
Freedman, J.L. 56, 91
Freedman-Doan, C. 142
Frenkel-Brunswick, E. 236
Frey, K.S. 146, 155
Fried, C.S. 120–121
Friedman, R.D. 113
Frome, P. 142
Frot, E. 203
Fu, V.R. 244
Furby, L. 173
Furnham, A. 179
Furnham, A.F. 44, 51, 54–56, 62–63, 84, 86, 154
Furth, H.G. 2, 3, 48, 73, 76, 175, 181–182, 189, 287, 291, 298

Gallatin, J. 72
Gallay, L.S. 71, 73
Garcia, I. 279
Garcia-Claros, E. 258, 272
Gardner, H. 110
Garner, P. 26
Garnier, H. 296

Garvey, C. 110
Garza, C.A. 225, 230
Geary, D. 138–140
Geiselman, R.E. 110, 112
Gellner, E. 259, 278
Gelman, S.A. 38, 69, 149, 200–201, 203, 213–214, 218, 289, 292
Genesee, F. 235
Gentner, D. 201
George, D.M. 230
Gerth, H. 171, 176
Giacomarra, M. 243
Gibbons, J.L. 146
Gibbs, J.C. 187
Gil de Montes, L. 279
Giles, H. 227
Gilligan, C. 300
Gimenez, A. 252, 254, 258, 260, 266–267, 271–272
Glachan, M. 190
Glascock, J. 154
Glick, P. 140, 151, 159
Golding, J.M. 105
Goldman, K.S. 146
Goldstein, N. 112
Goldstone, R.L. 201
Gonzalez, J.L. 279
Goodman, G.S. 107, 112–113, 115–116, 122, 126
Goodman, S.H. 152
Goodnow, J. 295
Goodwin, B. 90, 93
Gopnik, A. 115
Gordon, B.N. 112, 114, 117
Gordon, L. 213
Gorodetschnaya, N. 271–272
Gottfredson, L.S. 178
Gottfried, A.E. 239
Gottfried, A.W. 239
Govrin, N. 149
Grace, D. 151
Graf, P. 115
Grant, G. 230, 244
Green, B. 2, 73, 87
Green, S. 156
Greenfield, P. 157
Greenstein, F.I. 27, 70, 72, 78, 80
Grenkova-Dikevitch, L. 271–272
Grieser, D. 203
Grieve, R. 111
Griffiths, J. 277

Grisso, T. 91, 107–108, 112, 117, 119, 120–121, 125
Gross, E. 157
Gross, M.L. 89
Gruber, R. 149
Guajardo, J.J. 203
Guarnaccia, V. 79, 81–82, 88
Gunn, B. 179
Gunter, B. 84, 86, 154, 262
Guth, M. 112
Güth, W. 61

Halperin, J.J. 266
Halsted, N. 203
Halverson, C.F. 146–148, 153, 244
Hamilton, D.L. 200, 205, 207, 215
Hamilton, V.L. 19–21, 29, 38
Hammer, D. 158
Hammer, R. 291
Hammond, N.R. 117
Harbaugh, W.T. 61
Hardman, M. 157
Harris, B.E. 185
Harris, P.L. 295
Hart, D. 263
Hartman, E. 214
Haslam, S.A. 264, 276
Hatano, G. 52–53, 201, 214, 289–290, 292–293, 298
Hebl, M. 57
Heider, F. 204
Helms, J. 234
Helwig, C.C. 92, 260
Hepps, D. 112
Herold, C. 265
Hess, R.D. 2, 70, 80
Hesse, P. 266
Heyman, G.D. 149
Hill, D. 117
Hilt, L. 140, 151, 159
Hilton, J.L. 200, 205
Himmelweit, H. 176
Himmelweit, H.T. 265
Hines, M. 140
Hinkle, S. 276
Hinton, I. 107–108, 110, 115–116
Hirschfeld, L.A. 200, 202–204, 206–207, 209, 215–217
Hirschman, J.E. 112
Hocevar, D. 241
Hof, E. 26, 28, 31, 37

Hoffman, L. 154
Hogg, M.A. 238, 240, 276
Hogrefe, G.J. 115
Ho, C.N. 112
Holden, C. 296
Holmes, D.L. 112
Hopkins, N. 264
Hoppe, R.A. 230
Hook, J. 183, 186
Horenczyk, G. 223–224
Hornby, K. 265
Horowitz, R.E. 225
Hoskin, M. 87
Houghton, S. 28
Howarth, N. 109, 111
Howe, C. 189
Howe, M.L. 114
Howie, P.M. 111
Hraba, J. 230, 244
Hudson, J. 115
Hudson, R.L. 112
Huffman, M.L.C. 113
Hughes, M. 111
Humphrey, N. 189
Hurst, Y.G. 119
Hurtz, W. 154
Husfeldt, V. 71, 74, 84, 87
Huston, A. 142
Huston, A.C. 136, 150
Hutchins, G. 158
Hyde, J.S. 152
Hyman, H.H. 70
Hymel, S. 139

Inagaki, K. 201, 214, 289–290, 292
Inhelder, B. 183
Isen, A.M. 152
Ivanova, O. 270–271

Jackson, R. 75
Jacobs, J. 142
Jaenicke, C. 109, 112, 116
Jahoda, G. 2, 45, 48, 50–53, 73, 75, 81,
    173, 179, 181–182, 184–185, 189,
    242, 251–254, 256, 260, 262,
    265–267, 269, 276, 278, 295
Jarvie, G.J. 158
Jaspers, J.M.F. 251, 257, 267
Jeffrey, L. 159
Jencks, C. 177–178
Jenning, M.K. 89

Jertson, D. 290
Jhaveri, N. 174
Johnson, M.K. 114–115
Johnson, N. 244, 251, 256–258,
    266–267, 269, 276, 278
Johnson-Laird, P. 203
Johnston, J. 158
Jones, L.C. 240
Jordan, V.D. 230
Jules, V. 25, 31, 37
Junn, J. 70, 84, 86, 98
Jusczyk, P. 203

Kadirova, R. 271, 273
Kalin, R. 244
Kalish, C. 77
Kanagawa, C. 191
Karakozov, R. 252, 267–269, 271, 273,
    277
Karbon, M. 152
Karmiloff-Smith, A. 34, 37
Kassin, S.M. 113
Katz, P. 206–207, 239
Katz, P.A. 142, 237–238
Kay, P. 200
Kazdin, A.E. 120
Keating, D.K. 91
Kedar-Voivodas, G. 31–34, 36
Keeter, S. 70
Kehret-Ward, T. 48
Keil, F.C. 287
Kelemen, D. 292
Keltner, D. 152
Kempton, W. 200
Kenrick, D.T. 136, 139–140
Kessel, F. 295
Keys, W. 30
Khaneman, D. 56
Kiechel, K.L. 113
Killen, M. 208
King, M.A. 111–112
King, S. 265
Kingman, J. 114
Kipiani, G. 252, 267–271, 273, 277
Kirsh, B. 146
Kitayama, S. 201
Klineberg, O. 244, 251, 262–263,
    265–271, 276, 278
Klink, A. 276
Knight, G.P. 225, 230
Kobasigawa, A. 114

Koegl, C. 91
Kohlberg, L. 73, 77, 79, 81–82, 89, 121, 300
Kohlberg, L.A. 137, 144–147, 153, 159
Kovac, P. 112
Kozeki, B. 24, 26, 28, 38
Kramper, G. 88
Krause, K. 61
Kraut, R. 157
Krogh, H.R. 150
Kryazh, I. 270–271
Kuhl, P.K. 203
Kuhn, J. 116
Kutnick, P. 25, 31, 37
Kwon, P. 115

Lagattuta, K.H. 152
Lamb, M.E. 107
Lambert, W.E. 235, 244, 251, 262–263, 265–271, 276, 278
Lambertz, G. 203
Lang, P. 31
Laosa, L. 242
Lapsey, D.K. 94
Lare, J. 69, 72–73, 75, 76, 79–81
Larranaga, M. 279
Larus, D.M. 112, 114
Lassare, D. 54
Lattuada, R. 79, 81–82, 86
Lauer, R.H. 179–180
Laupa, M. 22, 77
Lea, S.E.G. 59, 63
Leahy, R.L. 173–174, 178–180, 185, 191
Leaper, C. 154
Lee, C. 54
Lee, P.C. 31–34, 36
Leeb, R.T. 142
Leekam, S. 77
Lee Kim, J. 208
Lehmann, R. 71, 74, 84, 87–88
Leichtman, M.D. 113
Leinbach, M.D. 136, 206
Leiser, D. 49, 54, 185
Leman, P.J. 189
Leonard, S.P. 146
Lerner, M. 181, 187
Leslie, A.M. 201
Leve, L.D. 142
Leventhal, G. 186
Levine, F.J. 2
Levine, L.J. 113

Levine, M. 116–117
Levine, R.M. 56–57
Levinson, D.J. 236
Levitt, M. 112
Levy, D. 49, 54, 185
Levy, G.D. 148, 150
Lewis, A. 56–57, 63
Lewis, M. 74
Liben, L.S. 147, 150
Liebkind, K. 223–224
Liebl, M. 149
Lindberg, M.A. 114
Lindsay, D.S. 113
Lindsay, S. 115
Lindsey, E.W. 139
Lintern, V. 153
Lipmann, O. 114
Lis, A. 175
List, J.A. 112
Little, J.K. 145
Livesley, W.J. 263
Liwag, M.D. 113
Lobel, T.E. 149
Lobliner, D.B. 240
Lo Coco, A. 224, 230–231, 242–243, 245
Loftus, E.F. 112–114
Lott, B. 141
Loucky, J. 296
Low, J. 109–110
Lowe, G.D. 119
Luce, C.L. 136, 139
Luecke-Aleksa, D. 156
Luise, B. 81
Lunney, G.S. 142
Luria, Z. 141
Lutz, S.E. 149, 151, 153, 158, 159
Lyons, E. 244–245, 252, 254–255, 257–258, 260, 263–264, 266–274, 276–278
Lytton, H. 142

Maass, A. 277
Maccoby, E.E. 136–137, 139, 140–142, 149, 152
MacDonald, K.B. 139, 141
Mack, J.E. 266
Magai, C. 152
Maianu, C. 94
Mak, T. 154
Malcuit, G. 141

Maluso, D. 141
Mandler, J.M. 117
Mann, L. 191
Mannheim, L. 185
Mant, C.M. 90
Marcia, J. 228
Marin, B.V. 112
Markham, R. 111
Marks, J. 211
Markus, H.R. 201
Martin, C.L. 136–137, 143, 145–154, 158, 244, 262
Mashraki-Pedhatzur, S. 149
Masson, K. 242
Maxfield, D. 114
Mazella, C. 154
McAleer, J. 262
McCauley, M.R. 112, 117
McFadden, S.H. 152
McGarrell, E.F. 125–126
McGarty, C. 264
McGlothlin, H. 208
McGraw, K.O. 158
McGuire, C.V. 231
McGuire, W.J. 231
McHale, S.M. 142
McLaughlin, M. 74
McLellan, J. 71, 74, 97
Medin, D.L. 201, 214
Mehler, J. 203
Melton, G.B. 91
Mendelsohn, H. 119
Menesini, E. 139
Merrett, F. 28
Messerschmidt, R. 114
Metzner, R. 57
Meyer, C. 110
Middleton, D. 244
Middleton, M. 251, 256–258
Miller, C.L. 206
Miller, G. 203
Miller, J. 54
Miller, P. 295
Mills, C.W. 171, 176
Milner, D. 240, 242,
Minuchin, P.P. 17, 37
Mischel, H. 57
Mischel, W. 57, 141
Mitchell, F.G. 235
Mitchell-Copeland, J. 152
Miura, K. 29, 38

Miyake, N. 291
Mize, J. 139
Moan, S. 116
Moan-Hardie, S. 110, 118
Moller, L.C. 139
Monaci, M.G. 52–53
Monreal, P. 252, 263, 270–273
Moodie, M.A. 261
Moore, B.S. 152
Moore, S.W. 69, 72–73, 75–76, 79, 80–81
Morash, D. 152
Morgado, L. 46–47
Morland, J.K. 208, 237, 240
Morten, G. 228
Mortimer, J.T. 54
Moscovici, S. 18, 22, 24–25, 27–28, 34, 38, 74, 78, 171, 188
Moss, N. 254
Mphuthing, T. 244
Much, N. 19–20
Mugny, G. 190
Mulder, M.R. 111
Mummendey, A. 276
Munn, P. 20, 152
Murnighan, J.K. 60–61
Murray, F.B. 189
Myers, J.E.B. 122–124

Nakhaie, M.R. 51
Narus, M.J. 114
Nelson, J. 117
Nelson, K. 115
Nemeth, C. 251, 267, 269, 276, 278
Nesbitt, M. 111
Nesdale, A.R. 240
Nesdale, D. 231, 240, 277
Neukee, S. 243
Newman, L.S. 157
Ng, S.H. 44, 52–53, 174
Nicholas, G. 116
Nicholls, J.G. 29
Niemi, R.G. 70, 84, 86, 98
Nigro, G.N. 117
Nikolic, C. 91
Nikolova, R. 71, 74, 84, 87
Nisan, M. 191
Nisbett, R.E. 201
Nolen, S.B. 29
Norenzayan, A. 201
Nucci, L. 73–74, 78

Nugent, B. 157
Nugent, J.K. 252, 255, 259
Nussbaum, M.C. 152

Oakes, P.J. 238, 240, 264, 276
Oberlander, L.B. 112
Ocampo, K.A. 225, 230
Ohana, J. 18, 22–25, 27–28, 34, 36, 38, 74, 78, 151, 185, 189, 191
Ohtsu, K. 296
Oliver, M.B. 156
O'Neil, R. 2, 73, 80, 82, 87
Ontai, L.L. 152
Oppenheim, A.N. 71, 84, 88, 176, 265
Orcutt, H. 126
Orcutt, H.K. 122
Ornstein, P.A. 112, 114
Ortiz, G. 279
Oswald, H. 71, 74, 84, 87, 88
Otis, M. 114
Otto, A. 50, 57
Ozbek, N. 107–108, 110, 115–116

Pace, U. 224, 230–231, 242–243, 245
Padilla, A. 225, 241
Padilla, A.M. 230, 240
Paicheler, G. 191
Palonsky, S.B. 36
Papadopoulou, A. 266–269, 277–278
Papastamou, S. 190
Pappas, A. 214
Paris, S. 118
Parker, J.F. 111–112
Pastorelli, C. 177
Patterson, J.N. 158
Pavlenko, V. 252, 267–271, 277
Peake, P.K. 57
Peek, C.W. 119
Pellegrini, A.D. 139
Peng, K. 201
Penny, R. 264
Perera, S. 252, 263, 270–273, 279
Perlman, N.R. 112, 154
Perner, J. 90, 111, 115
Perrow, C. 175
Perry, D.G. 136
Peter, N. 183
Peters, D.D. 105
Peterson, C. 112, 152
Peterson-Badali, M. 107–108, 119, 120
Petrakos, H. 152

Petty, J. 188, 190
Phelps, E. 110
Phinney, J.S. 223–227, 229, 232–233, 237
Piaget, J. 2, 69–70, 77, 89, 121, 182–183, 238–239, 244, 251–253, 256, 262–265, 271, 287, 296
Pickering, S. 158–159
Pietras, M. 64
Pintrich, P.R. 19–21
Pipe, M.E. 113–114
Plaisier, Z. 54–56
Planalp, S. 152
Plant, E.A. 152
Pliner, P. 56
Pomerleau, A. 141
Poole, D.A. 107, 113, 117
Porter, J.D.R. 226, 241
Poulin-Dubois, D. 146
Powell, M.B. 115
Powlishta, K.K. 149, 151, 153, 159, 240
Prencipe, A. 260
Price, D.W.W. 112
Priestley, G. 114
Pring, R. 98
Provenzano, F.J. 141
Purkhardt, C. 254–255

Quas, J.A. 113, 116

Raag, T. 153
Raaijmakers, Q.A.W. 89, 96
Rackliff, C.L. 153
Radford, M. 191
Ramsey, P.G. 239, 245
Rankin-Williams, E. 297
Reasons, C.E. 119
Regan, M. 264
Reicher, S.D. 238, 240, 276
Reizábal, L. 252, 267–268, 270–271, 273, 276, 278–279
Rejsking, F.G. 142
Repacholi, B. 158–159
Reppucci, N.D. 120–121
Reyna, V.F. 114
Rheingold, H.L. 141
Riazanova, T. 252, 267–269, 271–272, 277
Ricci, C.M. 114
Rice, A.S. 230, 240

Riddlesberger, M.M. 116
Rim, Y. 251, 267, 276
Roberts, D.F. 265
Roberts, S. 114
Robertson, S.J. 158
Robinson, J. 146
Rodgers, C.S. 136
Roebers, C.E.M. 111, 113
Roebers, C.M. 111
Rogier, A. 204
Romney, D.M. 142
Rose, H. 149
Rosenberg, M. 177
Rosengren, K.S. 214
Rosenthal, S. 74
Ross, D.F. 119
Rotheram, M.J. 225, 227, 232, 237
Roy, A. 189
Rubin, J.Z. 141
Rubin, K.H. 139
Ruble, D.N. 136, 143, 147, 149, 151,
    153–154, 156–159, 262
Ruck, M.D. 91
Rudy, L. 112
Ruiz, R. 225, 241
Ruiz, R.A. 230, 240
Russell, J.A. 152, 189
Rutland, A. 158, 251, 254, 267–268,
    276
Ryalls, B.O. 148
Ryan, M.K. 151

Sachsenmaei, T. 126
Sadovsky, A.L. 150
Sanford, R.N. 236
Sani, F. 151, 244–245, 252, 267, 271
Santini, C. 115
Savory, F. 74, 91, 93
Saxon, M.S. 60–61
Sayers, J. 138
Saywitz, K.J. 107–112, 116–118
Schlagman, N. 20
Schmitt, K.L. 156
Schneider, W. 111, 114
Schnell, S. 187
Schuessler, K. 44–46
Schulz, W. 71, 74, 84, 87–88
Schwartz, R. 108, 112, 117, 119, 121,
    125
Schwartz-Kenney, B.M. 112
Schweder, R.A. 19–20

Seavey, C.A. 142
Seidler, K.M. 111
Sell-Trujillo, L. 179
Semaj, L. 213, 215, 231, 239
Sen, M.G. 146
Serbin, L.A. 146
Sergienko, E. 271–272
Servin, A. 139
Sevón, G. 49, 54, 180, 185
Shakin, D. 141
Shakin, M. 141
Shapiro, C. 126
Shapiro, E.K. 17, 37
Shapiro, E.R. 107
Sharabany, R. 146
Shaw, L.A. 94
Sheatsley, P.B. 70
Sherif, C.W. 237
Sherif, M. 237
Sherman, I. 114
Sherman, S.J. 207
Shields, M. 175,176
Short, J. 244, 251, 262–263, 265–269,
    277–278
Shum, M.S. 214
Sidorowicz, L.S. 142
Siegal, M. 146, 180
Siegel, J.M. 105
Siegel, R.S. 87
Siegler, R.S. 49, 50, 62, 114, 287, 290,
    292
Signorella, M.A. 147
Signorielli, N. 109
Silbereisen, R. 74
Silberman, M.L. 19
Silverman, T. 265
Simmel, M. 204
Simmons, C. 181
Simmons, R.G. 177
Sivers, H. 114
Skerry, S.A. 231
Slaby, R.G. 146, 155
Slobogin, C. 117, 125
Sly, K. 290
Small, M.H. 118
Smees, R. 139
Smetana, J. 20, 77, 189
Smith, A.D. 259–260, 278
Smith, E. 113
Smith, P.K. 139
Smith, S.A. 112

Snarey, J. 191
Snyder, L. 111, 116–117
Sohn, M. 239
Sommerville, J.A. 203
Sonuga-Barke, E.J.S. 55–57, 63
Sopasakis, M. 115
Sorenson, S.B. 105
Spelke, E. 217
Spencer, C. 255, 257–258
Spencer, J.R. 122–124
Spencer, M.B. 231
Sperber, D. 217
Spinrad, T.L. 152
Sporer, S. 200
Springer, K. 214
Staats, A.W. 141
Stacey, B. 72, 75, 184
Staerklé, C. 74, 91, 93
Stake, J. 180
Stangor, C. 208
Statuto, C.M. 31–34, 36
Stein, J.A. 105
Stein, N.L. 113
Steinberg, L. 111, 120, 125
Stellwagen, L.D. 107
Stennes, L. 149
Stern, W. 114
Sterne, D. 265
Sternglanz, S.H. 141
Steuck, K. 94
Stevens, O. 36
Stevenson, H.W. 226, 231
Steward, D.S. 107, 112
Steward, M.S. 107, 112
Stewart, E.C. 226, 231
Stilwell, R. 255, 257–258
Stoddart, T. 147, 159
Stoler, A. 202
Stradling, R. 84, 86
Strandberg, K. 152
Strauss, A. 44–46, 175
Strauss, A.L. 2
Suarez, E. 258, 272
Subrahmanyam, K. 157
Sue, D. 228
Suthers, E. 237
Sweeney, J. 141
Szkrybalo, J. 136, 143, 153

Taebel, D. 180
Tait, H. 24, 26, 28, 38

Tajfel, H. 149, 172, 186, 192, 224,
    226–227, 237–238, 240–244, 251,
    256–258, 267, 269, 276, 278
Takahashi, K. 52–53, 293, 298
Tallandini, M.A. 76, 78
Tanaka, S. 260, 278
Tang, W. 28
Tapp, J. 73, 79, 81–82
Tapp, J.L. 2
Tate, C. 107–108, 110, 115–116
Tate, J.D. 223–224
Taylor, D.M. 244
Taylor, M.G. 149–150, 214
Taylor, S. 200
Taylor, T.J. 119
Thaler, R.H. 55
Thoden, K. 91
Thoma, S.J. 89, 96
Thomas, P. 54, 56
Thomas, S. 122, 126
Thompson, D.R. 49–50, 62
Thompson, R.A. 152
Thompson, S.K. 145
Thompson, T.L. 156
Thomson, D.M. 115
Thomson, S.S. 242
Tietz, R. 61
Tisak, M.S. 19
Tobey, A. 108, 117, 119, 121,
    125–126
Tobey, A. E. 122
Toglia, M.P. 119
Torney, J.V. 2, 71, 80, 84, 88
Torney-Purta, J. 71, 74–75, 84,
    87–89
Trautner, H.M. 136, 154, 262
Tribe, V. 180
Trivers, R.L. 138
Trolier, T.K. 200, 205, 215
Troseth, G.L. 150
Trost, M.R. 139, 141
Tsurumi, Y. 296
Tucker, C.J. 89
Tucker, G.R. 235
Tudor, W. 184
Turiel, E. 19–22, 73–74, 77, 89, 147,
    159, 187, 300
Turner, J. 149, 240
Turner, J.C. 238, 240, 264, 276
Turner, K.B. 119
Tversky, A. 56

Unbreit, M. 126
Ugolini, E. 79
Ullah, P. 226
United Nations General Assembly, 89

Valencia, J. 252, 267–268, 270–271, 273, 276, 278–279
Valentini, P. 76, 78
Van Ausdale, D. 206
Van de Geer, J.P. 251, 257, 267
Vanni, E. 75, 80, 82
Van Praag, B. 55
Van Putten, C.M. 26, 28, 31, 37
Varendonck, J. 113–114
Vaughan, G. 226–227, 239–240, 242
Vaughan, G.M. 240
Vedder, P. 223, 224
Verbogt, T.F.M.A. 89, 96
Veres, C. 204
Verkuyten, M. 242–245, 252, 267–268
Verna, G.B. 235
Verville, E. 105
Vila, I. 252, 254, 258, 260, 263, 270–273, 279
Vince, P. 176, 265
Vollebergh, W.A.M. 89, 96
Volovikova, M. 252, 267
Von Hippel, W. 200, 205
Vrij, A. 111
Vyskocilova, E. 46–47

Wackman, D.B. 56
Wagner, K.A. 69, 72–73, 75–76, 79–81
Wainryb, C. 94
Walker, A.G. 116
Wallace, G. 26–27
Wallen, K. 139
Ward, S. 56
Warin, J. 135–136, 153
Warnaar, M.F. 55
Warren-Leubecker, A.R. 107–108, 110, 115–116
Wartella, E. 56
Waterson, M.J. 55
Webley, P. 46, 50, 52–57, 59, 63, 251, 261
Weber, E.K. 78
Weckström, S. 180
Wegener, D. 188, 190

Weil, A. 238–239, 244
Weil, A.M. 2, 69, 251–253, 256, 262–264, 271
Weiner, B. 183
Weinreich, J. 224
Weinstein, E. 179
Weinstein, E.A. 2, 260
Weisner, T.S. 296
Wellman, H.M. 38, 69, 152, 214, 289–290, 292
Wendelboe, B. 290
Wertsch, J.V. 278
Weston, D.R. 21
Wetherell, M.S. 238, 240, 276
Wheldall, K. 28
Whennell, S. 273
Whitcomb, D. 107
White, L.T. 113, 117
Whitely, S. 265
Whiteman, S.D. 142
Widen, S.C. 152
Wiegand, P. 254
Wilberg, S. 252–253
Will, G. 172
Williams, J.A. 240
Williams, J.E. 208, 235
Wills, J.S. 262, 278
Wilson, E.O. 138
Wilson, H. 252, 263, 266–269, 272, 276–278
Wilson, J.C. 122
Wimmer, H. 111, 115
Winfree, L.T. 119
Winner, E. 110
Winocur, S. 180
Wirth, B.A. 119
Wong, M. 52–53
Woodward, A.L. 203
Woolard, J.L. 117, 125
Woerdenbagch, A. 254
Wosinski, M. 64
Wyatt, G.E. 105
Wyse, D. 32–33

Yasui, T. 296
Yates, J. 290
Yates, M. 71, 74, 89, 97–98, 296–299, 301
Yee. M. 151
Yoon, K.S. 142
Yoshida, N. 295

Youniss, J. 71, 74, 89, 97–98, 296–299, 301
Yuille, J. 111–112
Yung, S. 54
Yzerbyt, V.Y. 204

Zajonc, R.B. 152

Zalk, S.R. 142, 239
Zangl, R. 203
Zappulla, C. 224, 230–231, 242–243, 245
Zaragoza, M.S. 115
Zerbinos, E. 156
Zimler, J. 114

Subject index

Authority,
  attitudes towards police, 111–112, 119
  in schools, 21–23
  political understanding and, 77–78

Banks, 52–54, 293–294, 298
  bank profit, 52–53, 292
  cross-cultural differences in understanding, 53–54
  understanding of saving and, 58–59
Biculturalism, 242–243

Children,
  as agents in development, 15, 298–299
Child witnesses, 7, 112–116, 121–124, 126
Child offenders, 7, 124–125, 127–128
Citizenship, 37, 296–299
Civic knowledge, *see* Political knowledge
Cognitive architecture, 200–202
Cognitive development theory,
  comparison with social transmision theories, 187–192
  economic behaviour and, 62
  ethnic identification and, 225–226

gender role development and, 144–147, 159
national identity and, 275–276
political understanding and, 69, 73, 97
social inequalities and, 181–183, 185
societal cognition and, 289
understanding of the school and, 37–38
Compliance
  legal understanding and, 118–119
Conceptual limitations
  legal understanding and, 106–112
Countries, 13–14, 81
  affect for, 256–259
  'enemy' countries, 256–257
  personal travel to, 257
  geographical knowledge of, 257–259
  landscape and, 258–259
Crime, perceptions of, 109
Cultural context, 3, 5–8, 12–13, 46–47, *see also* Sociocultural context
  importance of, 64
  wealth differentials and, 174

Demand, *see* Supply and demand
Division of labour, 169–170

Domains of knowledge, 3–4, 14, 38, 49
  conventional domain, 73, 77
  core or privileged domains, 292–295
  domain-general approach, 3, 200, 294
  domain-specific approach, 4, 69, 73, 77, 97, 288–290
  moral domain, 73, 77
  peripheral domains, 293–294
  personal domain, 73, 78
  political domain, 82–88, 99

Earnings, see Income
Economic behaviour, 54–62
  altruistic behaviour, 61–62
  cognitive development and, 62
  economic theory and, 60–62
  mental accounts, 55–56,
  playground economy, 59–60, 296
  pocket money, 54–56
  saving, 56–59
Economic understanding, 5–6, 43–44
  cognitive development and, 62
  cross-cultural differences, 63
  direct experience, 51–52, 62–63
  naïve theory of, 49, 63–64
  societal cognition and, 64
  sources of information, 62–63
  within-culture differences, 63
Educational context, see Information sources
Educational intervention, 296–297, 301
Ego-identity, 228
Emotions, 4, 14
  cognition and, 4
  ethnicity and, 11
  gender and, 8, 136, 152–154, 160
  national groups and, 13
  societal cognition and, 291, 299, 301
Employment, 9–10, 170, see also Occupations
Ethnic attitudes, 232–245
  biculturalism and, 242–243
  egocentrism and, 239
  ethnic identification and, 243–245
  group social status and, 241–243
  inner state theory, 236–237
  measurement of, 233–236

social reflection theory and, 237
social identity theory and, 240–241, 243–242
self-categorisation theory and, 240–241
sociocognitive development and, 237–240
Ethnic categories, 225, 230
Ethnic constancy, 231
Ethnic identity, 11–12, 225–227
  cognitive-developmental theory and, 225–226
  ethnic attitudes and, 243–245
  measurement of, 229–232
  minority groups and, 227
  stage-based theories of, 227–229
  self-description, 229–230
  social identity theory and, 226–227
Ethnic labelling, 230–231
Exchange of goods, 48–52

Folk beliefs, see Naïve theory
Folk sociology, 217, 293–294

Gender, 8–9
  occupational choice and, 150, 178
Gender categories, 135–136, 213–214
Gender consistency, 145
Gender constancy, 144, 146, 155–156, 214
Gender labelling, 144–145
Gender schemas,
  theory of, 147–154
  naïve theory of gender and, 149–154
Gender stability, 145
Gender roles, see also Gender Schemas
  biological accounts of, 138–141
  cognitive developmental theories and, 144–147
  emotions and, 136, 152–153, 160
  environmentalist accounts of, 141–142
  familial influences, 296
  media influences on, 154–159
  morality and, 300
  self-categorisation theory and, 151, 153
  social-cognitive theory and, 142–144
  social identity theory and, 151, 153
  social learning theories and, 141–144

Geographical knowledge, 252–256
    cross-cultural differences in,
        253–254
    educational influence, 255
    gender differences in, 253
    individual differences in, 254–255
    national identity, 273

Hierarchical organisation, 79–81
    in schools, 27, 34

Implicit understanding, 4, 290
Income, 170
    occupation and, 174–179
    inequalities of, 179–183
    social class and, 183–185
    social transmission theories and,
        185–193
Information sources, 3–9, 13–14, 51–52,
    63, 108–109, see also Television
    educational practices, 5, 10, 14, 63
    indirect, 3, 6–8, 13, 63
    mass media, 9, 63, 108–110, 154–159,
        297–298
    personal experience, 5–8, 13, 51, 63
    selective attention to, 155–157
    socio-cultural influences, 3–4, 14,
        46–47, 63, 174, 191–193

Just world theory, 181

Labour contract, 294
Language limitations,
    understanding of the law and,
        116–117
Lay theory, see Naïve theory
Law, 7–8, 87
    cognitive limitations on
        understanding, 7–8, 106–117
    distinguished from rules, 79
    psycho-social factors, 119–121
    social factors, 118–119
Legal decision-making, 119–121
Legal orientation, 121
Legal system, 294
Legal understanding,
    conceptual limitations on, 106–112

Memory limitations
    understanding of the law and,
        112–116

Minority groups, 8, 117, 227, 241–243
Money, 44–47, 295
    cross-cultural differences in, 47
    environmental differences in, 46–47
Morality, 291, 299–300, see also Rules
    political ideologies and, 96

Naïve theory, 4–6, 8–11, 38, 201,
    214–215, 289–290, 292–293
    of economics, 49, 63–64
    of gender, 149–154
    of national group membership,
        264
    of politics, 82
Nation states, see Countries
National emblems,
    knowledge of, 259–262
National groups, 13–14
    affect for, 266–271
    enemies, 269
    individual differences, 270
    information sources, 265–266
    naïve theory of, 264
    nested group memberships and,
        264–265
    television and, 265
National identity, 271–275
    affect for national groups and,
        273–274
    geographical knowledge and, 273
    individual differences in, 272–273
    influences on, 278–280
    relative importance of, 272
    theoretical frameworks, 275–278
Natural cognition, 290–291

Occupations, 9–10, 171, 174–179
    choices of, 177–179
    earnings and, 174–176
    gender stereotypes and, 150

Piagetian theory, 2–4, 10, 12, 44, 69,
    73
    criticism of, 2–4, 10, 12, 37, 290
    equilibration, 52
    preoperational thinking, 76
    societal cognition and, 289
Political understanding, 6–7, 70–71,
    75–88
    early childhood development, 75–76,
        98–99

Political education, 70, 98
  training study, 83, 98
Political knowledge, 70
  civic knowledge, 71, 74
  definition of nation state, 81
  elections, 80
  geopolitical knowledge, 81
  interest and pressure groups, 88
  political domain, 82–88,
  political institutions, 82–85, 98
  political parties, 80, 82, 84–85
  roles, 79–82
  rights of citizens, 86
  types of government, 83, 86–87
Political values 88–97
  economic justice, 89–90
  rights, 90–93
  tolerance, 93–95
  ideologies, 95–97
Political socialisation, 70, 72
  political attitudes, 72
  political change, 72–74
  theoretical frameworks, 72–75
Poverty, 170–174
  cultural context, 174
Prejudice, 11–12, 233, 236–241
  racial prejudice, 199–200, 208
Prices,
  exchange of goods and, 48–49
Principle of relative need, 183–184
Profit, 45, 49–51, 295
  as income, 175
  personal experience and, 51–52
  profit seeking, 50
  training study, 51

Racial categories, 10–11, 199–200
  adult understanding of, 210–213, 215
  appearance of, 207–210
  awareness of, 206–207
  cognitive architecture and, 200–202
  developmental trends, 213
  realist perspective, 210–216
  social categories and, 202–206,
    215–216
  verbal information and, 209–210
Racial constancy, 215
Racial prejudice, 200, 208,
Restorative justice, 125–126
Rights,
  conception of, 108

Roles,
  boss, 27, 79, 175
  chief, 79
  shop-keeper, 50
  societal, 78–79
  political, 78–82
  teacher, 21–30, 78
Rules,
  academic rules, 19
  authority and, 21–23
  difference from laws, 79
  moral rule understanding, 19–21, 23,
    77
  prudential rules, 19
  school, 19–23
  social, 296
  socio-conventional rule
    understanding, 19–21, 23, 77

Saving,
  economising, 50
  by children, 50
Schools,
  as social system, 5, 17–18, 33–37
  citizenship and, 37, 299
  classroom norms, 28–30
  educational context of, 18
  pupils'evaluation of, 30–32
  school rules, 19–23
  variance between, 22, 35–36
School councils, 32–33
Scripts, 115–116
Self-categorisation theory, 151, 153,
    240–241, 276–277
Social categories,
  as embodied, 205–207, 210–218
  cognitive architecture and, 200–202
  development of, 202–205
Social class, 9–10, 191–193
  classroom processes and, 28
  income inequality and, 184–185
  perceptions of school and, 35–36
  wealth and poverty and, 171–174
Social-cognitive theory,
  gender and, 142–144
Social context,
  understanding of money and, 46–47
Social identity development theory,
    277–278
Social identity theory, 12,149,151,153,
    226–27, 240–241, 276

Socialisation,
  agents of, 9
Social justice,
  theory of, 180–183
Social learning theories, 141–144
Social reflection theory, 12
Social status, 172, 241
Social transmission theory, 10, 185–193,
  294
Societal cognition, 2–5, 14
  as domain of knowledge, 289–290
  children as agents, 298–299
  compared with 'natural cognition',
    290–291
  domain-specific approach, 288–290,
    294
  emotions and, 291, 299, 301
  experiential factors in, 295–298
  innate bases of, 293
  links with citizenship, 288, 299
  mental models and, 290
  morality and, 291, 299–300
  naïve theory and, 289–290
  Piagetian approach to, 2–3, 289
  problems with research in, 287–288
  significance of research, 299–301
  teleological explanations, 291–2
Sociocultural context, 3, see also
    Information sources
  family environment, 295–296
Stage-based development, 2–3
  distributive justice, 182–183
  Kohlberg's gender development
    theory, 144–147
  political understanding and, 97
  understanding of money and, 44–46
Stereotypes,
  national groups and, 262–266
  social groups and, 205–6
Supply and demand, 49–50
  competition between sellers, 50

Teachers, 22–24
  children's motivation and, 24–25,
    28–29
  classroom role, 24
  cross-cultural differences in
    perception of, 24, 28–30
  evaluation of, 25–27, 28–29
  head teacher, 22–23, 27
  rules and, 22–23
Teleology,
  societal cognition and, 291–292
Television,
  child witness testimony and CCTV,
    122–123
  gender role development and,
    155–159
  legal understanding and, 108–110
  national groups and, 265–266
  occupational roles and, 176,
  source of information 9, 108–110
Theories of development, see also
    Cognitive development theory,
    Naïve theory, Social transmission
    theory,
  contextualist, 74
  Erikson's theory of identity
    formation, 72–73
  Kohlberg's theory of gender
    development, 144–141
  Kohlberg's theory of moral
    development, 73
  lifespan developmental, 72
  Piagetian, 2–4, 10, 12, 44, 69, 73
  social representations, 74
Theory of mind, 111, 290–292
Transductive reasoning, 111

Verbal interviewing, 4, 11
  problems with, 4

Wealth, see Poverty